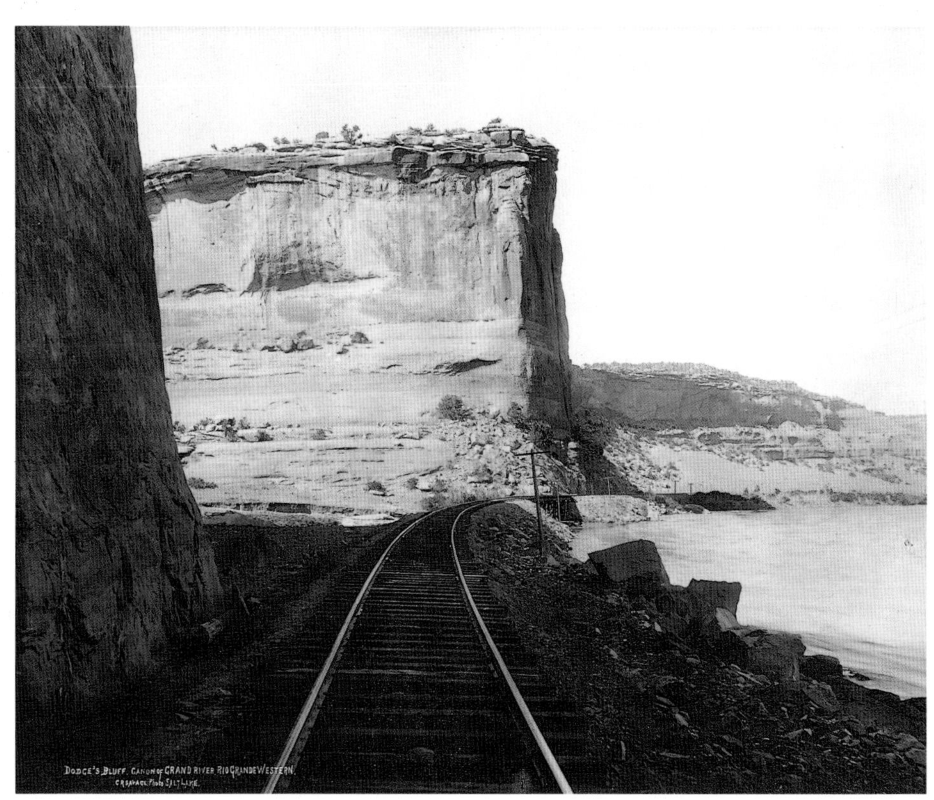
DODGE'S BLUFF. CANON OF GRAND RIVER. RIO GRANDE WESTERN.
C R SAVAGE. Photo SALT LAKE.

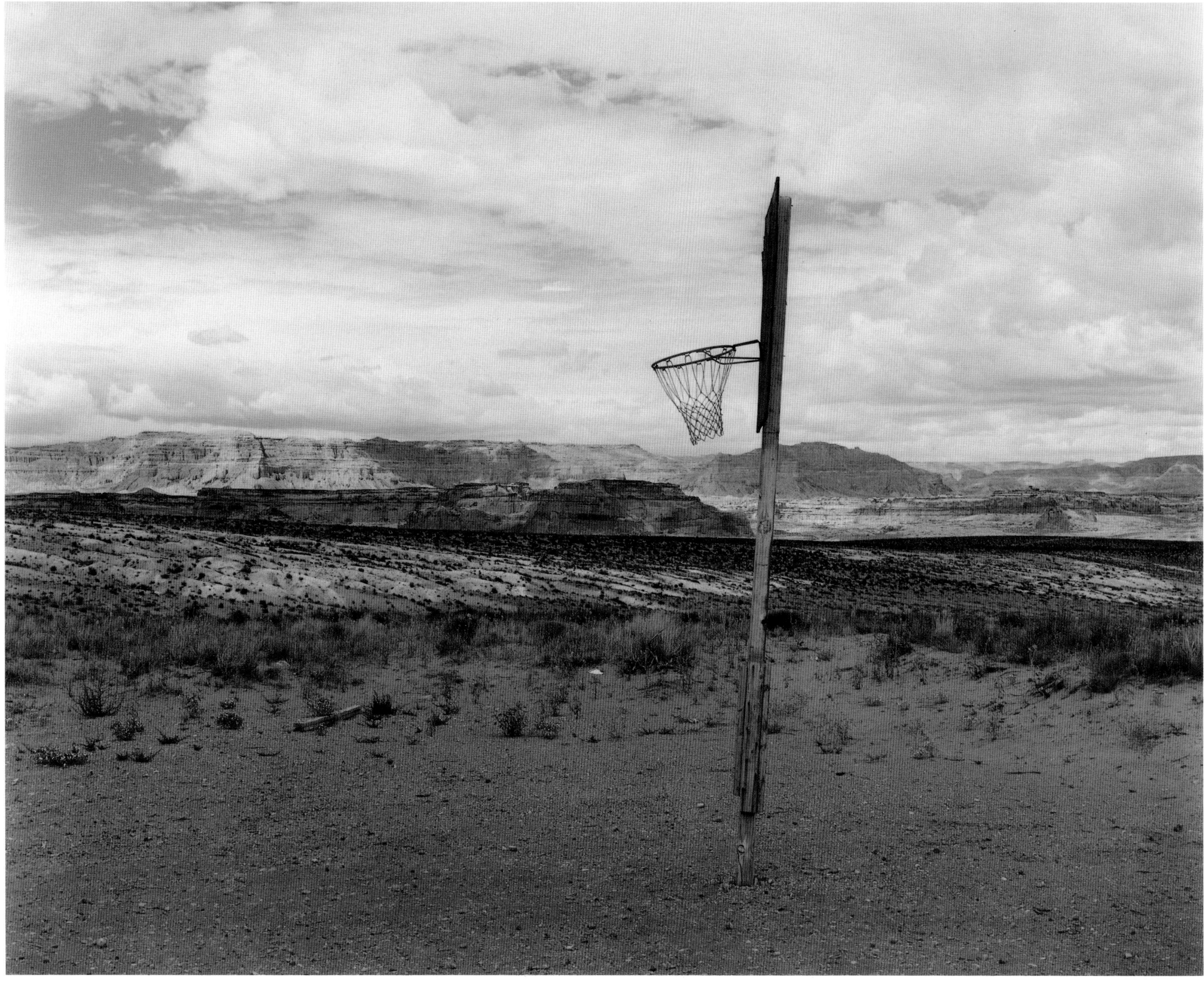

Crossing the Frontier

Photographs of the Developing West, 1849 to the Present

Sandra S. Phillips
Richard Rodriguez
Aaron Betsky
Eldridge M. Moores

San Francisco Museum of Modern Art • Chronicle Books

This catalogue is published on the occasion of the exhibition *Crossing the Frontier: Photographs of the Developing West, 1849 to the Present*, organized by Sandra S. Phillips at the San Francisco Museum of Modern Art.

EXHIBITION SCHEDULE

San Francisco Museum of Modern Art
September 26, 1996–January 28, 1997

Yale University Art Gallery
April 11–June 8, 1997

Phoenix Art Museum
July 12–September 27, 1997

Tokyo Metropolitan Museum of Photography
February 11–April 3, 1998

Crossing the Frontier: Photographs of the Developing West, 1849 to the Present is made possible by the Modern Art Council, the National Endowment for the Arts, a Federal agency, and the Foundation for Deep Ecology. Additional support is provided by Judy and John Webb, Evelyn D. Haas, and George and Leanne Roberts.

Chronicle Books, 275 Fifth Street,
San Francisco, CA 94103

Distributed in Canada by Raincoast Books, 8680 Cambie Street, Vancouver, B.C. V6P 6M9

10 9 8 7 6 5 4 3 2 1

Publication Manager: Kara Kirk
Editor: Gail Larrick
Designer: Robin Weiss
Cover Designer: Catherine Mills
Photography Coordinator:
Alexandra Chappell
Text Composition: Phoebe Bixler

Cover: detail of plate 39: Unknown, *Opening of Western Pacific Passenger Service between San Francisco and Salt Lake City, Sea of Salt, Utah*, 1910

Frontispieces:
Plate 1: Charles Roscoe Savage, *Dodge's Bluff, Cañon of Grand River, Rio Grande Western*, ca. 1870, albumen print, 17 1/4 x 21 in., (43.8 x 53.3 cm), PaineWebber Photography Collection

Plate 2: Joel Sternfeld, *Near Lake Powell, Arizona, August 1979*, 1979, Ektacolor print, 30 x 36 1/8 in. (77.8 x 91.8 cm), Collection of the San Francisco Museum of Modern Art. Fractional gift of David Breskin, 95.183

Library of Congress Cataloging-in-Publication Data:

Crossing the frontier : photographs of the developing West, 1849 to the present/Sandra S. Phillips ... [et al.].
p. cm.
"Catalogue ... published on the occasion of the exhibition ... at the San Francisco Museum of Modern Art"—T.p. verso.
Includes bibliographical references.
ISBN 0–8118–1420–3
1. Landscape photography—West (U.S.)—Exhibitions. 2. West (U.S.)—History—Exhibitions. I. Phillips, Sandra S., 1945– II. San Francisco Museum of Modern Art.
TR660.5.C76 1996
779'.3678'07479461—dc20 96–22072
CIP

Printed in Hong Kong

Table of Contents

Lenders to the Exhibition

Gordon Bennett
Ron Bommarito
Alexandra Bowes
Frances Bowes
David Breskin
Shawn and Brook Byers
California Historical Society
California State Library
Amon Carter Museum
Colorado Historical Society
DeGolyer Library, Southern Methodist University
Denver Public Library, Western History Collection
Carla Emil and Rich Silverstein
Betsy Gates
J. Paul Getty Museum
Evelyn D. Haas
Hallmark Photographic Collection, Hallmark Cards, Inc.
Matthew R. Isenburg
Prints and Photographs Division, Library of Congress
Jean McCusker
Nion McEvoy
Carl Mautz
Byron R. Meyer
Minnesota Historical Society Collections
Missouri Historical Society
Monsen Collection
Montana Historical Society
Merrill G. Burlingame Special Collections, Montana State University-Bozeman
Museum of Fine Arts, Santa Fe
Museum of History and Industry
Museum of the Rockies
National Archives
Nebraska Historical Society
Nevada Historical Society
Nancy and Steven Oliver
Eric Paddock
PaineWebber Photography Collection
Ron and Kathy Perisho
Prentice and Paul Sack
San Francisco Museum of Modern Art
Charles and Helen Schwab
Society of California Pioneers
Stanford University Museum of Art, Stanford Museum Collections
Department of Special Collections, Stanford University
Union Pacific Museum Collection
The Bancroft Library, University of California, Berkeley
Department of Special Collections, University of California Library, Davis
Special Collections, University of Nevada-Reno Library
Photography Collection, Harry Ransom Humanities Research Center, The University of Texas at Austin
American Geographical Society Collection, University of Wisconsin-Milwaukee Library
Utah State Historical Society
Whatcom Museum of History and Art
Stephen White Collection II
Cameron Whiteman
Photographic Archives of the World Museum of Mining
Private Collections

Artists in the Exhibition

Ansel Adams
Robert Adams
W. W. Alderson
Thomas Frederick Arndt
J. P. Babbitt
Lewis Baltz
E. J. Banks
Joseph Bartscherer
Virginia Beahan
Max Becher
William Bell
M. D. Boland
Henry P. Bosse
Barbara Bosworth
Bryan Studio
Bunnell Studio
Solomon Butcher
Evelyn J. Cameron
Lois Conner
Gregory Conniff
Asahel Curtis
Charles C. Curtis
William Thacher Dane
O. T. Davis
Robert Dawson
Joe Deal
Jack Delano
John Divola
Thomas M. Easterly
Edgerton, Germeshausen & Grier, Inc.
Augustus William Ericson
Terry Evans
Christopher Faust
George Fiske
Lee Friedlander
John Ganis
Alexander Gardner
William Garnett
Frank Gohlke
Peter Goin
Eugene O. Goldbeck
Wayne Gudmundson
Karen Halverson
David T. Hanson
Alfred A. Hart
Tim Harvey
Frank Jay Haynes
Anthony Hernandez
William E. Hook
Thomas Houseworth & Co.
Laton Alton Huffman
John Humble
William Henry Jackson
Geoffrey James
Len Jenshel
George Howard Johnson
Gene Kennedy
Darius R. Kinsey
Mark Klett
Larson Photo
Las Vegas News Bureau
Lawrence and Houseworth
Russell Lee
Jack Lueders-Booth
Skeet McAuley
L. C. McClure
Greg MacGregor
Laura McPhee
Richard Meisinger, Jr.
Francis Miller
Richard Misrach
Almeron Newman
Barbara Norfleet
Olson Bros.
Timothy H. O'Sullivan
Pacific Photo Company
Eric Paddock
Alfred Palmer
Harvey Patteson
Julius Patteson
John Pfahl
Andrea Robbins
Arthur Rothstein
Andrew Joseph Russell
Mark Ruwedel
Charles Roscoe Savage
Paul Shambroom
Shipler's Commercial Photographers
William Shrew
Charles Steale
Joel Sternfeld
J. E. Stimson
Tseng Kwong Chi
Carleton E. Watkins
Webster and Stevens
Charles Weitfle
Henry Wessel
Edward Weston
Herm Wilson
Garry Winogrand
Alfred S. Witter

Director's Foreword

JOHN R. LANE

Joining the work of contemporary artists with a historical survey of documentary images, *Crossing the Frontier: Photographs of the Developing West, 1849 to the Present* traces the ways photographers have confronted the visual realities of the western landscape over the past 140 years. Unlike other exhibitions of its kind, this one avoids approaches that see the land as a pretext for aestheticization and highlights those that address the land as it has actually been used. In recent decades considerable scholarship has been dedicated to the demystification of the American West and, while there has been the intention in some areas of the visual arts to pursue a similar project, it seems to be in the medium of photography that artists have been most clear-eyed.

This exhibition, organized by Curator of Photography Sandra S. Phillips, an art historian highly versed in the 150-year-old tradition of documentary photography, begins by delving into the nineteenth century to seek out a historical body of images depicting the western landscape. These photographs have been selected neither to illustrate the religion of nature (the sublime) nor the thesis of Manifest Destiny (the social and political imperative that rationalized the conquering of the frontier), but rather to shed light on the reality of land use. From the mid-nineteenth century until the Great Depression, photographers captured the excitement and optimism of the European-American development of the West, recording the advances of technology, the accomplishments of industry, and the mastery of the environment. It was not until the 1930s that documentary photographers began to acknowledge that the nineteenth-century cultural ideal of individualism had shaped the western landscape and the lives conducted on it—and not always for the best. This awareness revealed itself in works that were much more critical in their approach. Since the 1950s, with the urbanization, suburbanization, and industrialization of life in the American West, contemporary documentary photography of this landscape has become ever more personally expressive, at times sensitively appreciative of the new circumstances it finds, but more often environmentally concerned, manifesting itself in images conveying an ironic or frankly tragic sense of misuse.

It may, in fact, be argued that it is in contemporary documentary photography that the most revealing artistic interpretations of the West emerge in the visual arts. In films such as Sam Peckinpah's *The Wild Bunch* and Clint Eastwood's *The Unforgiven*, even as they deconstruct the western hero and offer a new version of a West inhabited by moral ambiguity, the landscape remains unchanged as a magnificent backdrop or mighty protagonist. In painting, the West recently has not been a serious subject, although some of the most important sculptural works of the past several decades—in particular, Walter De Maria's *Lightning Field*, Robert Smithson's *Spiral Jetty*, and James Turrell's *Roden Crater*—have not only been made out in the western landscape but have also literally been made *of* it. These grandly conceived pieces that rely on the scale of the space and the grandeur of its natural forms continue, within the language of modernism, the tradition of the sublime that distinguishes both nineteenth-century American landscape painting and post–World War II Abstract Expressionist art. But it is in the unconventionally poetic photographs by Robert Adams of suburban communities on the high planes along the Front Range of the Rockies in Colorado that we may see the best and the truest vision of what the real West is today.

I offer deep thanks to Sandra Phillips for conceiving and organizing this project and for having enriched the Museum's collection with many new acquisitions that are featured in the exhibition. Many staff members at SFMOMA assisted Dr. Phillips in the planning and presentation of *Crossing the Frontier.* I would particularly like to acknowledge the contributions of Jill Sterrett Beaudin, conservator; Virginie Blachère, intern; P. Chelsea Brown, former director of communications; Olga Charyshyn, associate registrar; Amanda Doenitz, intern; Suzanne Feld, curatorial assistant; Lori Fogarty, director of curatorial affairs; Tina Garfinkel, head registrar; Narelle Jarry, conservator; Barbara Levine, exhibitions manager; John Losito, former curatorial assistant; Jennifer Morgan, former exhibitions assistant; Douglas Nickel, assistant curator of photography; Ariadne Rosas, intern; Genoa Shepley, acting director of communications; Marcelene Trujillo, former secretary for the Department of Photography; John S. Weber, Leanne and George Roberts curator of education and public programs; Jane Weisbin, registrar, permanent collection; Greg Wilson, museum technician; and Samuel Yates, intern.

This publication is the result of the combined efforts of numerous individuals. The extensive research undertaken by Dr. Phillips to prepare this exhibition is brought to bear in the essay that serves as both an introduction to and a framework for this volume. Her text is complemented by three thoughtful essays whose authors deserve our deepest appreciation: Aaron Betsky, SFMOMA curator of architecture and design; Eldridge M. Moores, professor of geology at the University of California at Davis; and Richard Rodriguez, an editor, journalist, and cultural essayist. Museum staff members Catherine Mills, director of graphic design and publications, Kara Kirk, publications manager, and Alexandra Chappell, publications assistant; editor Gail Larrick; and designer Robin Weiss all contributed their expertise to this project, for which we are grateful. We also thank Annie Barrows, editor, and Karen Silver, associate editor, at Chronicle Books, this volume's copublisher.

On behalf of Dr. Phillips, I would like to extend warmest thanks to Martha Sandweiss, Merry Forresta, Ron Perisho, and Wanda and Joe Corn for reading drafts of her manuscript and offering their insightful comments. She would additionally like to acknowledge the generous assistance of May Castleberry, Donald and Dolores Cooney, Christopher Delaney, Terry Evans, J. B. Jackson, Wes Jackson, Mr. and Mrs. Mead Kibbey, Hilton Obenzinger, Peter Palmquist, Jenny Perlin, Christopher Phillips, Marc Reisner, Trudy Wilner Stack, Kevin Starr, Mary V. Swanson, William A. Turnage, Susan Swig Watkins, Terry Tempest Williams, and Donald Worster. And finally, Dr. Phillips owes a special debt of gratitude to John Szarkowski, director emeritus of the Department of Photography, The Museum of Modern Art, New York, for his friendship and good counsel.

An exhibition and publication of this complexity and scope could not have been undertaken without the generous support of the Modern Art Council of the San Francisco Museum of Modern Art, the National Endowment for the Arts, a Federal agency, and the Foundation for Deep Ecology. Additional support is provided by Judy and John Webb, Evelyn D. Haas, and George and Leanne Roberts.

We are beholden to the numerous institutional and private collections—listed on page six of this publication—for sharing their artworks with us. We are especially grateful to the following individuals for facilitating these loans: Lee Brumbaugh, curator of photography, and Nita Phillips, gift shop coordinator, Nevada Historical Society; John Carter and Jill Marie Koelling, respectively curator and assistant curator of photographs and audio/visual material, Nebraska State Historical Society; Keith F. Davis, fine arts programs director, Hallmark Photographic Collection; David Farmer, director, DeGolyer Library, Southern Methodist University; Roy Flukinger, curator of photography, and Ann Paterra, assistant curator of photography, Harry Ransom Humanities Research Center, the University of Texas at Austin; Susan Haas, registrar, and William McMorris, photograph archivist, Society of California Pioneers; Margaret Kimball, head of special collections and university archivist, Green Library, Stanford University; Gary Kurutz, special collections principal librarian, California State Library; Joel Leivick, honorary curator of photography, Stanford University Art Museum; Robert MacKimmie, curator of photography, California

Historical Society; Jim Masker, director, and Geraldine Walter, president of the board of directors and assistant director of photographic archives, World Museum of Mining; Augie Mastrogiuseppe, photograph specialist, Western History Collection, Denver Public Library; Delores Morrow, photograph archives supervisor, Montana State Historical Society; Doug Munson, director, Chicago Albumen Works; Toni Nagel, photograph archivist, Whatcom Museum of History and Art; Richard Ogar, head of duplication services, The Bancroft Library, University of California, Berkeley; Eric Paddock, curator of photography and film, Colorado Historical Society; Fred Pernell, assistant chief for Still Pictures Branch, and James Zeender, registrar, National Archives, Washington, D.C.; Terence Pitts, director, Center for Creative Photography, University of Arizona, Tucson; John Skarstad, head of the Department of Special Collections, Shields Library, University of California at Davis; Rod Slemmons, former curator of photography, Seattle Art Museum; Duane Sneddeker, curator of prints and photographs, Missouri Historical Society; Don Snoddy, director, Union Pacific Historical Museum; Joel Snyder, department of art history, University of Chicago; Kathryn M. Totton, curator of photography, University Library, University of Nevada–Reno; and Bonnie G. Wilson, curator of sound and visual collections, Minnesota Historical Society.

In addition, we are greatly indebted to the following individuals who made contributions to the Museum used for the acquisition of photographs included in the exhibition: Rena Bransten, Frederick P. Currier, Sidney Goldstein, Susan and Robert Green, Linda Gruber, Evelyn D. Haas, Lindsey Joost, Judy Kay Memorial Fund, Pamela and Richard Kramlich, Nion McEvoy, Robin Wright Moll, Jane and Larry Reed, Marsha Smolens, and Gary Sokol. Special thanks are also due to the Museum auxiliaries Foto Forum and Collectors Forum, to the members of the Museum's Accessions Committee and Photography Accessions Committee, and to the Columbia Foundation for their generous provision of funds used for the purchase of works included in the exhibition.

It is also our particular pleasure to have been the recipients of a number of artworks given on the occasion of the exhibition, and we thank the following individuals and organizations for their generosity: Robert Adams; David and Isabel Breskin, Frederick P. Currier; the Estate of Garry Winogrand; Fraenkel Gallery, San Francisco; Anthony Hernandez and Craig Krull Gallery, Santa Monica; Geoffrey James; Len Jenshel; Simon Lowinsky, Richard Meisinger, Jr.; Eric Paddock; Kathy and Ron Perisho; Charles and Helen Schwab; Joel Sternfeld; Terry Toedtemeier; United States Department of Energy/Nevada Operations Office; Stephen White; and Bruce Velick. We also would like to thank a number of people for supporting our efforts to bring photographs by Robert Adams into the Museum's collection, including Alexandra Bowes, Frances Bowes, Shawn and Brook Byers, Carla Emil and Rich Silverstein, Evelyn D. Haas, Jean McCusker, Nion McEvoy, Byron R. Meyer, Nancy and Steven Oliver, Ron and Kathy Perisho, Prentice and Paul Sack, and Cameron Whiteman.

Three other institutions have joined SFMOMA to present *Crossing the Frontier.* I would like to thank James K. Ballinger, director of the Phoenix Art Museum; Susan Vogel, director, and Richard S. Field, curator of prints, drawings, and photographs at the Yale University Art Gallery, and Miki Tamon, director, and Michiko Kasahara, curator, at the Tokyo Metropolitan Museum of Photography for uniting with us in this endeavor.

And finally, I would like to offer my thanks and appreciation to the many artists—listed on page seven—whose insight and interest in the western landscape have so illuminated this arena of American dreams and realities.

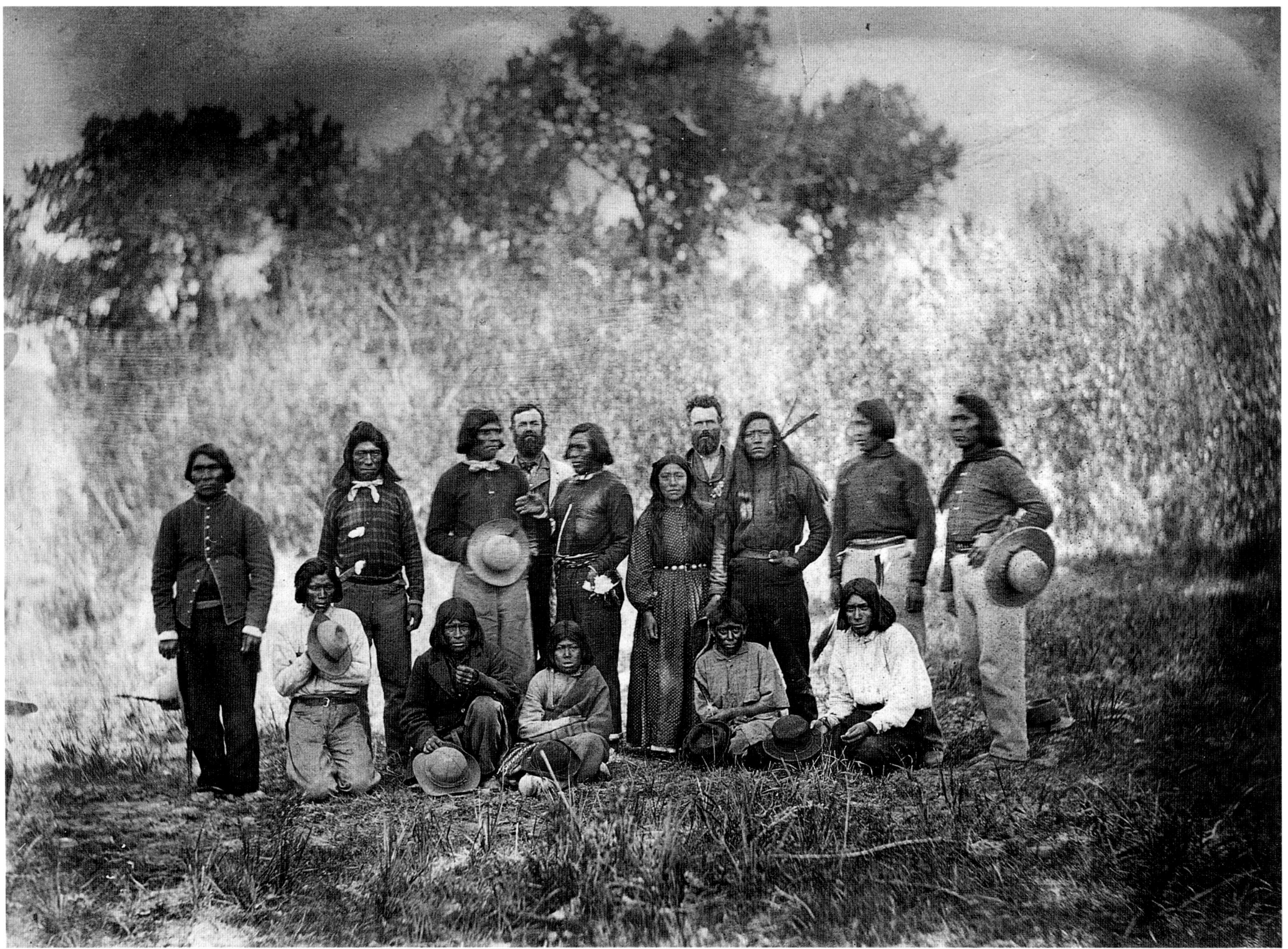

To Subdue the Continent: Photographs of the Developing West

SANDRA S. PHILLIPS

The untransacted destiny of the American people is to subdue the continent.
William Gilpin, *Mission of the People*[1]

Eastward I go only by force; but westward I go free.
Henry David Thoreau, *Walking*[2]

Until recently, a spirit of optimism has characterized American culture; it was confident optimism that provided the impetus to develop the second half of our nation in record time. William Gilpin, one of the original authors of the philosophy of the appropriation and settlement of land that we call Manifest Destiny, espoused a faith in corporate enterprise and shared mission that saw America's fate as preordained, a matter of God's will. Only later would it become clear that, as Henry David Thoreau hints, the ideals of personal ambition, individualism, and free-will often come into conflict with the nation's collective enterprise. The ambivalence between these positions is reflected in the way we have used and developed the western land. The irony we perceive today is largely the result of a failed optimism and a fuller understanding of the complexities of our history.

Crossing the Frontier: Photographs of the Developing West, 1849 to the Present explores the images and ideas of the vast and diverse western landscape and how it was used. It presents the photographic record of what we built: the rivers bridged, the western sod plowed under, the mineral resources mined, the irrigation systems developed, the rails and roadways constructed, and the ways of using the land that inform our own time. It documents what happened to "the wilderness" (a region, in fact, already occupied by indigenous peoples) and what we have inherited from that intense and amazingly inventive period during which the West was industrialized. One of the more remarkable facts about the development of the West was the speed of its "conquest." It happened in less than a lifetime.

There is a well-known tradition of western landscape photography, seen in the work, for instance, of Ansel Adams and Edward Weston, that looks to the land as a source of aesthetic, transcendent subject matter. The photography of land use, on the other hand, evokes a largely unacknowledged tradition, one closer to documentary photography in spirit and more likely to be found in anonymous works, in pictures by journeymen photographers, and in the lesser-known pictures of certain established artists. To reclaim this documentary tradition, we have consulted local historical societies and state university libraries, to begin to reintegrate the vernacular tradition with photographs already residing in art museums. Nonetheless, we are left with an incomplete record. The works in this show are mostly documents of the dominant culture, those of Anglo-European settlement. Photography was invented at the same moment as the economic development of the West. It was a technology introduced and practiced by settlers; it was an industrial tool used to record the larger industrialization of the land. This exhibition, comprising photographs that are essentially a white, male, Christian record of what was done to possess and civilize the land, thus omits in the main the territory's earlier possessors, Native Americans and the Spanish colonists.

But where is the West? If geography can define a cultural idea, the West is almost half of America. Some claim it begins at either the Mississippi River or the Missouri, but its border is generally considered the

PLATE 3
Timothy H. O'Sullivan
Kent Parker, Indian Agent, and some of his Pah Utes,
ca. 1867–69
albumen print
7⅝ x 10½ in. (19.4 x 26.7 cm)
Hallmark Photographic Collection, Hallmark Cards, Inc., Kansas City, Missouri

ninety-eighth or hundredth meridian, an almost traceable line that separates an area that gets sufficient rain to support the regular production of crops from that area of the Great Plains where, in the period before irrigation, farming was not a viable long-term prospect.

What is termed the "trans-Mississippi" West was developed and settled speedily after the Civil War. Its most distinctive aspect is the character of the land itself. This West comprises not only the arid West of the Plains, but also the Rockies and the Sierra, the Northwest, and the Southwest. Much of this western land was nearly treeless and lay exposed to a wide sky, but it is also an amazingly diverse landscape. Much of it was as flat as the receding glaciers could scrape it, but it also included the country's largest, newest, and highest mountain range, the Rockies, as well as the dense forest region of the Northwest enclosed in cloud, the Great Basin centered in Nevada, a rocky desert area, and the canyon lands and mesas of the Southwest. This grand, open land looked immense to those who passed over it in wagons, and it is still overwhelming to drive through its vast spaces, so different from the human-scaled ones of the Northeast or South.

GEOGRAPHY AND MYTHOLOGY If we consider the West as not only a cultural idea deriving from geography but as a mythology, then the West implies freedom, individualism, heroism. It includes what historian William Goetzmann called "the West of the imagination," an idea larger than that of mere geography. It implies that man (but usually not woman) bravely faces down the overwhelming odds and turbulent forces of nature, individually or as part of a small cluster of pioneering peoples, battling for possession of land with those who were occupying it already. The fortunate ones are those who survive.

The western myth has shaped much of our history and continues to play a significant, if often unrecognized, role in the way we think about ourselves. Although the myth is focused in the West, it is not limited to its geography but transcends both space and time. The Marlboro Man, alone in the wide open expanses, tough and self-reliant, continues to be effective in selling cigarettes around the world. In Oklahoma City, Timothy McVeigh, the resilient individual gone awry, will try to dismantle the government in an effort to bring about his own maverick version of "law and order." The conflict between individual ideals and corporate enterprise that shaped western history still informs our present. The added question of community needs or the general good and its relationship to western traditions of individualism and corporate industry have special relevance in the West.

Using the land with impunity, if not abandon—mining its resources, overgrazing its hillsides, overlogging, endangering water supplies and the health of its natural habitat and the human beings who live there—seems to have occurred more frequently in the West than in other American regions. In the West, land development coincided with new technology and methods of industry.[3] Attitudes toward the West were expressed in the language of control: We were to "conquer" nature, or as Gilpin put it, "subdue" its geography. Nature was in need of "taming"; she was "wild," "virgin," and often "dark"; she needed to be "penetrated" and "controlled." John L. O'Sullivan, who first used the term *Manifest Destiny* in 1845, did so in terms of an almost inevitable sexual claim: ". . . [it] is by the right of our manifest destiny to overspread and to possess the whole of the continent," he said.[4] Likewise, the eloquent geologist Clarence King wanted to use his scientific learning to "propel and guide the great plowshare of science on through the virgin sod of the unknown."[5]

The combination of conquest and paternalism affected attitudes toward the original inhabitants of the wilderness. It is made terribly clear in Timothy O'Sullivan's photograph of the Indian agent Kent Parker surrounded by "his Pah Utes" (pl. 3). Comparatively few photographs exist as records of the Spanish presence on the land. It is acknowledged as an ancient curiosity by the photograph of an inscription, the record of a Spanish party of exploration in the seventeenth century (pl. 17), but its history is more accurately expressed by such things as court records and photographs, such as those made by Watkins, that reveal property disputes with first the Spanish and then the Mexican governments over their relationships with Texas and California.

Western attitudes to nature and the wilderness, complex and potentially contradictory, came from the East. The Puritans felt they had a special "covenant" with God to build an enlightened, blessed community eked out of the hostile wilderness they first encountered when they arrived in New England.[6] Calvinist minister Jonathan Edwards found that nature could also be charming and pleasurable and embraced these seemingly anti-Puritan values.[7] In the nineteenth century, Romanticism in literature, philosophy, and art promoted an aesthetic regard for nature in America. We are, Perry Miller noted, "Nature's Nation." According to the Romantic French visitor Vicente François Auguste-René de Chateaubriand, "There is nothing old in America except the trees, children of the earth, and liberty, mother of all human society; these are as important as ancient monuments and ancestors."[8] Wilderness, not history, is what gave the New World its identity.

One of the earliest to appreciate the special implications of nature to Americans was the British-born painter Thomas Cole. In 1835 he delivered a lecture in which he declared:

> *... the most distinctive, and perhaps the most impressive, characteristic of American scenery is its wildness ... those scenes of solitude from which the hand of nature has never been lifted, affect the mind with a more deep toned emotion than aught which the hand of man has touched. Amid them the consequent associations are of God the creator—they are his undefiled works, and the mind is cast into the contemplation of eternal things.*[9]

In his memorial painting for Cole, his friend Asher Durand placed Cole and the Romantic nature poet William Cullen Bryant on a rocky platform overlooking a favorite Catskill glade, the distant wilderness radiantly illuminated (fig. 1). Nature in this work is a beautiful and holy eminence, still untouched. As a contemporary would state, for the landscape artist "... his picture is a representation of moral principles and sentiment; not merely an imitation."[10] But the wilderness was being invaded, or tamed, as it was also being appreciated. Even Cole admitted this:

> *... I cannot but express my sorrow that the beauty of such landscapes are quickly passing away—the ravages of the axe are daily increasing—the most noble scenes are made desolate, and oftentimes with a wantonness and barbarism scarcely credible in a civilized nation. The way-side is becoming shadeless, and another generation will behold spots, now rife with beauty, desecrated by what is called improvement; which, as yet, generally destroys Nature's beauty without substituting that of Art. This is a regret rather than a complaint; such is the road society has to travel. ...*[11]

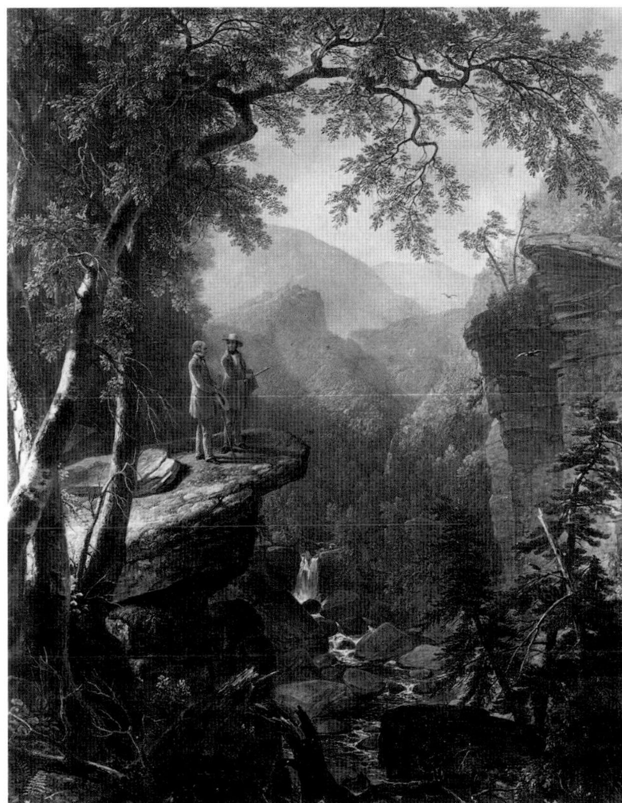

FIGURE 1
Asher Durand
Kindred Spirits, 1849
Collection of the New York Public Library

Cole's idealization of the wilderness began when he lived in New York City; later, when the area was no longer wild, he moved to the Catskills. The American painter of South American wilderness, Frederic Edwin Church, started building across the Hudson from Cole's home in 1860. German-born Albert Bierstadt constructed his eastern mansion nearby in 1865 while finding his subjects in the Far West (fig. 2). The artists who painted the sublime wilderness, and their patrons, were visitors to this landscape, not residents of it.

The wilderness as Cole understood it changed location dramatically in the nineteenth century. The continental West became a physical presence when Thomas Jefferson purchased the Louisiana Territory from France in 1803. When James Fenimore Cooper wrote his "Leatherstocking Tales," the wilderness was in western New York State. Before the Civil War, the agrarian ideal was aided by the opening of the Oregon Trail in 1846 and the annexation of Texas in 1845.

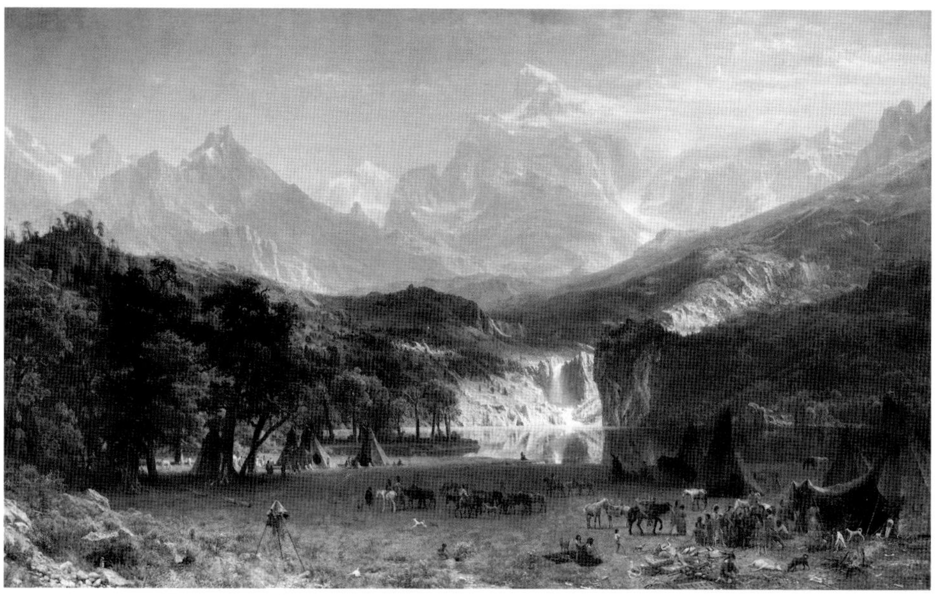

FIGURE 2
Albert Bierstadt
The Rocky Mountains, Lander's Peak, 1863
Collection of The Metropolitan Museum of Art, Rogers Fund, 1907

MANIFEST DESTINY The doctrine of Manifest Destiny, one of the great motivating forces that promoted rapid development of the West, held that the American land was providentially favored and its potential wealth destined for fruitful use. Cole's sublime wilderness was thus enthusiastically transformed into a garden, and Jefferson's dream of a yeoman nation was fulfilled. This swift overtaking of the wilderness was cast in the language of the Bible: In the book of Genesis, God directs his newly created man and woman to "be fruitful, and multiply, and replenish the Earth, and subdue it; and have dominion over the fish of the sea, and the fowl of the air, and over every living thing that lives upon the face of the earth." Manifest Destiny may have been irrational, even arrogant, but it was highly imaginative, and its perceived divine imperative made it appear that much was at stake. In 1835, Lyman Beecher, father of Harriet Beecher Stowe, declared:

> *The West is a young empire of the mind, and power, and wealth, and free institutions, rushing up to giant manhood, with a rapidity and a power never before witnessed below the sun. And if she carries with her the elements of her preservation, the experiment will be glorious—the joy of the nation, the joy of the whole earth—as she rises in the majesty of her intelligence and benevolence and enterprise, for the emancipation of the world.*[12]

The mythology of the West embodied two basic, contradictory tenets: one, that the individualist, agrarian ideal of continuous, divinely ordained progress would transform wild nature into a civilized garden; the other, that man's materialist, capitalistic development and the technology it possessed (its machines, its engineering) would be the agent that would harmoniously open the West. Instead of the easy progress of the "Civilizing Ax," settlers were confronted by the vast geography and relatively arid land beyond the hundredth meridian, which proved unworkable for much early agricultural settlement. Thus, the Great American Desert had to be transversed as quickly as possible to get to the rich ports of the Far East. The railroad would provide what Walt Whitman called the "Passage to India." The idea of the frontier was central to both the mythology of the farmer's civilizing ax and the railroad's industrial pathway through the desert.

THE TURNER THESIS OF THE FRONTIER Frederick Jackson Turner, probably the most famous western historian, first formulated in 1893 what is now designated the "Turner thesis." He saw the frontier as a "line between savagery and civilization":

> *The frontier is the line of most rapid and effective Americanization. The wilderness masters the colonist. It finds him a European in dress, industries, tools, modes of travel, and thought. It takes him from the railroad car and puts him in the birch canoe. It strips off the garments of civilization and arrays him in the hunting shirt and the moccasin. . . . Thus the advance of the frontier has meant a steady movement away from the influence of Europe, a steady growth of independence on American lines.*[13]

Turner found the landscape a symbolic setting for the evolution of American character. He saw development as being born of this wild state that began with farming and ended with cities, when the development of the trans-Mississippi West in fact often started with cities. He saw settlement beginning in the East and moving westward.

Yet Western settlement was far from linear. At mid-century, settlers poised to cross the wide Missouri at the ninety-eighth meridian often continued across the continent instead, searching for more fertile fields. Utah received its great wave of Mormon settlers, chiefly farmers, as early as 1847. Oregon and Texas were also settled by Americans in the 1840s. Most development grew from mining and railroad settlements, rather than farms. Turner's thesis, while hopeful, democratic, and idealizing the frontier farmer, never fully recognized the power of industry to transform the West.

THE MINING FIELDS AND THE CITY THEY PRODUCED In 1848, gold was discovered on the American River in the Sierra. Within months California ceased to be a "pastoral haven" (in the words of explorer John C. Frémont) and was opened to exploitation. News of the goldfields was continuously present in newspapers around the nation. Within a year San Francisco grew from a modest, rather sleepy, western outpost to become the largest city west of Chicago—a raucous, bawdy mining town, home both to fabulous wealth and the desperate, luckless poor.

San Francisco's early trade had been in furs destined for the East. In 1839 the town had perhaps fifty residents. It was not until after 1845, when California was acquired by the United States from Mexico, that San Francisco began to prosper. San Francisco was the West's first true mining town, preceding Denver by ten years and others by more. Despite its many steep hills, the city was laid out in grids, providing its nineteenth-century citizens a convenient way to acquire property rapidly. The open, rational grid structure that made property easy to sell became a characteristic of the western city.

Early photography documented not only the emergent city but the source of its insurgent wealth, the goldfields. They were truly international. Chinese, Europeans, South Americans, Hawaiians, Native Americans —all were in the rivers competing for space to pan the elusive metal. (The miners intruded on the territory of the Indians and sometimes hunted them for sport.) Albert Sands Southworth, of the eminent Boston daguerreotype firm Southworth and Hawes, spent time in gold country and may have turned to his former trade, either in the Sierra foothills or in San Francisco, before returning to the East. However, most of the daguerreotypes were made by entrepreneurs like the miners themselves. The number of gold-rush daguerreotypes is astonishing. These pictures reveal the early days of gold mining when it was truly an individual enterprise and the allure of personal fortune proved compelling to many (pls. 16, 18, 19). Everyone had a chance in the field: Women worked alongside men, blacks worked their placers, and so did the Chinese.

Although heroic individual mining or claims made by small groups of entrepreneurs soon gave way to larger, capitalized, and highly organized, often hard-rock mining operations, the ideal of the singular miner whose success depended on skill, hard work, and luck was curiously long lasting. Within about five years, most of the gold flowing freely in the Sierra rivers was panned out. The thoughtful nineteenth-century California philosopher Henry George considered the effect of the placer miners on California's history:

> *The miner working for himself owed no master; worked when and only when he pleased; took out his earnings each day in the shining particles which depended for their value on no fluctuations of the market, but would pass current and supply all wants the world over. When his claim gave out, or for any reason he desired to move on, he had but to shoulder his pick and move on. Mining of this kind developed its virtues as well as its vices. If it could have been united with ownership of land and the comforts and restraints of home, it would have given us a class of citizens of the utmost value to a republican state. But the "honest miner" of the placers has passed away in California. The Chinaman, the mill-owner and his laborers, the mine superintendent and his gang, are his successors.*[14]

San Francisco had its portrait taken more frequently than any other city of its time. Unintentionally, its gridded hills made splendid vistas, and the multiplate panorama, adapted from the painted Victorian form, seemed most appropriate to represent the graceful lay of the land and the dynamic growth of the city. The many depictions of early San Francisco were not derived only from civic pride or a historic desire to record the rapidly changing metropolis. They were also meant to assure those who lived far from the West that, although the city might suffer frequent devastation by fire, an unsettled, multinational, uncouth population, and a corrupt or ineffective local government (depending on the year), San Francisco still promised a good return on investment.[15]

A PHOTOGRAPHIC VISION OF THE WEST With its new wealth, San Francisco attracted and supported a surprisingly large number of skilled photographers, willing to try their luck with this financially risky venture. Not only did they make pictures of people who came to their studios for likenesses, but they took their cameras out of doors, into the streets, and to the countryside beyond.

Who would buy such pictures? A limited audience made their creation an expensive business. Even after the singular daguerreotypes had been supplanted by the wet-plate process, supplying potentially limitless quantities of albumen prints on paper, who (or what agency) would support a photographer making that kind of picture? Some saw their work as a service (much as portraiture by hire was a service). George R. Fardon worked (with now unknown interests) as the city's "booster." Robert H. Vance, usually a portrait photographer, also made a daguerreotype panorama of the West, a series of three hundred views that he showed, probably as entertainment, to paying viewers. Carleton E. Watkins, the greatest of them, was the first successful landscape photographer in the West. A man of artistic ability, he originally approached his work as a trade, and his photographs engage us not only by their quality but by their originality.

As a child in upstate New York, Watkins had befriended Collis Huntington, a local trader who became one of the "Big Four" railroad magnates for the Central Pacific. In 1851, in touch with the older man, Watkins traveled to California to keep Huntington's store in Sacramento. Chance led him to a position at Vance's San Jose daguerreotype studio, and later to other photographers. He probably participated in the earliest paper-print documentation of San Francisco, an album containing a series of views published by George Fardon. His earliest documented photograph was made to settle a land claim in 1858 for the Guadalupe mercury mine, near San Jose, where he was employed.[16]

By 1858 panning for gold had progressed to the more complex, capitalized techniques of hard-rock and hydraulic mining. The mercury ("quicksilver") mines in New Almaden provided the necessary ingredient for extracting gold from pulverized ore. California had only recently achieved statehood; Watkins' dispassionate pictures of the mining lands, the first of his large-format photographs, were used in court to sort out claims of the original Mexican owners and the newly arrived white occupants. Watkins was also hired to photograph the Mariposa mines by associates of John C. Frémont, the conqueror of California, in an effort to attract investors needed to raise capital. Frémont was the son-in-law of Thomas Hart Benton, the bristly Missouri senator who embodied Manifest Destiny. From the outset, Watkins was allied with the capitalists who developed the land with impunity.

Watkins made mining pictures from the beginning to the very end of his career. In the 1870s he photographed extensive hydraulic mining operations in the Sierra foothills north of Sacramento. This potentially lucrative technique demanded capital: The high water pressure that tore at the mountainside was achieved by extensive damming and flume operations, and the force of water from the hoses could kill or maim a man. Watkins' picture of the Malakoff Diggins is posed for aesthetic effect (his other pictures of hydraulic mining show the hoses more profitably directed at the gold-bearing cliff). The log present in other pictures was moved to the center to complete the photographer's sense of abstract design (pl. 20).[17]

Watkins' entire career paralleled his connections with mining and railroad interests, which explains his difficult and distant trips as an older man to Arizona and Montana, and his steady employment with Huntington and his associates. George Hearst's involvement in Virginia City and its Comstock Lode, the laying of the railroad into Oregon along the Columbia River (and the development of the river transport systems), and the projects to photograph the agricultural development—the early agribusiness—in Kern County are all examples of this circle of associates (pl. 24). Watkins' later pictures of mines and railroads have a new sense of enveloping atmosphere and, in some cases, a dramatic, deep darkness that by its emotional overtones departs from his earlier intellectual removal and reserve.[18] Some of this emotional sense was present in his late landscapes of Yosemite as well. But his chief reputation was not gained in industrial pictures; then, as now, it was the Yosemite pictures that brought him artistic acclaim.

THE WILDERNESS PARKS James M. Hutchings, an Englishman and former miner who had become a journalist, was first to write about Yosemite Valley, during his 1855 visit with Thomas Ayres, an artist who illustrated Hutchings' article. The piece was published in the first issue of *Hutchings' California Magazine* in 1856. Thrilled with what he saw, Hutchings became an ardent promoter of the valley. In 1859 Hutchings took Charles Leander Weed to Yosemite and he became the first photographer to depict it successfully. Sponsored by Vance, Weed made both salable stereos and large views. In 1864 Hutchings became the proprietor of a hotel in the valley. Gradually, an elite clientele developed, curious to see Yosemite's incandescent beauty and evidence of divine presence in its geologic forms.[19]

Watkins made his first of eight photographic visits to Yosemite in 1861 (fig. 3).[20] Undertaking such a venture with cumbersome, mammoth-size glass plate negatives was physically difficult and costly, but Watkins must have thought the results would make the considerable expense worthwhile. Yosemite was not far from the Frémont mines, and the valley was ripe for another kind of exploitation: tourism.

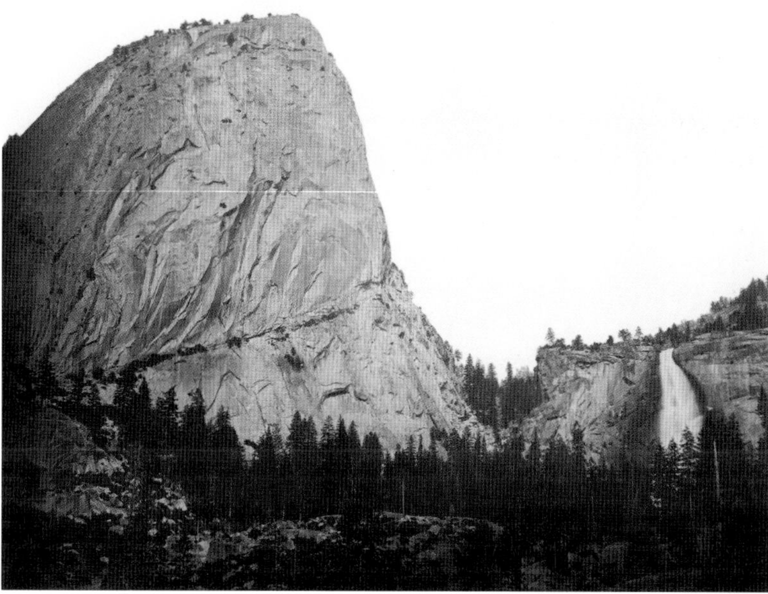

FIGURE 3

Carleton E. Watkins
Mt. Broderick, Nevada Fall, 700 ft. Yosemite, 1861
Collection of the San Francisco Museum of Modern Art. Purchased through a gift of Judy and John Webb, Sande Schlumberger, Pat and Bill Wilson, Susan and Robert Green, the Miriam and Peter Haas Fund, Members Accession Fund, and Mr. and Mrs. Max Herzstein and Mrs. Myrtle Lowenstern in honor of Mr. and Mrs. Stanley Herstein's Fiftieth Wedding Anniversary, 95.98

Watkins' familiarity with the pictorial rhetoric of the sublime assures the acceptance today of his work as valid art expression. But what, one wonders, was Watkins thinking when he made his big pictures? He was often referred to as "Watkins the artist," and his large pictures were sold in frames as well as in albums. When he opened his own establishment in 1872, he called it Yosemite Art Gallery. The scale of the big pictures, part of the largest consistent body of landscape work made by a nineteenth-century American photographer, and their exhibition at the prestigious Goupil's, an art gallery in New York, the year after they were made was surely an implied challenge to the older medium of painting.

When he packed twelve mules into the valley in 1861, Watkins included his stereo camera. The stereos he made at this time pleased a mass audience and popularized the large views made by frontier photographers. They also influenced the visual ideas in other arts—and photography itself. The pure geometric reading of space and of the separateness of the viewer from the scene that we find in many of Watkins' images and attribute to modernist vision may actually have been his way of assimilating qualities of the stereo into his larger format pictures, as others had done before him. Watkins' sense of emotional detachment (so uncharacteristic of both Bierstadt and Eadweard Muybridge, who followed him to Yosemite) was probably enhanced by the stereo view, with its dual sense of rushing to the far distance while remaining at the edge of the scene. This intellectual detachment, even contemplation, separated Watkins' photographs from the theatrics encountered in the work of many nineteenth-century photographers and painters.[21]

In the summer of 1863, driven by a need to make money and to avoid the fractional politics of a New York City embroiled in the Civil War, Frederick Law Olmsted, this country's first landscape architect, accepted Frémont's invitation to serve as superintendent of the Mariposa estate. The mines had recently been prosperous, and Watkins had photographed them in 1860 with the express direction to show "everything that contributed to income and possible future income from Las Mariposas."[22] However, they turned unproductive virtually at the moment of Olmsted's arrival. His task was to diversify the activities, disentangle the accounts, and make the enterprise successful. Frémont had recently lost his presidential bid, and would continue to engage himself in grandiose schemes, with a concerted lack of interest in business detail. In the summer of 1864 Olmsted first visited Yosemite Valley with his family and was moved by its special beauty. He wrote:

> *The union of deepest sublimity with the deepest beauty of nature, not in one feature or another, not in one part, or one scene or another, not in any landscape that can be framed by itself, but all around and wherever the visitor goes constitutes the Yosemite the greatest glory of nature.*[23]

Dedicated admirers sought to protect the valley as a national treasure from the sort of cheap development suffered by Niagara Falls. A month before Olmsted's visit, Abraham Lincoln signed a bill in Congress giving Yosemite to the state of California ". . . that the premises be held for public use, recreation, and restoration and shall be held inalienable for all times."[24]

Olmsted was the ideal candidate to plan the future of Yosemite. He had come to California because of problems surrounding his innovative plan for Central Park; a year later he was called back East to complete it. Olmsted's recommendation was to ensure that the general public had access to the beneficent enjoyment of Yosemite and that the natural setting be as protected as possible. Olmsted solicited advice from artists Virgil Williams and Thomas Hill, both of whom had accompanied Bierstadt on his 1863 visit and were familiar with Yosemite, as well as from Watkins.

The Mariposa estate continued to decline. From the window of his home on the estate, Olmsted viewed the flux of this typical mining town:

> *Since I have been here, the District Attorney's office has been twice vacated by resignation and is now filled by the third incumbent. The two leading lawyers in the county have left it; four other lawyers have changed their residence. Three citizens previously engaged in other occupations have entered upon the practice of law. The principal capitalist, the largest merchant, and three other leading merchants have left the county; at least a dozen storekeepers have sold out and many more come in. The men of my acquaintance who were running mills of various kinds (saw, grain and stamp) when I came here have left them. . . . The justice of the peace, the seven successive school committeemen, three out of four of the physicians, the five butchers, the five innkeepers, eight out of twelve tradesmen and their assistants, the blacksmith, the two iron founders, the two barbers, the daguerreotypist, the bathing house keeper, the seven livery stable keepers, the three principal farmers, the three school teachers and about seventy out of one hundred miners and laboring men who have lived nearest me or who have been most readily accessible and observable to me have moved from one house, office or shop to another, or have left the country within two years. I count in this village forty-seven separate places of residence and of business which have been occupied by eighty-seven persons, not including housewives and children. Of these eighty-seven, eighty-five have changed their residence or place of business within two years.*[25]

Yosemite's prospects, on the other hand, seemed bright. In October, when Olmsted returned to New York, he took some of Watkins' pictures to hang in his new home. Olmsted's Yosemite recommendation was the first to acknowledge the spiritual heritage of beautiful natural settings and their appropriate use for recreation.

With both these views—Yosemite as the idyllic valley, and the consistent documentation of the industrialized landscape—did Carleton Watkins feel any environmentalist glimmerings of conscience? Were he or his contemporaries aware of the destructiveness of industry? Did they care? One can only wonder whether Olmsted found conflict in working for the Mariposa mining estate while sequestering land not many miles away against the kind of use he was supervising. The only clues are in the photographs.

Watkins' earlier pictures, before his bankruptcy (1874–75), are more formal in composition and possess a beautiful sense of clarity and distance. The later New Series group is moodier, even melancholy. Between his second visit to Yosemite (1865) and the seizure of his work during bankruptcy proceedings, the destructive consequences of hydraulic mining became apparent. It had rendered the Sacramento River impassable, flooded towns, and destroyed thousands of acres of farmland. In 1884 the government brought suit and outlawed the method, making the so-called "Sawyer Decision" (*Woodruff v. North Bloomfield*) the first environmental decision in the United States.[26] The promise of western opportunity was being compromised by expansionist industry.

Watkins' late pictures of mining on the Golden Gate and Feather River claims reflect this ambivalence about the use of this land (pl. 4). On the one hand, they show massive constructions of machinery and scaffolding, monuments to the technological creativity and dominion of the land. Yet human activity, including the tiny, distinctive figures of Chinese miners, is subsumed in deep Blakean shadow. Pictures of mill owners with their stacks of bullion replaced daguerreotypes of prospectors with pick, shovel, and pan (pl. 19). Hard-rock mines, built for profit with little regard for workers' safety, drew forth a restless labor force (pls. 16, 18). Mines in Idaho and Montana became strongholds of what became the Industrial Workers of the World (the IWW, or "Wobblies"). His sympathies obvious, Watkins disguised himself as a placer miner for his only documented self-portrait. The darker, moodier late pictures suggest a landscape where such individualism is overcome by large industrial forces.

The move to protect, enjoy, and develop certain pleasure grounds for tourist use, soon abetted by the railroad industry, segregated nature into special reserves. This encouraged the treatment and exploitation of the wilderness as a curiosity rather than as an essential part of the common experience of living in a country that both valued nature and needed to develop it. The West was vast, the resources seemingly limitless, and the effects of man appeared trivial. Within his lifetime, Thomas Cole's vision of the untouched sublime was in conflict with a power more efficient than the ax but motivated by the same impulse: the technological sublime—the awe-some control of land by machine. Beyond mining came the railroad.[27]

THE RAILROAD The Pacific Railroad Act of 1861 had its seeds in the rhetoric of Manifest Destiny, the dream of an overland route to the China trade (later obviated by the Suez Canal), the lure of rich mines, the inefficiency of transportation around Cape Horn, and the outbreak of the Civil War.

The rush to connect East and West was inspired after the Louisiana Purchase by Jefferson's interest in discovering, through Lewis and Clark, a viable trade route to the Pacific. Many railroad surveys were undertaken and publicized before the Civil War (one historian estimated the cost of producing the 1853–55 transcontinental railroad survey publication at one million dollars—twice the cost of the survey itself).[28] By this time, the rail issue was politicized by the slavery question. The Union and Central Pacific lines won the right to initiate the northern route over the more efficient southern route proposed by Jefferson Davis, then secretary of war (and later president of the Confederacy), but this route crossed both the Rocky and Sierra mountains, the latter of which would require expensive grading and tunneling.

The drive to connect East to West was powerfully renewed after the war. With bardic energy, Walt Whitman celebrated the technological mastery of the vast western spaces by the railroad in 1871 in his poem "Passage to India":

> *I see over my own continent the Pacific railroad surmounting every barrier,*
> *I see continual trains of cars winding along the Platte carrying freight*
> *and passengers,*
> *I hear the locomotives rushing and roaring, and the shrill steamwhistle,*
> *I hear the echoes reverberate through the grandest scenery in the world . . .*

The railroad embodied Manifest Destiny. Thomas Hart Benton and others encouraged the government to spend large sums of money in surveys, several directed by Frémont, "the Pathfinder," and then to implement the railroads. There was little expectation that the underpopulated interior could ever support the enormous financial costs of laying track. Besides, the region was home to hostile tribes and enormous herds of bison.

After the Civil War, in 1866, the transcontinental railroad was presented by its backers as a constructive way to achieve political unity. Congress had granted the Big Four—Leland Stanford, Mark Hopkins, Huntington, and Charles Crocker, of mercantile and banking interests—incentives to construct the Central Pacific from Sacramento through Nevada to meet the Union Pacific line from the East. The government agreed to subsidize the enormous cost by land grants and advantageous loans, which proved insufficient and led to the scandal of the Credit Mobilier, a corrupt financial scheme on the part of the Union Pacific

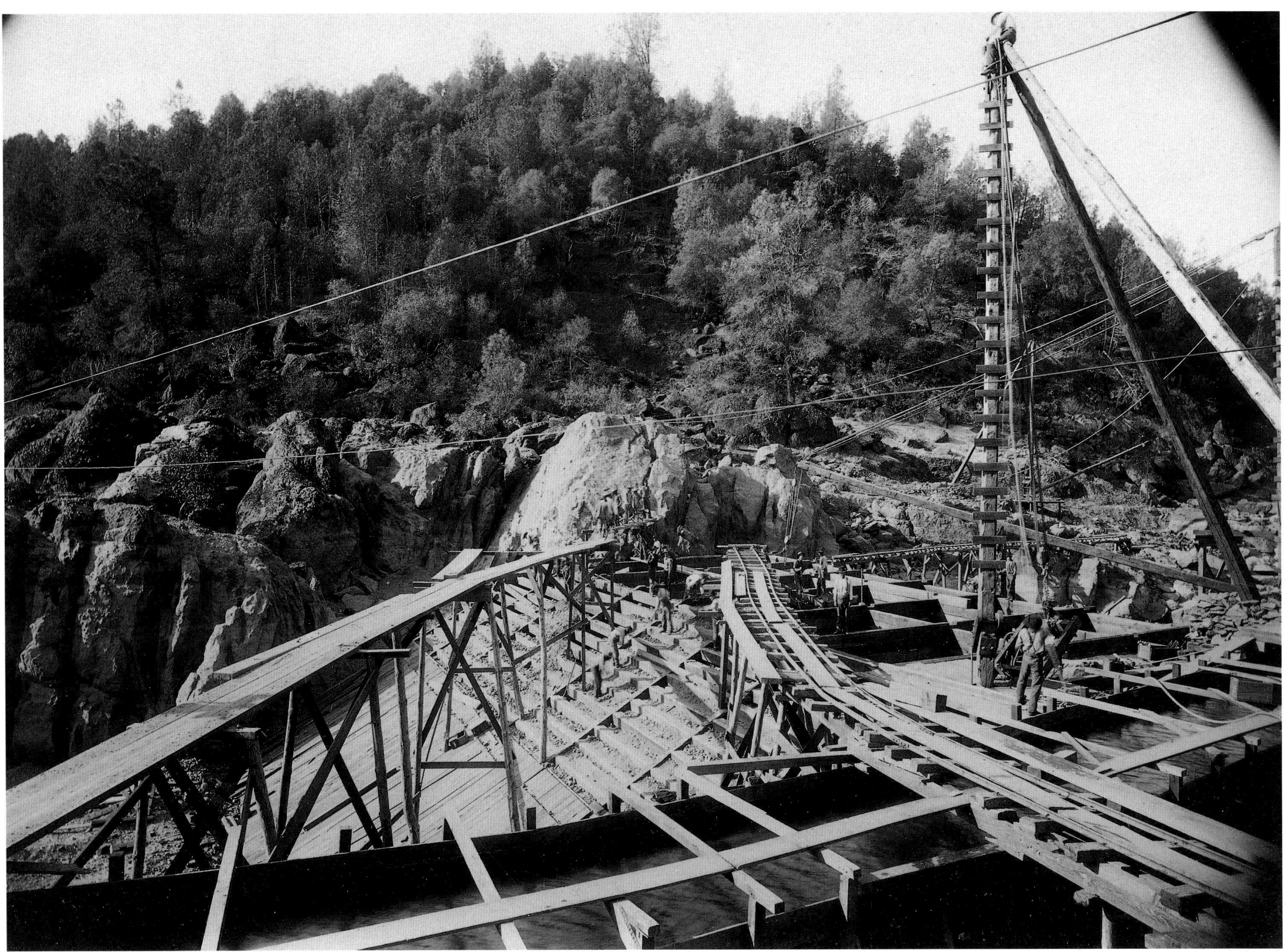

owners. The Union Pacific, staffed mainly by Irish emigrants, and the Central Pacific, which employed as many as ten thousand Chinese "coolies," joined track at Promontory, Utah, on May 10, 1869 (pl. 31). The Golden Spike reunited the country after the divisive experience of war.

THE SURVEYORS What was the interior like? Before it was photographed, the delineation of the land was made by artists who accompanied the early surveys and private exploring parties. They illustrated the flora and fauna of the interior, its geological and geographical character, and depicted the Native American inhabitants less in conscious artistry than as anthropological records. Their pictures are not ecstatic but documentary. The painters of these scenes considered themselves recorders of views and curiosities. Karl Bodmer, the greatest, was an enlightened and for the most part self-taught Romantic scientific illustrator. So was George Catlin. Seth Eastman was trained by the army as a surveyor.

The Victorian artist Albert Bierstadt, the archetypal painter of high moral sentiment and scientific accuracy, had an uncanny knack for the rhetoric of nationalism, if not bombast. His first major aesthetic statement, *The Rocky Mountains, Lander's Peak*, was painted in 1863, after he accompanied the explorer Frederick W. Lander to the western wilderness. The picture is enormous. At six by ten feet, it relays accurate information about what the area looked like and embodies the oracular nationalism of Manifest Destiny, in the accent of someone familiar with the European sublime (fig. 2). In 1859 gold had been discovered near Pike's Peak, and Bierstadt capitalized on interest in the region to promote his work.

Bierstadt, both artist and populist, took a stereoscopic camera to the Rockies on the Lander expedition, along with the usual means of making field notes, as much for publicity as for potential sales.[29] His theatrical paintings owe much to photography. He made photographs, and his two brothers were photographers (one particularly interested in quality photographic reproduction, the other in stereos). Bierstadt seems to have regarded *The Rocky Mountains* in a context similar to the large panoramas of the period, allied to science for their accurate delineation of distant and unknown territory and to the theater for their popular entertainment value. Many expeditions recognized the potential importance of photography, which had not earlier proven practical but soon would become essential. Furthermore, illustrated magazines, also for entertainment and self-improvement, emerged at about the same time as photography, serving a similar audience.[30] Bierstadt also commissioned a large chromolithograph of *The Rocky Mountains* for the potential middle-class clientele.[31]

In 1863, in the midst of the Civil War and as *The Rocky Mountains* was prominently displayed in the East, Bierstadt returned to the West on a more extended visit, accompanied by the writer Fitz Hugh Ludlow. Their visit was at least partly inspired by Carleton Watkins' Yosemite pictures, described in the press the year before: "Nothing in the way of landscape can be more impressive or picturesque."[32] Bierstadt had seen the photographs in New York, as he would also in San Francisco. The two artists probably knew each other but there is no evidence that Watkins had anything but a passing interest in the painter's work.

The last surveys to determine and delineate western resources and topography began with the close of the Civil War and ended in 1879. Four major teams employed scientists, topographical surveyors, artists, and photographers, most of whom had field experience in the Civil War. The territories under exploration stretched from Nebraska to California, and extended from Montana to the Mexican border. Large-format photographs were made for use in reports, but the surveys usually publicized their work through the sale of stereos. The George Wheeler expedition (1869–79), for instance, distributed stereos to members of Congress, friends, and associates, and also sold them commercially. William Henry Jackson retained the negative rights for stereos made for the Ferdinand V. Hayden surveys (1867–78) and provided Hayden with pictures for friends and influential persons. Stereos were mainly used for instructional purposes in schools and for parlor entertainment. Rights to the stereos, held by the photographers, were often considered so potentially lucrative that no salary was deemed necessary. It was in the interest of the photographer to develop this market.[33]

Concentrated attention on the geological history and character of this wide, diverse area was inspired not only by commercial interests and the need to have good maps, but by the imaginative hold of geologic science on the public. This science revealed the history of creation, a divine universal plan, and the role of the American continent within it. The geologist-

PLATE 4
Carleton E. Watkins
Golden Feather Mining Claim, No. 19, Feather River, Butte County, California, 1891
albumen print
15½ x 21 in. (39.4 x 53.3 cm)
Collection of the Bancroft Library, University of California, Berkeley

Detailed view of sluicing elevator, discharging water and gravels downstream through sluices across foot-dam

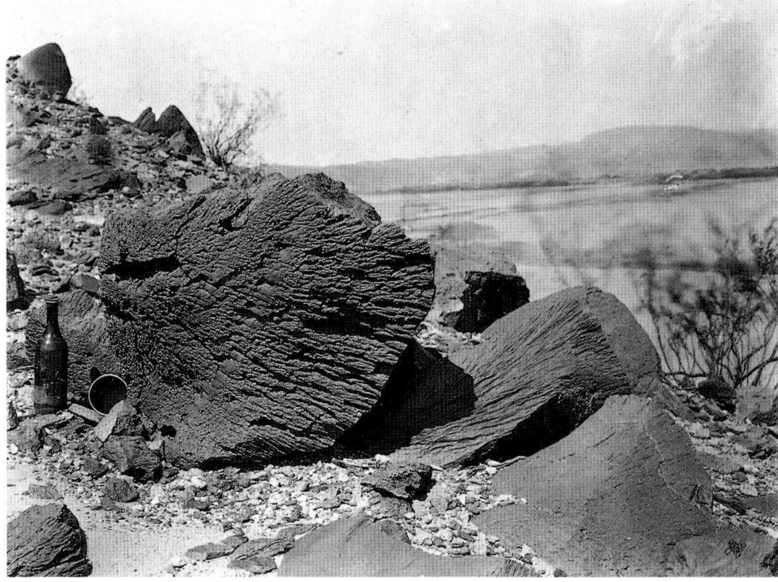

FIGURE 4
Timothy H. O'Sullivan
Rock Carved by Drifting Sand, Below Fortification Rock, Arizona, 1871
Collection of the San Francisco Museum of Modern Art, gift of Randi and Bob Fisher, 95.283

explorer and survey leader Clarence King, who led an expedition from 1867 to 1872, was an eloquent admirer of the American landscape and an active, impassioned proponent of the theory of "catastrophism." Geological change, he believed, occurred over vast periods of time but included moments of rapid, violent change, where raw forces flung up mountain ranges or created wastelands. This most popular nineteenth-century science was infused with religious idealism. The less dashing, more scholarly and conservative Grove Karl Gilbert, geologist with the Wheeler expedition from 1871–74, was a "Uniformitarian" who saw geologic evolution as an infinitely slow, gradual transformation (fig. 4).

The photographer Timothy O'Sullivan was hired to work with King from 1867 to 1869. He spent 1870 and 1871 with the Wheeler expedition, 1872 with King, and 1873 and 1874 with Wheeler again. O'Sullivan's pictures reveal an intelligence confronting the barren enormity of the interior wasteland and the rational approach to it: taking measurements, analyzing the phenomena objectively, and finding the relationship of these curiosities to the measure of man (pl. 17). O'Sullivan was repelled by the vastness of the desert lands. Their barrenness and strangeness moved him to make intellectually distanced pictures of a mysterious, frightening landscape, its wonders often eclipsed in terror.[34]

Other photographers followed to record the physical incursion of the railroad into the wilderness. Some of the railroad surveys were made before the more thorough, scientific, state-supported expeditions. Straight from the Civil War, Alexander Gardner followed the Kansas Pacific on its push westward and into Indian territory. His pictures record the power brokers—the deal-making railroad commissioners—at the state line (pl. 30) and the inevitable forward march of track. One picture is explicitly entitled *"Westward the Course of Empire Takes Its Way," Laying Track 300 Miles West of Missouri River, 19 October, 1867* (fig. 5). Its forward impulse is as inexorable and unstoppable as the dynamic sweep of the civilizing railroad in Fanny Palmer's famous and popular 1868 Currier and Ives print of almost the same name (fig. 6). Both titles quote Bishop George Berkeley's poem on the future of civilization. As a nineteenth-century defender of the necessity of railroads wrote:

> *In the Great West, where continuous settlement is impossible, where instead of navigable rivers we find arid deserts, but where nevertheless spots of great fertility and the richest prizes of the mineral kingdom tempt men onward into those vast regions, railways become almost a necessity of existence—certainly of development; and the locomotive has to lead instead of follow the tide of population.*[35]

The landscape painter Alfred A. Hart made an extensive set of stereo views as the crews of the Central Pacific blasted their way through the granite peaks of the Sierra. Hart owed his commission to his friendship with Edwin Bryant Crocker, and it ended with Crocker's retirement, but Carleton Watkins appreciated the quality of these views and purchased the negatives, which he printed and sold (fig. 7). Andrew Joseph Russell was hired by the Union Pacific. His volume, *The Great West Illustrated*, records the inevitable push of track laying; the bare, open landscape; and the inventive, innovative projects: spanning great rivers, dynamiting through rock walls, erecting elaborate trestles—first of wood, then of steel—large and complex engineering masterworks (pl. 35). The Credit Mobilier, which financed the Union Pacific's final push westward (and precipitated the scandal), may also have encouraged hasty, shoddy construction of the tracks, as seen in Russell's photographs.[36] In a variant of this album at the DeGolyer Library, the message of empire building is very clear: The photographs on the right

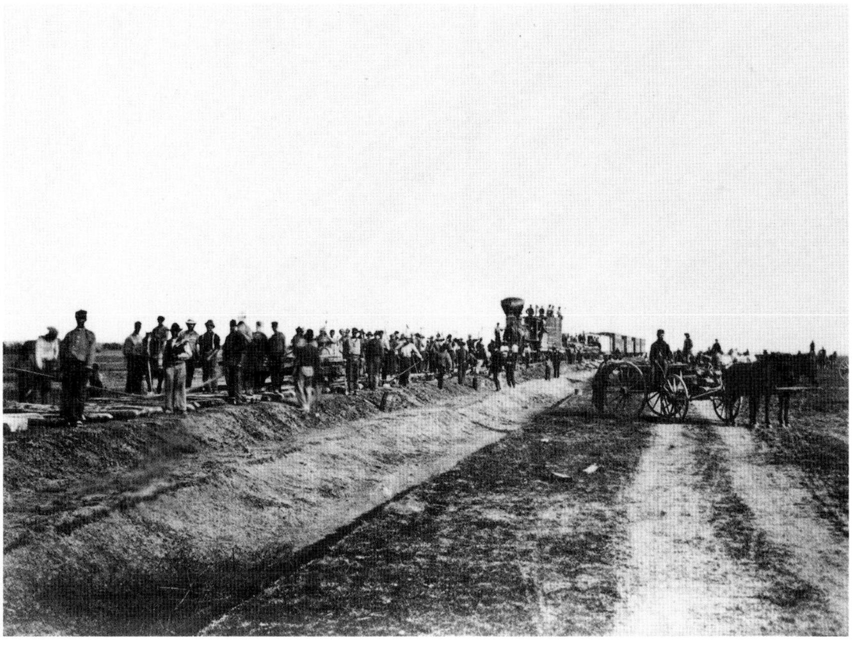

FIGURE 5

Alexander Gardner
"Westward the Course of Empire Takes Its Way," Laying Track, 300 Miles West of Missouri River, 19 October, 1867, 1867
Collection of the Boston Public Library

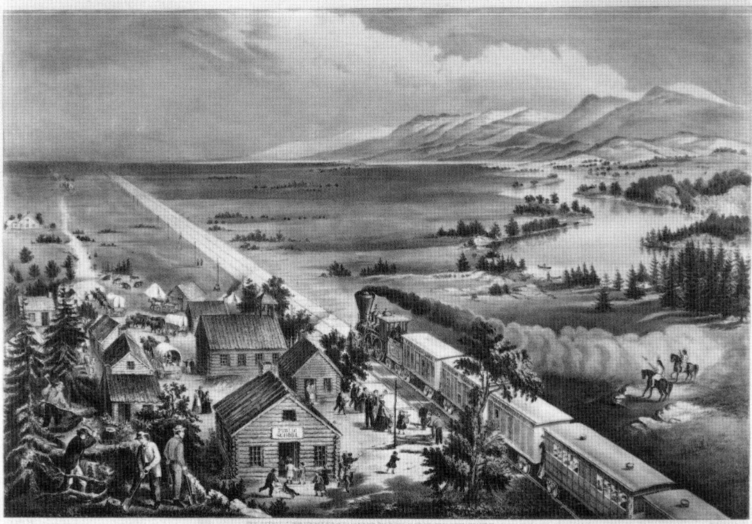

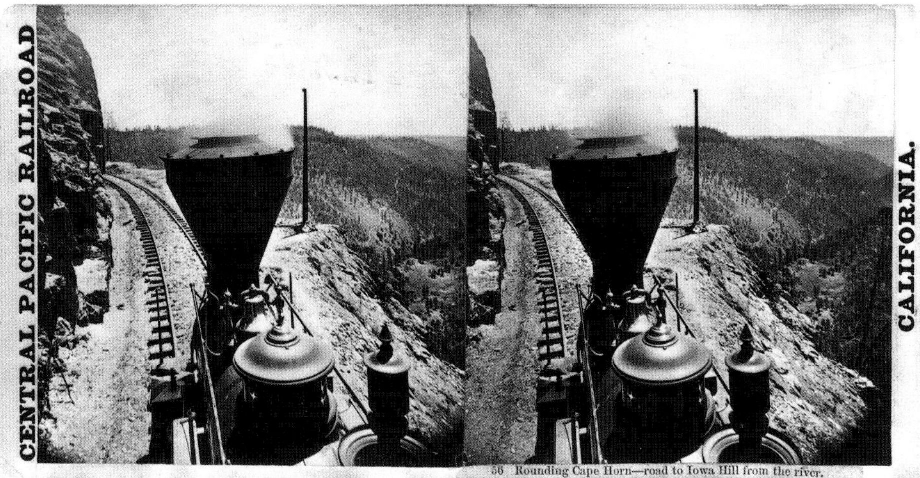

FIGURE 6

Fanny Palmer
Across the Continent. "Westward the Course of Empire Takes its Way," 1868
Museum of the City of New York, The Harry T. Peters Collection

FIGURE 7

Alfred A. Hart
No. 56 Rounding Cape Horn—road to Iowa Hill from the river, from the series *Central Pacific Railroad, California,* 1860s
Collection of Jim Crain

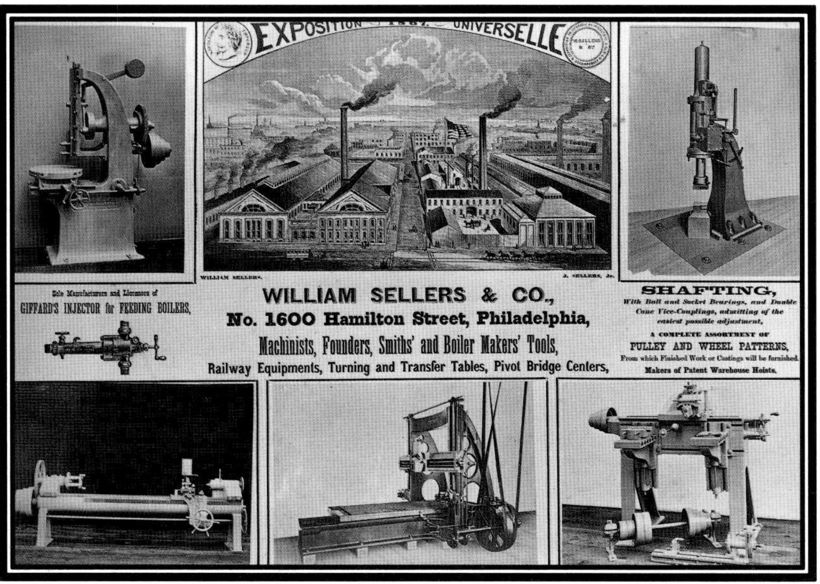

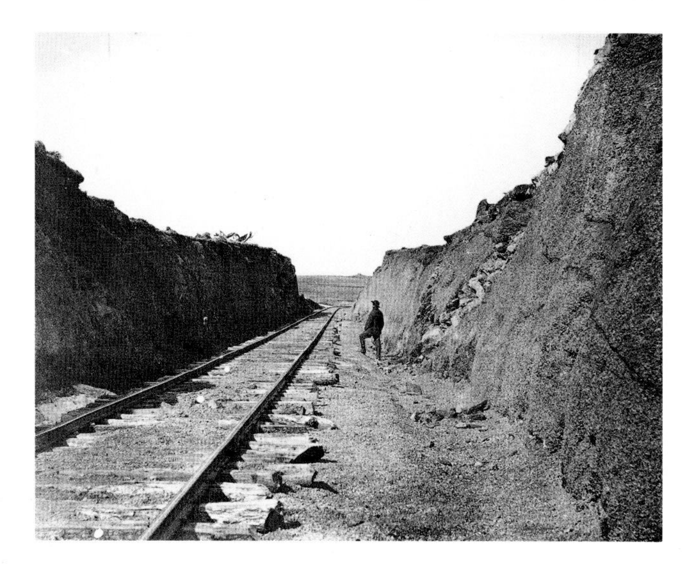

FIGURE 8

Facing pages from the album *Union Pacific Railroad Illustrations*, 1869
Collection of the DeGolyer Library, Southern Methodist University

(left) Advertisement for William Sellers & Co.

(right) Andrew Joseph Russell, *Carmichael's Cut, Granite Cañon*

depicting the incision of the railway into the barren, limitless desert are opposed on the left with gaudy illustrations of industry and towns, advertisements of what could come to this uninhabited land (fig. 8).

The photographs that Jackson made on the Hayden survey of the Yellowstone area were, like Watkins' pictures of Yosemite, effective in reserving that land for public use, withholding it from development to create a national park (technically the country's first) in 1872. Hayden had the perspicacity to hire both Jackson and the painter Thomas Moran. The two became friends, and Moran helped Jackson select the appropriate vantage points and taught him the artifice of picturesque and sublime composition. Jackson was transformed from a very good topographic photographer to one who learned and adapted the aesthetic lessons of landscape painting.

As a young photographer Jackson had sold his Indian portraits to ticket agents for resale to tourists. In 1870 he joined Hayden's survey and continued to work with him until he moved to Denver in 1880 to be close to the Rockies and to the many mining towns growing in the valley, where he transformed himself from government contractor to small businessman. He hoped to find markets for his pictures among the tourist trade and other industries in this rapidly growing city.[37] Jackson's career was complemented by the railroad: He photographed, along its lines, the spectacular scenery it served, and the towns and cities it connected. Jackson manufactured stereo views, mammoth pictures, panoramas, and eventually postcards, and traveled widely to photograph the burgeoning civilization that came from winning the war with the wilderness. (It helped that his wife's uncle, William Gilpin, was the mystic booster of Manifest Destiny.) Jackson eventually became a copier and warehouser of photographic images made for sale to as wide an audience as possible.

THE BUFFALO, THE TOURIST, AND THE RAILS The railroad transformed the trans-Mississippi West quickly and dramatically, in particular by hastening the decline of the Native Americans. Their territory, from which they were eventually removed, was physically invaded by the railroad. Furthermore, the vast herds of buffalo upon which their nomadic livelihood depended were decimated—as beavers had been trapped almost to extinction by the earlier frontiersmen, and deer had been hunted for the money their hides brought (when a "buck" was the price paid). Hunting represented the profound cultural divide between the attitude of Native Americans to land and its use and that of the eastern encroachers. The

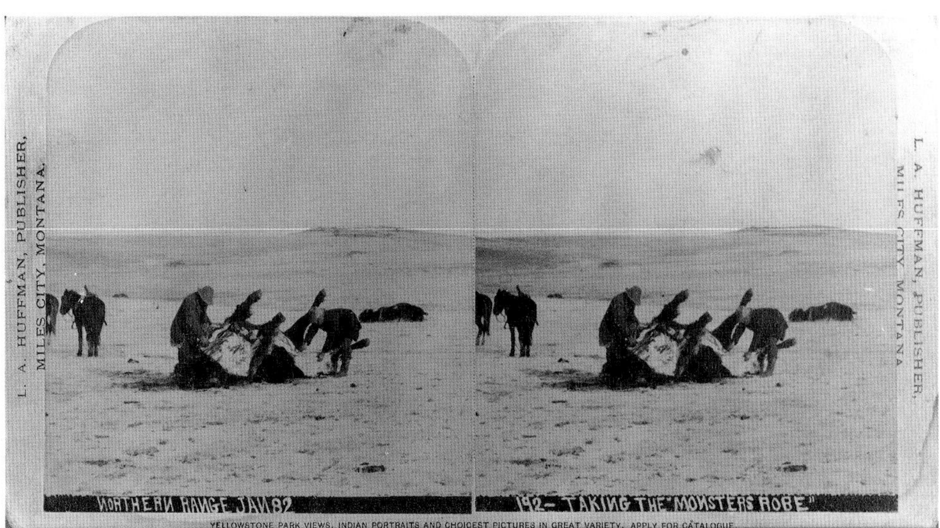

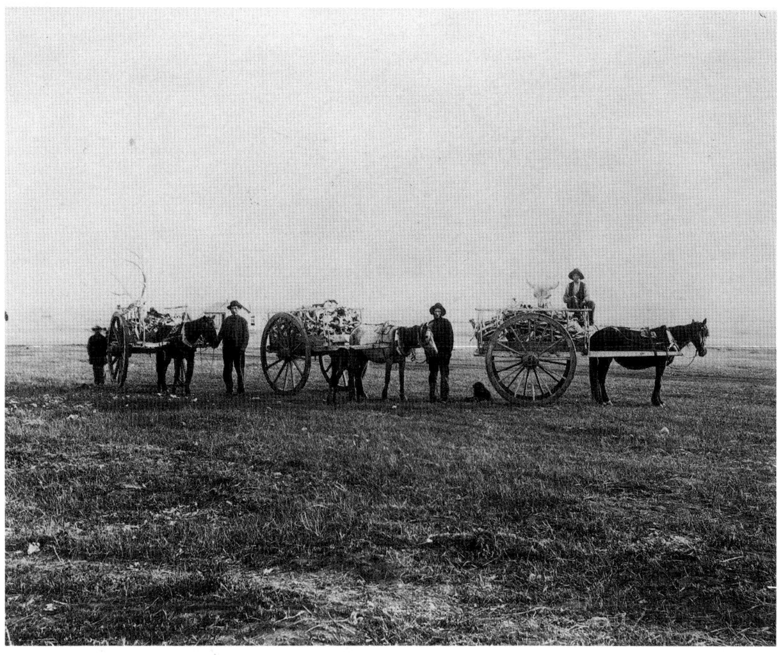

PLATE 5

Laton Alton Huffman
Taking the "Monster's Robe." Skinning Buffalo on the Northern Range, Montana, 1882
stereographic albumen prints
3⅞ x 7 in. (9.8 x 17.8 cm)
Collection of the Montana Historical Society, Helena

FIGURE 9

Frank Jay Haynes
Half-breed Buffalo Bone Pickers. Minnewaukan, Dakota Territory. N.P., 1886
Collection of William Reese

introduction of capitalist attitudes to natural resources—mining the land of its riches until there were no more—was practiced to perfection by the professional buffalo hunters (pl. 5). Hunting expeditions for visiting aristocracy and wealthy easterners were organized by the railroads. At first hunters took hides for robes or tongues (considered delicacies) or killed the animals simply for sport. In a mere few years, crews would gather up the bones that littered the plains to sell them for fertilizer (fig. 9). Barbed wire, introduced in 1874, confirmed the end of the free range and marked the beginning of the ranching and farming industries.

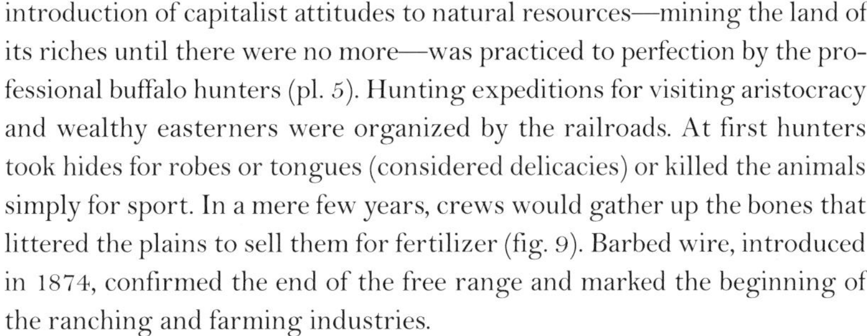

The railroads were, to a great extent, financed by outsiders, usually from the East. The Ames brothers, Massachusetts entrepreneurs and primary capitalists for the Union Pacific, were embroiled in the Credit Mobilier scandal of the 1870s. H. H. Richardson, the architect of the great public monuments of his day—churches, libraries, railroad stations—was commissioned in Boston to design a monument to the brothers with bas-reliefs by the eastern beaux-arts sculptor Augustus Saint-Gaudens. It was placed at the highest altitude achieved by the Union Pacific (fig. 10). Today the rusticated granite pyramid, a Victorian anomaly, stands in the bleak Wyoming plains three miles from the track, which was relocated in 1901.

Industry grew up around the track as it was laid, generating an enormous flow of wealth to eastern investors such as the Ames brothers. But the railroad also industrialized the experience of travel itself. Stepping into a railroad car, the passenger was absorbed into a larger industrial plan, a mechanized system rather than a personal experience of a particular landscape.[38] The railroad created an appetite for travel from East to West. As the speed of travel increased, the intense relationship of the traveler to the traversed space decreased. Going through the landscape was now peripheral to getting there. Wolfgang Schivelbusch remarks that the traveler could now sleep through the voyage. Instead of promoting an awareness of community, he says, train travel promoted a sense of solitude. The experience of travel by railroad—sitting in a dark room and watching the unfurling panoramic landscape—was like the experience of a diorama, and not unlike the sensuous pleasure we now take in film and television.[39] The tourist trade, driven by descriptions of curiosities and natural beauty—and by photographs—became an important nineteenth-century industry.

After the Union Pacific line was completed, the next two decades brought massive rail building, including the Northern Pacific, developed by Henry Villard. In 1876, Frank Jay Haynes, a young photographer, obtained

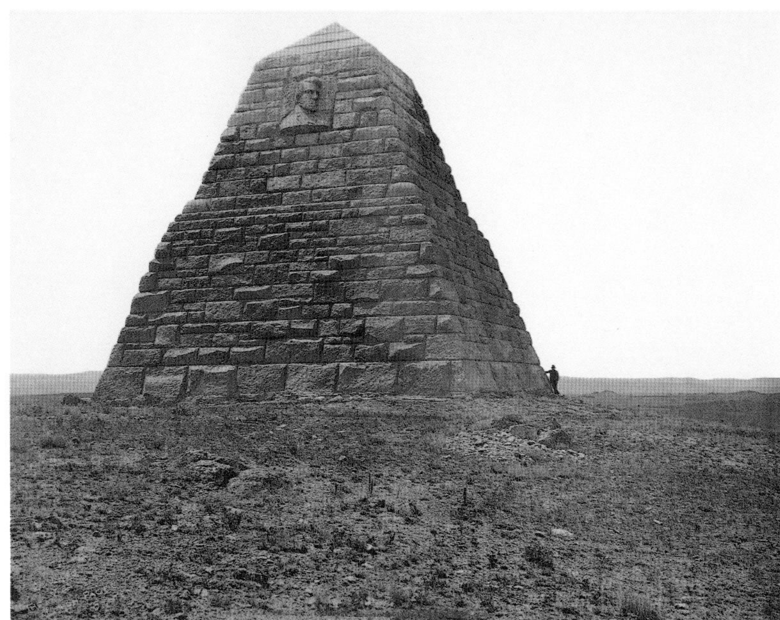

FIGURE 10
Unknown
Ames Monument reached via Union Pacific System, Sherman, Wyoming, ca. 1890
Union Pacific Museum Collection

a free pass from its superintendent at Brainerd, Minnesota. In about 1880 he was appointed official photographer for the line. In proposing this position, he wrote to a manager, Charles Fee:

> *You know as well as I do that the people back East are still describing this part of the country as the great American desert. My pictures are going all over the country; they are even going all over the world, and what I am doing is to show people that this is no desert, but a rich wonderland for tourists to marvel at, and for settlers to make their living in. If you will make me your official photographer, it will give me a standard that I don't now have. I can sell more pictures. You can do more business.*[40]

Haynes leased a Pullman car, outfitted it as a studio, and traveled the length of the line, making much of his money from the sale of stereos. His 1879 catalogue cites "all important places between Lake Superior and Missouri River," and "great wheat farms in Red River Valley, a specialty."[41]

Since the Northern Pacific owned the concessions at Yellowstone National Park, Haynes became Yellowstone's official photographer; eighty percent of his stereos were made in Yellowstone.[42] As he traveled the western states, photographing placer mining operations in Idaho, smelters in Montana, bonanza wheat farms in the Dakota and Montana territories, and large ranching operations, he was also commissioned by wealthy tourists visiting the "wild" West to be their guide. In 1884 he built a photographic studio at Yellowstone; two years later he formed a partnership to run a stage line into the park from Cinnabar, the nearest railway stop (pl. 33). Haynes' views publicized the park, and after E. H. Harriman asked Haynes to escort him through Yellowstone, he determined to lay track between Pocatello and West Yellowstone on the Union Pacific line.[43]

At first tourism was a luxury only the wealthy could afford, but soon it opened to the middle class. Scenery along the railroads was reproduced in popular weekly magazines such as *Harper's* and Frank Leslie's *Illustrated Newspaper*, as well as in the many guidebooks published in the 1870s and onwards.[44] Reproductions of William Henry Jackson's photographs proliferated in such places, and the public avidly bought stereo views and copies of William Cullen Bryant's lavishly illustrated, two-volume essay on the glories of American scenery, *Picturesque America*, published in 1874. Pictures of Yosemite, Yellowstone, the Rocky Mountains, and all the known wonders and curiosities of nature became important commodities, testimonies of the original—or the hoped for—sight.[45] Pleasure in nature offered contact with the divine origins of beauty or wonder; it was moral, instructive, and enjoyable. Such sights differed from the ordinary experience of nature, and photographs of the major natural tourist sites of the nineteenth-century West, Yosemite and Yellowstone in particular, emphasized isolation, curiosity, or wilderness, separated from, but within reach of, civilization (pls. 14, 42).

According to a popular travel guide, the vast territory of the West was neatly divided into marvels of nature, race, enterprise, mining, stock raising, and agriculture (fig. 11).[46] However, these "categories" were not seen as being at cross-purposes, but rather as parts of a large whole. According to the guidebook's author, "The remarkable growth of the New West is one of its marvels." He wrote further:

> *It seems as if God had concentrated His wisdom and power upon this part of our country, to make it His crowning work of modern civilization on this Western Continent. . . . Mammonism, Mormonism, Socialism, Skepticism, and Atheism are mighty obstacles to the rise and progress of our Western domain; but the holy trinity of Liberty, Education, and Christianity, in which the Anglo-Saxon race believe, will prove more than a match for them*

The industrialization symbolized by the railroad in the West occurred at every level and virtually all at once. It set systems in place that still exist, and it radically changed relationships with nature and community. Although its destructive aspects were acknowledged, in general the railroad was considered a positive, civilizing force. The energy and determination with which this change was accomplished were seen as part of the divine will, evidence of the superior traits of the culture behind it.

AGRICULTURE With the completion of the transcontinental railroad, no theoretical impediment remained to the agricultural conquest of the remaining West. Jefferson's persistent myth of the self-sufficient yeoman farmer energized the Freesoil movement that culminated in the Homestead Act of 1862, granting a 160-acre parcel to anyone who could live on it for five years. The railroads accelerated the process of homesteading, clearly suited to settling the Midwest. But it was vainglorious and painfully destructive to settlers who crossed the hundredth meridian, beyond the area of normally feasible agriculture.

Yet the agrarian ideal was not to be dismissed by inconvenient scientific fact. Once the railroad was built, its financiers had a vested interest in developing the area it crossed. Recent scholarship suggests that, rather than only exploiting the wealth of the West and importing it opportunistically to the East, the railroad interests, including the "robber barons," sought to develop stable economies in the West. Idealism and opportunity led the most vociferous propagandists to suggest, defying science, that "rain follows the plow," and that gardens would spring up magically after the plow turned the virgin sod.[48] Even after agricultural disasters ensued—drought and extreme winter and, on the plains, plagues of insects or ravages by natural predators (pls. 51, 52)—the myth of the garden persisted.[49]

Rain generally failed to follow the plow, but the railroad brought the culture of industry. Eastern boosters in favor of transforming the endless, treeless plains into a garden were forced to reconcile with the West's ocean-like sweep of space. The scale of the Great Plains, without trees, hills, vales, streams, was a new landscape; it encouraged a different kind of garden. The homesteaders that Solomon Butcher pictured—brave, proud families who

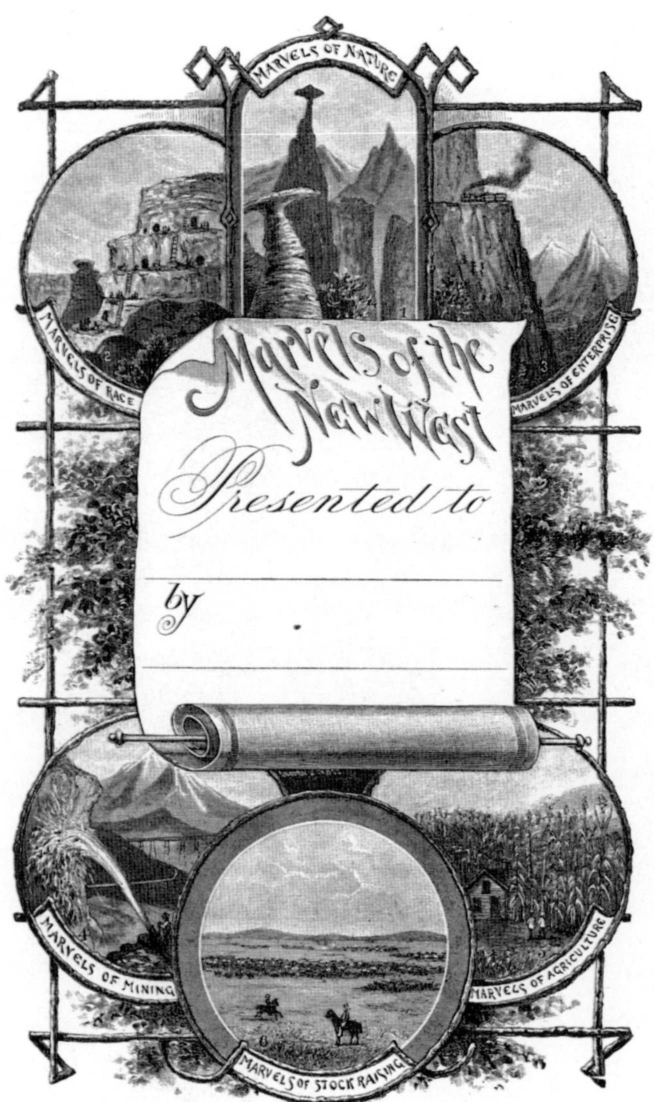

FIGURE 11

Unknown
Frontispiece of *Marvels of the New West: A Vivid Portrayal of the Stupendous Marvels in the Vast Wonderland West of the Missouri River,* 1888, William M. Thayer (author)

lived in dark sod homes where the snow blew without respite in the winter (pl. 47)—were pioneers of the old type. The new pioneer was the agricultural industrialist.[50]

Large-scale farming was the result of vast acreage, usually railroad property sold or leased to capitalists in the Northwest, the Dakota Territory, and California, and made into enormous wheat farms. These "bonanza" farms were usually operated by gangs of itinerant men, housed in communal lodges, fed communally, and transported from one area to another to plow, tend, and reap the harvest.[51]

Efforts were made to change the Homestead Act to help the individual farmers to better compete with this incipient agribusiness. This involved changes that would better reflect the climatic character of the trans-Mississippi West and alleviate persistent and flagrant abuses. John Wesley Powell, who published the *Report on the Lands of the Arid Region of the United States* in 1878 after leading his survey team down the Colorado River, suggested that the land of this area be classified by the government as best suited its use. Areas for stock raising, for instance, should be allotted more acreage than the 160-acre parcel, and fertile areas within range of irrigation projects should be given less.[52] This proposal, an argument for public planning of the West's most precious resource—water—proved unacceptable both to the railroad interests and their associates and to those who spoke for the small farmer, still the idealized pioneer.

The railroad bought industry to agriculture. The subsistence farmer, to survive, had to produce enough for his family as well as a surplus to sell. By the 1880s methods of plowing, fertilizing, producing hybrid seed, and marketing brought higher yields with less labor. This, combined with the markets opened up by the railroad, brought more money to the small farmer, and thus even he became a capitalist. In 1847 the Deere factory in Moline, Illinois, began producing a plow designed to cast off the heavy clayey soil of the prairie. But this was only the beginning of enormous technological inventiveness. Gang plows, more advanced harrows, seed drills, Cyrus McCormick's mechanical reaper—patented in 1845 and improved when he fashioned a machine that combined reaping and winnowing in the 1850s—led to other inventions. Harvesters, reaper-threshers, and combines—the enormous machines used particularly in the grain-farming centers of the Pacific Northwest and the Dakotas in the 1880s—were drawn by gangs of twenty horses over hundreds of acres of ripened grain.[53] Steam was introduced to power these giant machines, and, after World War I, gasoline (pl. 54). Towering over the horizon, the grain elevator appeared in the 1880s, a concrete symbol of the industry of farming.

Is extensive farming appropriate to the plains and the prairie? The question persists today as periods of certain drought follow periods of relative rainfall and water is mined from ancient aquifers below the earth.

THE COWBOY AND THE INDUSTRIAL RANCH Advanced technology fed the perception that the railroads favored larger mechanized operations, promoting sentiments that resulted in the populist movement. A parallel perception evolved in ranching and the growth of the cattle and sheep industries, where the mythology of the cowboy is virtually synonymous with the culture of the West. This mythology idealizes the hardworking, lonely figure created out of Hispanic predecessors on the Texas plains, where cattle roamed freely and a successful market was not developed until after the Civil War. Then the natural ability of the Texas longhorn to withstand the long distances of a cattle drive, the existence of open range, and the encroachment of the railroad led to a large-scale industry.

The first cowtown was Abilene, Kansas, characterized like the mining towns by its wildness, its colorful lawlessness, and its impermanent, diverse population. The cowboys who drove the cattle were used to hard, generally solitary work in the outdoors, and when they came to their port of call they tended to blow their earnings on booze and gambling. The "end of the trail" changed frequently, in part because of the cowboy's lack of neighborliness with the resident community.

Once the cowboy life evolved, it began to change. The Homestead Act, encouraging the establishment of farms, meant less free range; city growth meant a demand for good-quality meat. And so evolved stockyards, canning factories, more rail routes, and, in 1874, barbed wire, which promoted large-scale land holdings. Beef more tasty than the free-roaming longhorns resulted from breeding. The windmill obviated the need for natural accessible water sources.

Improvements required capital, and the lure of great profits brought heavy investment from the East and Europe. In the late 1880s, drought and, in the north, severe cold struck the plains. Thousands of cattle died. By the mid-1880s cattle raising was a business rather than a colorful, individual way of life.[54] Still, the personal ruggedness and courage of the cowboy, the value he placed in the reliable companionship of his horse (pl. 48) and in the manly communal rites of roundups and branding (pl. 49), and the beauty of experiencing the open plains (pl. 50) are indelible elements in the American cultural landscape. Cowboys (many were Hispanic or African American) soon became hired laborers on the large ranches, working for companies, in contrast to profiting as small-time entrepreneurs through hard work and luck. Their attempted strike in 1883 was easily broken.[55] The Taylor Grazing Act of 1930, intended to preserve what remained of the free range as land to be owned by government and leased to ranchers at advantageous rates, has proven to be a subsidy more for large-scale businesses than smaller operations. Yet the mythology prevails.

Laton Alton Huffman arrived in eastern Montana in about 1878 and spent most of his career around Miles City. Still-hostile Sioux remained in the area, although war with the Indian tribes soon would be over, and the northern buffalo still roamed the land Huffman called "The Big Open." By the end of the decade the hide-hunters had begun to kill as many bison as possible (pl. 5).[56] Huffman, who witnessed the slaughter, reported as many as 120 of the animals killed in under two hours. In 1883 it was all over. Wolfing also paid a bounty, and the slaughter of the wolves was photographed by Huffman as well. Wolves were killed by strychnine poison rubbed into buffalo carcasses. As the natural predators were removed, other kinds of pests persisted, especially on agricultural land (pls. 51, 52).

Huffman saw that the range was closing in on the large cattle ranches, and often on horseback, using dry (glass) plates he recorded these ranches extensively. He photographed the conquered Indian and the invading railroad, acutely aware that he was recording the end of a wild state, and he sold collotypes of these pictures to tourists and eastern admirers of cowboy life including his friend, the artist Charlie Russell. In 1907, Huffman said, "I would that there were yet a few waste places left untouched by the settler and his cursed wire fence. Good in its way, but not for me."[57]

Evelyn Cameron, a modest and private Montana photographer, documented ranch life on the high northern plains. She and her husband, Ewen, minor British aristocrats without much money, arrived in Montana for their honeymoon in 1889 and essentially never left. They planned to raise polo ponies on the open grassland, newly released from the buffalo and the Indian, and ship them to Britain. Investors, including British ones (and, soon, Theodore Roosevelt), were interested in developing what seemed such propitious markets. Overstocked grasslands and the terrific blizzards of 1886 and 1887 checked unrealistic speculation, and the Camerons settled on more modest ranching aspirations. Evelyn Cameron began to photograph in 1894, working consistently with dry-plate negatives and a folding four-by-five-inch view camera (she later used a Graflex), and contact printed on printing out paper. Because of the couple's financial straits, Cameron sold some of her photographs to local people, as she sold vegetables from her garden. Though modest, her images reveal her robust appreciation of that landscape and its extraordinary solitude. She documented the ranching and railroad operations, as well as the introduction of dry-farming techniques, about which she was dubious (pls. 45, 46).[58]

LUMBER CAMPS AND OIL RIGS With the railroad's incursion into the interior, the lumber industry developed in the Pacific Northwest (pl. 6) and the Northern California redwood forests. Lumber was needed for building and for ship construction, another major industry (pl. 63); for mining, to feed the smelting operations; and to produce steam power on the railroads. Originally confined to waterways, lumbering moved gradually inland with the railroads. When the steam donkey was introduced, the instinct to mine this resource and eliminate the lumber supply led to an 1891 Congressional bill to establish forest reserves. Still, only a handful of the giant fir trees, on protected land, now exist in the Northwest. Not only were all trees cut, but a secondary industry of harvesting the stumps eliminated all evidence of those forests.

Forest workers were usually single, young immigrants in dangerous and exacting conditions; thus lumber camps were sites of "Wobbly" activity. Probably because he was ardently religious, Darius Kinsey was trusted by the camp owners to enter the logging areas to photograph.[59] Kinsey worked in Washington state with his wife, Tabitha: he, to make pictures in

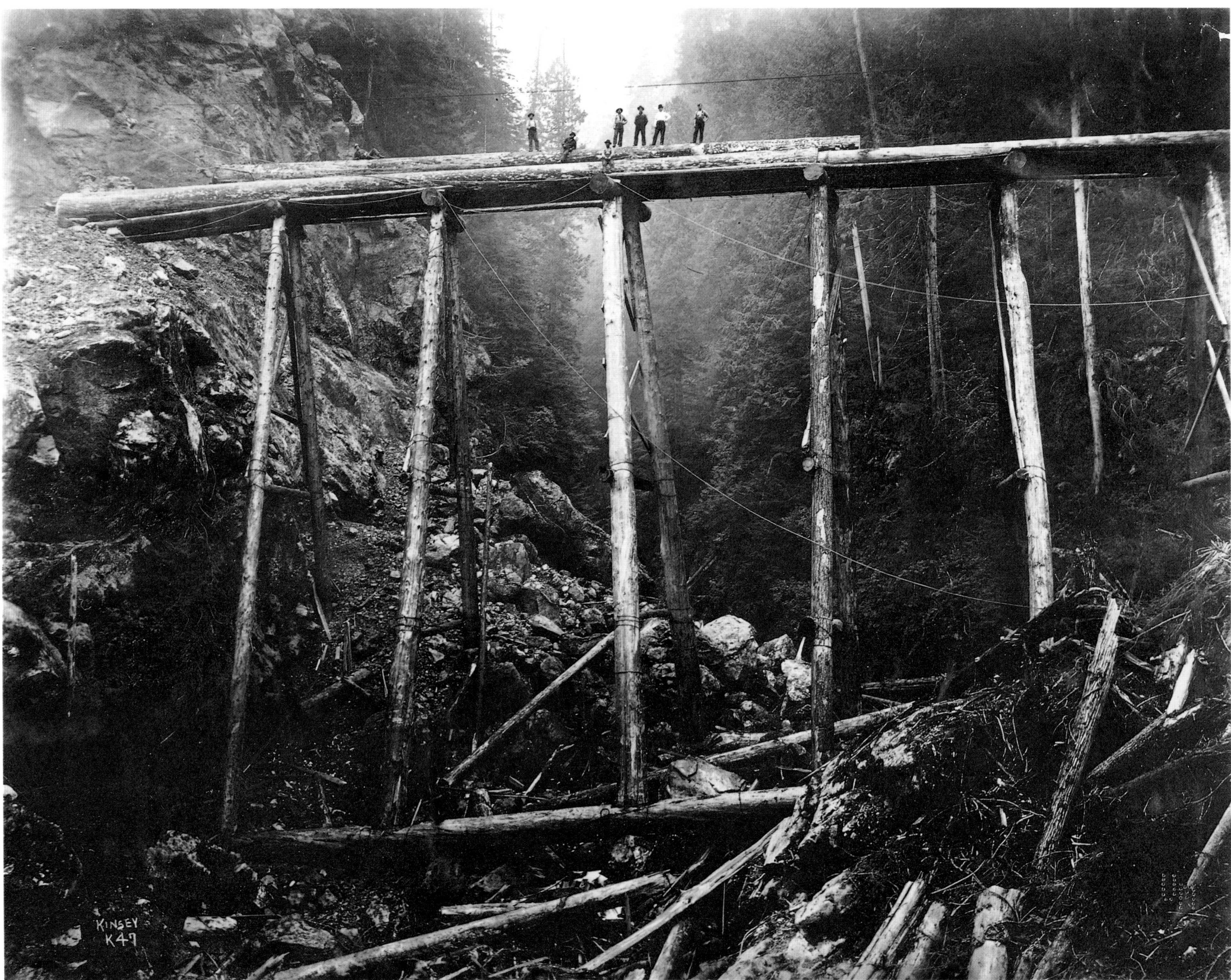
KINSEY
K47

the field; she, to do the processing. In this way they made a living photographing workers at their trade. For reasons of economy, Kinsey often put as many people into the picture as he could, intending to sell many prints of the same picture to those who were in it. His sympathies lay with the men who lived plain, spartan, heroic, and often lonely lives, with the companionship almost exclusively of other single men. The sawyers standing beside their cut trees are proud and modest conquerors.

California mill owners were photographed by the Bunnell firm, which specialized in industrial subjects. Spreading his arms out to the sides of a solid redwood plank like Leonardo da Vinci's Vitruvian man, one capitalist of the redwood forests, in his hat and topcoat, has taken control of the wilderness and reduced the wild trees to the measure of man (pl. 60).

At the turn of the century another form of mining evolved, with as profound an influence as the discovery of gold: petroleum. Southern California's fields were developed by E. L. Doheney, and a major strike in 1901 at Spindletop, in Texas, followed significant finds in Wyoming and the Indian Territory (Oklahoma). Oil produced instantaneous wealth on the plains, contributing to the development of major western cities, including Los Angeles (close to the Kern County fields in Bakersfield) and Houston. Most photographs of the industry were made by commercial photographers, many unknown except by their companies, who worked either as specialists or adept regional workers. Later, mining engineers and inspectors also made such photographs themselves.[60] Technological developments—lighter, simplified cameras and improved film, particularly roll film, that was easier to work with—made the process of photography less difficult. The photography market was increasingly directed to the amateur.

PANORAMIC VIEWS The original painted panorama, invented in 1785, was viewed in a circular room with controlled light, optically recreating the experience of viewing an expansive scene from above. Like their painted predecessors, most early photographic panoramas took the city as their subject. The static optical-panoramic form implied a continuum of vision, but the related narrative panorama, painted movies on canvas that were unrolled before an audience, implied a narrative of travel. This narrative was adapted to photography by sequencing photographs in an album. A sufficient market existed for these photographic panoramas, as well as their close relative, the diorama, despite their expense. Panoramic photography was employed in the service of industrial development.[61]

The great nineteenth-century panoramas made by Watkins and Muybridge focus mainly on the vital growth of San Francisco. However, some of the survey reports included panoramas of western landscape phenomena. O'Sullivan, piecing together several views made with a large-format camera, was especially inventive. He also recorded his subjects in sequences of time, or the progress of looking through the view (downstream, midstream, and upstream of the Black Canyon, Colorado River, 1871), suggesting a panoramic sensibility. A. J. Russell made a panorama of the open land in the Wyoming Territory as the railroad was passing through, inserting a tiny figure in the center to accentuate the modest scale of human accomplishment. Only the right half of this "panoramic" was included in Russell's promotional publication, *The Great West Illustrated*, because the full diptych revealed a barren, vast wasteland (pl. 11).[62] Watkins (as well as Russell) photographed Virginia City, site of the rich Comstock Lode, arisen Phoenix-like from the ashes of a fire a year before, a monument to the tremendous energy of enterprise (pl. 24).

By the 1880s the industrious, market-sensitive William Henry Jackson was reproducing not only city views but also the splendors of American scenery on a large, panoramic scale (pl. 40)—views probably intended for the decoration of public places. At the 1893 Chicago World's Fair, Charles Close exhibited his electric cyclorama, surrounding the viewer with a large-scale, 360-degree screen. Panoramas became widely popular when, in 1902, the Cirkut camera was introduced. Before this, the photographic panorama comprised many individual pictures placed end to end; the Cirkut produced a long, continuous image. However, while it was an effective, reliable instrument, it was not an amateur amusement but a professional tool for making panoramic views.

Eugene O. Goldbeck, located in San Antonio, Texas, an army base and incipient aviation center, found the Cirkut camera he had purchased in 1912 ideal for recording experiments in aviation (pl. 64), local industry, city views, and scores of uniformed men, each of whom wanted a yearly class picture. Goldbeck exploited the panorama. He saw that it was especially adaptable to formal group portraiture and made pictures of police departments, firemen, schools, and other community organizations. Much of his

PLATE 6
Darius R. Kinsey
Building Logging Railroad Bridge over a Canyon, Using Fir Bents 100 Feet Long, from an untitled album of logging pictures of the Northwest, early 1900s
gelatin silver print
10⅝ x 13¾ in. (30 x 34.9 cm)
Collection of the San Francisco Museum of Modern Art

income came from military groups, whom he visited regularly. He also made panoramas of famous sites, from the Grand Canyon to the Pyramids. But his most memorable pictures record the small communities of his native Texas and their traditions, as daffy as the bathing-beauty contest in Galveston and as fearsome as members of the Ku Klux Klan who posed for their portrait in his hometown.

Other photographers adapted the panorama camera to industry. Some, such as the Patteson Company, continued in Goldbeck's tradition and produced works such as the hand-tinted photograph of the spinach field in West Texas, with the laborers leaning over the crop, the owner in his hat and suit (pl. 56). Panoramas were ideally suited to render forests of derricks in California or Texas, huge open-pit copper mines in Utah, smelters in Montana, or logging operations in Washington and California (pl. 66), views, no doubt, proudly displayed in corporate offices.

URBAN GRIDS While popular mythology associated the West with wide open spaces, cities in the West grew with industrialism. Popular sentiment railed against cities, but exclusively those in the East, which were thought to keep the small farmer in bondage. William Jennings Bryan, the great populist, said in 1896: "The great cities rest upon our broad and fertile prairies. Burn down your cities and leave our farms, and your cities will spring up again as if by magic; but destroy our farms and the grass will grow in the streets of every city in the country."[63] By 1890 the majority of westerners were urbanites, and the West was the most urban region of the country. The character of their cities was different from that of cities in the East. Almost universally, their grid forms disregarded the specific character of the landscape.

One of the most distinctive western cities is Salt Lake City, Utah, established on a plain between the Wasatch Range and the Great Salt Lake, where the Mormons ended their long years of wandering. Under Brigham Young's direction, following Prophet Joseph Smith's city of Zion plan, with modifications, Salt Lake City was laid out in lots of ten acres, centered on the temple block, with streets 132 feet wide—enough space to turn an ox-driven wagon around. By the summer of 1849 the city housed about 8,000 persons. Temple Square was the focus of worship and church presence; Brigham Young and his polygamous family resided nearby. In 1864 work began on the Tabernacle, the large domed structure designed for perfect acoustics and the site of regular religious services and community functions (pl. 73). Construction of the Mormon Temple, a Victorian building of fortress design, was begun in 1853 and completed in 1893. These buildings are absolutely foreign to the landscape, just as the grid was an imposed ideal (pl. 72). Young and his successors were town builders; they planned 500 communities in the Great Basin area and beyond. When Young died in 1877, the Mormons had established 358. But Salt Lake City and the communal, generally agrarian society developed by the Mormons, so influential in the development of Utah, were not characteristic.

More truly western were the less centralized frontier towns created by industry. Popular archetypes were Dodge City, Kansas, a cattle town, or Deadwood, South Dakota, organized around mining—boom-and-bust towns where lawlessness, violence, and vigilantism played brief but significant roles. The predominantly male populations and their ethnic diversity affected the culture of the region. The miner's interest in extraction of resources, his fondness for risks and lavish living, and his restlessness characterize the extreme individualism of this culture. An English observer feared that in these towns "the unrestfulness, the passion for speculation, the feverish eagerness for quick and showy results, may so sink into the texture of the popular mind as to color it for centuries to come."[64]

The little railroad town of Corinne, Utah, seen in A. J. Russell's photograph as a series of tents (pl. 34), or the mining towns staked out in built homes and tents in Wonder, Nevada, are typical of the region's impermanent aspect. Many railroad towns constructed at the end of track were called "hells on wheels" because dormitory shacks and other buildings were literally put on the tracks to conveniently move them along as the railroads were constructed. Most towns that began in this way were as violent as they were temporary; only a few grew to substantial size. Many disappeared within months of the railway's relocation. Ghost towns also flourished at the end of a mineral vein.

By their scale, many of these raw urban centers projected an imperial intention. They had wide boulevards with imposing blocks and capitol buildings. Bigger was often better in the West. Almost without exception they were platted in grids, most without acknowledgment of topography, often ignoring open public space but providing for schools and religious and government buildings. Where the topography was deemed inconvenient and technology existed to modify it, changes occurred. In St. Louis, an older, established city and "gateway" to the West the site of an ancient Indian burial ground called "the Mound" was painstakingly leveled, its remains used for railroad fill. The Denny Hill area of Seattle was attacked by hydraulic technology learned from mining to grade the steep hills (pls. 70, 71). Like the imposition of the grid, these measures symbolized intellectual, even racial, control of the area and its domination by the superior skills and wisdom of the frontiersmen.

THE AUTOMOBILE AND THE IRRIGATION DITCH Two radical twentieth-century modifications of the land—the invention of the internal combustion engine and the design of large-scale irrigation systems—affect the way we now use this land as much as did mining and the railroad. In the early twentieth century automobiles enabled the middle class to own a comfortable, relatively inexpensive form of transportation that quickly became a necessity (pl. 7). Cars necessitated better roads, bridges, and the proliferation of gas stations, and they begat an increasingly mobile culture. Los Angeles and San Francisco, transformed by the car, sold out their efficient public transportation systems to make room for it. The automobile was the living symbol of individual mobility (pl. 79). By the 1930s it made possible migratory labor—the "factories in the fields" of the Depression. It provided Dust Bowl emigrants the means of finding employment and often served as their shelter.

By the 1920s the world-weary city dweller could own a country home or plan a vacation at Lake Tahoe or Yellowstone. With expanded popularity, these natural sites became increasingly man-centered. "Inconveniences" of the wilderness—grizzly bears and wolves—were trapped and killed. The "taming of the West" came to mean accessibility to wild places; motels, diners, and roadside tourist kitsch engendered a view of nature domesticated for human consumption. Films of talking deer and Disneyland itself were not far away. Closer to our own time, the "authentic" understanding of "nature," usually wilderness, by well-educated city folks has became something of a class practice. They were apt to disdain the recreation of ordinary citizens—drinking beer in trailer camps, jet-skiing in man-made lakes, or making indelible marks in the desert with all-terrain vehicles (pl. 88).

Photography, too, experienced a major technological change when, in 1888 George Eastman's Kodak camera revolutionized the industry. Suddenly anyone could make a photograph. Company advertising declared "You Press the Button, We Do the Rest." Professional photographers had to define themselves. Many became specialists (wedding or press photographers), or, like Goldbeck, concentrated on the panoramic group portrait. Regional journeymen recorded local industry, beauty spots of the area, and its tragedies—an earthquake, a train wreck, the passage of a tornado.

However, another kind of photographer also emerged at this time—the artist photographer. For this, much credit must be given to Alfred Stieglitz, born of German-Jewish parents in Hoboken, New Jersey. Art photography was an international, aristocratic phenomenon. By the turn of the century it was a practice mainly of well-heeled amateurs—"Pictorialists"—who made blurry pictures that looked like Whistler portraits or Symbolist paintings. As Stieglitz became interested in modern art, the photographers he had sponsored either withdrew or became, like him, keen to investigate the relationship of photography to modern painting, especially Cubism. Thus, through his galleries (291 and, later, An American Place) and his magazine *Camera Work*, photography as a modernist art form became known in New York and well beyond.

In Northern California, f/64, a group of professional photographers—specifically (and most importantly) Edward Weston, Imogen Cunningham, and Ansel Adams—were influenced by Stieglitz's example. Weston and Cunningham practiced a fully formed Pictorialist style before they, like their New York contemporaries, rejected "arty" Pictorialism, and in their own fashion became interested in Cubist-derived modernist abstraction. This interest, along with their respect for the particular properties of the medium—sharpness, close-up, and the glossy, industrial-looking print—were formulated in f/64 exhibitions and became characteristic of what they called "straight" photography. These exhibitions were the main aesthetic events of Northern California art in the early 1930s.

For Group f/64, nature was a more important, consistent subject than for their colleagues in the East. Weston examined vegetables—peppers, cabbages, radishes—in closeup, discovering their abstract sculptural properties in studio pictures, taken indoors. Even in nature, Weston (and Cunningham too) most often photographed the microcosmic detail—form

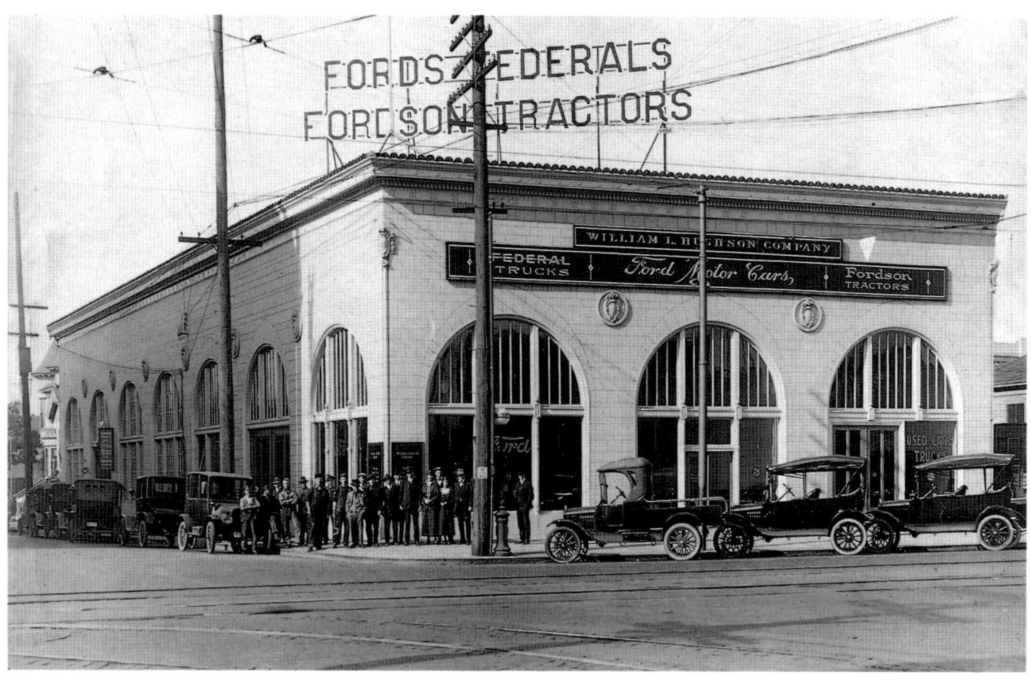

PLATE 7

Unknown
Untitled, ca. 1920
gelatin silver print
10 x 15⅜ in. (25.4 x 39.1 cm)
Collection of the San Francisco Museum of Modern Art. Members of Foto Forum, 95.450

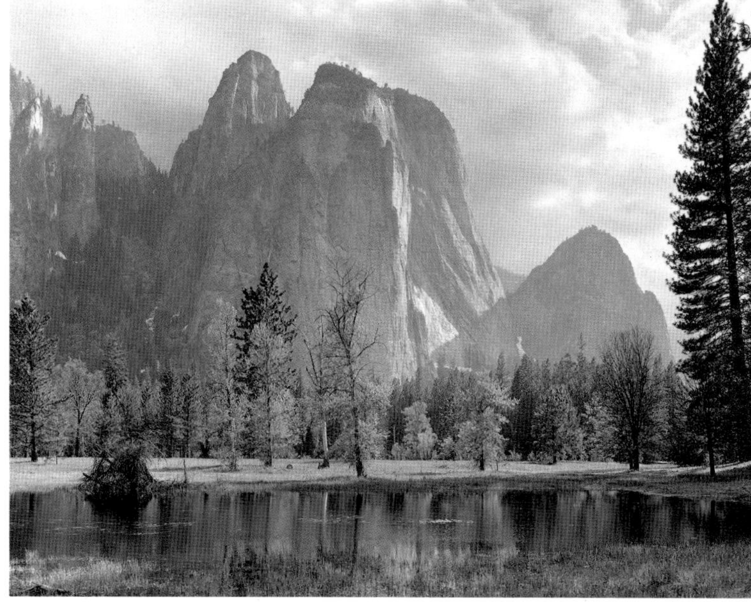

FIGURE 12

Ansel Adams
Cathedral Rocks, Yosemite Valley, ca. 1949
Courtesy of the Ansel Adams Publishing Rights Trust

rendered abstract—converted into a photographic modernism. Weston's Guggenheim grants in 1937 and 1938, and the pictures he made and included in his book *California and the West* in 1940, enlarged the detail to include the context, usually the landscape—most often wild desert places or lush agricultural valleys—as well as the traces and ruins of man's incursion.

Ansel Adams was different. He was younger, more articulate, and less comfortable with Weston's ascetic, marginal lifestyle and the conventions of artistic bohemia. He had turned to photography seriously after attempting a career as a concert pianist. His early pictures, called "Parmelian" prints, are stylistically similar to the symbolist painting of his friend Gottardo Piazzoni, and his early book, *Taos Pueblo* of 1930, is allied to Arts and Crafts publications. After his visit to New York in 1933, Adams was granted an exhibition at An American Place in 1936 and, of the westerners, it was he who maintained the closest ties to Stieglitz. The pictures he showed there were mostly small-scaled, carefully made modernist works within the tradition of Stieglitz and Paul Strand, whose experience of nature was intimate and within the reach of civilization. Later, Adams would turn to the more romantic, inclusive pictures of Yosemite and the Sierra, as the country slid from the Depression into war and then into the uncertain, disturbing period of McCarthyism (fig. 12). The spectacular effects of light, the more operatic manipulations of the print would come even later.

As a teenager, Adams had daily roamed the 1916 Panama Pacific Exposition in San Francisco (he considered this experience equivalent to a high school education), where American landscape painting was granted special attention.[65] He had haunted Yosemite in childhood with a small camera and later married Virginia Best, whose father was a painter of the wild park area and the West in general. Adams' vision of the western wilderness as the untouched sublime—the primal, God-given American landscape—was formed as the land was developed by the federal government during the Depression—its wild Colorado River controlled by the erection of the Hoover Dam, the western wilderness made more accessible through government-supported projects.

By the time Adams had evolved his wilderness ideal, he was supporting himself as a commercial photographer, many times depicting the man-used or man-inhabited landscape (pl. 83). With the death of his father-in-law, he took over Best's studio and promoted the Yosemite landscape in part by sales of his own work. In his mind and heart, he divorced the pure landscape of art from the commercial landscape of man's development.[66] Adams understood that the painters of the western sublime—Bierstadt, Moran, William Keith, Thomas Hill—were imbued with a reverential sense of the spiritual power of the western landscape. He appropriated this view as both justification and warning for the spiritual condition of his countrymen.

With the Depression, many artists turned to social subjects. Paul Strand, engaged in leftist activism in the 1930s, left the country after the war, profoundly troubled by what he saw as political regression. Dorothea Lange, deeply involved in easing the suffering of the Depression in California, rankled at her friend Adams' aloof stance and his insistence on "aesthetic" landscape subjects. Government projects for writers and artists of the thirties provided an opportunity to reexamine the American past, especially its regional history. In 1934, Bernard DeVoto, a friend of Adams, published in *Harper's Monthly Magazine* an incendiary, scholarly article, "The West: A Plundered Province," a culmination of years of perceived regional exploitation. In it he wrote: "From 1860 on, the western mountains have poured into the national wealth an unending stream of gold and silver and copper, a stream which was one of the basic forces of national expansion. It has not made the West wealthy. It has, to be brief, made the East wealthy."[67] This was old-fashioned populism brought up to date.

Photographers of f/64 or the Stieglitz circle, including Weston and Cunningham, experimented with industrial subjects as appropriate forms of modernist aesthetic expression. Adams, who took delight in photographing dams, mines, and even tourists in his commercial work, understood a need to accommodate the imperative of development. In 1936 he also began to use his pure landscape work to approach the government, lobbying on behalf of the Sierra Club for the establishment of King's Canyon National Park.

Adams was a man of contradiction. He was eminently of his time, believing, on the one hand in the good and wise technological mastery of nature and the possibility—even necessity—of multitudes to enjoy it, and, on the other hand, the special spiritual benefits of its untouched state. Yet for so stalwart a believer in the spiritual necessity of wilderness, Adams was a mechanically burdened photographer with a sophisticated collection of gadgets. Convinced of the viability of atomic energy, Adams also advocated an even-handed approach to land development. He worked within the park system, as well as through his commercial enterprise, to encourage visitors to nature. Adams' vision, essentially a nineteenth-century idealism, became profoundly influential as his interest shifted from making personal, expressive art to using his pictures in a more focused engagement with environmentalism, as the work of Carleton Watkins and William Henry Jackson had been used earlier in establishing parks. His wilderness vision still informs most of the photography published by the Sierra Club.

PUBLIC PROJECTS Tight, even excessive control of water—specifically a western phenomenon—defines the western experience. To survive in almost half of our nation one must transcend this basic necessity and find and collect it from snowpack rather than rain. The Mormons were able to thrive through a social structure that led them to develop communal irrigation systems, permitting Mormon farmers to form a prosperous agricultural economy, which the elders soon diversified with industrial projects. However, the history of water rights and use in the West is not characterized by the community planning of the Mormons or the Spanish. John Wesley Powell, later to be the second chief of the United States Geological Survey, wanted government to radically rethink its land-sale policies in order to reduce abuses and provide a more equitable system.[68] A different policy has steadily evolved, particularly since the Works Progress Administration projects of the 1930s. Government was brought in as an agent to subsidize large irrigation systems, providing water for farming, urban use, and power, and water became a form of capital and a means of extracting profit. It even has its own robber barons, depicted in the movie *Chinatown*. Of all the western myths, it is the myth of the family farmer, for whom the dams were claimed to be built, that has taken the longest to vanish.

During the 1930s, Franklin Delano Roosevelt initiated a major works program to develop jobs and provide cheap energy, an improved road system, and accessible parks with more amenities. The immediate enthusiasm with which the dams and enormous road-building projects were received comprised the last great creative impulse toward the construction of sublime technological wonders—those we believed could exert a beneficent control over nature—before the advent of nuclear power. Nothing so symbolized this as the beauty and power of the hydraulic dam, Hoover most of

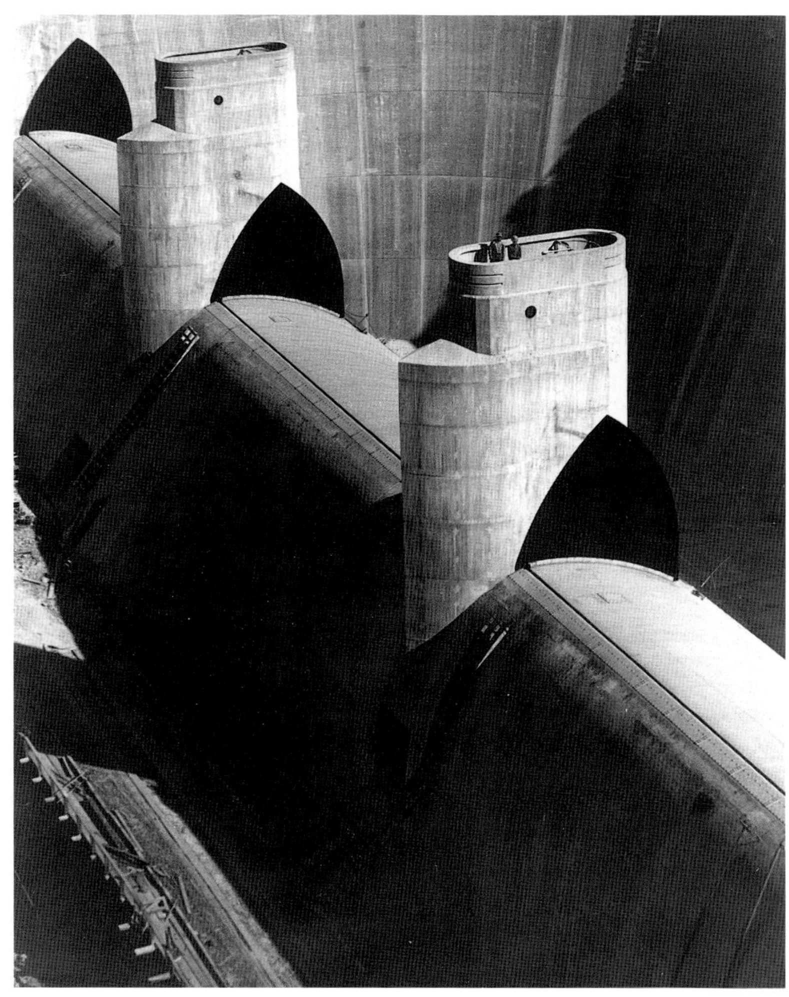

FIGURE 13
Ben Glaha
Boulder Dam, 1930s
Collection of Camera Works, Inc., New York

all. Henry Ford had declared that with his invention, "We shall learn to be masters rather than servants of Nature," and the same idealization of the control of natural forces—in this case energy rather than speed—vitalized the hydraulic engineers.[69] As factories developed in the Northeast, visiting tourists admired equally the hydroelectric power plants and the natural scenic beauty of Niagara Falls, which empowered the great industries of Buffalo in the early twentieth century.[70] Adams, Weston, and the easterner Charles Sheeler all photographed the more massive, more modern Hoover Dam. Even many Pictorialists, some of whom worked for the government, pictured the dam as a work of modern art (fig. 13). As many tourists came to watch its construction as visited the Grand Canyon.

The dam was considered a technological wonder of the world and a monument of great beauty. Pictorialist Ben Glaha presented a unique album, richly decorated with hand-prepared prints, to Harold L. Ickes, secretary of the interior. Journeymen photographers described the scale of workers to the larger master plan, detailing the shapes of its construction (pls. 85, 88). Amateurs joyfully recorded the excitement of the opening ceremony, when the newly contained waters leaped over the gates (pl. 84). These pictures, descriptive and positive, participate in the progressivist idealism of modernism and the New Deal.

Since the 1930s, the government has been a willing partner in the hydraulic environment of the West. Rivers and lakes, which receive spring runoff from melting snows, provide irrigation, power, and refreshment to the cities and to industries and agriculture. In 1902 the Newlands Reclamation Act established the Reclamation Service to construct irrigation dams in arid regions, funded by the sale of public lands. One early project on the Truckee River was intended to develop Reno and provide an agricultural community for local Paiute Indian tribes (pl. 81). This complex web necessitated a high level of control both by entrepreneurs and the government. The resulting system has made the desert blossom but in the highly capitalized conditions of industrialized agriculture. It also has provided, until recently, abundant water for Los Angeles lawns by extracting it from the wild rivers of Northern California.

Private adulation of the wilderness may have been a reaction, perhaps unaware, to centralized control, the anti-individual forces at work in the Central Valley and beyond, next door to Yosemite and the High Sierra.[71] In

Ansel Adams' time, the West rapidly became more deeply industrialized. The vast gardens and agricultural economies that flourished from the irrigation system called the Central Valley Project were not far away from the protected "wilderness" areas Adams photographed. Despite the great expanses of open space, it was a relatively closed, centralized, and hierarchical economy.

THE DISSONANTS Following Weston and Adams, some photographers of the western land—including Wynn Bullock, Paul Caponigro, and William Clift—have made personal, reflective, quiet pictures of lyrical grace and formal invention. Others have pursued commercial or local careers, photographing landscape for magazines, regional industry, or as amateurs. Before the 1960s, only two dissonant voices intruded, both from the East.

The earliest to articulate the changed character of the land, from the optimistic, confident "mastery" of resources to the human implications of technological and industrial control were the Farm Security Administration photographers, especially Dorothea Lange, Russell Lee, and Arthur Rothstein, who all worked extensively in the West. FSA photographs were mainly centered on people, and in the West they usually showed the effects of industrialized agriculture on the small entrepreneur, or the misfortunes of drought and soil erosion. Lange, especially, was committed to the persistent myth of the Jeffersonian farmer and the effect of industrialization on farm families and agricultural communities. But the FSA photographers were still optimists and resolutely believed in the power and integrity of the individual, and the necessity of government to enact just, progressive reform.

The displaced Swiss photographer Robert Frank received a Guggenheim grant in 1955 to work for a year photographing the United States. His book *The Americans* was published in the United States in 1959 (and a year earlier in Paris). Of the 83 photographs, only 33 are of western subjects, most made in Hollywood or greater Los Angeles. Another picture, published later (fig. 14), depicts a postcard stand near Hoover Dam holding three cards: a scenic panorama of the Grand Canyon, a picture of the dam, and a detonated atomic bomb. They constitute three contemporary uses of western lands: the commodified tourist's view; land as a source of power for human consumption; and the figurehead of the exuberant new Atomic Age, the bomb that brought an end to World War II, and a potential source of new wealth and energy in the 1950s. Hoover Dam electrified Las Vegas; that extravagant, unreal boomtown owed its existence to Roosevelt's public works. Not far away, in the desert, the federal government financed the secret testing of atomic power and gradually assumed control of vast acreage to perfect and produce nuclear weapons. The government became the largest single landowner in the postwar West, and much of it was devoted to military use. Frank's existentialist picture was a stunning comprehension of the dilemma of landscape in the postwar West.

Two years later, Garry Winogrand photographed a decidedly western suburban home, bare and new, surrounded by the craggy peaks of some unnamed western range, illumined by a dirty cloudy sky (fig. 15). The sun is bright and hot, parching the desert earth, blankly illuminating a "U" engraved on the side of the distant mountain. It casts a glare on the concrete slab that leads to the garage and stills a blond-headed child in diapers, wandering in this suburban wilderness, accompanied only by an overturned tricycle and an oil stain on the pavement. Winogrand's photographs were exhibited at the Museum of Modern Art in 1967, in a show titled *New Documents.* In the brochure John Szarkowski described the work of Winogrand, Lee Friedlander, and Diane Arbus:

> *In the past decade a new generation of photographers has directed the documentary approach toward more personal ends. Their aim has been not to reform life, but to know it. Their work betrays a sympathy—almost an affection—for the imperfections and the frailties of society.*[72]

Winogrand's particular, remorseless view of inhabited land was somewhat modified by the appearance, in 1974, of a modest book, *The New West*, by Robert Adams.

THE NEW TOPOGRAPHY Plain-spoken, the pictures in *The New West* are slightly tempered by the dyspeptic melancholy of Edward Hopper and by Ansel Adams' profound appreciation of wintry western light. Robert Adams' photographs are almost antithetical to those of Ansel Adams. For both, the open western sky, almost treeless, and the bare ridges of rock were palpable wonders. Ansel Adams was awestruck and grand, while Robert Adams looked at the foreground: he cherished the modest, prefabricated

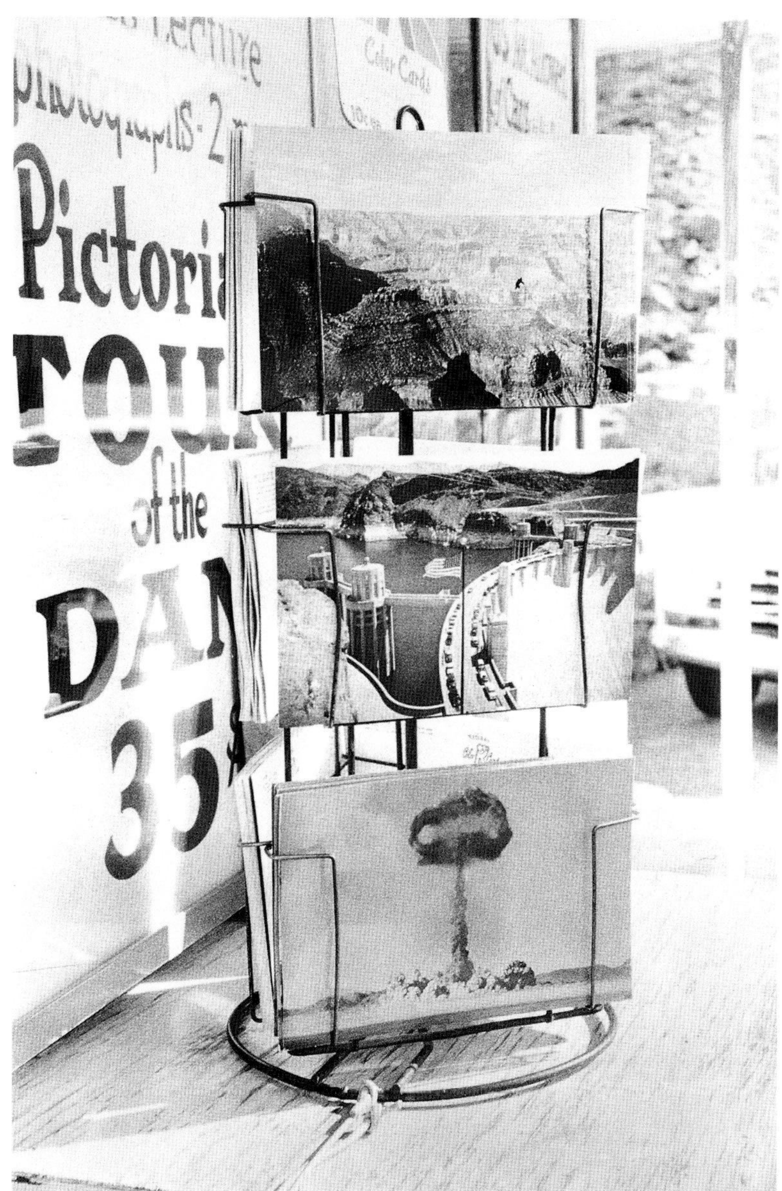

FIGURE 14

Robert Frank
Hoover Dam, Nevada, 1956
Collection of the Museum of Fine Arts, Houston. Gift of P/K Associates

homes, the trailers, the stretches of suburbs encroaching on the front range, even the roadside cluttered with plastic and neon. He recognized the fiction of Ansel Adams' idealized, segregated wilderness. Every Robert Adams picture is modified by identifiable western light, clear and warm, and by a modesty that poses as the intransigent truth.

By the time his book was published, Adams had moved to Denver. The pictures in *Denver*, published in 1977, are grimmer, the light more bleak, the tract housing colder—pathetically fragile, immodestly sterile. These pictures are more existential, less tender, made in boom times, when tract housing was constructed on a large scale for a new wave of western immigrants. They are brave and tragic, with a puritan edge. They reveal a social disregard for the people who will live in the houses, for the lack of human considerations with which these communities were planned, deep in the Watergate era and during the final contortions of the Vietnam War, and for the moral indifference of the society that produced it all.

In 1975 the George Eastman House in Rochester, New York, held an exhibition titled *New Topographics: Photographs of a Man-Altered Landscape.* It included the work of five of the photographers who appear in *Crossing the Frontier:* Robert Adams, Lewis Baltz, Joe Deal, Frank Gohlke, and Henry Wessel, Jr. The curator, William Jenkins, realized a sea change in the approach to landscape photography—an approach that was descriptive and, it seemed, emotionally removed. It lacked wholly the self-consciousness and inflection of the mature, developed work of Ansel Adams and those who took aesthetic direction from him. These photographers, certainly very different from each other, all share stylistic similarities: the convention of emotional distance, the depiction of commonplace subjects, and an interest in the descriptive property of photography. In the catalogue, Jenkins quotes Robert Adams:

> *Pictures should look like they were easily taken. Otherwise beauty in the world is made to seem elusive and rare, which it is not. . . . I admire the work of many photographers, but none more than that of O'Sullivan and Lange.*[73]

He admires, in other words, what we have come to recognize as documentary photography.

Robert Adams proposes that photographs approach the facility and uncomplicated appreciation of those made by an amateur. Otherwise, he cautions, "beauty in the world is made to seem elusive and rare." He is, in fact, an old-fashioned transcendentalist. Lange and many of her colleagues made pictures of what they saw that needed to be changed. In the 1960s and 1970s, this kind of photography was labeled a "style." *Let Us Now Praise Famous Men*, the book Walker Evans made with James Agee on families of white Southern sharecroppers, relevant to the generation of the New Topographers, was republished in 1960. In 1971, when Evans was given an exhibition, with catalogue, at the Museum of Modern Art in New York, he protested that his work was not "documentary" but in the "documentary style."[74] He was, after all, an artist, and he was not interested in using his talents to achieve political change (an attitude that got him into trouble with the government agency that hired him). He was an aristocrat by choice, by his emotional aloofness and even coolness to his subjects—which is not to say that he was insensitive or unappreciative. The demonstrative warmth Agee felt for the tenant families, his insistent engagement in their lives, was complemented but not shared by Evans.

By the 1970s, the public university systems in California and New York were booming and so were art departments, in whose arms the photographer was frequently embraced. As popular pictorial magazines diminished and television became the preferred visual currency, academia provided relative security and the company of colleagues and students. Photographers were treated as artists in this context, and some of the best were not only teachers but sold prints, published books, and continued to do some commercial work—in other words, they continued the entrepreneurial tradition with a new twist.[75]

At the same time, photography entered—or reentered—the art world of museums and galleries, spaces conducive to the meditative appreciation of pictures. But photographs present a further challenge. The subject of Robert Adams' picture is his reason for making it. To group his pictures, as in the Rochester exhibition, with the work of Bernd and Hilla Becher is to see in them a stylistic or formal cohesion but not to recognize their social content—in Adams' case, a brave one (pls. 120, 121, 123). To fail to question their motives or subjects is to deny the ironic humor of Henry Wessel's pictures, or Bill Dane's, or the fascinated horror of Lewis Baltz's *Industrial Parks* (pls. 127, 103, 122). Even the presumption of recording the world out there, existentially, is a concern with subject, and some, such as Joe Deal, find their subject beautiful (pl. 101). The reticence of their pictures indicates passionate conviction and sometimes dread at the implications of truth. Photography, as it was put into the context of art as another modernist enterprise with its "photographic" properties analyzed, seemed closer to the formal experimentation of painters of the same era.

Many photographers of the 1970s elected to make "art photographs," pictures that hung on a wall like a painting and whose content was in their formal invention. At the same time the new photographers of the social landscape and their often modestly produced books became increasingly engaged. They focused on a subject sequentially, even contextually, reintroducing narrative into photography. Reading photographic images to formulate a cumulative understanding was a nineteenth-century practice, forgotten through the exhibiting of pictures individually, on museum walls.[76]

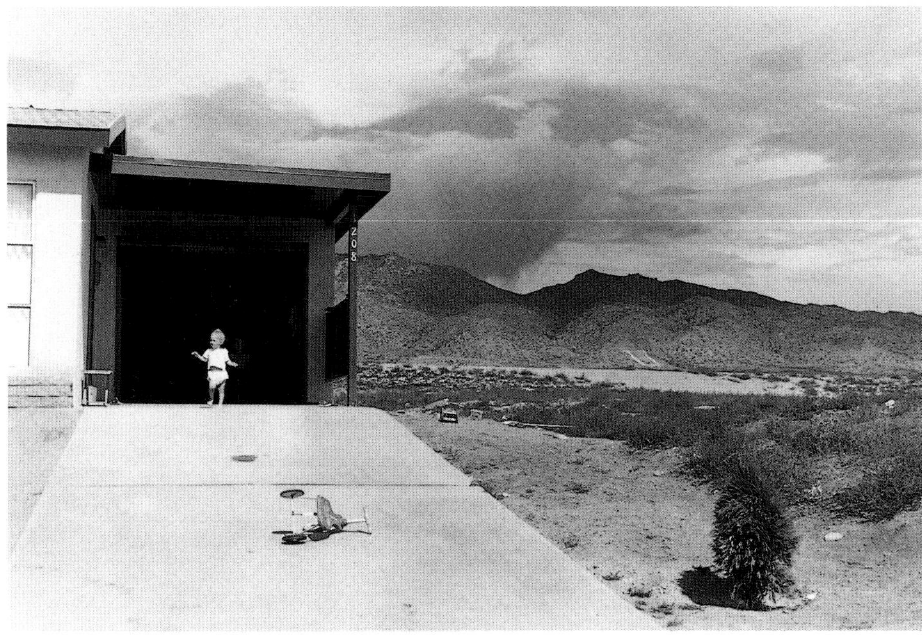

FIGURE 15
Garry Winogrand
New Mexico, 1957
Courtesy of the Fraenkel Gallery, San Francisco

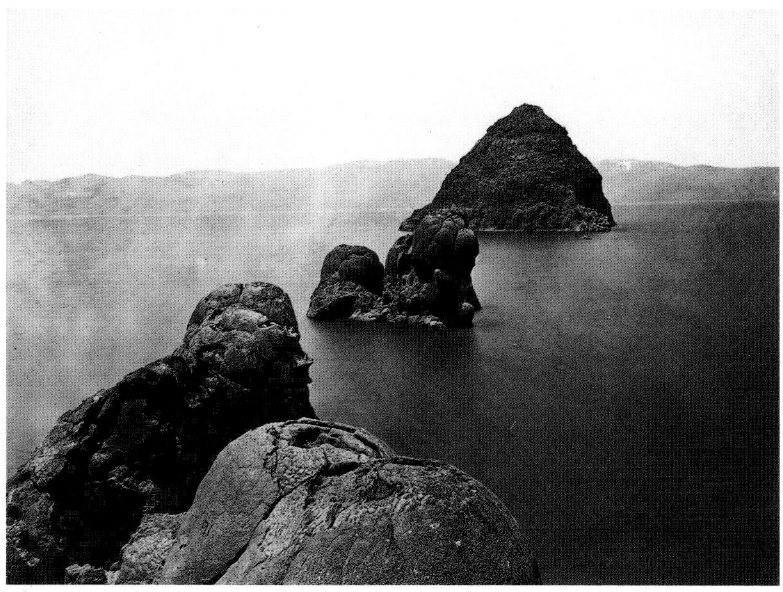

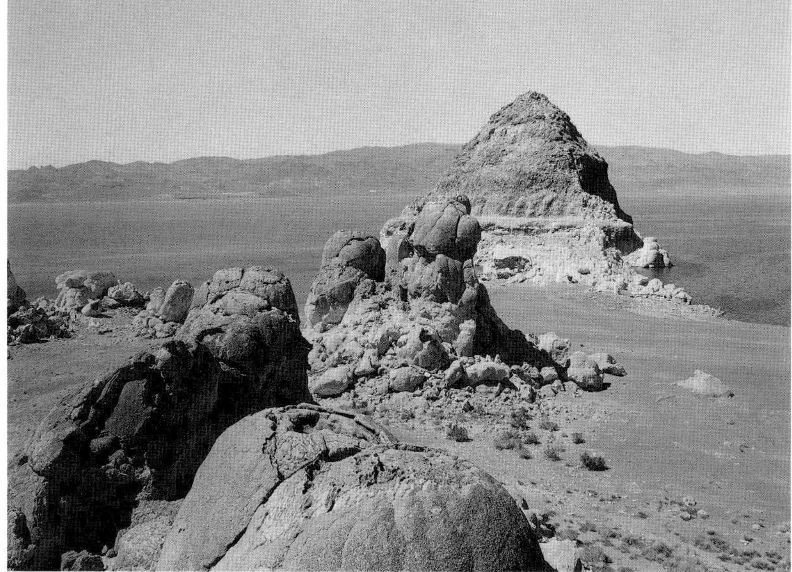

FIGURE 16
From the book *Second View: The Rephotographic Survey Project*, 1984

(left)
Timothy H. O'Sullivan
Rock Formations, Pyramid Lake, Nevada, 1867
Collection of the Massachusetts Institute of Technology

(right)
Mark Klett
Pyramid Isle, Pyramid Lake, Nevada, 1979
Courtesy of the artist

One of the decade's more revealing and relevant books, *Second View: The Rephotographic Survey Project*, was published in 1984.[77] It rerecorded the nineteenth-century western survey views to reveal what had happened in the intervening century. The work downplayed the personal, individualistic view or focus on "style," to create a narrative from one century to the other. Surprisingly, most of the sites remained virtually the same, untouched, at least within the limited frame of the picture. But the differences are instructive. Paved roads have displaced or destroyed impressive rock formations, such as Hanging Rock and, near it, Pulpit Rock, from which Brigham Young declared that a scouting team had discovered, not far away, the promised land at Salt Lake.[78] In another spot, an entire gold mine was removed, making the place virtually unrecognizable, but also reclaiming it from earlier industrial use. The comparison between Pyramid Lake photographed by O'Sullivan in 1867 and by Mark Klett in 1979 is subtle but important (fig. 16). In the intervening period the lake fell because water from the Truckee River had been diverted to Reno and for the Newlands Reclamation project.

Such mini-narratives imply a larger social landscape while maintaining the presumption of scientific observation. Ed Ruscha, in a series of books, elected to photograph *Every Building on the Sunset Strip* (fig. 17), the *Twentysix Gasoline Stations* he encountered on a drive from Los Angeles to Oklahoma City, and *Thirtyfour Parking Lots in Los Angeles*, a visual directory seen from the air. These books are like flat-footed puns. They describe the banal appearance of the city—an aggregation of parking lots and real estate touched by seediness. They constitute a reality check on inflated Hollywood melodrama, for which the camera is ideally suited. In the 1960s, Ruscha, like Andy Warhol, Robert Rauschenberg, John Baldessari, and many other artists, challenged what he felt to be overused modernist ideals.[79] The skirmish continues, past postmodernism to the present.

Although the Ruscha generation of artists can hardly be said to be socially conscious, postmodern artists such as Cindy Sherman and Richard Prince use the medium to enact or excerpt a critique of the pervasive media culture. Most recently, photographers Nan Goldin and Larry Clark represent the usually unknown, "white trash" culture or, in Goldin's case, flamboyant "high livers"—her friends among the cross-dressers and drug users—who are seen with the intimacy of family snapshots. These photographers, although they are the art world's latest media stars, have undertaken a social questioning that focuses less on the role of the artist than on the proper role of the gallery or museum, beyond enriching and enshrining the chosen artists.

These issues are relevant, and are shared by a number of photographers included in this exhibition who are uncomfortable with an elitist aes-

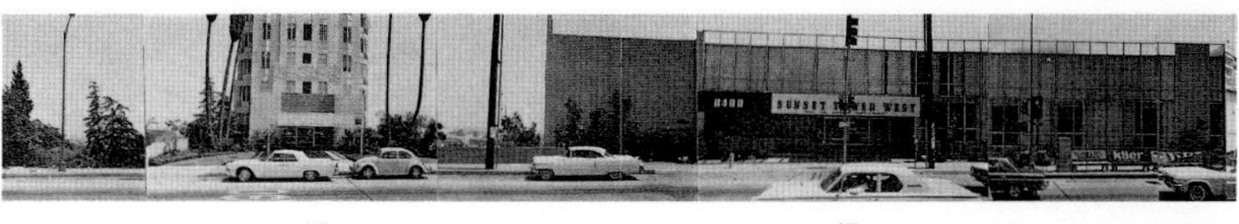

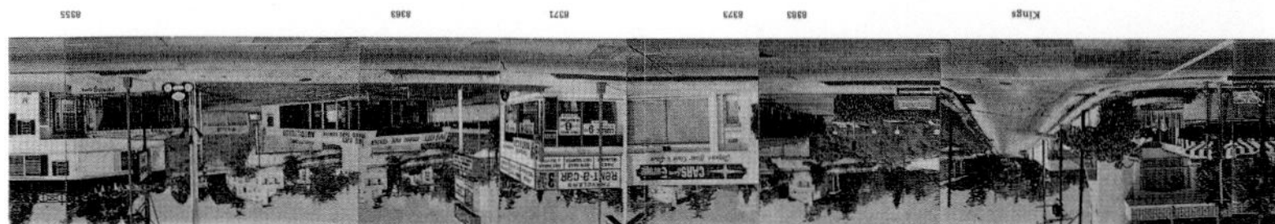

FIGURE 17

Edward Ruscha
Every Building on the Sunset Strip (book detail), 1966
Collection of the San Francisco Museum of Modern Art

theticism. The role of these photographers and the system within which they operate is opened (or reopened) to scrutiny. Some do not deign to exhibit in art galleries or, in this case, the museum. Are catalogues, or the pages of an art magazine appropriate venues for presenting major social issues? The question remains unanswered. Are museums the most effective places to stimulate thought and advocate change? Unlike the "artist photographers," they find themselves in an ambiguous position. Freed, however modestly, by the art world's tolerance of photography but not (or not yet) elevated to the upper reaches of art stardom, many of these photographers are as interested in the social meaning of landscape as they are in contemporary questions of art making. As was Carleton Watkins in the nineteenth century, they are poised between art and commissioned work, between landscape as salvation and as a source of profit. Perhaps it would be more accurate to call them photographers of the social landscape.

Some have elected to become environmental historians or local activists, using their work as propaganda, with text, to oppose activities they deem wasteful or harmful. Richard Misrach's book *Bravo 20* is an example. It is something of a legal brief against the government's appropriation of large stretches of public land (which sometimes encroaches on private land) for bombing practice.[80] Many of these photographers address the now-depleted mythology of the land as it affects the largely undeveloped, rural landscape or as it relates to western cities and suburban development. Geoffrey James finds the industrial sublime in asbestos mines in Canada; John Pfahl's nuclear power plant is enshrouded in cloud and sunset color worthy of Frederic Church or Albert Bierstadt, and an abstract, Richard Diebenkorn–like form is discovered in the aerial view of a toxic waste site by David Hanson (pls. 8, 110, 111). Mark Ruwedel's diptychs owe some of their astringent grandeur to Richard Long, but he also inscribes the history of the land on the photograph's mount, describing the invisible: the wartime transformation of the small town of Hanford, Washington, into a nuclear weapons plant; the unseen, unfelt presence of nuclear seepage; the earlier history of the place as an encampment for the Nez Percé (pl. 112). Barbara Norfleet finds the military use of land fairly ridiculous and unreal (pl. 114).

The federal government, involved since the nineteenth century in land development, has had a continuing presence in the West on military reserves and in the contorted, political management of resources such as grazing rights and water. Robert Dawson's picture of Pyramid Lake, photographed also by O'Sullivan and Klett, reveals a rare western lake on a reservation, depleted for a city and a complicated land reclamation project (pl. 117). Joseph Bartscherer's meditations on newly reclaimed desert land in East Oregon acknowledge the government's questionable presence in western agriculture (pl. 107). Frank Gohlke's photographs of Mt. St. Helens after the 1980 eruption acknowledge the nineteenth-century awe at sublime nature and the complex web of relationships between the timber companies, who clearcut and replant forests with single species (making them vulnerable to pests), the government ownership and management of forested land, and the fragile and increasingly taxed equilibrium between people and their planet (pl. 13).

The uses of land have expanded since the frontier opened. We see the segregated (and now overused) natural wonders of Death Valley through a car window, with lunch on the dashboard (pl. 94). We move mountains at tremendous expense to create an artificial, environmentally costly golf course (pls. 95, 125). We idolize our pioneer past through the tourist industry in a process called "Disneyfication." We fetishize or commodify the landscape of our history (pl. 9) and the culture of individualism (pl. 92). Self-sufficiency, even violence, is present in the way we live on the land, and the way in which some of us seek hostile or remote isolation in it (pls. 96–98). Others farm or ranch in increasingly depopulated, isolated places, undermining the supportive community structure that has sustained rural America for most of its history. Some mine water resources under the earth, treating both land and water as commodities to use and exhaust. The map of roads and high-tension wires that cross the countryside is a sign of internationalism and dispersion as much as of communication (pl. 108).

The land's suburbanization or urbanization is inevitable. Cities and towns have always been part of the West, but they have a different character than most other parts of the country: they are more open-ended in design, less centralized, looser, freer. They reflect the mobile society that produced them.

Everyone has an opportunity in the West, at least more so than elsewhere, but the human cost can be great. Lewis Baltz noticed this in a picture that appears in Robert Adams' book *Denver.*

> *Denver is a devastating photograph, though in such a quiet and understated way that one might pass by it several times before it engages the full measure of one's attention. . . . The context in which Adams has placed this remarkable photograph . . . allows us to make certain suppositions about the world [his] nameless shopper inhabits . . . this is a suburban setting, a world of enforced solitude in an environment as impersonal as modern packaging technology can deliver. . . . The city looks temporary, shoddy, and comfortless . . . , [a] metaphor of interpersonal relationships, which must also obey the laws of expediency and the demands of transience. It is as though habitation and development have made the vastness of the American land even emptier and lonelier than it was before we arrived.*[81]

PLATE 8

John Pfahl
Rancho Seco Nuclear Plant, Sacramento County, CA, June 1983, 1983
chromogenic development print
13½ x 18½ in. (34.3 x 47 cm)
Collection of the San Francisco Museum of Modern Art. Purchased through a gift of an Anonymous Donor, 93.116

Faceless homes, chilly modernist industrial parks, exotic landscapes of suburban developments that more resemble ziggurats on the arid plains of the ancient Near East than any edifice on our continent, strange contraptions that alight on the landscape for recreation or cruelly disfigure it—all have exerted an impersonal coldness and irony to the term "taming the landscape" (pls. 100, 125). The people who live in these solid middle-class developments seem almost unerringly bland and more distant than the gentle working-class woman, cheerful, beautiful, and relaxed, who poses next to her modest trailer park (pl. 99). The fragile basketball hoop near a trailer encampment in the open desert is set against a backdrop of mountains where Charlton Heston accepted the Ten Commandments (pl. 2).

Photographs record the strange sights of Las Vegas, the curious habits of those of our species who find amusement in playing slot machines in swimming pools located in a city of bombastic water fountains with chipping, peeling paint (pls. 102, 103). Many photographers have concentrated on Los Angeles. Big, diverse, flamboyant, exuberant, tragic, it exemplifies the urban West. It is relatively new, built around the automobile, which provides enormous fluidity to its citizens while also serving to isolate them. Garry Winogrand lived in L.A., a city inhabited by cars, after years of working as a street photographer in New York, a city of streets inhabited by people. He saw it as a freeway city, isolating its inhabitants, or a boardwalk culture of strange, amusing characters clustered around Venice and Santa Monica, some of the few places where people actually walk for pleasure (pl. 128). Some of its inhabitants see a new landscape whose empty streets are possessed by stray dogs or the unmentionable homeless camped under bridges or finding shelter in deserted spaces near the roads or by the sea.

Many photographers of this new documentary landscape shy away from the old contact with people in the full complexity of social situations. They look at the traces, leavings, as an archeologist unearths the culture of a distant past, then painstakingly examines the clues. Anthony Hernandez has looked at public parklands where people go to shoot cans of paint, toys—anything. He shows not just a marvelous fabric of abstract color but a place of real violence (pl. 97). A large diptych reveals a horrifying number of cigarette butts, a plastic spoon, a roasted bone, a blanket (perhaps with someone in it?) with delicacy and honesty, more disturbing than if the photographer had forced himself (and us) on the man or woman who sleeps there, roasts the bone, smokes the cigarettes (pl. 129). Disturbing too is the image made by a white man of an inauspicious city streetcorner in the full, beautiful light of day. He gives us only the address: It is the site of Rodney King's brutal altercation with the L.A.P.D. (pl. 130). Probably the most fruitless gesture of all is the vain attempt against geology, geography, and history to fence off the culture to our south (pl. 131).

The intellectual control of the land, our mastery of it, appears to be

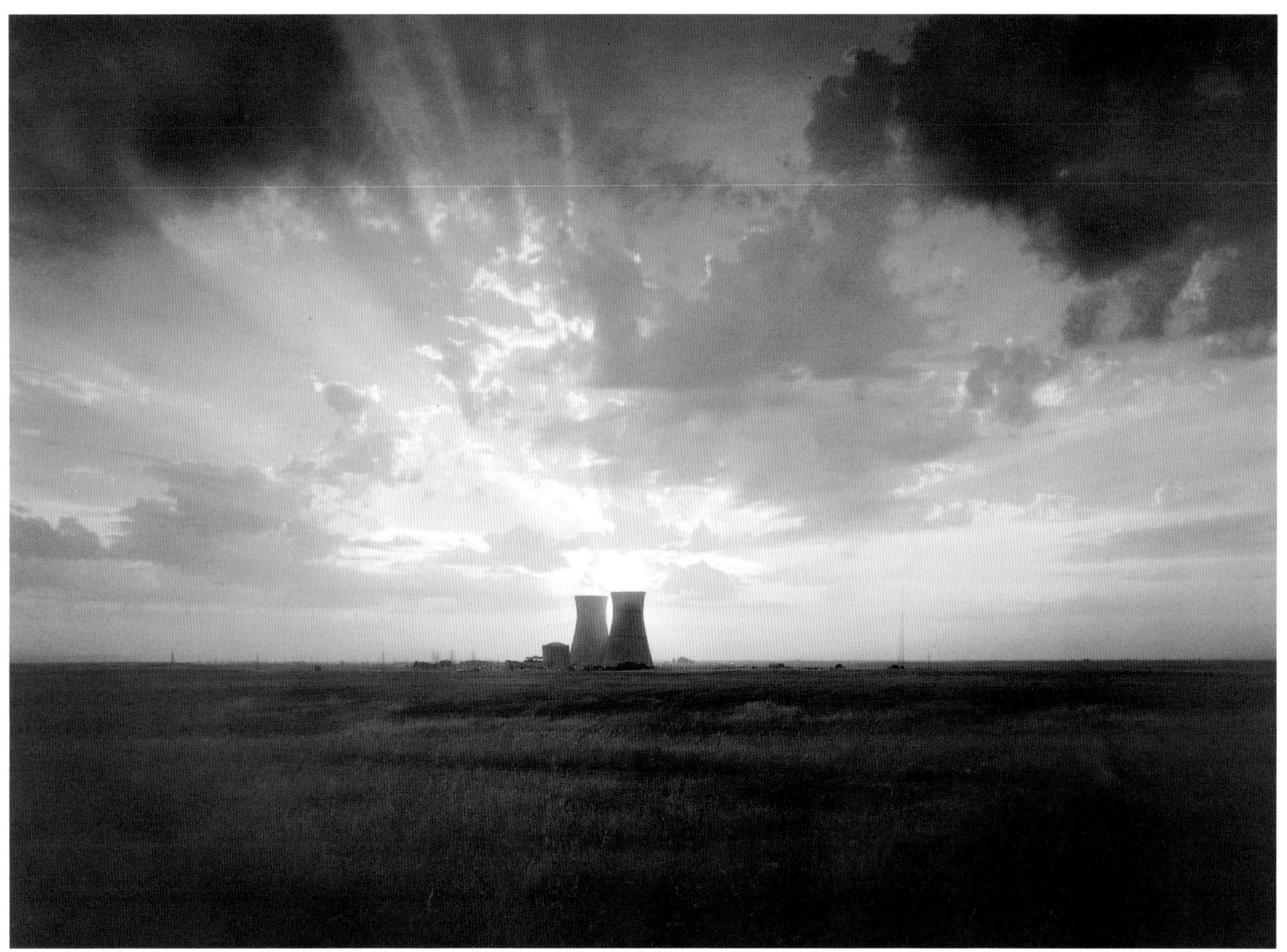

coming apart at the seams. The idealization of individualism and of corporate enterprise, so vividly optimistic in nineteenth-century photographs and so important even to the work of Ansel Adams, has become despairing, and reveals a flawed and damaged landscape that is only occasionally brightened by an appreciation of the fragile beauty of what remains. The optimism that energized Dorothea Lange and her colleagues to rally for change has been transformed into a weary acceptance of what exists and what we have done.

Curiously, the minimalist, uninflected aesthetic of contemporary photographers bears a closer relationship to the nineteenth-century photographers' desire to document the changing, developing landscape and unearth its geometric, intellectual order than to the impassioned approach of photographers of the 1930s. But perhaps this recently achieved "realistic" objectivity reveals the very same conflicts that informed the work of their predecessors: a resignation to the exploitation of wilderness as an inalienable right, and the attendant mythology of a frontier of individual promise.

NOTES

1. William Gilpin, *Mission of the North American People: Geographical, Social, and Political* (1873; reprint, Philadelphia: J. B. Lippincott, 1874), p. 130.

2. Henry David Thoreau, "Walking" (1862), in *The Portable Thoreau*, ed. Carl Bode (New York: The Viking Press, 1968), p. 603.

3. Alan Trachtenberg, *The Incorporation of America: Culture and Society in the Gilded Age* (New York: Hill and Wang, 1982), chap. 1. See also *The West as America: Reinterpreting Images of the Frontier, 1820–1920*, ed. William H. Truettner (Washington, D.C.: The Smithsonian Institution Press, 1991).

4. John L. O'Sullivan, 1845, as quoted in *God's New Israel: Religious Interpretations of American Destiny*, ed. Conrad Cherry (Englewood Cliffs: Prentice Hall, 1971), p. 129. O'Sullivan coined the term in a discussion of the annexation of Oregon. See also Cadwallader D. Colden, *Memoir . . . at the Celebration of the Completion of the New York Canals* (New York: W. A. Davis, 1825), p. 55; Leo Marx, *The Machine in the Garden: Technology and the Pastoral Ideal in America* (New York: Oxford University Press, 1967), esp. p. 29; and Ernest Lee Tuveson, *Reedeemer Nation: The Idea of America's Millenial Role* (Chicago: University of Chicago Press, 1968); and Donald Worster, *An Unsettled Country: Changing Landscapes of the American West* (Albuquerque: University of New Mexico Press, 1994), chap. 3.

5. As quoted in Michael L. Smith, *Pacific Visions: California Scientists and the Environment, 1850–1915* (New Haven: Yale University Press, 1987), p. 87. See also Patricia Nelson Limerick, *The Legacy of Conquest: The Unbroken Past of the American West* (New York: W. W. Norton and Co., 1987).

6. See Frederick Turner, *Beyond Geography: The Western Spirit Against the Wilderness* (New Brunswick, N.J.: Rutgers University Press, 1994), and Sacvan Bercovitch, *The Puritan Origins of the American Self* (New Haven: Yale University Press, 1975).

7. See Hans Huth, *Nature and the American: Three Centuries of Changing Attitudes* (1957; reprint, Lincoln: University of Nebraska Press, 1990), p. 6–9.

8. Quoted in Huth, *Nature and the American*, p. 216.

9. Thomas Cole, "Essay on American Scenery" (1835), reprinted in *American Art 1700–1960: Sources and Documents*, ed. John W. McConbrey (Englewood Cliffs, N.J.: Prentice-Hall, Inc., 1965), p. 102. See also Barbara Novak, *Nature and Culture: American Landscape and Painting, 1825–1875* (New York: Oxford University Press, 1980).

10. From "The Relation between Geology and Landscape Painting," *The Crayon*, no. 6 (1859), pp. 255–56. See also William Cullen Bryant's poem "To Cole, the Painter, Departing for Europe."

11. Cole, "Essay on American Scenery," p. 109.

12. Lyman Beecher, "A Place for the West," in *God's New Israel: Religious Interpretations of American Destiny*, p. 120.

13. Frederick Jackson Turner, "The Significance of the Frontier in American History," paper read in 1893 at the Chicago World's Fair, reprinted in *The Frontier in American History*, foreword by Wilbur R. Jacobs (1920; reprint, Tucson: The University of Arizona Press, 1994), pp. 3–4.

14. Henry George, "What the Railroads Will Bring Us," in *Unknown California*, ed. Jonathan Eisen and David Fine (New York: Macmillan, 1985), p. 67.

15. See especially *San Francisco in the 1850s: 33 Photographic Views*, ed. George R. Fardon and Robert Sobieszek (New York: Dover, 1977); and Peter Bacon Hales, *Silver Cities: The Photography of American Urbanisation*, 1839–1915 (Philadelphia: Temple University Press, 1984), p. 50. See also Martha A. Sandweiss, "Undecisive Moments: The Narrative Tradition in Western Photography," in *Photography in Nineteenth-Century America*, ed. Martha A. Sandweiss (New York: Harry N. Abrams, 1991), esp. pp. 99–129 on the profound role of the panorama in photographic views and series. There was an implied narrative to the panoramic form.

16. See Peter E. Palmquist, "Carleton E. Watkins: Photographer of the American West," in catalogue of the same title (Fort Worth: Amon Carter Museum of West-

ern Art, 1983), pp. 5–7. See also John Coplans, "C. E. Watkins at Yosemite," *Art in America* 66, no. 6 (Nov./Dec. 1978), pp. 100–8.

17. See the aesthetic appreciation of this in "Photographic Mining Views," *Mining and the Scientific Press*, 4 (November 1871), p. 281, quoted in Palmquist, "Carleton E. Watkins," p. 46.

18. See T. J. Jackson Lears, *No Place of Grace: Anti-Modernism and the Transformation of American Culture, 1886–1920* (New York: Pantheon Books, 1981).

19. Information derived from Hank Johnston, *The Yosemite Grant 1864–1906: A Pictorial History* (Yosemite National Park: Yosemite Association, 1995); Mary V. Hood, "Charles L. Weed, Yosemite's First Photographer," *Yosemite Nature Notes* xxx.viii, no. 6 (June 1959), pp. 76–87; and Peter E. Palmquist, "California Peripatetic Photographer: Charles Leander Weed," *California History* 58, no. 3 (Fall 1979), pp. 194–219.

20. Palmquist notes trips in 1861, 1865, 1866 (with J. D. Whitney and the California State Geological Survey), 1872, 1875, 1878, 1879, and 1881.

21. See Weston J. Naef in collaboration with James N. Wood, *Era of Exploration: The Rise of Landscape Photography in the American West, 1860–1885* (New York: Albright–Knox Art Gallery and the Metropolitan Museum of Art, 1975), pp. 80–81. See also Douglas Nickel, "Francis Frith in Egypt and Palestine" (Ph. D. diss., Princeton University, 1995) for his description of the relationship of Frith's large views to his stereos, and Martha A. Sandweiss, "Foreword," in "Carlton E. Watkins," esp. pp. x–xiv.

22. As quoted in Ferol Egan, *Frémont: Explorer for a Restless Nation* (New York: Doubleday, 1977), p. 512.

23. Frederick Law Olmsted, "The Yosemite Valley and the Mariposa Big Trees: A Preliminary Report" (1865), reprinted with an introduction by Laura Wood Roper, in *Landscape Architecture* 43 (Oct. 1952), p. 16. See also Hans Huth, "Yosemite: The Story of an Idea," *Sierra Club Bulletin*, v.xxxiii (1948), pp. 47–8.

24. Carl P. Russel, *One Hundred Years in Yosemite: The Story of a Great Park and Its Friends* (Berkeley: University of California Press, 1947), pp. 148–49.

25. As quoted in Laura Wood Roper, *F. L. O.: A Biography of Frederick Law Olmsted* (Baltimore: Johns Hopkins University Press, 1973), p. 255.

26. See Waverly Lowell, "Where Have All the Flowers Gone? Early Environmental Litigation," Prologue 21, no. 3 (Fall 1989), pp. 247–55; and Marilyn Ziebarth, "California's First Environmental Battle," California History (Fall 1984), pp. 275–79. See also Peter E. Palmquist, "Robert Vance: Pioneer in Western Landscape Photography," American West 18, no. 5 (Sept./Oct. 1981), pp. 22–27.

27. See David E. Nye, *American Technological Sublime* (Cambridge, Mass.: The MIT Press, 1994).

28. See Clyde A. Milner II, "National Initiatives," in *The Oxford History ofthe American West*, ed. Clyde A. Milner II, Carol A. O'Connor, and Martha A. Sandweiss (New York: Oxford University Press, 1994), p. 161.

29. Albert Bierstadt was specifically interested in effects with magic lantern slides. He presented *The Rocky Mountains, Lander's Peak*, to the public under a spotlight, with living Indians in attendance and with an informational brochure, in other words, with the same kind of supportive material as the popular entertainment of dioramas and panoramas.

30. *The Illustrated London News* began publication in 1842. Frank Leslie's *Illustrated Newspaper*, which began publication in 1855, and *Harper's Weekly*, which began in 1857, were the most important and persistent American illustrated weeklies. Both had copies of daguerreotypes and illustrative material abundantly present.

31. He commissioned the eminent graphic artist James Smillie. See also Richard N. Masteller, "Western Views in Eastern Parlors: The Contribution of the Stereograph Photographer to the Conquest of the West," *Prospect* 6 (1981), pp. 55–71.

32. As quoted from the *New York Post* (December 11, 1862), in Nancy K. Anderson, "Wonderously Full of Invention: The Western Landscape of Albert Bierstadt," in *Albert Bierstadt: Art and Enterprise* (New York: The Brooklyn Museum, in Association with Hudson Hill Press, 1991), p. 79. See also Fitz Hugh Ludlow's essay, "Seven Weeks in the Great Yo-semite," *Atlantic Monthly* 13, no. 80 (June 1864), p. 740.

33. For information on stereos, see William C. Darrah, *The World ofStereographs* (Gettysburg, Pa.: William C. Darrah Publishing, 1977), pp. 93–94.

34. See Joel Snyder, *American Frontiers: The Photographs ofTimothy O'Sullivan, 1867–1874* (Millerton, N.Y.: Aperture, 1981); and Kim Sichel, *Mapping the West: Nineteenth-Century American Landscape Photographs from the Boston Public Library* (Boston: Boston University Art Gallery, 1992).

35. William A. Bell, *New Tracks in North America*, vol. 1 (London: Chapman and Hall, 1869), p. xxv.

36. See Susan Danly Walther, " The Railroad in the Western Landscape," in *The Railroad in the American Landscape, 1850–1950* (Wellesley, Mass.: The Wellesley College Museum, 1981), p. 41.

37. For a comprehensive analysis of Jackson and his career, including a discussion of his adaption to changing markets, see Peter B. Hales, *William Henry Jackson and the Transformation ofthe American Landscape* (Philadelphia: Temple University Press, 1988), esp. p. 143.

38. See Wolfgang Schivelbusch, *The Railway Journey: The Industrialization of Time and Space in the 19th Century* (Berkeley: University of California Press, 1986), chap. 3.

39. The interrelationship of panoramas, dioramas, and photography, and the scientific and entertainment value they share are discussed in Schivelbusch, *The Railway Journey*, pp. 62–63, and *Panoramania* (London: Trefoil Publications, in association with the Barbican Art Gallery, 1988). See also Schivelbusch, p. 63, "Thus the intensive experience of the sensuous world, terminated by the industrial revolution, underwent a resurrection in the new institution of photography."

40. As quoted in Freeman Tilden, *Following the Frontier with F. Jay Haynes, Pioneer Photographer of the Old West* (New York: Alfred A. Knopf, 1964), pp. 11–12.

41. Ibid., p. 30.

42. See Darrah, *The World of Stereographs*, p. 96.

43. Tilden, *Following the Frontier with F. Jay Haynes*, pp. 396–7.

44. See Walther, *The Railroad in the American Landscape, 1850–1950*, pp. 45ff.

45. See Dean MacCannell, *The Tourist: A New Theory of the Leisure Class* (New York: Schocken Books, 1976), esp. chap. 1.

46. William M. Thayer, *Marvels of the New West: A Vivid Portrayal of the Stupendous Marvels in the Vast Wonderland West of the Missouri River* (Norwich, Conn.: Henry Bill Publishing Co., 1888).

47. Thayer, *Marvels of the New West*, pp. 710, 715.

48. Henry Nash Smith, *Virgin Land: The American West as Symbol and Myth* (New York: Vintage Books, 1957), chaps. XVI–XVIII.

49. Ferdinand V. Hayden, who led a survey team that included William Henry Jackson, gave this theory scientific plausability in his report of 1867. See Smith, *Virgin Land*, pp. 209–10.

50. The conflict between the traditional yeoman farmers and the emigrant, bourgeois, small-scale capitalist farmers is discussed in Allan Kulikoff, *The Agrarian Origins of American Capitalism* (Charlottesville: University Press of Virginia, 1992). John Carter of the Nebraska Historical Society suggests that this duality is not entirely accurate, and that the farmers photographed by Solomon Butcher were mostly incipient bourgeois families.

51. Frank Norris' novel *The Octopus* (1901) is about the conflict of bonanza farmers with railroad interests.

52. See Wallace Stegner, *Beyond the Hundredth Meridian: John Wesley Powell and the Second Opening of the West* (1954; reprint, New York: Penguin Books, 1992).

53. See John T. Schlebecker, *Whereby We Thrive: A History of American Farming, 1607–1972* (Ames: Iowa State University Press, 1972), on farm technology and land use.

54. See Walter Prescott Webb, *The Great Plains* (Lincoln and London: University of Nebraska Press, 1981), p. 240, and Richard White, "Animals and Enterprise," in *The Oxford History of the American West*, pp. 237–73.

55. Richard White, "Animals and Enterprise," in *The Oxford History of the American West*, p. 262.

56. See Mark H. Brown and W. R. Felton, *The Frontier Years: L. A. Huffman, Photographer of the Plains* (New York: Bramhall House, 1955), pp. 66–67.

57. Brown and Felton, *The Frontier Years*, p. 52.

58. See Donna M. Lucey, *Photographing Montana, 1894–1928: The Life and Work of Evelyn Cameron* (New York: Alfred A. Knopf, 1990).

59. Labor organizers often presented themselves as photographers. For Kinsey's political sympathies in conjunction with contemporary labor history, I thank Rod Slemmons. See also Wallace Stegner's autobiographical essay *Where the Bluebird Sings to the Lemonade Springs: Living and Writing in the West* (New York: Random House, 1992). Stegner's family owned a restaurant business that moved with the sawyers' camps. It was finally put out of business when they ran out of trees. See also *Kinsey, Photographer: A Half Century of Negatives by Darius and Tabitha May Kinsey*, eds. Dave Bohn and Rodolfo Petschek (San Francisco: Chronicle Books, 1982).

60. The University of Wyoming has an extensive collection of photographs made by an inspector for the petroleum industry.

61. Albert Boine, *The Magesterial Gaze: Manifest Destiny and American Landscape Painting, c. 1830–1865* (Washington: Smithsonian Institution Press, 1991), p. 5, and the illustration on p. 46 entitled *Westward the Course of Empire Takes Its Way*, with McCormick Reaps in the van.

62. Information from May Castleberry, the Whitney Museum of American Art.

63. Quoted in Allan G. Bogue, "An Agricultural Empire," in *The Oxford History of the American West*, p. 305. For the conflicting idealism of nature and cities, of society and freedom, see John Brinckerhoff Jackson, "Jefferson, Thoreau, and After," in *Landscapes: Selected Writings of J. B. Jackson*, ed. Ervin H. Zube (Boston: The University of Massachusetts Press, 1970), pp. 1–9.

64. James Bryce, *The American Commonwealth*, Vol. II (New York: MacMillan, 1906), p. 839.

65. The exhibition included two paintings by Bierstadt. See chapter two, "American Landscape Painting," in *Catalogue Deluxe of the Department of Fine Arts: Panama-Pacific Exposition*, Vol. I, ed. John E. D. Trask and J. Nilsen Laurvik (San Francisco: Paul Elder and Company, 1915).

66. He included a commercial picture in his show at 291. He also had a longstanding, eventually difficult, relationship with Yosemite Park and the Curry Company, for which he made commercial work. See also his "colorama" pictures for Kodak, many made at tourist sites in national parks.

67. Bernard DeVoto, "The West: A Plundered Province," *Harper's Monthly Magazine* (August 1934), p. 358.

68. For an account of Powell's efforts see Stegner, *Beyond the Hundredth Meridian*.

69. Henry Ford, *My Life and Work* (London: Heineman, 1924), p. 280.

70. See Nye, *American Technological Sublime*, pp. 135, 137–42.

71. The hydraulic empire has received attention recently in Marc Reisner, *Cadillac Desert: The American West and Its Disappearing Water* (New York: Penguin Books, 1987); and Donald Worster, *Rivers of Empire, Water Aridity and the Growth of the American West* (New York: Oxford University Press, 1985).

72. From the brochure *New Documents: Diane Arbus, Lee Friedlander, Garry Winogrand* (New York: The Museum of Modern Art, 1967).

73. As quoted in William Jenkins, "Introduction," in *New Topographics: Photographs of a Man-Altered Landscape* (Rochester: International Museum of Photography at George Eastman House, 1975).

74. Evans makes the distinction in a 1971 interview with Leslie Katz in *The Camera Viewed: Writing on Twentieth-Century Photography*, Vol. 1, ed. Peninah R. Petrick (New York: E. P. Dutton, 1979), p. 127.

75. Social questions of the changing economics of photography are addressed in John Szarkowski, *Photography Until Now* (New York: The Museum of Modern Art, 1989).

76. See Martha A. Sandweiss, "Undecisive Moments," in *Photography in Nineteenth-Century America*, pp. 99–129.

77. Mark Klett served as chief photographer, with Ellen Manchester, project director; JoAnn Verburg, project coordinator; and Gordon Bushaw and Rick Dingus, project photographers.

78. *Second View: The Rephotographic Survey Project* (Albuquerque: University of New Mexico Press, 1984).

79. See Abigail Solomon-Godeau, "Photography after Art Photography," in *Photography at the Dock: Essays on Photographic History, Institutions and Practices* (Minneapolis: University of Minnesota Press, 1991), pp. 103–23.

80. Richard Misrach, with Myriam Weisang Misrach, *Bravo 20: The Bombing of the American West* (Baltimore: John Hopkins University Press, 1990). The first museum show and brochure of this work, to my knowledge, is Robert A. Sobieszek, *The New American Pastoral Landscape Photography in the Age of Questioning* (New York: International Museum of Photography at George Eastman House and Whitney Museum of American Art, 1990). See also Merry A. Foresta et al. *Between Home and Heaven: Contemporary American Landscape Photography* (Washington, D.C.: Smithsonian Institution, 1992).

81. Lewis Baltz, "Konsumterror," *Camera Austria*, 18 (1985), p. 17.

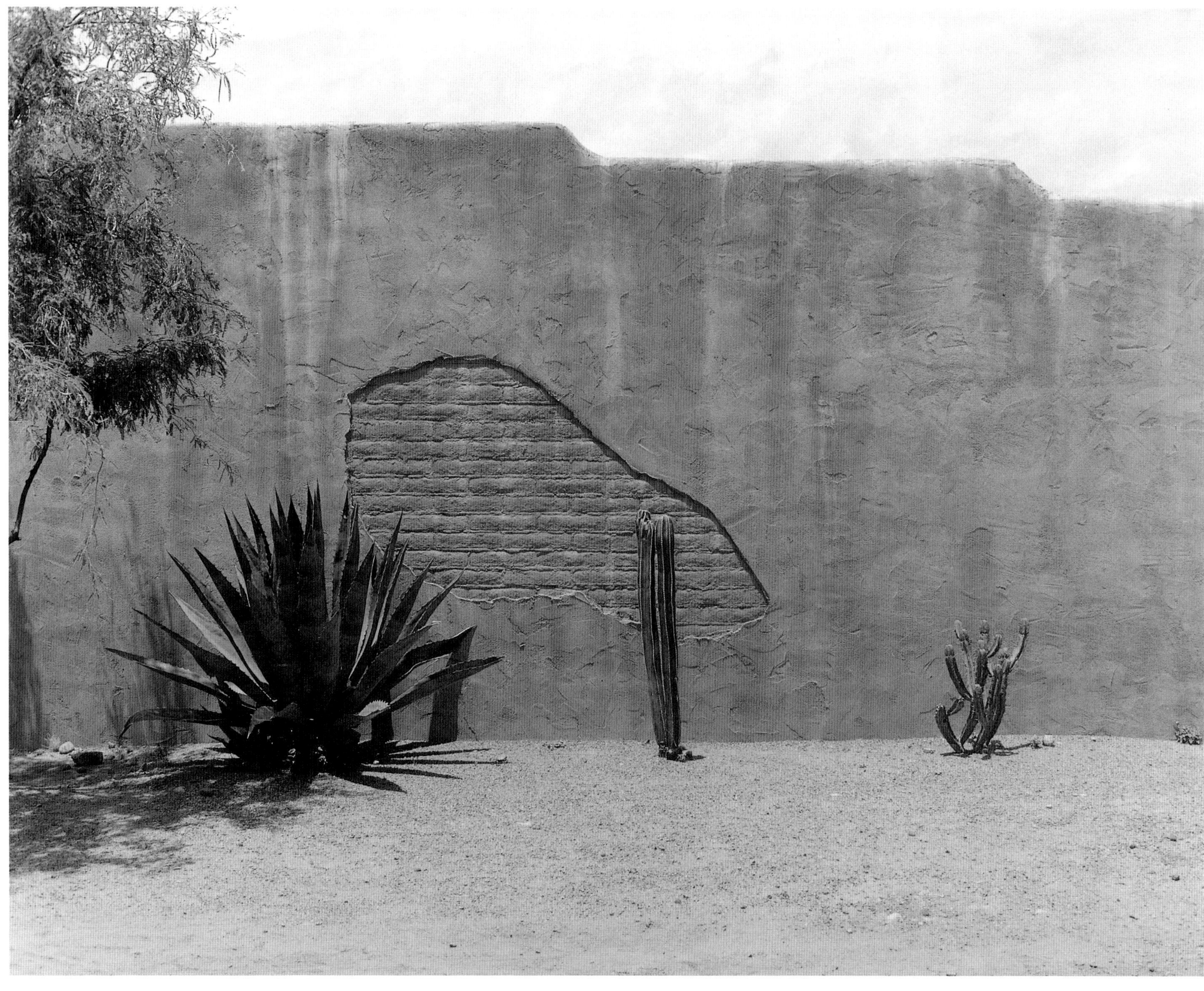

Ralph Lauren's Teepee

RICHARD RODRIGUEZ

Several seasons ago Ralph Lauren produced fashion layouts of high WASP nostalgia that were also confused parables of Original Sin. Bored, beautiful children pose upon the blue dappled lawns of Long Island, together with their scented, shriven parents. All are washed in the Blood of the Lamb—cashmeres, linens, muslins. The parents have rewon Eden on credit for the sake of the children—"...understand, all this will be yours." The knowing children, however, have obviously found the disused apple under a hedge and swallowed it.

Mr. Lauren's more recent work attempts a less complicated innocence; he has had himself photographed astride his horse, alongside his horse. The *mise-en-scene* is the American West. According to *W* magazine, in real life (as we say, allowing for variance), whenever Mr. Lauren wants to escape the mythology business he repairs to his Double RL Ranch, a 14,000-acre spread outside Telluride, Colorado.

On a meadow within that reserve, Mr. Lauren has constructed a Plains Indian teepee, inside which he has placed genuine Navaho rugs and club chairs from London, electrical outlets, phones, faxes, CDs—"stuff an Indian never dreamed of," as one tickled ranchhand remarks.

I do not mock Mr. Lauren's *Trianon sauvage*. It may represent an authentic instinct for survival, like the family-built nuclear shelters of the 1950s. Leaving all that alone, I should confess I have not made my own peace with wilderness, never liking to be more than two miles from restaurants and theaters. From an air-conditioned car, I often regret the suburban sprawl—sometimes so much as to blast my horn at it. That is an aesthetic regret. As a westerner, I approve the human domination of nature.

I have been to Telluride only once—for the film festival. But I have often enough visited the chic little towns that nestle in the mountain states of the West. A friend's wedding in Idaho, most recently—the guests had flown in from Los Angeles and London. On the Saturday morning, nearly everyone rode into the foothills on horseback. I don't ride.

It was a hot Labor Day weekend, with a parade in Ketchum; but the forest was dark and cool. I trudged one mile, perhaps two—whichever, it was in the direction of loneliness. A noise stopped me. I don't remember what kind of noise, a crackle or something, a pinecone dropping, a blue jay —it's just that I was alone. I think I did discover an anxiety the white pioneers could have known in these same woods a century ago. Whose woods these are? Injuns? Or was I the Indian? Well, I am an Indian. My shoes were getting scuffed. Maybe the woods were dangerously settled—Snow White and the Seven Militiamen. And then an idea, even more unsettling, fell upon me in rank and ancient coils: The forest was empty.

There was no design.

Except the trail. I turned and quickly walked back to the lodge, where Ella Fitzgerald's voice flitted through several speakers in the eaves of the lobby.

Mr. Lauren, quoted in *W*, speaks in oracular puffs from beneath designer blankets: "I'm just borrowing the land." (...) "You can never really

PLATE 9

Max Becher and Andrea Robbins

Old Tucson: Catcus and Wall, ca. 1992
chromogenic development print
28 x 32 in. (71.1 x 82.6 cm)
Collection of the San Francisco Museum of Modern Art

own it." (...) "It's only yours for a short time." (...) The *W* article notes the Double RL Ranch is circumscribed by fifteen miles of white fence.

In nineteenth-century daguerreotypes of the American West, the land is the dropped rind from a transcendently fresh sky. Time is evident: bleaching centuries have withered the landscape. There is no evidence of history except the presence of the camera.

The camera is debris, the pristine image "taken" is contamination. The camera can look only backward. Our backward glance is pure and naively fond. The camera cannot look forward. To see the future we must look through Ray-Ban darkly. Smog, literally. There is smog in Phoenix, Vegas, Modesto. Smog is everywhere. It is hard to see the West the pioneers imagined. It is more difficult to imagine their terror. But not impossible, as witness my dude-ranch vastation.

The Puritan theology of America predisposed pioneers to receive the land as "virgin." The happy providence of God had provided them a new Eden. The gift must have inspired exhilaration as well as terror. Evidence of exhilaration remains. Settlers dammed the waters. They leveled mountains. They broke their backs to build our regret.

Some neighbor's house in Sacramento, a summer evening. I have come to collect for the newspaper. "Come on in, honey," the wife said through the screen door, and, "I've got goop on my hands. Hold a sec." I watched as she finished rubbing the liniment into her husband's shoulder. She noticed my fascination (though she interpreted it incorrectly), said, "Labors of Hercules," which even as a child I could interpret as meaning she was comically rearming her husband for battle with nature. Nature meant labor. All he'd been doing was working on the lawn.

An acquaintance in his eighties had pits of cancer dug out of the side of his nose. My friend lamented his disfiguring fate in the present—"I use sun screen, never go out without a hat." The young doctor's prognosis harkened to a pristine West: "This damage was done a long time ago, when you were a little boy and stayed too long in the sun."

I believe those weathered westerners who tell me over the roar of their air conditioners that the wilderness is no friend. They seem to me to have at least as true a knowledge of the West as the catechism of the Sierra Club. A friend, an ex–New Yorker, now a Californian, tells me she was saved from a full-scale panic attack while driving at night through a remote stretch of New Mexico by the sudden appearance of writing in the sky: BEST WESTERN.

I was driving myself to the sea on a twisting road in Northern California. Each mountain turn revealed new curtailed vistas, kleigs of sunlight trained down forest aisles, rocks spilled at the side of the road. Then another turn and, in a clearing, a bungalow, a lawn, a coiled hose, a satellite dish, a bed of roses. What an absurdity, thought Goldilocks, to plant Pasadena amidst such splendor!

Something in the heart of the westerner must glory in the clamor of hammering, the squealing of saws, the rattle of marbles in aerosol cans. Something in the heart of the westerner must yearn for lost wilderness, once wilderness has been routed. That in us which is both most and least human—I mean the soul—cannot live at ease with oblivious nature, nor do we live easily with what we have made. We hate both the world without us and the world we create.

So we mythologize. Ralph Lauren has built roads on his ranch, sunk ponds, cleared pastures. "My goal is to keep and preserve the West." A modern heresy, an arrogant self-hatred is rampant in the West: the idea that we can create landscapes vacant of human will when, in fact, protection is human intrusion. When we celebrate the land as an alternative to the city, we encircle it with our will. Our ultimate picket fence, the ultimate domestication, is the modern ability to say: "Rage on here, but not elsewhere." Any tending of wilderness makes of the wilderness a lawn.

Ralph Lauren's teepee of "commercially farmed buffalo hide" was painted by a "local mountain man" with figures representing Mr. and Mrs. Lauren and their three children.

In hippie times, my friend Peter moved up to Guerneville to live among the redwoods with his wife and their baby son. Peter's impulse was to smoke dope and commune with the All in All. When communion palled a bit, in winter, he enrolled himself in the local J.C. Within two years, he moved back to the city, without wife or son or diploma—and with the extraordinary explanation that redwoods tap all human ambition. He had become pale, morose, furtive, and finally—his word—an adulterer.

Once the shopping center is up and the meadows are paved over and the fries are under the heat-lamp, we park in a slot, take our bearings, and go watch *Pocahontas* at the Cineplex. We feel ourselves very sympathetic with the Indian, a sympathy we extend only to the dead Indian. Necrophilia thrives throughout America, especially in the West, certainly as one approaches the Mexican border. The *New York Times* best-seller list abounds with pale-face channelers of Cro-Magnon metaphysic—the medium in Sedona, Shirley MacLaine's alter ego in Beverly Hills, the *brujo* in a novel of Cormac McCarthy.

The dead Indian, Weeping Conscience, has become the patron saint of an environmental movement largely made up of the descendants of the pioneers. More curiously, the dead Indian has become a stand-in for Nature in an argument made by some environmentalists against "overpopulation" (the fact that so many live Indians in Latin America are having so many babies and are moving north).

William tells me—he's a movie-guy—in a smoke-free, fat-free, vegan cantina (hi-ho, Silicon) that cowboy movies will shortly make a comeback "Big Time." The busboy, an Indian, approaches our table balancing two possible futures: regular or decaf?

That part of me I will always name *western* first thrilled at the West in VistaVision at the Alhambra Theater in Sacramento, in those last years before the Alhambra was torn down for a Safeway. In the KOOL summer dark, I took the cowboy's side.

The odds have shifted. All over the West today Indians have opened casinos where the white man might test the odds. Skinheads, the last American Puritans, head for the Northwest seeking, not the world, not manifest destiny, but a fence to keep the world out. Not so many miles away are New York millionaires on horseback. And me, in cordovan loafers.

Another summer day, late in the 1960s, I was driving a delivery truck to a construction site at the edge of suburban Sacramento, already by then a maze of freshly carved streets that had streetlights but no names. Most of the lots were numbered. On several lots construction had begun. Making a sharp turn right, I saw a gray snake keeling upon the watery concrete.

I make no apology for the snake. It is no literary device I conjure to make a theological point. It was really there—in my path on that hot summer afternoon for the same reason that Wyoming sunsets resemble bad paintings.

I hadn't time enough to swerve or to stop. Bump. Bump. Front wheels; rear wheels. Looking into the rear-view mirror, I saw the snake writhing upon the pavement, an intaglio of pain. I drove on. I came to the end of a street with no name. I was lost in my hometown, in a delivery truck, parked where pavement ran to dirt.

Eventually, I found the lot where I made my delivery. After a few minutes, I returned to my truck, retraced my way out of the maze. Only then did I remember the snake—look for it where I had slain it. But the snake was gone. Or was I mistaken?

Several construction workers were standing alongside a sandwich truck, drinking sodas. One man, a dark Mexican, shirtless, had draped the snake I killed over his shoulders, an idea that had not yet occurred to Ralph Lauren, who at that time was just beginning to be preoccupied with WASP nostalgia.

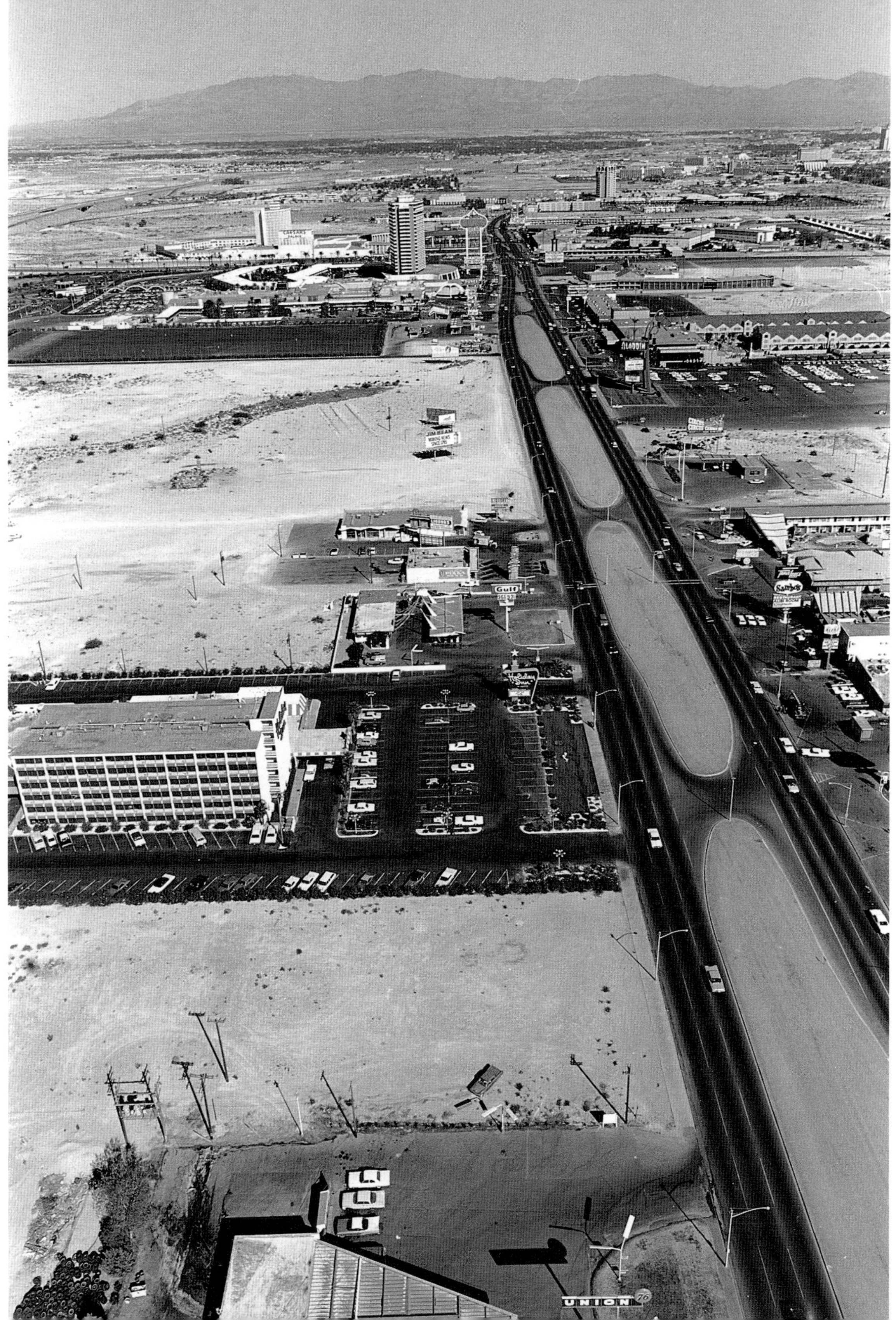

It was March, near the beginning of April. The heat wave held. I went into two atmospheres. Five times a day, or eight, or sixteen, there was a move from hotel to car, a trip through the furnace with the sun at one hundred and ten, a sprint along the Strip (billboards the size of a canyon) a fast sprint in the car, the best passenger car racing in America, driving not only your own piece of the mass production, but shifting lanes with the six or seven other cars in your field of collision. It was communal living at its best, everybody ready for everybody else, and then an aces fast turn off the Strip to land in the parking lot of the next hotel . . . where the second atmosphere was on, the cold atmosphere, the seventy degrees of air-conditioned oxygen, that air which seemed to have come a voyage through space as if you were in the pleasure chamber of an encampment on the moon. . . .

Lived in this second atmosphere for twenty-three hours of the twenty-four—it was life in a submarine, life in the safety chambers of the moon. Nobody knew that the deserts of the West, the arid empty wild blind deserts, were producing again a new breed of man.

Norman Mailer, *An American Dream*[1]

Emptiness on the Range: Western Spaces

AARON BETSKY

Las Vegas is the *locus classicus* of Western space.[2] Here America is reinventing itself into sprawl held together by a "themed" strip.[3] This is one of the two fastest growing cities in the country. It is the sunshine and *noir* that have been shadow boxing in Los Angeles raised to the multimillion-volt level of a Strip that beckons beyond the desolate stretches of stuccoed subdivisions hiding behind their palm-lined gates. It is also the site of the Hoover Dam, the most famous, if not in reality the largest, monument to man's desire to completely transform the American West, where man was not intended to live, into a home to millions by harnessing its water. Finally, it owes its life to the hidden force in the American West: the military-industrial complex that brought the first audience into the casino, that used the void of the desert as the testing ground for its proposal to turn the rest of the world into a deserted void through nuclear bombs.

Each of these forces has conspired to create a spatial configuration that is a profound challenge to those looking for traditional urban environments. It does not present a pretty picture. Picture Las Vegas. It is the many myths of the American West turned into a city where more than a million people live. It is a place where the mechanistic inhabitation of the void has created new phenomena: strips, compounds, sprawl, icons.

The basic elements that make up this stretched-out world are highly visible. First is the Strip: a linear space that organizes the major commercial life of the community. It follows the railroad lines, the first dividers of space to arrive, then veers off to accommodate the interstate and establishes its own place right past city control, on county land where the laws were once as lean as the land. The growth of the Strip has been amply documented,[4] but notice the space: It flows. Not only does it proceed forward, along the line of movement of the car, but it oozes out the sides, with nothing to impede it. In most strips, parking lots ring the street, leaving only the scrims of signs to mark the difference between public and private territory. In Las Vegas, space oozes into casinos, spreading out into a world of machinery that, in a surreal commentary on the assembly line, seduces millions to pull levers all night and all day long. Night and day, in fact, blend together, as do the casinos, leaving only the signs to differentiate between them. An artificial, flowing space traces the desert, offering neon versions of its tonalities.[5]

Beyond the Strip lies sprawl. Construction costs are low, a logic that might direct growth in a rational pattern is absent, and the warped grids of developments spin off their curved accentuation of isolation from arterials that still follow the Jeffersonian grid. Hundreds of thousands of middle-class refugees from the economic wars of California and the weather of the Midwest come every year to drown in a sea of sameness. Land costs are low, the geography and climate offer few challenges air-conditioning cannot fix, and transportation, whether along the network of broad, empty roads or through the fastest-growing airport in the country, is easy. Business is following the flight, making Las Vegas into a node in the international network of back office–based service industries that process credit cards, sell

FIGURE 18

Amorphous Space: The Las Vegas Strip circa 1970

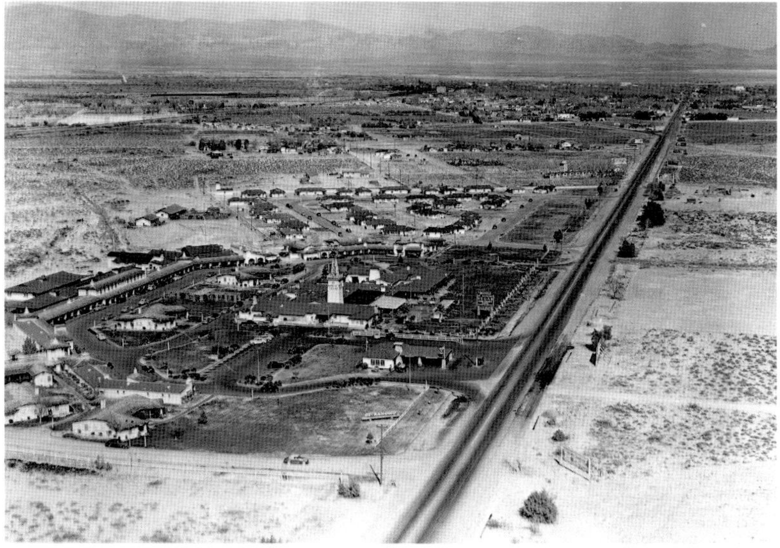

FIGURE 19
The Las Vegas Strip circa 1941: El Rancho Vegas (Wayne McAllister, architect), the first hotel on what was to become the Strip, was a rambling collection of highway buildings that presaged and condensed the sprawl that was to follow

things over the telephone, or facilitate consumption in ways that leave no physical trace beyond bland office buildings.

The overwhelming sensation of sameness, emptiness, and ephemerality conceals the carefully designed confines of each element in these developments, whether they are residential or commerical. Turned away from the landscape and from any reality that might offer itself up for representation, these air-conditioned, completely controlled worlds look toward the very engine of representation: the television or computer screen. A virtual space replaces built reality. As a result, little civic structure might allow these communities to represent themselves, despite a $200 million expenditure on schools in the last five years. Those funds have only bought educational bunkers that serve to prepare their denizens for more sprawling lives.

Between the intensity of the Strip and the emptiness of sprawl lie the public works that make it all function: the airport, already one of the busiest in the country, the freeways, and the commercial nodes of the shopping malls. The mass of construction evidences itself not in heroic spaces or grand edifices but in snaking ramps, in assemblies of people processing lobbies, in security screens. The city comes together purely as a succession of signs that funnel, spread, direct, control, command your attention.

These spaces turn away from the camera, from criticism, from our awareness. They are, however, our new landscape, waiting to be formed and built upon by both business and culture. And this is the point: Las Vegas offers the West as it is traditionally not pictured, because picturing the West has always meant representing what it is *not:* its construction, its utopian ideals, its fears—even the gritty reality belies the blankness of its vast spaces. What can be pictured is Hoover Dam, the test sights, the lushly landscaped golf courses of the rich. These heroic counterpoints result in the reality of space that eludes us, that slips away, that you see framed only in the rearview mirror.

This is the dilemma with space in the West: reality escapes us. Only its construction and its projection are of interest. We picture ourselves building new worlds and then creating luscious escapes from the worlds we inhabit, but we never can quite grasp the reality of what we have done, which is to create, in the words of Mike Bell, "Space that escapes us."[6]

THE GRIDDED WEST The West is Las Vegas writ large. Las Vegas is the true capital of the West. It assembled itself out of lines of flight, down the road away from confined spaces that imprisoned inhabitants within social and economic realities. They found what they perceived as empty space, ranging from horizontal plains to vertical barriers, rather than rolling hills marked by places of fertility connected by rivers. They used technology to impose an order on this world that was most visible as a grid and most effective, in time, through the invisible zones of air-conditioning. This assault was not a planned or careful colonization but a swarming transformation of land into real estate. Community and connection had little place in this brave new world. What did was the sprawling assembly of the ephemeral places of momentary inhabitation that were left behind as the dream moved on. A speculative landscape, Las Vegas is the Avalon of the West, its Strip and sprawl the mandala of this particular universe.

There is a history to this process, but it is not one just of cowboys and Indians. The making of the West has, until recently, occurred in a series of dualities: heroic constructions and romantic escapes, rapacious manipulations of the land and recreations of a garden of Eden. Recently, this dichotomy has given way to a supposed realism that responds to the unification of the previous dialectic in the technocratic planning visions of the 1960s. Now the debate is between the evocation of a conservative realism and a critical one, leaving us to wonder what happened to our ability to reimagine the West.[7]

The first proposals for the West were abstract, and this legacy, as J. B. Jackson has pointed out, informs every aspect of the current urban landscape west of the Alleghenies.[8] The Jeffersonian grid converted the continent into territory, in which the scale of the whole country specified itself down to states, communities, neighborhoods, farms, building sites, and finally into the rooms within each balloon frame structure. America became the Descartian Eden, where every aspect of reality presented itself as a grid, from the street to the room, from the social space of the town square to the furrowed land. The undulations of geography, the vagaries of discovery, and the peculiarities of site disappeared below this invented spatiality.

Most fundamentally, the grid meant that all the world was developable. Fallow land became unfulfilled space, waiting only to give up its potential within a gridded reality. The great mountains were the only boundary to this rule. They rose suddenly out of the West and gave it its heroic backdrop against which the potential of the land could be measured—until the mountains themselves could be mined either for minerals (becoming, in the process, part of the gridded plain) or for entertainment value as locales for recreation.

The land was waiting to become either a furrowed field or a home site, the basis for either transformation or superimposition. This marked western American space as fundamentally different from European spatiality, since its basic module was not the defensible space that each activity formed, nor the abstract syntax of power defined by the elite architecture of palaces, but empty, invisible, and highly tradable space. In the words of Henri Lefebvre, this was modernist space, which in the end produced nothing but itself.[9] The very engine of American society is its own development, whether through its conquest of ever more space (its "Manifest Destiny") or through the development of its already existing territories into ever more generous and ever more technologically determined (air-conditioned and secure) private space.

The problem with the grid was that it did not attract memory. Activities left little trace, since every change of ownership meant that a place reverted to its potential as developable space. As a result, an emptiness

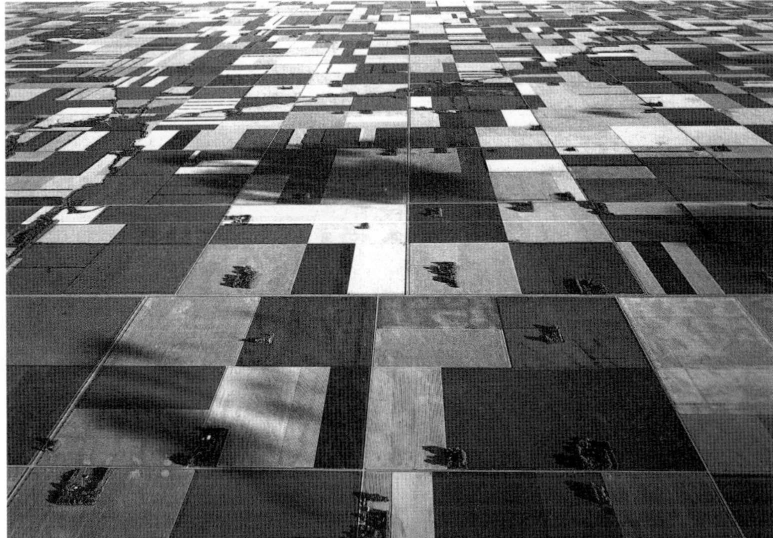

FIGURE 20

The Gridded Land: farmland in the Red River Valley, North Dakota, represents the translation of the Jeffersonian grid into agricultural reality

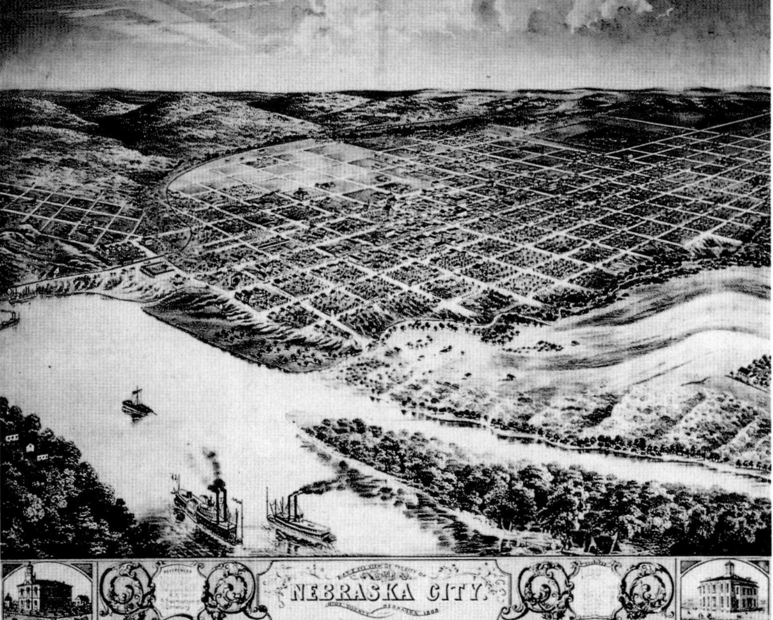

FIGURE 21

Urban Intensification: Nebraska City established its metropolitan ambitions within a subdivision of the grid that faded out into the limits of river and mountain

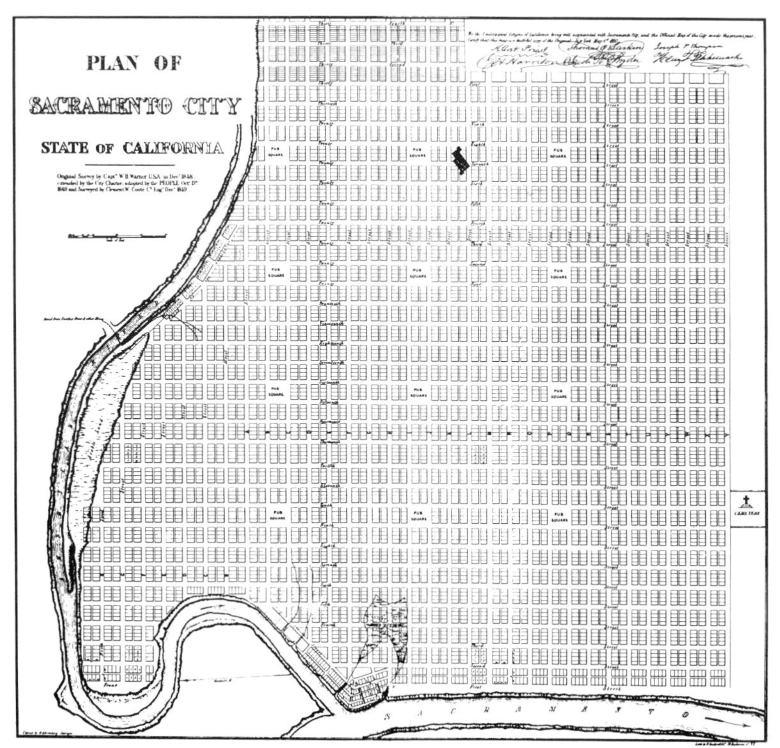

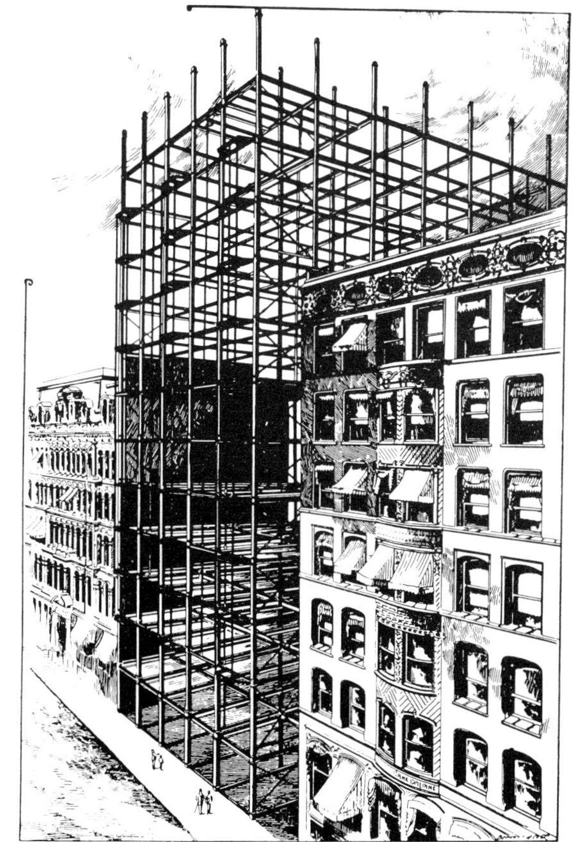

FIGURE 22

The Grid Realized: Sacramento, the capital of California, was laid out as a complete grid that contained within its order voids (parks) and densities that served as shopping streets

FIGURE 23

The Skeleton Rises: Chicago's Unity Building (1891–92, Clinton J. Warren, architect) was haunted by the specter of its gridded corset—the steel frame that has defined the arrangement and appearance of most office blocks since the late 1880s

FIGURE 24

The Road: a rural road in Colorado draws the restless rider toward the limits of space through an empty landscape waiting to be experienced, tamed, and speculatively inhabited

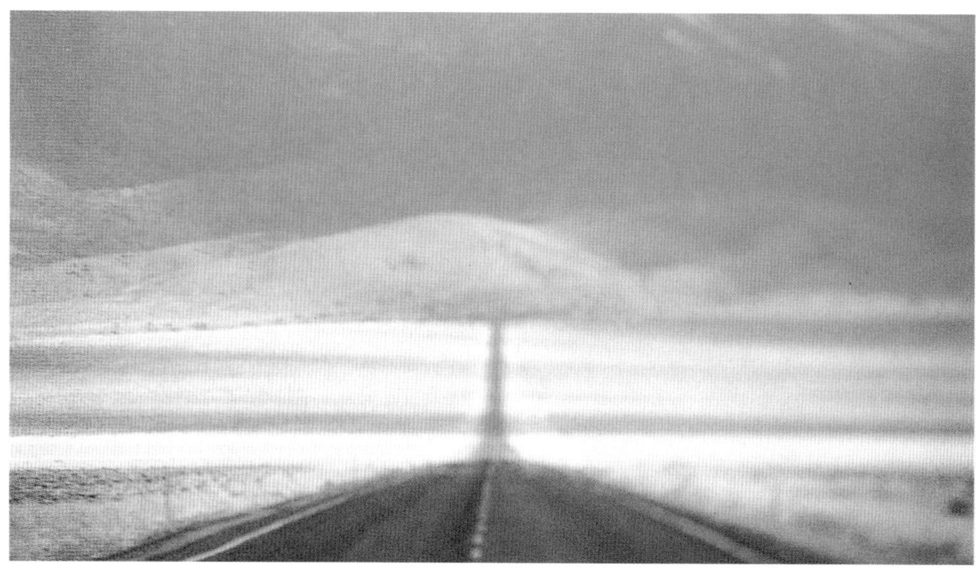

is central to all picturing of western space. It is an absence not just of things but of the texture that comes out of layering. The materials that cover in the grid are thin, frequently mass-produced, and often only signs for other building blocks: wood meant to look like stone, stucco meant to look like adobe. Other times and places are framed within the gridlike pictures at an exhibition.

What did attract association was the building of the grid. The laying out and later replication of the grid was itself the cornerstone of an architectural culture that reached its culmination in the corporate cleanliness of the Miesian grid as it was propagated throughout the West in the work of Skidmore, Owings, and Merrill, Helmuth, Obata & Kassenbaum, C. F. Murphy, and, later, I. M. Pei. It generated a certain romance of absence that was codified by the Miesian *beinahe nichts* (almost nothing) that, though formulated in Germany, found its natural home in the Midwest.[10]

But this was the refined pursuit of architects and their elite clients. The grandeur of vernacular space-making was informed by structural bravura to a degree unequalled anywhere in the world. Leo Marx has traced the profound love for progress as it could become embodied in the machinery of spatial conquest, especially the railroad train.[11] Vincent Scully has taken this notion further by showing how this machinery became embodied in buildings that range from Frank Furness's Philadelphia Academy of Art, which still looks like a Gothic steam engine, to the skyscrapers themselves, which became the great road West turned back and up into the sky.[12]

More important than the mechano-morphic implications of form was the enclosure of whole spaces by structures that seem to be continually under construction. Although structural expressionism is by no means an American invention (it harks back at least to the work of Eugène-Emmanuel Viollet-le-Duc), it became tied in the American West to a profound instability in spatial configurations that found its final, if rather attenuated, expression in the split-level home. The Chicago School is famous for its ability to express grids, but it is just as much a way of making buildings that refuses to accept the stability of the floor plane, replacing it with voracious staircases that eat up space, spinning it off into space, and finally fracturing it into the puzzling geometries of Frank Lloyd Wright.[13] In the work of Wright's heirs, who range from Louis Kahn to Paul Rudolph, this spatial instability held together by expressive construction and very little else, as well as the realization that there is no there there, only the continual appropriation and building of space itself, haunt American architecture.

STRUCTURED SPACE Outside of the realms of clearly delineated architecture, this romance of construction finds few takers. Most of the inhabited landscape of the West is not just superficially but intrinsically bland. What does attract the eye, however, is either the thrust-up ranges of mountains, the result of clearly visible geologic action, or a series of infrastructural constructions.

First, the *road* is not merely a line in American space but a serial repetition of railroad ties, a ribbon of life that derives its name and reality from songs ("Route 66") and, later, the largest construction project in most western communities. The railroad pushed up into the grain silo that marks the crossing point where communities form, and there the gantries, chutes, and abstract geometries replace the church as the most clearly designed structures in the field. As the road becomes larger, it distorts the grid as it opens up into a flow of parking lots surrounded by stores, motels, and, later, industrial buildings. These in turn stretch over boundaries and establish their own geometries related to a phenomenon of flow: the turning radius of the car or truck. The interstate highway system then turns that flow into form, raising itself up into viaducts, cloverleafs, overpasses, and dams that course right through the grid. By the time these ribbons of concrete reach the West Coast, they take on heroic proportions whose elegance turns them into the natural symbols of achievement.

Second, the *control of water* is the most fundamental activity in the West, as it allows for inhabitation in what is mostly a semi-arid or desert terrain. As Marc Reisner has pointed out, water distribution systems in America soon departed from the more traditional adherence to riparian rights common to Mediterranean lands as well as from the communal management of water common in, for instance, Holland. Water was spatialized, which is to say dammed and distributed, by corporate means; that is, it was centralized. The result was a spate of heroic structures starting at the beginning of the twentieth century that, once they had been put into place right before the Second World War, created the opportunity for the trans-

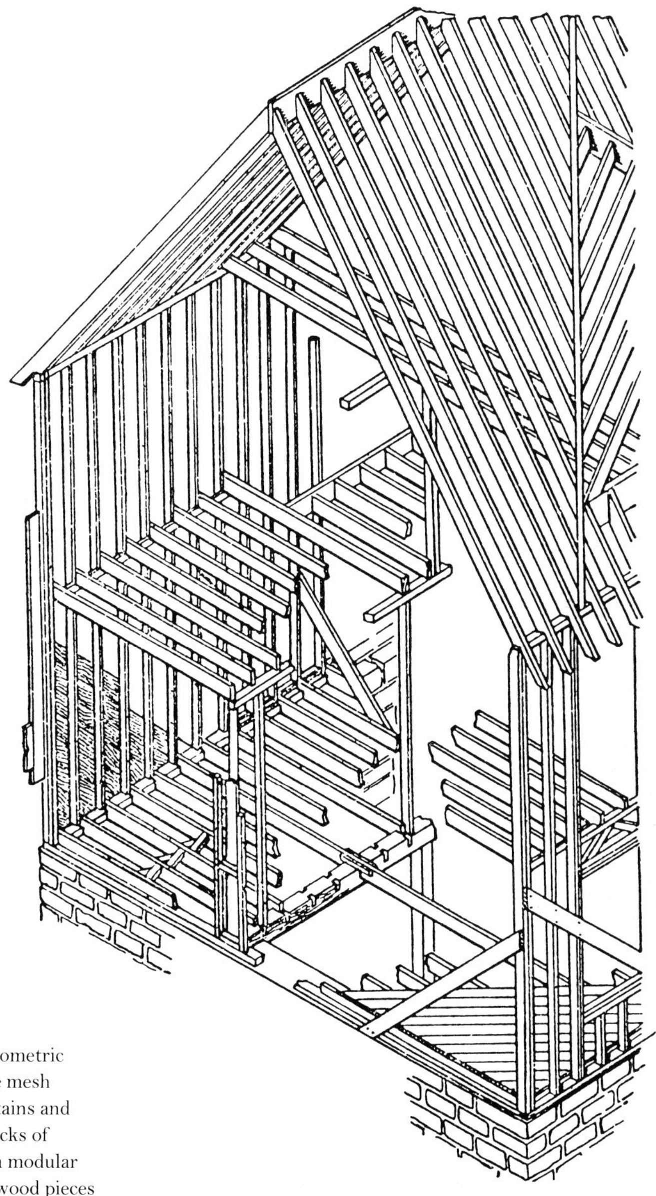

FIGURE 25

The Balloon Frame: An isonometric drawing reveals the intricate mesh of structural forces that contains and orders the basic building blocks of American domesticity with a modular system composed of simple wood pieces

formation of the West into an attractor of larger populations.[14]

To understand that such a strategy was deliberate, one has only to turn to the example of Los Angeles, which financed its imperial growth by exploiting the economy of the grid (land speculation) to create something very different: sprawl. The architect of the initial stages of the project, William Mulholland, had wanted his work to be invisible and beneficent by pumping the water into the Los Angeles aquifer, where anyone with his own quarter-acre and a well would have access to it. His financial backers, however, convinced him to dam the water up into giant reservoirs from which they could parcel out the water while generating electricity from its flows. The result was disastrous—at least in the case of the St. Francis Dam in the San Francisquito canyon, a hastily constructed structure that collapsed, causing several hundred deaths.[15]

These great works of earth and concrete also became the monuments of the West, an answer to the forms of the mountains that supplied them with a reason and framework. Taller than any skyscraper, bigger than any palace, and stranger in form than any cenotaph, the Boulder, Grand Coulee, and other dams truly spoke to the imagination of the West. The only problem was that they existed, like the mountains, of necessity at the very fringes of civilization, so that one could see them only by going on a pilgrimage. They were not a visible part of everyday life; thus they became more famous *in* than influential *on* the visual culture of the American West.

The third romance of construction that rose out of the grid was *exploitation*. Agriculture had followed the grid (at least until the rotating irrigation devices were introduced). Mining dug underneath the grid, though it was defined by stakes that themselves followed the Jeffersonian precepts. Mining made the West rich, and mines became its greatest destroyer. The clear expression of the skeletal constructions hovering over the mine entrances, which looked like hopeful constructions, soon gave way to the more efficient destruction of the land. The washing of the soil in the California gold mines, which created lunar landscapes in the foothills of the Sierra, then gave way to strip mining. The land itself opened up into vortices of exploitation whose size defied the imagination. These were negative spatialities; they did not encase space so much as they opened it up and down.[16]

Forestry, the other great source of wealth (and therefore attractor of people) in the West, created similar negativities. It turned the dense spaces of the forests into openings ready for further development. Its heroic structures, which included sawmills, skids, and processing harbors, were puny compared with the overall spatial effect of clear-cutting. Ironically, these voids are now turning into what amount to parodies of the grid as companies replace the forest with fast-growing plantations of homogenous firs.

The only physical articulation that one could hold onto in all of this work was the act itself, whether that was the act of building the railroads, roads, dams, and aqueducts or the act of mining and forestry itself. One could see machinery transforming space with a spider's nest of scaffolding that offered an articulate artificiality answering to the grandeur of the West. Such construction turned the grid into something indeed heroic. Yet it was evanescent, disappearing into the great lines of escape, the big holes and killing fields of the American West. It left little trace beyond the photographs collected in this exhibition or the persistent architectural desire for such unstable structural expressionism. It reached perhaps its high point in Frank Gehry's discovery that "buildings under construction are much more beautiful" and his ten-year-long attempt (now abandoned since he moved to a less western-based practice) to design structures that would not just picture, but realize, such profoundly western constructions.[17]

No wonder, then, that many westerners sought to escape from the grid and from the machinery that exploited it. They turned instead to an invocation of all that they thought had been there without them, but which they had replaced, and which was, in any case, only a myth. They sought, first, to resurrect the Eden they had thought the West embodied, but which their very settlement had destroyed. This mythic spatiality was based, like the grid, on the notion of motion—in this case the meandering and ultimately circuitous (if the traveler were lucky) movement of the explorer. Meriwether Lewis and William Clark named much of the West, and then John Muir turned their travels into iterative tramps that were meant to offer the westerner an escape from the grids of the city and return him or her to it, fully restored by a realization of boundless space.[18] Although this romantic (in the Burkian sense of the term) notion was by no means unique to the West, it achieved a cult status that eventually gave birth to a whole industry of outdoor gear. It also gave the West a cohesive mythology. The American West, if it were ever to be a separate nation, would have "America, the Beautiful" as its anthem, the bear as its symbol, and either the Grand Canyon or Yosemite as its shrine. Land, the embodiment of freedom, and the both physical and economic freedom to move through it, became a secular religion.

In architecture, such spaces became embodied by the bungalow, which deconstructed the balloon frame into flung-out concatenations of sleeping porches and strings of rooms in which structural expression evoked not just the grid but the very landscape in which these machines for living sat. The physical tracing of the land became the roof, which, starting with the vacation retreats of the Eastern Shingle Style, took on a plasticity that sheltered and replicated the spread of the land. This architecture of the American West is horizontal, spreading, and curved. Perhaps its purest form is the "organic architecture" that Frank Lloyd Wright pioneered at his Taliesin West and that Bruce Goff, Bart Prince, and Paolo Soleri took to delightfully absurd lengths.

VOIDS AT THE HEART OF THE GRID Outside such extreme articulations, the evocation of this limitless landscape, through which one toured as in the one-way loops that still define almost every national park in the West, became fixed in an elaborate system of reserves that included the national park system itself, national forests, Native American preservations, military reservations, and state and community parks. These replaced the small town square that had been the traditional center of most American cities and found their smallest version instead in city parks that existed, more often than not, on the flood plane of the local river. The space of Central Park and the lawns of Capability Brown became something outside the place of inhabitation and their only limit. In states such as Nevada, where the government controls most of the land, such voids are the only stops to sprawl, and they might turn out to be the natural border of Los Angeles as it continues to spread over whole mountain ranges and across deserts.[19]

Such voids that open up at the vast scale of the grid also replicate themselves at the local level in the suburban lawn. American houses do not organize themselves around courtyards, nor do they group themselves together in rows. Instead they sit back behind miniature versions of the great spaces of the West and open up to this privatized fragment of infinity through great picture windows. The lawn is the last remnant of the Jeffersonian subdivision, but it is also a romantic evocation of much larger spaces. It is as destructive of the original land as anything man has done; it requires immense amounts of water and has changed the climate of urban areas such as Phoenix. It is not meant to be a place of work, as communities that forbid their inhabitants from working on their cars in the yard will attest, and it is not even a place to play (you play basketball in the driveway, baseball in the street). Instead, it is a place of absence, a place that sets off the machines.

One should not forget that those machines also became embodied in the landscape. The activity of opening up of space became an ironic return to the landscape of the West. Tracing that landscape with a car is only the modern version of the Muirian *derive*, and its forms became billboards for what was lost. The sweeps and curves of the railroad and roads followed the contours and arched off into infinity. The dams held back bodies of water that precisely marked the edges of the mountains, creating a smooth but clearly limited expanse within those confines. The clear-cuts evoked the prairies where the buffaloes roamed in song, and the open-pit mines aspired to the status of man-made Grand Canyons. The geography of the American West became re-presented in grand voids.[20]

SPACES OF FEAR Not until after the Second World War did a new element enter into American spatiality: enclosure. The advent of air-conditioning and the closing of the frontier combined to create an inward turn that itself fed on a long American tradition of turning to the inside in defense against the sheer size of space.[21] In the West, this movement took a decidedly paranoid turn: the Wild West became a place where one avoided the showdown on Main Street by outfitting oneself with security systems and never leaving the car. One experienced the land itself as inimical, so that one had to stay in the world of air-conditioning or, as in Houston and Minneapolis, stay away from the grid itself in bridges and tunnels.

The result of this inward turn was the emergence of certain fluid objects. These are not structures that are meant to define space and represent activities. They only *contain*, in as efficient and anonymous a manner as possible. The car, with its flowing, mass-produced lines, is the prototype, and the shopping mall is its epitome. The optimistic grids of corporate modernism became replaced with "Defensible Space," and the flowing forms of the bungalow solidified into stucco boxes with small windows.[22] Eventually, the two merged into the secure compound, or "luxury laager," which isolated itself completely.[23]

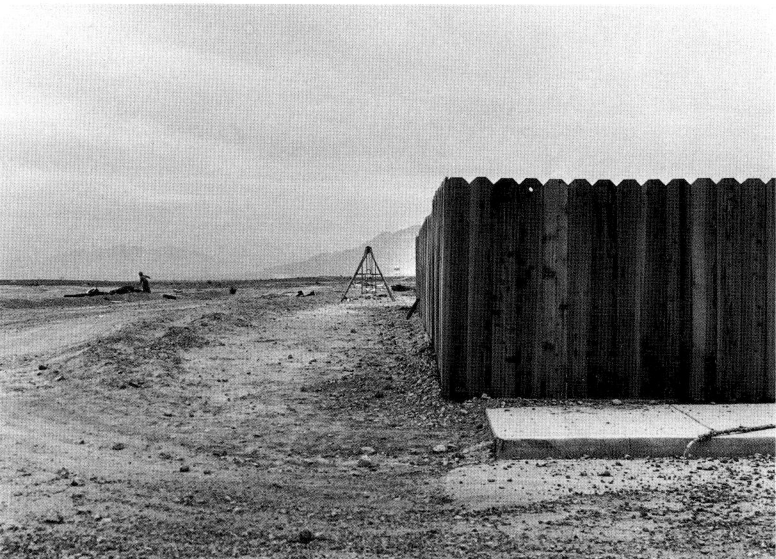

FIGURE 26

The empty space of fear, as it marks itself in the walls of privacy the denizens of sprawl throw up in the desert landscape of the American West

The aggregate of such isolations, each contained within its own little section of the grid, is sprawl. Sprawl transforms the Jeffersonian grid into the flowing spaces of conditioned air, motorized movement, and the panoptic cone of the security camera. The curving roads now lead to nodes of coherence that are neither part of the grid itself nor an escape from it. Instead, the office buildings, shopping malls, and hospitals that form the places where western communities find their focus are concatenations of curved and angular geometries. They share a lack of hierarchy and definition found in the traditional reactions to western space. They add a sense of blob-like solidity that elides the emptiness of the landscape and the technology of inhabitation into something difficult to define, name, or even judge. The logic that underlies these spaces appears to be that of epigenetic landscapes[24] and rhizomes,[25] but such pseudo-scientific explanations do little to explain the sheer slickness of the current forms of western space.

The closest definition of such space is that it is an assemblage of premade materials, usually bought at a store such as Home Depot. Unlike the former methods of importation, including buying one's plans at Sears, these spaces do not cohere into a system. Instead they just grow to the form an inhabitant can afford. The same can be said for industrial space. Instead of the large forms of spatial exploitation, the West now sprawls into light industrial parks whose tilt-up concrete elements are serial and can contain any number of activities.

At the heart of these postmodern machines for isolation, a new kind of space opened up: the lobby, the golf course, the shopping arcade, and, at a heroic scale, the playing field. The lobby is the spatial version of the sign and the entrance to town that western communities rarely had, turned into a holding pen that bleeds off into corridors. The golf course became a ritualistic evocation of the Muirian circuit, devoid of any association with Eden and, instead, more often than not reflecting its elderly and retired users' nearness to the final void of death.

The shopping mall became a space evoking the flows of the road and the limitless possibilities through which one cruises with a credit card rather than a car, but it is an assembly of semi-transparent and open fragments of form. Shopping mall designers avoid corners, articulated roofs, or any other delineation of limits; they "theme" their environments to look like places that usually have nothing to do with the West, whether it be Olde England or even older Italy. The West, seen by its conquerors as an empty void waiting to be filled with culture, has produced the most outrageously artificial version of culture in such themed environments. Based on Disneyland and the stage sets of the elaborate restaurants of the 1950s, "themed" shopping malls were pioneered by architect Jon Jerde and the Rouse Corporation in the 1970s; by now they are making shopping in Hong Kong and London a unified experience. The mobility and malleability of space has reached such an extent that you can, indeed, be anywhere everywhere, and the West has been the progenitor of such space.

The modern equivalent of the heroicism of the dam and the road are the convention center and the stadium. As David Harvey has pointed out, such large constructions are the prime methods by which communities can define themselves, both economically and in terms of local identity.[26] The convention center is the modern equivalent of the marketplace, turned inward, themed for different trades, and blown up to a vast scale that presents itself as acres of sprawling booths huddled under a heroic construction of trusses and girders that disappear into the mists far above. These spaces are bunker-like from the outside, completely cut off on the inside, and often the largest building in town.

Stadia, convention centers, and golf courses, are, according to some studies, the prime reasons why corporations choose their locations. Stadia and convention centers are also the largest constructions in most western cities. They are not much more than constructions: cantilevered scaffolding for viewing a ritualistic conquest of space (football) or circuit through it (baseball) on a gridded void. Yet even these moments of playful heroicism are disappearing as communities try to turn them into themed evocations of an urban past that cities such as Denver never had.

ICONS IN THE SPRAWL Las Vegas offers an alternative, though it might not be a palatable one. In this city, the road, the grid, the circuit, the shopping mall, the assemblage, the place of play, and the inhabitation merge into what is still rather quaintly called a casino. The Strip gave birth to these behemoths, which now are as large as anything the West has ever produced. They house tens of thousands of people in gridded anonymity above a sea of games through which they move as if through an electronic forest, looking for liberation through cash, the most abstract embodiment (if one is a good Marxist) of land. Space is both profoundly fragmented and flows, all the way from the street into the heart of the machine. Water becomes visible in giant fountains and waterfalls and lakes. The themed versions of reality come out into the open and take over the street as electric circuses (the Fremont Street Experience), visions of Avalon (Excalibur), or sea battles in which rapaciousness is rewarded (Treasure Island).

A new kind of space appears in Las Vegas that incorporates as well as destroys the desert, turning it into a communal, air-conditioned, and carefully guarded carpet of free-floating signs. The space of paranoia and the dreams of escape become coincident in this "clean" place of sin, where even day and night disappear into the pulses of an "electronic expressionism."[27]

At the heart of this new space sits the Luxor, a dark emblem of what this space really is, which is desert. In its black glass it makes even the

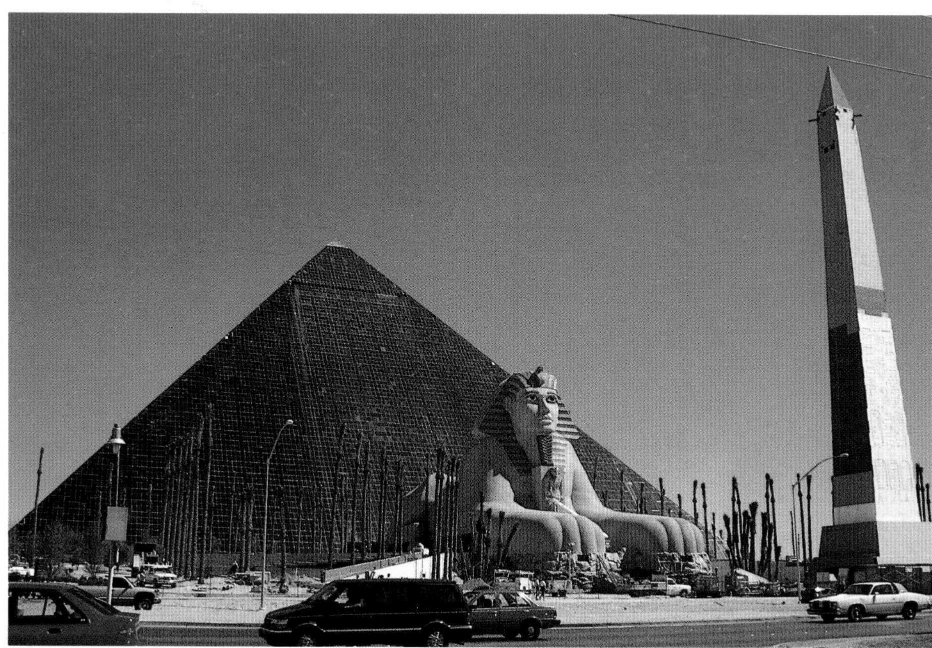

FIGURE 27

The Inhabited Tomb: The Luxor Hotel, Las Vegas, presents the most abstract form of the serious business of entertainment. Here the grid turns in on itself and becomes a shrine to the voids of the West.

pyramid more expressive of what it contains, which is death. One can inhabit this monument. It creates a new kind of space in the desert where one cannot so much find one's self as escape into a manifest destiny as ominous as our forefathers thought the march toward the setting sun was luminous.

The Luxor is so dark that they have not yet figured out how to illuminate it. Similarly, it is difficult to represent the spaces of Las Vegas. A new realism evident in most forms of art turns its back on the Strip, back to the sprawl and, preferably, the very edges where it fades back into the "real" desert. With a loving eye, our culture tries to give material reality to spaces that slip away from an observer who is not equipped with a machine of visual exploitation, framing and voiding. Our culture is now in love with the reality of the desert, its harsh forms and its emptiness. An "aesthetics of poverty" is becoming popular at certain architecture schools, and films such as *Leaving Las Vegas* delight in the moral as well as physical voids at the heart of the western city.

We assume that by finding the physical embodiment of the ephemeral absences of the West, we will be able to fill them with meaning. Architects make "real" buildings out of the material around them: concrete block, tilt-up concrete, fragments of the sprawl itself. Critics search for the places where the void reveals limits that seem real, such as prisons and the crystal palaces of the Edge City malls. Photographers caress such planes and places as they find them.

To all such pioneers of a western neo-realism, the Sphinx in front of the Luxor, laser-eyed and monstrous in its tacky abstraction, asks: "Who am I...?"

NOTES

1. Norman Mailer, *An American Dream* (New York: The Dial Press, 1965), pp. 268–69.

2. It was the subject of Robert Venturi, Denise Scott Brown, and Steven Izenour's influential *Learning from Las Vegas* (Cambridge: The MIT Press, 1972), and the site of Hunter S. Thompson's most important ranting assessment of American culture, *Fear and Loathing in Las Vegas* (New York: Random House, 1971).

3. "Theming" is a word probably coined by the architect Jon Jerde to denote environments that have been designed around a central theme or "look." It has its roots in Walt Disney's phrase "imagineering," which he used to describe the process by which his theme parks were designed.

4. Alan Hess, *Viva Las Vegas: After-Hours Architecture* (San Francisco: Chronicle Books, 1993).

5. These characteristics were first documented by Robert Venturi, Denise Scott Brown, and Steven Izenour in *Learning from Las Vegas.*

6. Michael Bell, "Slow Space," unpublished essay, 1995.

7. The importance of utopian impulses, particularly in the development of California, has been most thoroughly documented by Kevin Starr in *Material Dreams: Southern California through the 1920s* (New York: Oxford University Press, 1990); see also my "Riding the A Train to the Aleph: Eight Utopias for Los Angeles," in *Heterotopia: Postmodern Utopia and the Body Politic,* ed. Tobin Siebers (Ann Arbor: The University of Michigan Press, 1994), pp. 96–121.

8. John Brinckerhoff Jackson, *A Sense of Place, A Sense of Time* (New Haven: Yale University Press, 1994); see also John W. Reps, *The Forgotten Frontier: Urban Planning in the American West Before 1890* (Columbia: University of Missouri Press, 1981).

9. Henri Lefebvre, *The Production of Space*, trans. Donald Nicholson-Smith (1974; reprint, Oxford: Blackwell, 1991).

10. For the best collection of analyses of both the sources and influences of Mies van der Rohe's abstractions, see *The Presence of Mies*, ed. Detlef Mertins (New York: Princeton Architectural Press, 1994).

11. Leo Marx, *The Machine in the Garden: Technology and the Pastoral Ideal in America* (New York: Oxford University Press, 1964).

12. Vincent Scully, *American Architecture and Urbanism* (New York: Praeger Publishers, 1961).

13. Cf. Carl W. Condit, *The Chicago School of Architecture. A History of Commercial and Public Buildings in the Chicago Area, 1875–1925* (Chicago: University of Chicago Press, 1964). This "nervous" spinning out of the grid does seem to offer an American alternative to the European dialectic between *raumplan* (the concatenation of functional spaces) and the Corbusian order of the *plan libre*.

14. Marc Reisner, *Cadillac Desert: The American West and Its Disappearing Water* (New York: Penguin Books, 1987).

15. Cf. Margaret Leslie Davis, *Rivers in the Desert: William Mulholland and the Inventing of Los Angeles* (New York: HarperCollins, 1993).

16. Margaret Crawford has pointed out the one exception to this process, which was the spate of company towns that arose in New Mexico and Arizona around the turn of the century. These were small attempts to import a sense of (company-defined) community and even traditional spatiality into the West. Margaret Crawford, *Building the Workingman's Paradise: The Design of American Company Towns* (London: Verso, 1995).

17. Frank Gehry and Peter Arnell, "No, I'm an Architect," in *Frank Gehry Buildings and Projects* (New York: Rizzoli International Publishers, 1985), p. XVIII.

18. Muir's most influential book was probably *The Mountains of California* (1875; reprint, New York: Barnes and Noble Books, 1993).

19. Cf. Ed Soja, "It All Comes Together in Los Angeles," in *Postmodern Geographies: The Reassertion of Space in Critical Social Theory* (London: Verso, 1989), pp. 190–221.

20. This might be a version of what Gilles Deleuze and Félix Guattari refer to as "retroactive smoothing." Gilles Deleuze and Félix Guattari, *A Thousand Plateaus: Capitalism and Schizophrenia*, trans. Brian Massumi (1980; reprint, Minneapolis: The University of Minnesota Press, 1987).

21. Cf. T. J. Jackson Lears, *No Place of Grace: Antimodernism and the Transformation of American Culture, 1880–1920* (New York: Pantheon Books, 1981).

22. The strange relationship between the needs for defensible space and the aesthetic tenets of postmodernism have been well documented by Mike Davis in his *City of Quartz: Excavating the Future in Los Angeles* (London: Verso, 1990).

23. Steve Flusty, *Building Paranoia: The Proliferation of Interdictory Space and the Erosion of Spatial Justice* (Los Angeles: The Los Angeles Forum for Architecture and Urban Design, 1994).

24. The relation of emerging forms of spatiality and biological models for the emergence of form has been most succinctly traced by Manuel De Landa in his "Nonorganic Life," *Zone* 6 (1992), pp. 128–67.

25. The notion of rhizomes as models for all kinds of urban forms has been popularized by Deleuze and Guattari in their *A Thousand Plateaus*.

26. David Harvey, "Flexible Accumulation Through Urbanization: Reflections on 'Post-Modernism' in the American City," *Perspecta* 26 (1990), pp. 251–73.

27. The phrase is from *Learning from Las Vegas*, p. 28; the importance of fear or perceived danger as an element that draws people to the casinos of Las Vegas was emphasized by Veldon Simpson, the designer of the Luxor, Excalibur, and MGM Grand, among other hotels, in an interview with the author in September 1994. According to Simpson, the sense of danger is tied both to the "free-wheeling traditions" of the desert Southwest and to the violence inherent in "big money" and its instability.

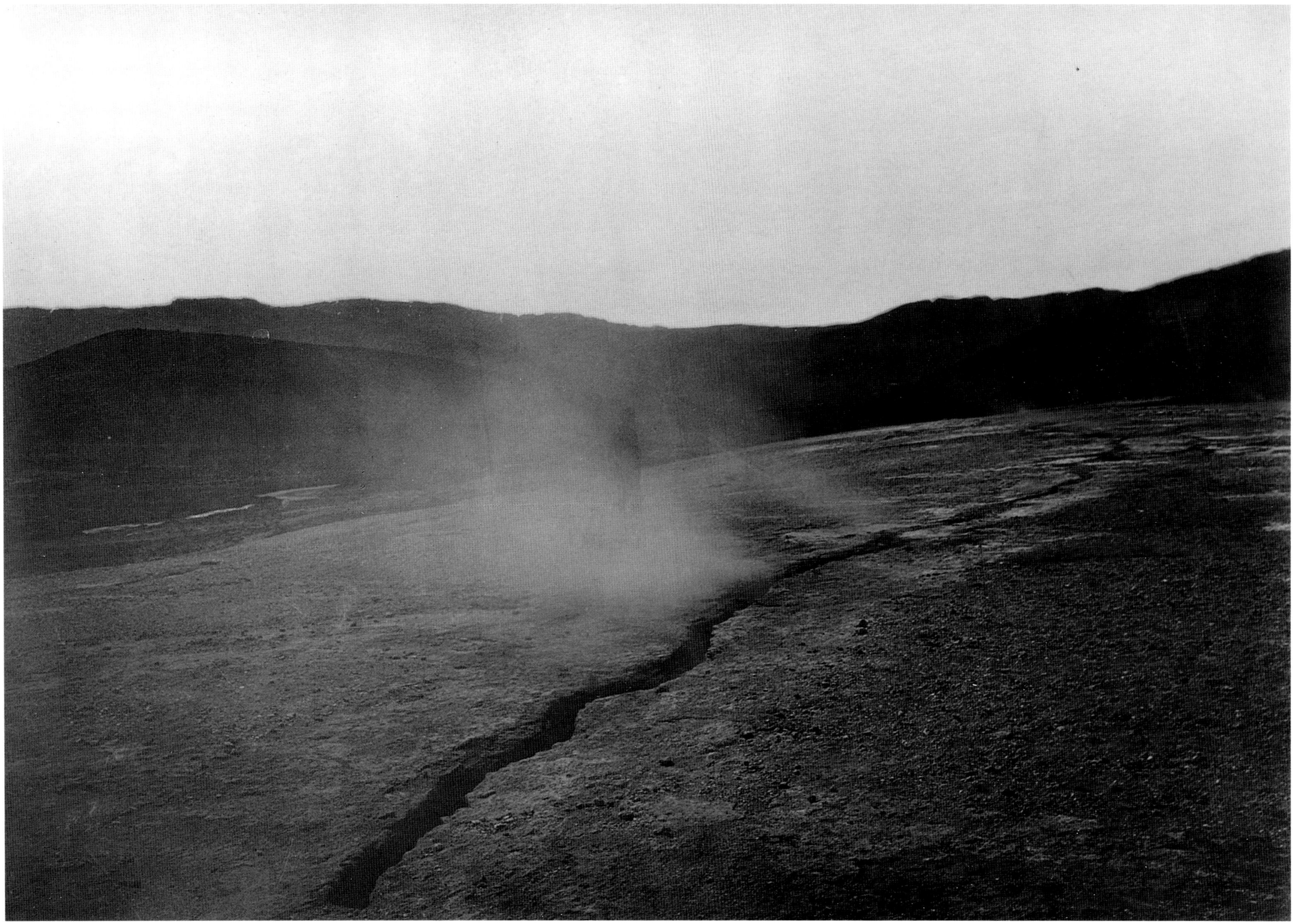

Geology and Topography of the American West: Its Impact on Development

ELDRIDGE M. MOORES

Civilization exists by geologic consent—subject to change without notice.
Will Durant

The Euro-American settlement of the American West was one of the most rapid and profound migrations of people in human history. It arose primarily through several factors: the discovery of mineral wealth, the farming potential of land given free by the federal government under the Homestead Act, and the warm climate of the "sun belt."

With increased settlement, farmland and water became increasingly important. The indigenous native populations had sustained their existence for thousands of years but never with numbers like those that developed starting in the 1840s. The American West is a region of generally scarce water resources. Farmland is abundant where water is abundant, but farming is hampered by a short growing season in many states where the elevation is greater than 3,000 feet above sea level.[1] Many regions of the West today remain thinly populated because of difficulty of access (high mountains, steep canyons), short growing seasons, and lack of water. Settlement of this region has been difficult, and human ingenuity has been challenged to come up with engineering structures to "bend" nature to the perceived human needs. This "bending" has come at the price of environmental degradation of the landscape, depletion of resources, and large-scale engineering structures that transfer water from one region to another.

THE ACTIVE EARTH Like the rest of the Solar System, Earth is about 4.5 billion years old.[2] Earth is also unique in the Solar System. No other planet has Earth's tectonic activity: its earthquakes, its moving plates carrying continents and oceans, its number and variety of volcanoes. Slow movements in the interior (an inch or two per year, about as fast as the growth of a fingernail) cause jerky motion of rocks at the surface in the form of earthquakes. Earthquakes cluster along the edges of huge segments of Earth's outer layers, the crust and outer mantle, called *lithospheric plates,* which are in motion with respect to each other and interact at their boundaries (fig. 28). Most of Earth's quakes occur along such boundaries.

Along mid-oceanic ridges, called *divergent* or *constructive boundaries,* plates move apart. Material fills the void by moving up from Earth's interior to the surface, where it forms new oceanic crust and mantle, representing new plate material. Hot springs along these boundaries produce metal deposits—zinc, copper, gold, silver, and manganese.

Along a *convergent* or *consuming boundary* (also called a *subduction zone*), one plate slides beneath another back down into Earth's interior. A convergent boundary is marked by an inclined zone of earthquakes and a row of cone-shaped volcanoes spaced roughly 50 miles apart. As the plate descends into Earth's interior, some of it melts to form bodies of molten rock, called *magma,* which rise toward Earth's surface. This melt cools and solidifies below the surface or erupts as volcanoes and then cools to form igneous rocks. A convergent boundary produces a chain of volcanoes (such as the Cascades of the Pacific Northwest) along the edge of a continent, or a curved line of islands (an island arc) within an ocean. Mineral deposits form in bodies of cooling magma or in hot springs formed from water heated by the magma.

At a third kind of boundary, called a *transform fault* or *conservative bound-*

PLATE 10
Timothy H. O'Sullivan
Steamboat Springs, Ruby Valley, Nevada, 1867
albumen print
18 x 23 15/16 in. (45.6 x 60.8 cm)
American Geographical Society Collection, University of Wisconsin–Milwaukee Library

FIGURE 28

Three-dimensional sketch of the major plate boundaries. Divergent or mid-oceanic ridge, transform fault, and convergent boundaries are located either at a continental margin or within an ocean. Volcanoes form where one plate descends beneath another.

FIGURE 29

Generalized plate boundary map of western North America. Convergent margins or subduction zones are present south of Alaska, along the Pacific Northwest, and along central Mexico. Spreading ridges are present west of the Pacific Northwest and in the eastern Pacific extending into the Gulf of California. The San Andreas fault system is present along the West Coast of the United States and extends into the Gulf of California. Plate movement along the San Andreas is about one to one-and-a-half inches per year. The internal region of the United States, called the Basin and Range Province, is widening about three-eighths of an inch per year.

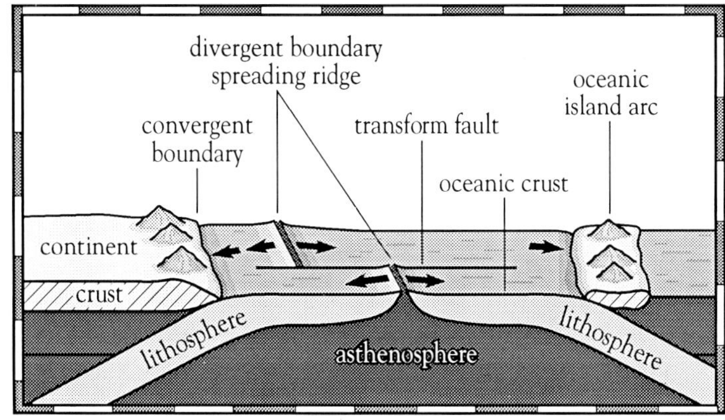

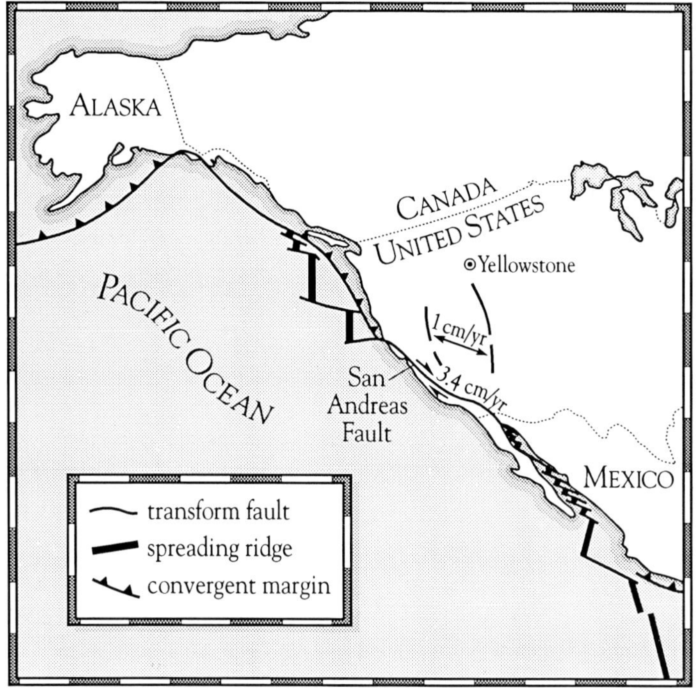

ary, plates slide past each other with little or no creation or destruction of lithospheric plates. These boundaries are characterized by abundant earthquakes at fairly shallow depths. The San Andreas fault zone that runs through most of California is a good example. Added features of the San Andreas include volcanic rocks, hot springs, and mineral deposits.

As plates move, continents move with them as passive riders. Continents move apart along some plate boundaries and converge toward each other along others. When they collide, high mountains are formed. Oceanic island chains also approach, collide with, and deform continental edges. This process, which has happened several times along the western edge of North America, is reflected in the geology, geography, and mineral resources.

As geologic processes continue to act, Earth's geography slowly but inexorably changes. At present six continents—Antarctica, Australia, South America, North America, Africa, and Eurasia—stretch from one pole to another. As the geologic features and ore deposits of the western lands were forming over hundreds, even thousands of millions of years, Earth's geography went through many changes. Some 750 million years ago, western North America may have been next to eastern Australia and East Antarctica, with the present South Pole within walking distance of Death Valley. About 500 million years ago, there were four or five continents generally located along the equator.

Approximately 200 million years ago all Earth's land masses were assembled into a single large supercontinent, which we call Pangea, that stretched almost from pole to pole. Pangea separated about 150 million years ago into two huge continents called Laurasia (including North America, Europe, and Asia), and Gondwana (including Africa, South America, India, Australia, and Antarctica). These huge continents subsequently split apart to form the present continents. The Atlantic and Indian oceans formed and widened, while Africa and India converged and collided with Eurasia to form the mountain ranges stretching from Spain to the Himalayas.

The climate of Earth and of individual continents changes as the location and distribution of continental regions change. Mountains thrown up by plate activity are broken down. The debris is transported by wind and water and laid down by streams, lakes, or oceans in a series of horizontal sedimentary layers.

As mountain-building occurs through plate motions, pre-existing igneous or sedimentary rocks are buried to depths of 12 to 18 miles, where high heat and pressure cause them to recrystallize to become metamorphic rocks. Water driven out of the rocks in this process dissolves metals from them, which it carries to other sites in Earth's depths. Usually along faults, long thin veins of quartz are deposited that contain metals dissolved from the rocks as the hot water passes through them. Thus were born many of the mineral-bearing quartz veins of the deep hard-rock mines of the West.

In places, large volcanoes form in the middle of plates, away from the plate edges. These *mid-plate volcanoes* are thought to result from columns of molten rock rising from very deep within Earth, possibly as deep as 1,500 to 1,800 miles down. These pipelike columns of magma burn their way through the overlying plates to erupt on the surface. Yellowstone National Park, full of young volcanic rocks and active hot springs and geysers, appears to have formed over such a hot spot. We see the trail of its passage under the continent in volcanic rocks in eastern Washington and Oregon and in southern Idaho.

GEOLOGIC OVERVIEW The western region long supported a nomadic native population that traditionally depended upon the local resources, such as the buffalo, for its existence. More recent increased population in the western Great Plains is supported by tapping underground water in a widespread sand and gravel layer formed by streams draining off the mountains to the West. This layer is called the "Oglala," after one of the Sioux tribes. Streams flowing eastward from this high region along the backbone of the continent eroded valleys that have served as pathways for indigenous people, Euro-American hunters and trappers, wagon trains, railroads, and finally, interstate highways (pl. 29).

Western North America lies along a complex boundary between the North American, Pacific, and other oceanic plates (fig. 29). The region's mountains, deserts, earthquakes, and volcanoes are recent manifestations of activity along that boundary. But our studies of the geology of the western United States tell us that plate activity of a different sort, present for a great length of time, has played an important role in the development of the landscape.

It is popular to talk of the San Andreas fault as being the boundary between the Pacific and North American plates. The plate boundary is not a single fault but a whole family of faults that runs along the Coast Ranges of western California from offshore to about 40 miles inland. All these faults are active, with earthquakes along them. They are not the only earthquakes in the western United States, however. Zones of earthquakes are present in central Nevada, central Utah, central New Mexico, and the Pacific Northwest. Active or recently active volcanoes are found in many parts of the West. Think of the entire western portion of the continent as part of a messy plate boundary, some 1,000 miles wide in places, between plates in the ocean to the west and North America. All of this region is susceptible, to varying degrees, to earthquakes, volcanic eruptions, or both.

Much of the middle part of North America consists of ancient rocks, more than a billion years old, overlain by younger deposits, ranging in age from about 500 million to a few hundred thousand years. Very old rocks are exposed in Canada and adjoining parts of Minnesota, Wisconsin, and Michigan; they also appear in Missouri, the Rocky Mountains, the inner gorge of the Grand Canyon, the deserts of southeast California and western Arizona, and in the mountains near Los Angeles. They record a complex history of tectonic activity, formation of oceanic island chains, collisions, and finally relative quiescence and erosion to produce a low-lying plain on which younger sediments were deposited.

The edge of this ancient continent extends from southeastern California through central Nevada, eastern Idaho, western Montana, and western Canada to northern Alaska. All of the rocks west of this ancient continental edge have subsequently been added to the continent in one form or another. Some added rocks formed as islands or deep sea sediments and volcanoes that approached and became attached to North America as the plates that carried them disappeared beneath the edge of the continent. Others formed by the melting of down-going plates to form

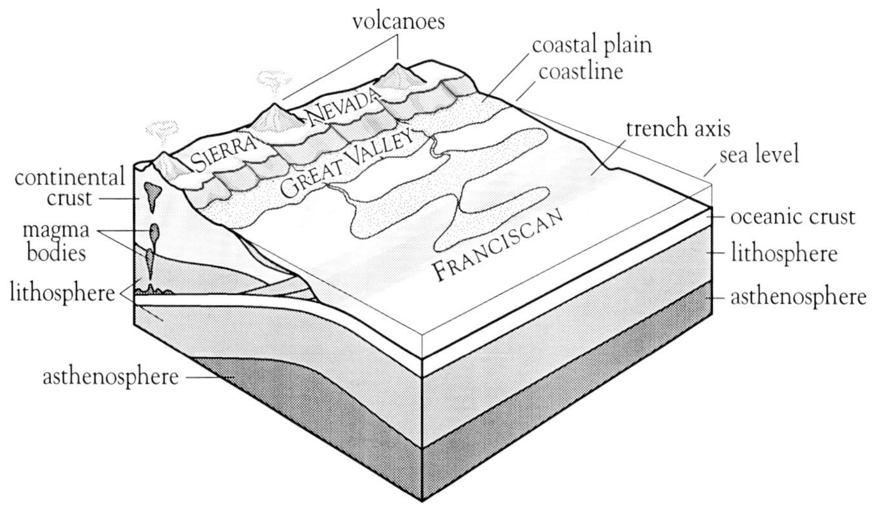

FIGURE 30

Diagram showing formation, about 100 million years ago, of ancestral Sierra Nevada and rocks of western California along a convergent margin. Melting of the down-going plate forms magma bodies that rise to form granitic bodies within the crust or volcanoes at the surface.

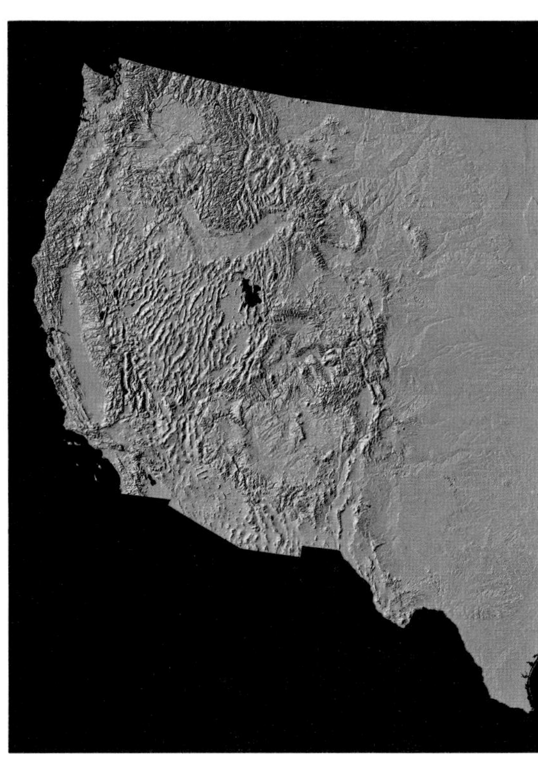

FIGURE 31

Relief map of the western lands showing principal topographic features.

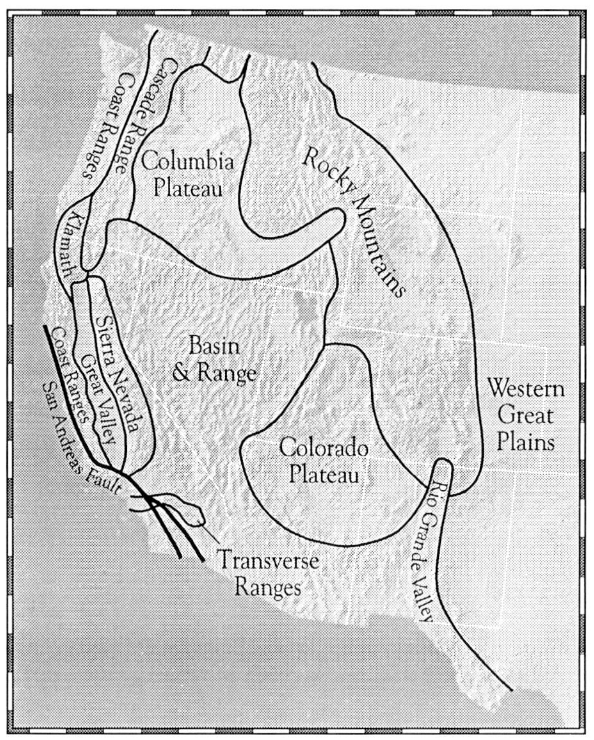

FIGURE 32

Relief map of western lands showing major geologic provinces.

magma that rose toward the surface to form volcanoes or granite-intrusive rocks within the crust (fig. 30). Most of this addition of material has occurred in the past 200 million years, which is also the time of formation of most of the geologic structures we see around us.

Much of the West is high, standing more than 2,000 feet above sea level (fig. 31). Even the western Great Plains gently rise from near sea level in the Mississippi valley to 5,000 feet at Denver or central Montana. The mountains to the West are even higher, over 14,000 feet in the Rockies and Sierra Nevada and over 13,000 feet in Nevada and Utah. Even many valleys are high, 4,000 to 10,000 feet in the western interior. Much of this area has risen up fairly recently—in the past five million years—and uplift is still going on today. High mountains block moisture-laden winds coming in from the ocean and force them to dump their precipitation as they rise. This phenomenon forms a so-called rain shadow in the downwind direction. Most of the deserts of the western interior and their short growing seasons there are caused by this uplift and its effects.

GEOLOGIC PROVINCES The western lands are a complex series of mountains, deserts, plateaus, and canyons, each with its own unique character and its own characteristic geology. Every landscape has its geologic explanation—land forms are there for a reason. The land that the natives inhabited, the Spanish, Russian, and North American explorers encountered, and the nineteenth-century migration settled reflects its complex geologic history. It is an extension of written history preserved in the rocks extending to vastly greater lengths of time in the past. Think of rocks as a kind of historical archive, preserving parts of the history of the planet that can be "read" by those who understand the language.

For descriptive purposes, geologists separate this diverse region into a series of provinces, each with a characteristic geologic history (fig. 32).

ROCKY MOUNTAINS The high mountains of Montana, Wyoming, Colorado, and northern New Mexico stretch along the backbone of the continent, forming the continental divide—the boundary between streams draining to the Pacific and those draining to the Atlantic. The high mountains and valleys formed formidable barriers to transport and commerce. The main western migration routes tended to go around the mountains to the north and south (pl. 93). This southern end of the Rockies includes a series of mountains reaching heights of 14,000 feet or more, separated by wide, flat valleys, called *parks* by the nineteenth-century explorers (pl. 53). The valleys are usually at elevations of 5,000 to 7,000 feet. These ranges consist of rocks more than a billion years old and, here and there, 200 to 500 million years old, overlying sedimentary rocks laid down on the ancient rocks before the mountains were formed. For example, in the Garden of the Gods, sedimentary rocks are tilted up by the rise of Pike's Peak (pl. 40). In Jackson's picture, one is looking down on the top of these tilted sediments toward progressively older strata that were deposited on an originally flat erosion surface on top of the much older (more than a billion years) Pike's Peak granite.

The wide valleys contain thick sedimentary deposits formed by rivers draining off rising mountains some 50 to 80 million years ago. A tropical ocean shoreline that existed approximately 80 million years ago near the present location of these mountains led to formation of thick coal deposits in this region.

The southern Rocky Mountains of Wyoming, New Mexico, and Colorado formed by squeezing the continental crust, causing it to break along fractures, uplifting some pieces (the mountains) over others (the valleys). The originally horizontal sediments were tilted up to steep inclinations by this process. Forty to fifty million years ago, huge lakes in this region were the sites of the deposition of fish-rich, salt-lake sediments, called *oil shale* for the hydrocarbons contained within the rocks (pl. 11). Large volcanoes of the same age in southwestern Colorado were the locus of the deposition of rich silver and gold deposits. Other rich Colorado mineral deposits formed along a series of zones of rock fractures that cross the mountains from southwest to northeast.

The northern Rocky Mountains of Montana (for example, Glacier National Park) consist of a region of bent and broken sedimentary rocks, mostly deposited 200 to 1,300 million years ago along the edge of North America. Squeezing of the continental edge by plate movements some 100 million years ago caused structures—long linear "rumples," or *folds*, and fractures, or *faults*, with steeply inclined sedimentary rocks—to form in

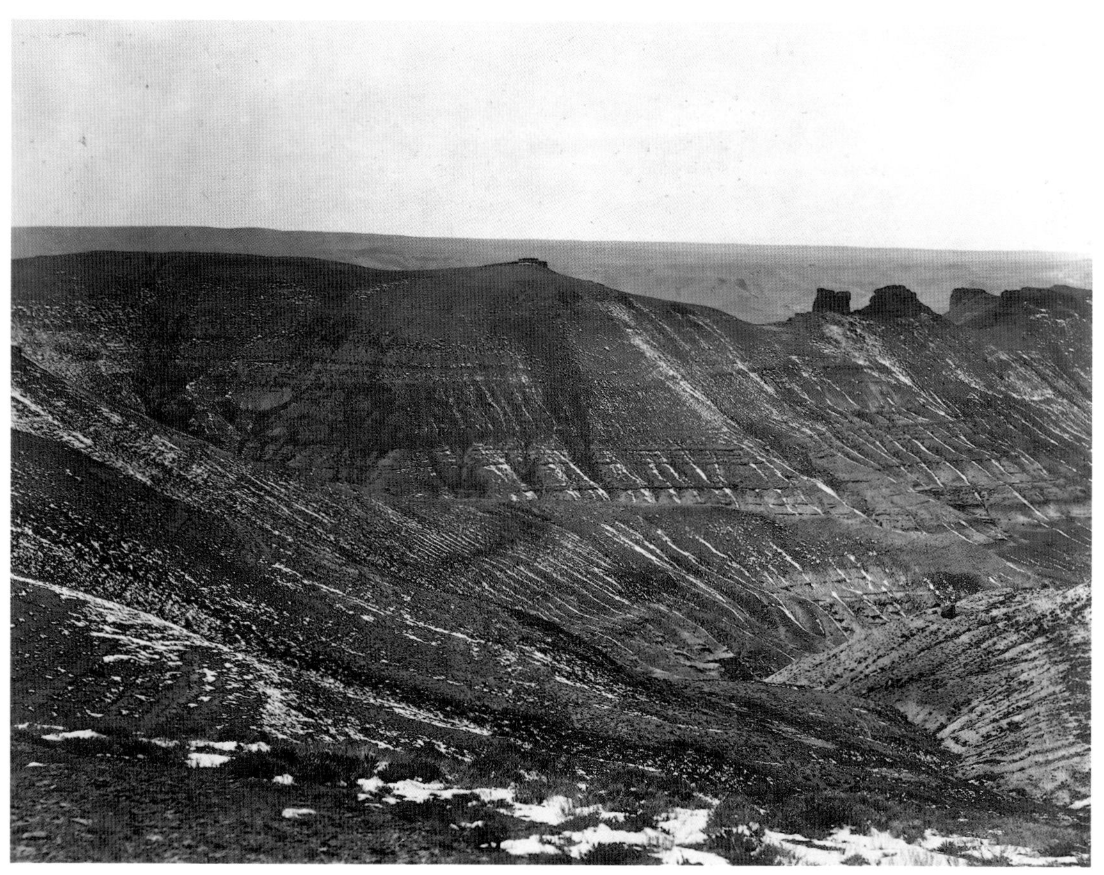

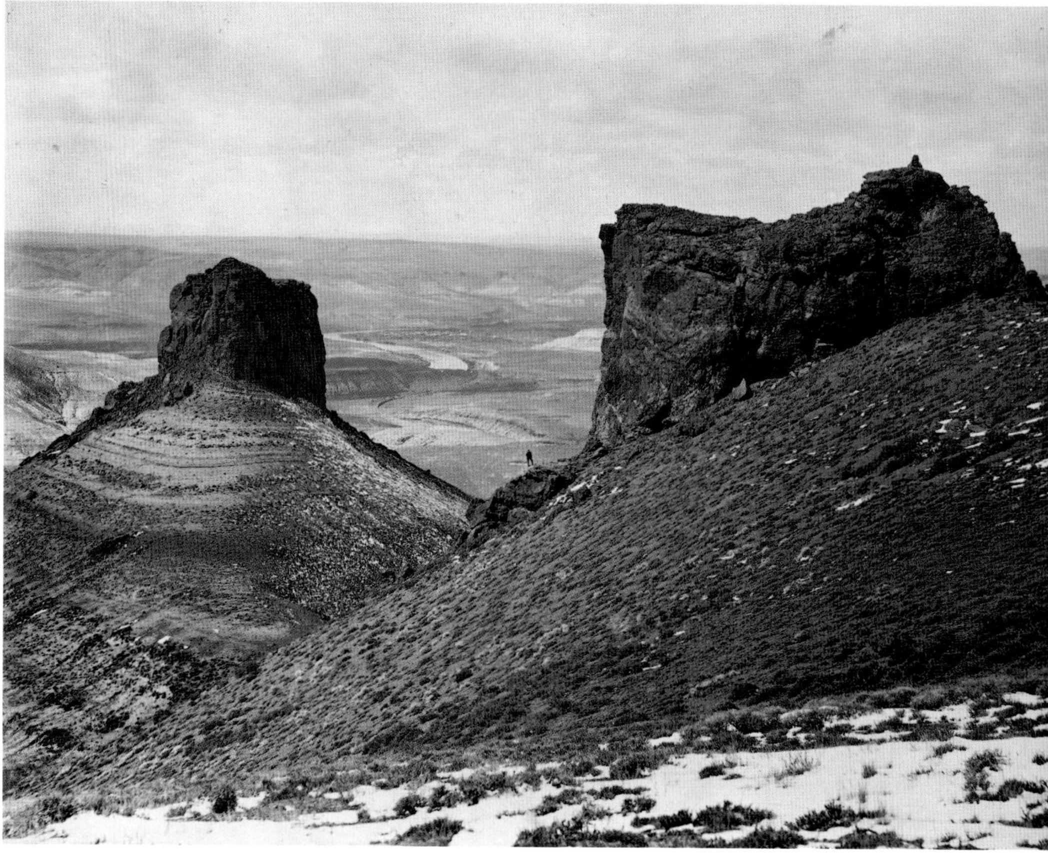

PLATE 11

Andrew Joseph Russell
Bitter Creek Valley [Wyoming] and *On the Mountains of Green River, Smith's Butte in Foreground*, 1868–69
albumen prints
8⅝ x 11¾ in. (21.9 x 29.8 cm) each
Union Pacific Museum Collection

these rocks (pl. 33). Some structures create natural reservoirs for gas and oil. Voluminous magmas intruding into these rocks some 65 to 100 million years ago resulted in widespread granitic rocks in western Montana and central Idaho. Ore deposits are present in some of these igneous rocks and in fractures that have affected the older sedimentary rocks.

COLORADO PLATEAU The Colorado Plateau country has long been the home of such native peoples as the Navaho and Hopi, and before them the Anasazi. The dry plateau country with its steep, deep canyons was a formidable challenge to travel, let alone settlement. One of the last regions to be settled by Europeans, its population is still sparse.

The high plain of southwest Colorado, northwest New Mexico, southeast Utah, and northeastern Arizona generally exhibits a flat-lying sequence of sedimentary rocks, mostly 50 to 500 million years in age, that overlies ancient rocks (over one billion years old) of the North American continent (pl. 2). The ancient rocks are exposed, for example, in the inner gorge of the Grand Canyon. This plateau is "canyon country," the site of many national parks and monuments (Bryce Canyon, Zion, Grand Canyon, Canyonlands, Cedar Breaks, Capitol Reef, Mesa Verde, Arches, Natural Bridges, Petrified Forest). The sedimentary rocks in this region attest to alternately tropical and Sahara-like desert conditions over the time period 50 to 200 million years ago. The vivid colors of the region's rocks arise from the varying abundance of red or green minerals containing iron and the lack of thick soil and vegetation. Similarly colored rocks are present in the East (in, for example, New York, Pennsylvania, and Virginia), hidden by thick soil and plant cover. For some reason, the Colorado Plateau mostly escaped the folding and faulting or "deformation" that affected the rocks to the West and East.

BASIN AND RANGE In earlier times when rainfall was more plentiful, parts of the Basin and Range province supported earlier civilizations along river valleys such as the Gila (in Arizona and New Mexico) and the Rio Grande (in western Texas and New Mexico). With climatic change and less water available, some of these civilizations (Anasazi and Hohokam) disappeared; others have adapted and survived to the present day (Pueblo cultures of New Mexico, Pima people of Arizona).

This region, consisting of elongate ranges and intervening valleys, trends mostly north-south and extends from northern Mexico through western Arizona, eastern California, all of Nevada, western Utah, through Idaho and eastern Oregon and Washington into Canada. The continent is coming apart in this region. The distance from the Sierra Nevada to Salt Lake City has roughly doubled, from about 180 to 360 miles, in the past 10 to 15 million years at the rate of only a fraction of an inch per year. The rocks in these ranges and beneath the sediments filling the valleys consist of ancient continental margin rocks in the east and remnants of oceanic plates in the west. On top is a huge pile of volcanic deposits, some 3,000 to 6,000 feet thick, deposited by explosive eruptions of magma formed by melting of the base of the continent some 20 to 40 million years ago. Granite formed in Earth's crust beneath the centers of these eruptions (pl. 74). The potential high-level radioactive disposal site at Yucca Mountain is on the Nevada Test Site within these volcanic rocks (pl. 115). Ward Valley, a designated low-level nuclear waste repository, is also within this region.

With the Sierra Nevada mountains of California acting as a rain shadow, the Basin and Range Province has become a high, cold desert in which erosion has been unable to keep up with mountain uplift (pl. 96). Most moisture that falls collects in the many valleys. This region of "internal drainage" is called the *Great Basin.* During the last ice age, some 10,000 to 100,000 years ago, huge lakes formed in these valleys. Remnants of these ancient lakes are found in the Bonneville Salt Flats of the Great Salt Lake in Utah, Humboldt and Carson sinks, Pyramid Lake (pl. 117) and Walker Lake in western Nevada, the borax and trona-bearing sediments of Death Valley, and nearby valleys of southeast California. Most of these valleys contain groundwater beneath the surface, collected thousands of years ago during the last glacial period when the climate was wetter. This water is a finite resource. It is now being mined to support agriculture and population centers such as Las Vegas.

Earthquakes are prevalent in four general zones of this province: along its western margin east of the Sierra, another extending north from Death

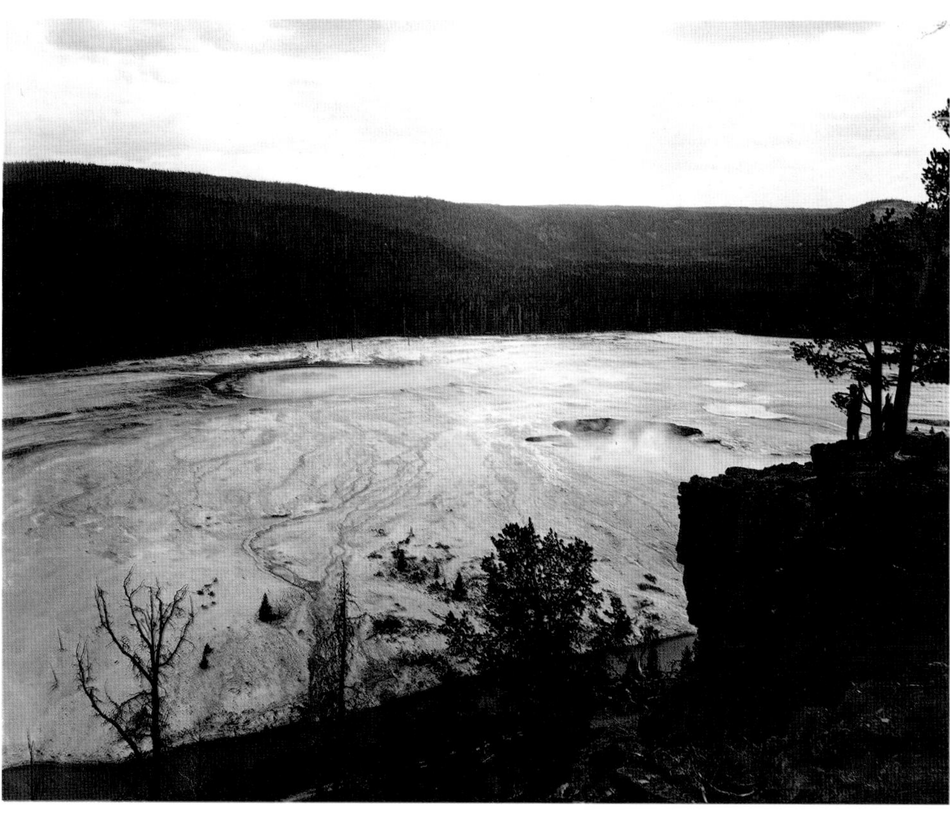

PLATE 12
Frank Jay Haynes
Hell's Half Acre, Prismatic Spring, Yellowstone National Park, 1884
albumen print
17¾ x 21½ in.
(45.1 x 54.6 cm)
Collection of the Montana Historical Society, Helena

Valley into central Nevada, from southern Nevada through central Utah and the Salt Lake Valley to Yellowstone, and along the Rio Grande valley of central New Mexico. Active or recently active faulting is evident in such places as the Salt Lake Valley, the Nevada Test Site, and Los Alamos National Laboratory (pls. 34, 72). An active fault runs along the edge of the mountains in both of these photographs.

Ore deposits are abundant in many parts of the Basin and Range province. Huge Mt. Shasta-like volcanoes reflecting convergent plate activity off California once were active along western Nevada. Rich gold and silver deposits that formed in these volcanoes, which eventually became famous mines (Comstock Lode, Goldfield, Bodie, Bingham Canyon), are associated with volcanic or intrusive igneous rocks thought to be the product of convergent plate activity (pl. 24). The same is true of many large low-grade, open-pit copper mines of Arizona and New Mexico, such as Silver City, Globe-Miami, Bisbee, San Manuel, and others, which are often near or within intrusive bodies that contain small amounts of copper compounds. These deposits range from 20 to 80 million years in age. In the 1980s a new type of low-grade gold deposit was recognized to be associated with active or recently active hot springs. These deposits turn out to be quite abundant, and they have resulted in a new "gold rush," principally in Nevada. All these low-grade mining operations require the movement and processing of enormous quantities of barren rock, called *waste* or *tailings,* and result in huge human-made holes, some as much as one cubic mile in volume. These mining operations are truly changing the landscape for a long time to come.

Although active volcanoes in the Basin and Range province are not numerous, several small runny-lava volcanoes and cinder cones exist in and around Death Valley and in central Nevada. Three large, still active, explosive, and potentially dangerous volcanoes in this province are worthy of mention.

The Yellowstone Volcano is located along the eastern edge of the Basin and Range Province, above an active hotspot in Earth's mantle (pl. 12). Volcanic activity began about two million years ago and continues. The volcano has produced three huge explosive eruptions, one of which was one of the largest eruptions known on Earth (620 cubic miles), equivalent to six Mt. Shastas in one eruption or 2,500 Mt. St. Helens eruptions! The latest cycle began about one million years ago and ended about 70,000 years ago, during which about 250 cubic miles of new volcanic material was erupted. A hot reservoir of molten rock probably still exists beneath Yellowstone, and it may well erupt again someday with devastating effect.

The second volcano, called Long Valley Caldera, is located along the western boundary of the Basin and Range province. This volcano includes part of Owens Valley and the ski resort of Mammoth Lakes, California. Its elliptical crater is about 20 miles long and 10 to 15 miles wide. Associated with it are some smaller volcanoes near Mono Lake, called the Mono Craters. These latter volcanoes erupted violently about 600 years ago, and they could do so again. Long Valley Caldera produced a huge eruption about 140 cubic miles in volume roughly 700,000 years ago. Ash from this eruption overtopped the Sierra Nevada to the west and covered about 600 square miles of central California and western Nevada with a thick layer of ash; some ash made it as far east as Nebraska. This volcano is still active.

Small earthquakes occur almost daily, and a body of magma lies a few miles below the surface. We don't know when it will erupt again or how big an eruption might be.

A third very large volcano, the Valles Caldera, about 40 miles northwest of Santa Fe, New Mexico, measures 12 by 15 miles in dimension. About 900,000 years ago it produced a very large eruption, similar to that of Long Valley. There is no reason to believe that it will not do so again. Los Alamos, the famous "home" of the atomic bomb, perches atop this volcano (pl. 114).

COLUMBIA PLATEAU About 10,000 years ago, toward the end of the most recent ice age, an ice dam formed repeatedly in the mountains of western Montana. It caused the formation of a huge lake hundreds of cubic miles in volume in the valleys surrounding the present town of Missoula, Montana. When the dam broke the water was suddenly released in a catastrophic flood that raced down the Columbia River Valley, probably in only a few days, causing waterfalls many times larger than Niagara Falls. It scoured the land for miles around, eroding channels hundreds of feet deep, and leaving giant gravel bars hundreds of feet high. Over what is now western Montana, eastern Washington, and nearby parts of Idaho and Oregon, the flood formed scour marks and huge current ripples over a 30,000-square-mile area. Geologists have called this region the *Channeled Scabland* and speak of the "Spokane Flood." Many such floods may have occurred after humans had migrated from Siberia to western North America. How many native settlements along the Columbia River Valley were wiped out by such floods will never be known, but the effects on a huge area of the Columbia River Valley must have been truly devastating (pl. 112).

In eastern Washington and Oregon, southern and western Idaho, northeasternmost California, and northern Nevada a pile of old lava flows, several thousand feet thick, mostly horizontal and little faulted, underlie an upland plateau surface averaging about 3,000 feet high. They are especially well-exposed along the Columbia River Gorge and Hells Canyon of the Snake River. They represent the products of Hawaii-type quiet, runny lava eruptions mostly one to fifteen million years ago. A small amount of activity is still present in such places as Craters of the Moon National Monument, Idaho. Geologists think that these lavas represent the outpourings of a hotspot volcanic center that erupted beneath eastern Washington and Oregon and moved slowly inland beneath the Snake River Plain of southern Idaho as the North American plate moved westward over it. This hotspot currently is beneath Yellowstone National Park, giving rise to the recent volcanic and current hot spring and geyser activity.

Older rocks are present around the edges of the Columbia Plateau in northern Washington, eastern Idaho, northern Nevada, and northern California. Similar older rocks poke up through the Columbia Plateau volcanics in a few places, such as the Blue and Wallowa mountains of northeast Oregon. These older rocks are part of an earlier complex chapter of the saga of the North American geologic evolution.

The Columbia Plateau volcanics contain little in the way of economically important mineral wealth. Except for the clues from the older rocks around the edges and in the mountains of northeast Oregon in the middle, we have little idea of the nature of the rocks beneath the lavas.

CASCADE RANGE At least 20 cone-shaped volcanoes, from 8,000 to more than 14,000 feet high, extend from Mt. Lassen in California to Mt. Garibaldi in southern British Columbia. This volcanic chain includes Mt. Shasta, Mt. Hood, Mt. St. Helens, Mt. Adams, Mt. Jefferson, Mt. Rainier, Mt. Baker, and Glacier Peak. These peaks are the latest volcanic products of a convergent plate boundary off the coast of the Pacific Northwest, from Cape Mendocino to Vancouver Island. The Juan de Fuca oceanic plate is descending beneath North America. This plate and its predecessor, the Farallon plate, have been disappearing beneath this part of North America for about the past 50 million years. The continuation of this process of *subduction* of a plate along a convergent plate margin off the North American coast is evidenced by the activity of these volcanoes and by infrequent but very large earthquakes beneath the Pacific Northwest coast.

Recently, Mt. St. Helens has been the most active of the Cascade volcanoes (pl. 13). Eleven of these volcanoes have erupted in the past 250 years. Their lavas are stickier and gooier than those of Hawaii or the Columbia Plateau. Eruptions tend to be more explosive. They have included clouds of hot glowing ash that flow along close to the ground incinerating everything in their paths. Because the volcanoes are high and often covered in snow, eruptions often also include huge hot or cold *mudflows* of a slurry of melted snow and rock debris that can travel for tens of miles and inundate large areas. Many areas affected by the most recent eruptions of Mts. Hood, Rainier, Baker, Shasta, and Glacier Peak are now well populated by towns with thousands of people. Mt. Mazama, a volcano in central Oregon, erupted about 7,000 years ago. This eruption of some 40 cubic miles (200 times the 1980 Mt. St. Helens eruption) was the largest volcanic eruption in the United States since the end of the last ice age. The eruption left a void into which the top of Mt. Mazama collapsed to produce a huge caldera, which filled with water to become Crater Lake.

Each Cascades volcano has an individual history of eruptions that make any prediction of the next eruption virtually impossible. On the average, they erupt every few hundreds or thousands of years. There is no magic to the average. In principle, an eruption can occur just about any time.

The western slope of the Cascade Range receives a large amount of rain from moisture-laden winds coming from the Pacific Ocean, producing the extensive forests for which Washington and Oregon are famous.

OLDER ROCKS OF THE WEST COAST Older rocks are found in the North Cascades of Washington, the Wallowa and Blue mountains of Oregon, the Klamath range and the Sierra Nevada of northern and central California, parts of western Nevada, and the Transverse and Peninsular ranges of southern California.

These mountainous regions have a distinctive history; they all contain rocks that began life somewhere away from the North American continent. Each shows a history that reflects collision of volcanic islands, fragments of former oceanic crust and mantle called *ophiolites*, or pieces of continental crust, or *microcontinents*, with North America over the past 500 million years, but especially between 200 and 40 million years ago (figs. 33, 34). After arrival of these pieces and their attachment to North America, molten rock produced by melting of downgoing plates rose and came to rest in these recent arrivals to form thick, vast areas of granitic rock called *batholiths*. Subsequent uplift and erosion exposed deeply buried rocks at Earth's surface. Continued uplift has led to steep slopes and widespread landslides, particularly in earthquake-prone regions.

KLAMATH MOUNTAINS The Klamath mountains of southwest Oregon and northwestern California (and parts of the Sierra Nevada in western California) contain a distinctive series of ophiolites, as old as 600 million years, together with volcanic rocks laid down along a consuming margin some 200 to 400 million years ago. Some of these rocks developed at intraoceanic convergent margins and were later swept into the continent. Some volcanic rocks developed along a convergent margin along the edge of North America after older rocks were attached. In the western Klamath mountains along the California-Oregon border, ophiolites preserve a history of formation of a small ocean basin, akin to the Sea of Japan separating Japan from Asia, some 150 million years ago. The Trinity Alps of the southern Klamath mountains are formed of granitic rocks intruded into older rocks that have been uplifted and sculpted by glaciers.

Oceanic crust and mantle rocks in the Klamaths contain deposits of chrome and copper. Gold deposits are associated with stream gravel and ancient fractures in older rocks. The entire Klamaths are a region where many mountains of about the same elevation are separated by steep, narrow stream valleys. It appears that a relatively low-lying, gently rolling region was sharply uplifted as a single block starting less than five million years ago and continuing today. Deep red soils on some mantle rocks of ophiolites (*peridotite*) contain economic deposits of nickel.

Chemical addition of water to the peridotite of ophiolites produces serpentine, which is so abundant in California that it has become the state rock. Some serpentine is present as commercial asbestos deposits. Ophiolites thus altered are also present in the Appalachian mountains of New England and Quebec, Canada, where they record a plate history some 400 to 500 million years ago that is similar to the more recent history of California (pl. 110).

SIERRA NEVADA The Sierra Nevada extend for approximately 250 miles along the eastern part of California. The range represents the western edge of the Basin and Range province; it has a steep eastern side and a gentler western slope. The western slope catches the moisture coming off

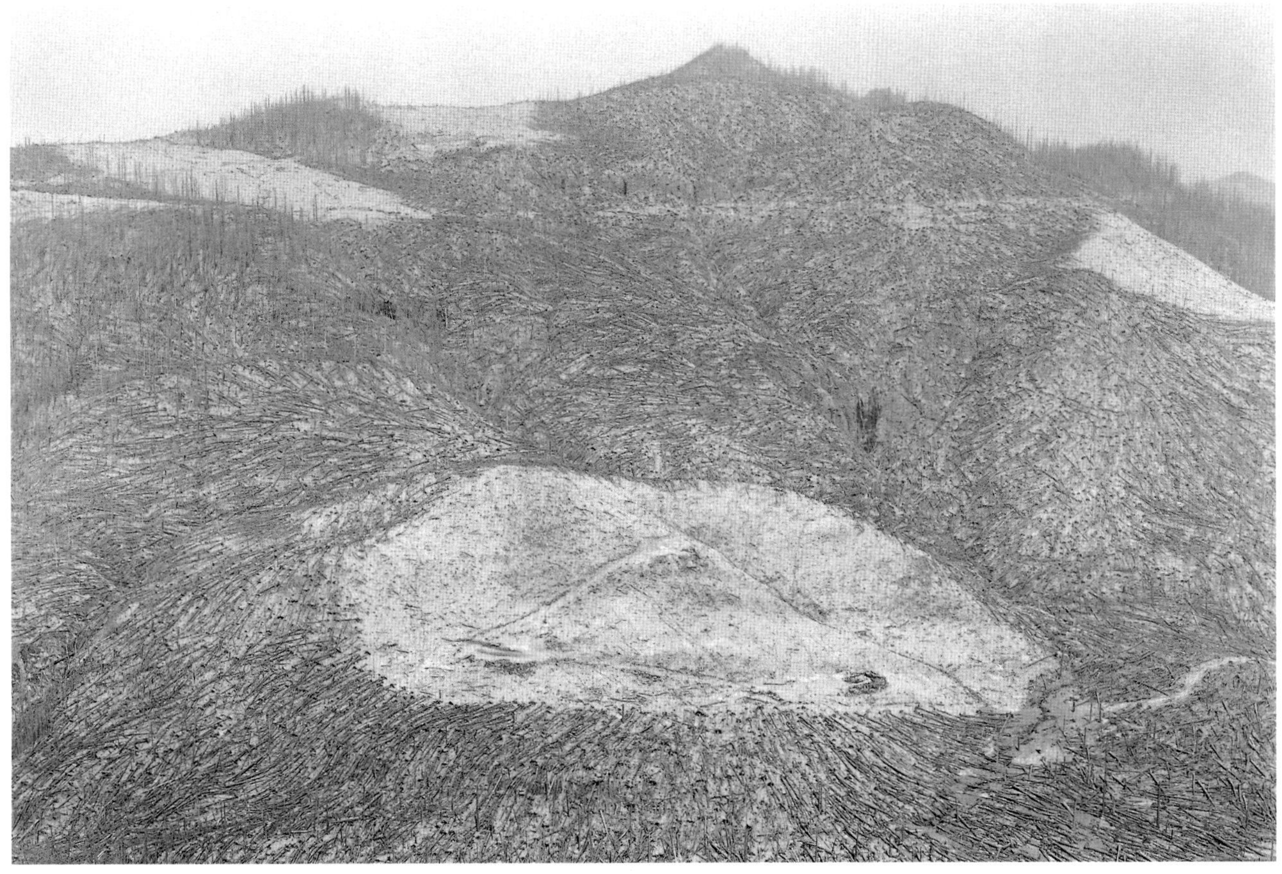

PLATE 13

Frank Gohlke

Area clearcut prior to 1980 eruption surrounded by downed trees; salvage in progress—valley of Clearwater Creek, 9 miles E of Mt. St. Helens, Wash. 1981
gelatin silver print
20 x 23¾ in. (50.8 x 60.3 cm)
San Francisco Museum of Modern Art. Purchased through a gift of the Judy Kay Memorial Fund

FIGURES 33 AND 34

Sketch maps illustrating the tectonic evolution of much of the West in California and neighboring states. (Left) Possible scenario approximately 170 million years ago. Edge of continent was in eastern California and central Idaho. An off-shore oceanic island chain approached the coast from the west. (Right) Possible scenario approximately 100 to 140 million years ago. A new convergent margin developed to the west after collision of the offshore island chain.

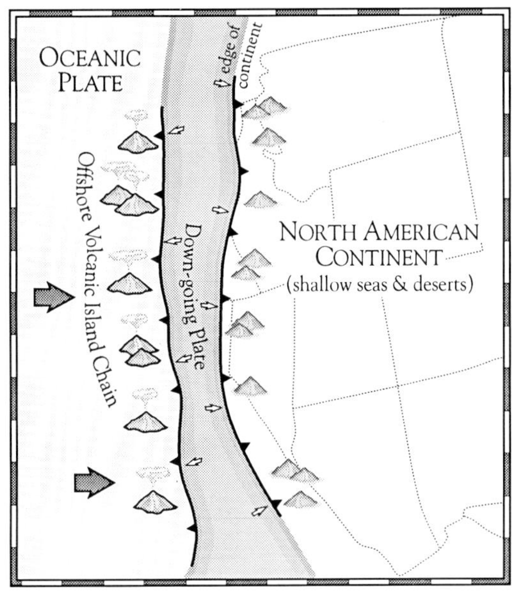

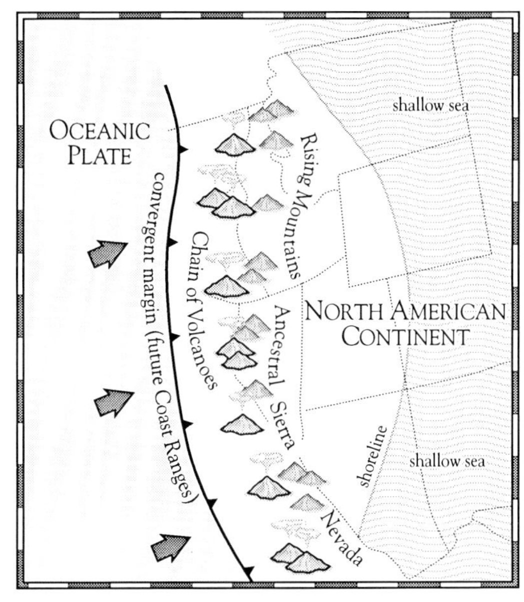

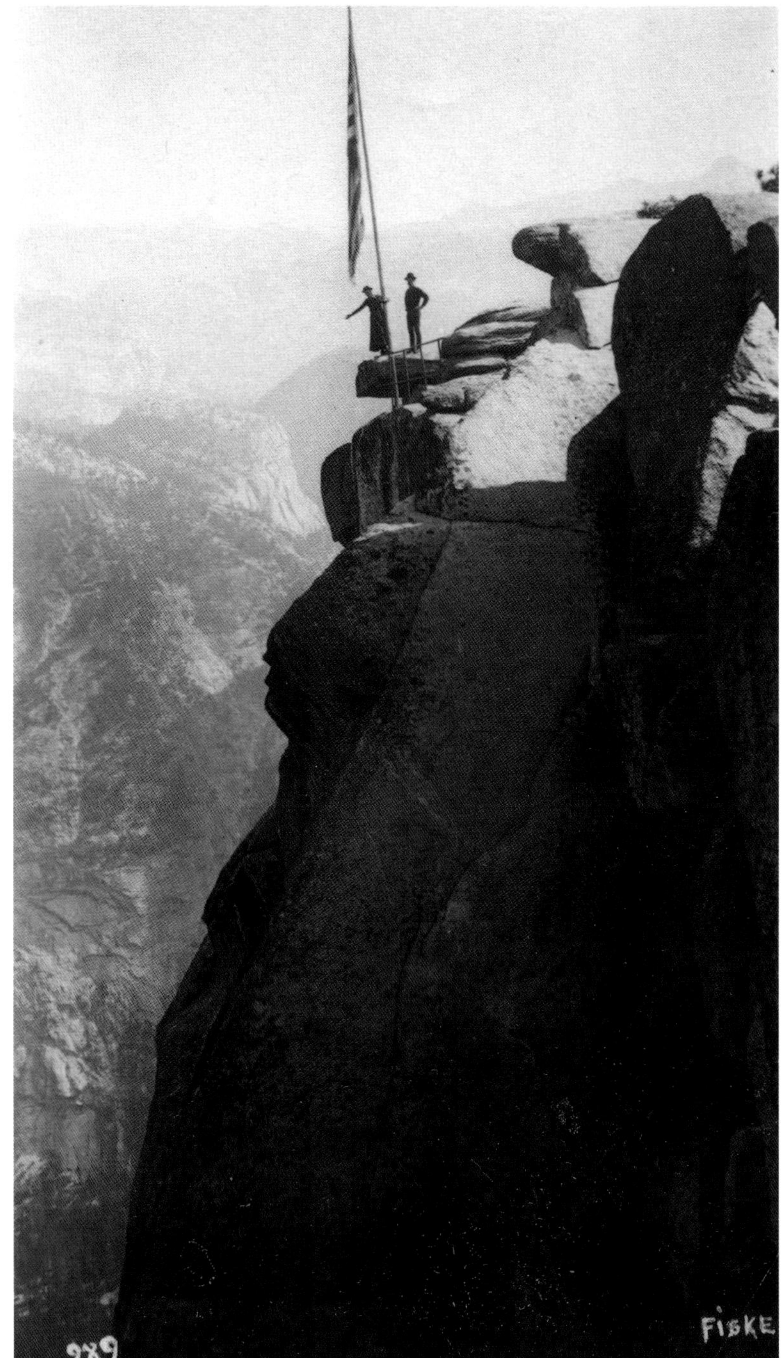

PLATE 14
George Fiske
J. McCauley and Mrs. Lettie Hill, Glacier Point, Yosemite, ca. 1885
albumen print
7⅛ x 4¼ in.
(18.1 x 10.8 cm)
San Francisco Museum of Modern Art. Study Collection, s.142.83

the Pacific Ocean, which has led to thick forests and steep river canyons draining westward. The Sierra block the moisture from the desert regions of the Basin and Range province to the east.

Rocks in the Sierra Nevada include an older sequence of igneous and metamorphic rocks overlain by younger series of sedimentary and volcanic deposits. The older igneous rocks consist chiefly of a vast region of granitic rocks, thought to have developed over a descending oceanic plate some 60 to 200 million years ago. These rocks, called the Sierra Nevada batholith, are generally light in color and fairly uniform in texture. They have given rise to the smooth, light-colored mountains and valleys of such regions as Yosemite, Kings Canyon, and Sequoia national parks. In these regions, the granitic rocks were sculpted by glaciers in the last ice age, some 10,000 to three million years ago (pl. 14). The older metamorphic rocks represent the crustal rocks into which the magmas of the batholith were intruded. In the south, these rocks include deposits that probably formed along the edge of North America up to 500 million years ago. In the north, the pre-batholithic rocks mostly are highly contorted ophiolites, volcanic, and associated sedimentary rocks exotic to North America. Squeezing of these older rocks produced many folds and faults or fractures in the rocks. The faults and fractures served as conduits for hot gold-bearing solutions that gave rise to the gold deposits of the "Mother Lode" of the western foothills of the Sierra Nevada. Copper deposits in places in the western Sierra were formed in oceanic environments before the rocks were attached to North America.

For the most part, the younger sedimentary and volcanic rocks were deposited by streams flowing westward out of Nevada prior to the rise of the Sierra Nevada. Some 50 million years ago, huge streams flowed westward from a highland in Nevada, depositing a series of gold-bearing gravels, called the *Auriferous Gravels.* These gravels form a second source of California gold. Between the 1860s and 1880s they were mined by diversion of whole streams through ditches and pipes into huge nozzles called *monitors* that were used to wash the gravels down and over a concentrating device where the gold was recovered (pl. 20). More than a billion tons of gravel, sand, and mud were washed away from their original location into the streams, valley, and bays below. This caused tremendous changes in the level and nature of streams and infilling of the eastern part of the San Francisco and Suisun bays, which can still be seen.

PENINSULAR RANGES The Peninsular Ranges along the coast of southern California south of Los Angeles represent essentially a continuation of the Sierra Nevada geology without the high peaks and abundant gold deposits. Mining activity has been less in this region. In places, special kinds of granitic rocks, called *pegmatites*, contain deposits of exotic minerals, some of which are of gem quality.

GREAT VALLEY The Great Valley of California represents a thick pile of sedimentary rocks overlying the gently west-plunging slope of the Sierra Nevada. The oldest parts of these sedimentary rocks to the west were laid down in several thousand feet of water on oceanic crust, now preserved in places as ophiolites, off the edge of the North American continent. Oil and gas are abundant in some places, particularly along the west side of the Valley (pl. 15). The most recent sediments were deposited by streams, including the Sacramento and San Joaquin river systems in the north or by inland lakes in the south.

The Willamette and Puget Sound regions of Oregon and Washington bear a similar relationship to the Cascade Range. These flat valleys, with their deep, rich soils and abundant water, are ideal farming country.

COAST RANGES Most of the Coast Ranges of California, Oregon, and Washington have steep slopes, rounded hills, and narrow canyons eroded by small streams. Rapid rise of the land and weak rocks have led to widespread landslides and slow downhill creep of loose rock debris. Such natural processes make these regions hazardous for intense urban development.

The coastal mountains are characterized by material that has been swept into the North American Continent by convergent plate movement. The Olympic Mountains of Washington and the Oregon Coast Ranges exhibit the remnants of a series of mid-plate or hotspot-type volcanoes, like the Hawaiian Islands, which were attached to North America some 40 to 50 million years ago.

The California ranges, on the other hand, reflect a history of plate convergence that began some 150 million years ago and continues today off northwestern California, Oregon, and Washington. In California, the Coast Ranges contain a vast sequence of diverse rocks, called the Franciscan, that represents the material scraped off the downgoing plate in a subduction

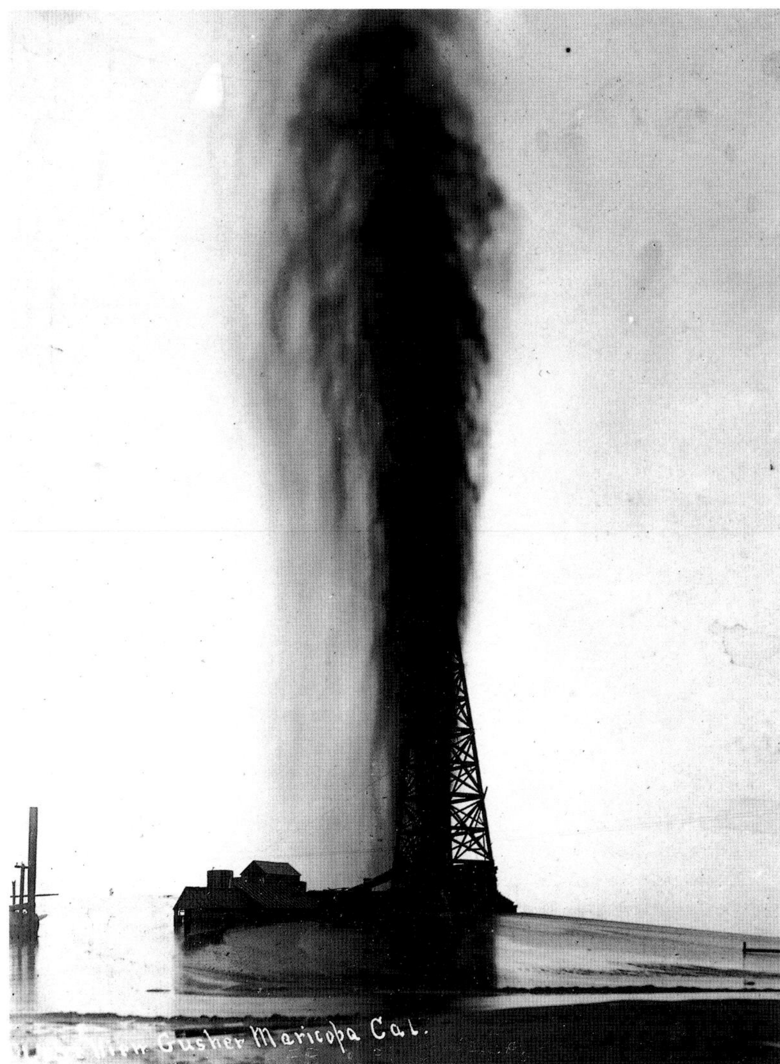

PLATE 15
Unknown
Lake View Gusher, Maricopa, California,
ca. 1905
gelatin silver print
8 x 6⅛ in.
(20.3 x 15.6 cm)
San Francisco Museum of Modern Art. Gift of Stephen White, 96.121

zone. The Franciscan, named for exposures in and around San Francisco, contains many rocks of separate histories (pl. 69). Some, such as at the north end of the Golden Gate Bridge, have come from thousands of miles away. Others, such as the rocks of Telegraph Hill, Mount Sutro, Twin Peaks, and Alcatraz, are sedimentary deposits that probably were derived from North America but were deposited out away from the continent on the down-going oceanic plate. Some rocks, such as along the Tiburon Peninsula and Angel Island, show evidence of having been buried some 12 miles down and spit out again to make up part of our present landscape.

Franciscan rocks extend from northwestern California some 300 miles south to the area around Santa Maria, San Luis Obispo, and Vandenberg Air Force Base. South of the Transverse Ranges, similar rocks are present in a few places around Los Angeles, on Catalina Island, and along the western edge of Baja California.

Mostly along the eastern edge of the Coast Ranges, a vast series of sedimentary rocks, called the Great Valley sequence, are present. These rocks, mostly turned up on edge, are thought to be exposed equivalents of those beneath the surface of the Great Valley itself. They appear to have been deposited on oceanic crust between the margin of North America and the offshore subduction zone.

SAN ANDREAS FAULT Two of California's largest historical earthquakes, the 1906 San Francisco and 1857 Fort Tejon earthquakes, as well as the 1989 Loma Prieta earthquake, were caused by movement on the San Andreas fault. Other faults of the San Andreas family have been active also, however. In particular the Hayward fault, which is located at the foot of the hills in the East Bay, is actively moving and last experienced a large earthquake in 1868.

The Coast Ranges of California include a number of northwest-trending ranges and intervening valleys. This structural "grain" is a product of the San Andreas fault and its satellite faults. The present motion between the Pacific and North American plates amounts to about two inches per year. This motion is thought to be caused by slow, smooth motions within the interior of the earth. But at and near the surface, the movement takes place in jerks that result in earthquakes.

TRANSVERSE RANGES North of Los Angeles the San Andreas fault and plate boundary curves into a more east-west direction. This change in direction causes compression between the plates and has caused the rise of steep, high mountains (in and around Los Angeles) separated by valleys underlain by large thicknesses of marine sediments, such as the Los Angeles and Ventura regions. This uplift and compression accounts for much of the motion between the Pacific and American plates in this region. Earthquakes such as the 1971 San Fernando and the 1994 Northridge events occurred between the mountains and valleys in this region along hidden faults, which have no obvious surface features and may remain unknown until they actually move.

Because the mountains in the Los Angeles area extend east-west, they are at an angle to the coast, and for that reason they are called the Transverse Ranges. Ancient rocks, as old as one billion years, are found in these mountains. The sediments in the valleys in between are mostly much younger, some five to ten million years old. The mountains, some of the fastest rising in the world, rise some five to ten millimeters per year.

Oil was abundant in the rocks beneath the valleys. Extraction of oil in the Los Angeles–Long Beach, Ventura, and Bakersfield regions has added considerably to the region's economic wealth. This has come at a price. It has caused the land to sink, leading to flooding in the Long Beach region. Oilfield waste sites have contaminated groundwater in several spots.

The attractive climate of the Transverse Ranges has led to a large and growing urban region. The region is dry, however, and water must come from elsewhere to support the population and development.

Volcanic rocks are present in the Coast Ranges from the Transverse Ranges northward. Ranging in age from about 20 million years in the south to a few hundred or thousand years in the north, the rocks have contributed to the rich soils of much of California's wine country, especially Napa and Sonoma counties. Associated with these volcanic rocks are hot springs. One region of springs, the Geysers in Lake County, has become the world's largest geothermal power source. Associated with these hot springs are young (a few thousand years old) deposits of mercury and gold. Mercury was mined in the Coast Ranges during gold-rush days to help in the recovery of gold in the Sierra Nevada. Abandoned mercury mines have caused considerable contamination of surface waters in the northern Coast Ranges. Active today, the McLaughlin gold mine, about 100 miles northeast of San Francisco, is one of the largest mines in the West.

FINAL WORD The landscape of the continent, its mineral wealth, its patterns of water distribution and climate are all direct or indirect reflections of the geologic processes that formed the rocks at and beneath Earth's surface. These processes continue today at the same rate as before, as seen in such features as earthquakes, mountains, erosion, transport and deposition of sediment, volcanic activity, and hot springs. The time between major events, such as large earthquakes, volcanic eruptions, or landslides, is long compared with the average human lifetime. We can do nothing, really, to change these processes or to prevent their occurrence, and at present our ability to predict when major events will occur is poorly developed. We can only prepare ourselves so that when major geologic events do happen, their effects upon our infrastructure and our society are minimal.

NOTES

1. The geologist, explorer, and ethnologist John Wesley Powell pointed out in 1878 that west of 100° longitude the overall water supply was insufficient to provide for large populations without tapping groundwater or importing it from elsewhere. He suggested a frugal series of self-sustaining societies based on each watershed's land and water supply.

2. A big number—roughly the number of seconds in thirty-two years, or the number of millimeters from San Francisco to New York.

PLATE 16

George H. Johnson
Mining on the American River, near Sacramento, ca. 1852
whole-plate daguerreotype
approx. 6½ x 8½ in.
(16.5 x 21.6 cm)
Collection of Matthew R. Isenburg

PLATE 17

Timothy H. O'Sullivan
Historic Spanish Record of the Conquest. South Side of Inscription Rock, N.M., 1872
albumen print
16 x 20 in. (40.6 x 50.8 cm)
Collection of the San Francisco Museum of Modern Art. Accessions Committee Fund, 95.410

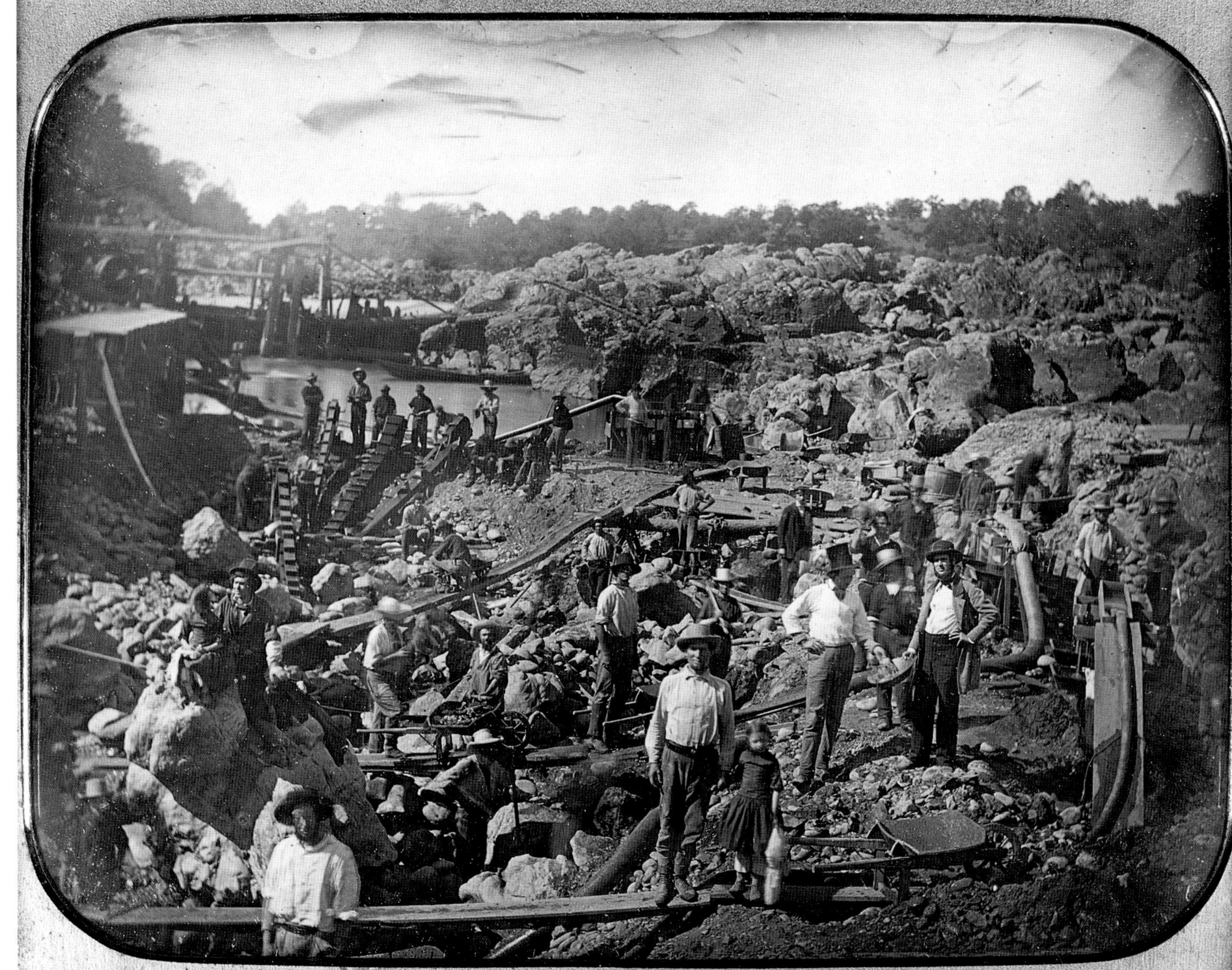

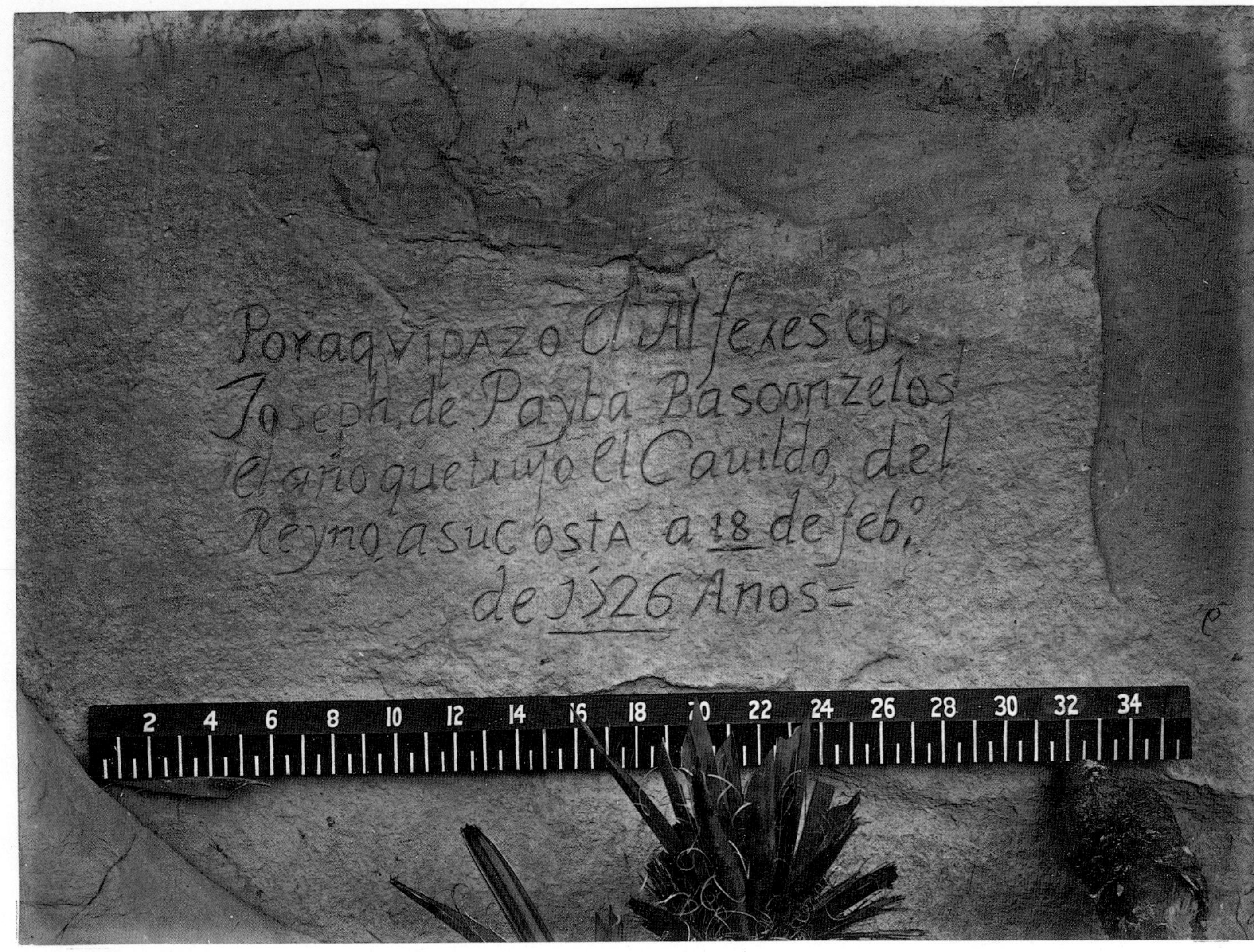

T.H.O' Sullivan, Phot. No 13

HISTORIC SPANISH RECORD OF THE CONQUEST.

South Side of Inscription Rock. N.M. No 3.

PLATE 18

William Skew
Mining Scene near Lincoln, California, ca. 1849
half-plate daguerreotype
approx. 3¾ x 5 in.
(9.5 x 12.7 cm)
Collection of The Bancroft Library, University of California, Berkeley

Shows 39 miners, including Wm. Pickett, brother of Gen. George E. Pickett (tall man with suspenders)

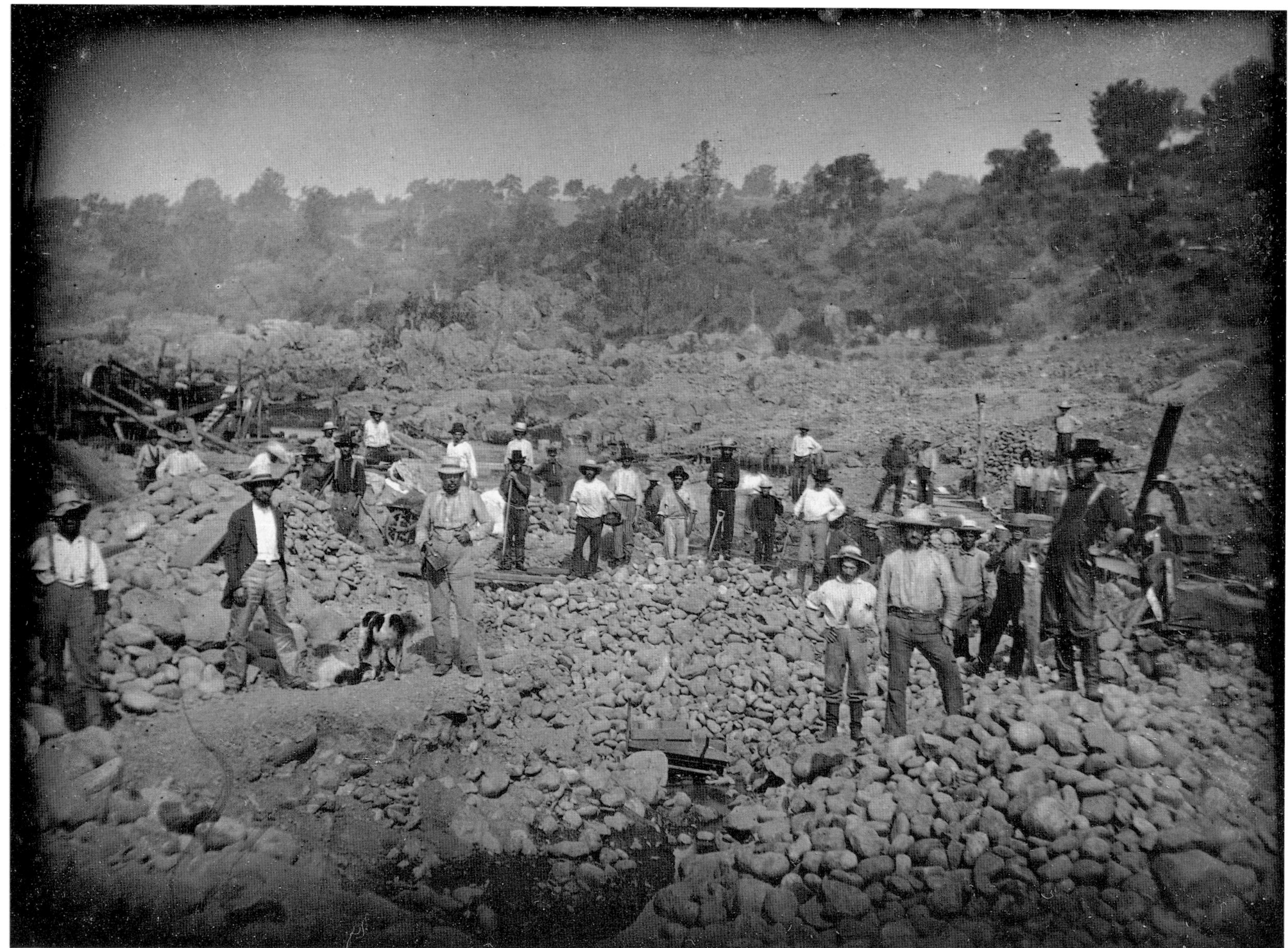

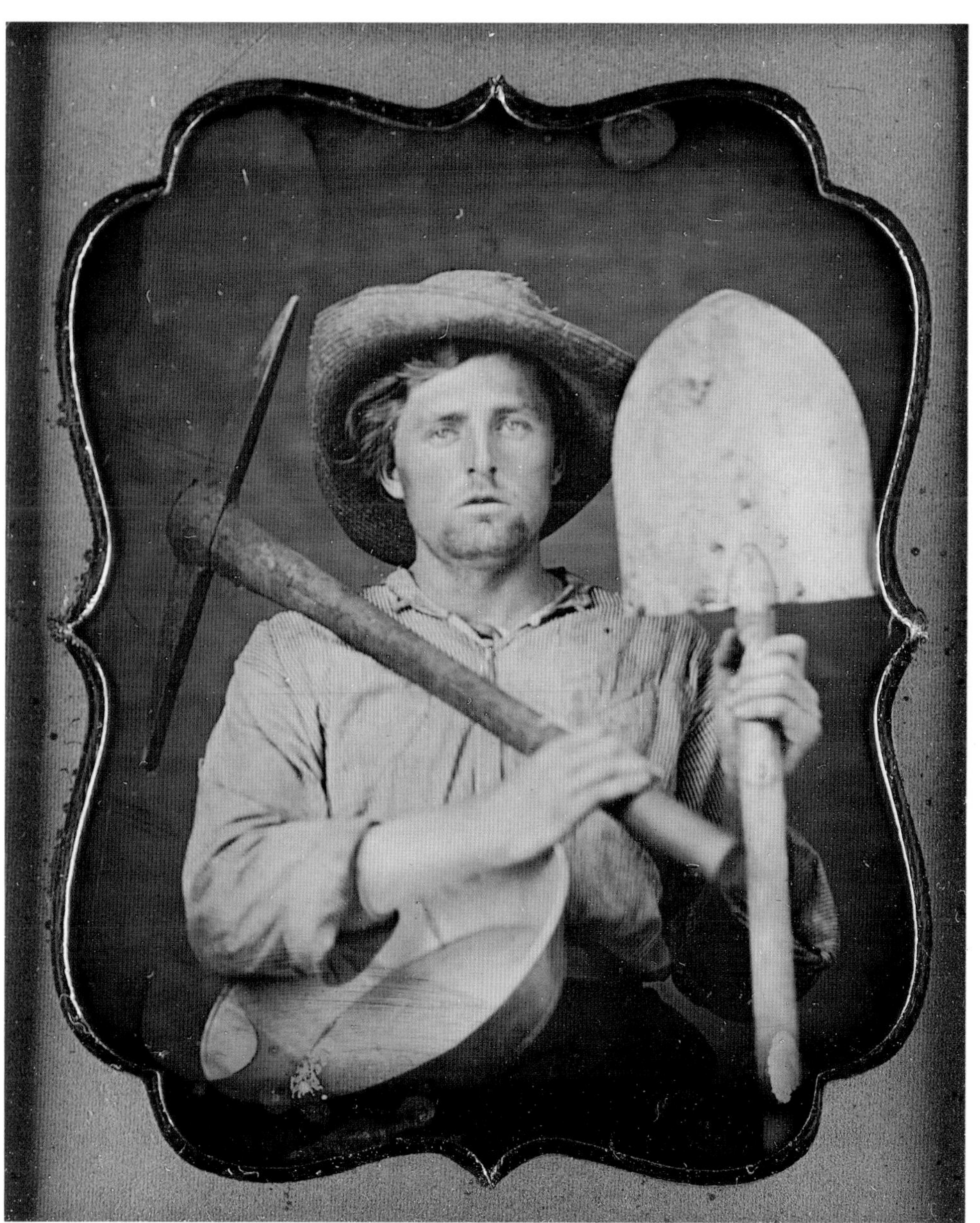

PLATE 19

Unknown
Untitled, ca. 1850
sixth-plate daguerreotype
2¾ x 3¼ in. (7 x 8.3 cm)
Collection of Matthew R. Isenburg

PLATE 20

Carleton E. Watkins
Malakoff Diggins, North Bloomfield, Nevada County, California, ca. 1871
albumen print
15⅞ x 20¾ in. (40.3 x 52.7 cm)
Collection of the San Francisco Museum of Modern Art. Purchased through a gift of the Judy Kay Memorial Fund, 96.125

PLATE 21

Carleton E. Watkins
The California Pan Mill, 1876
albumen print
15½ x 21 in. (39.4 x 53.3 cm)
Collection of The Bancroft Library, University of California, Berkeley

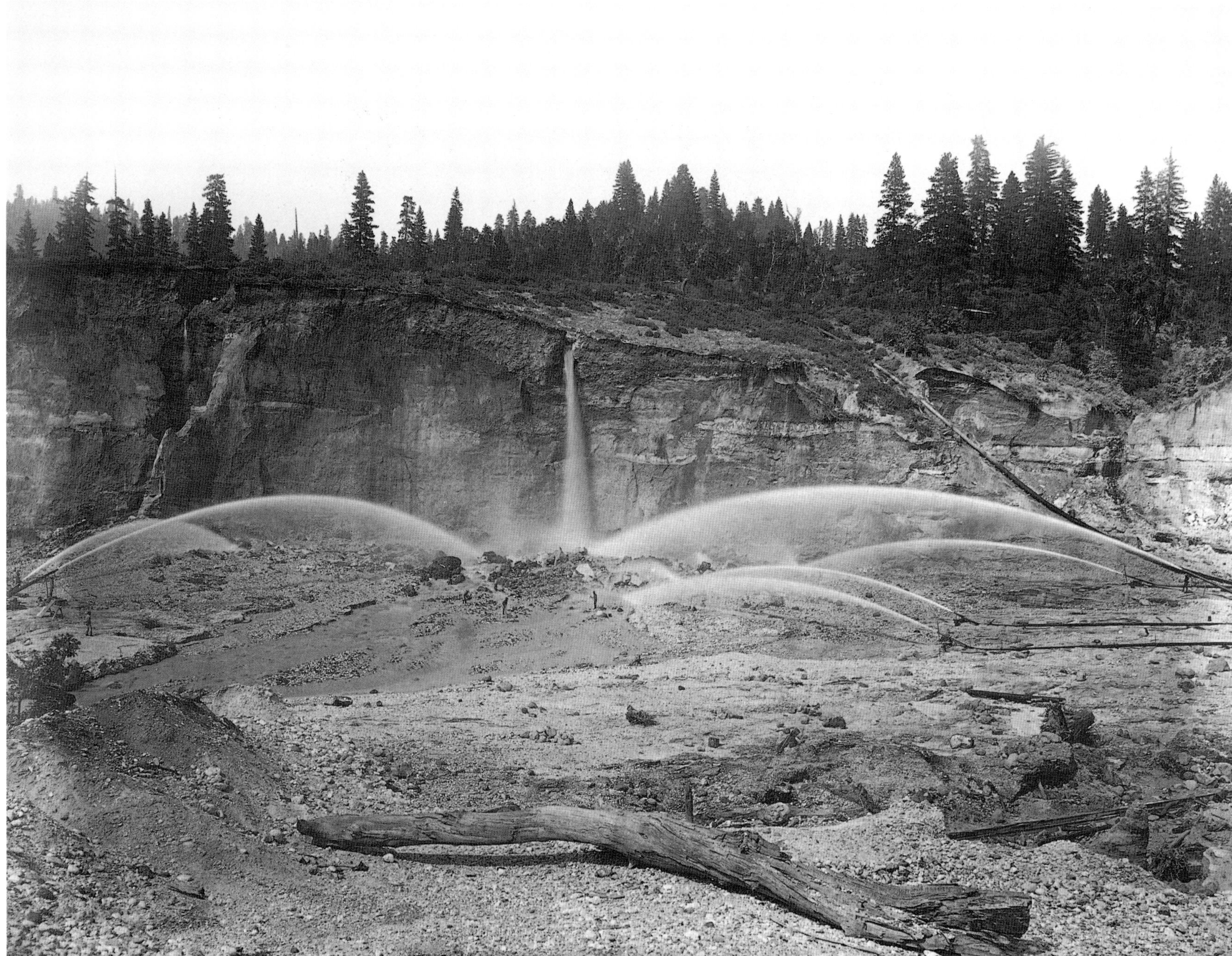

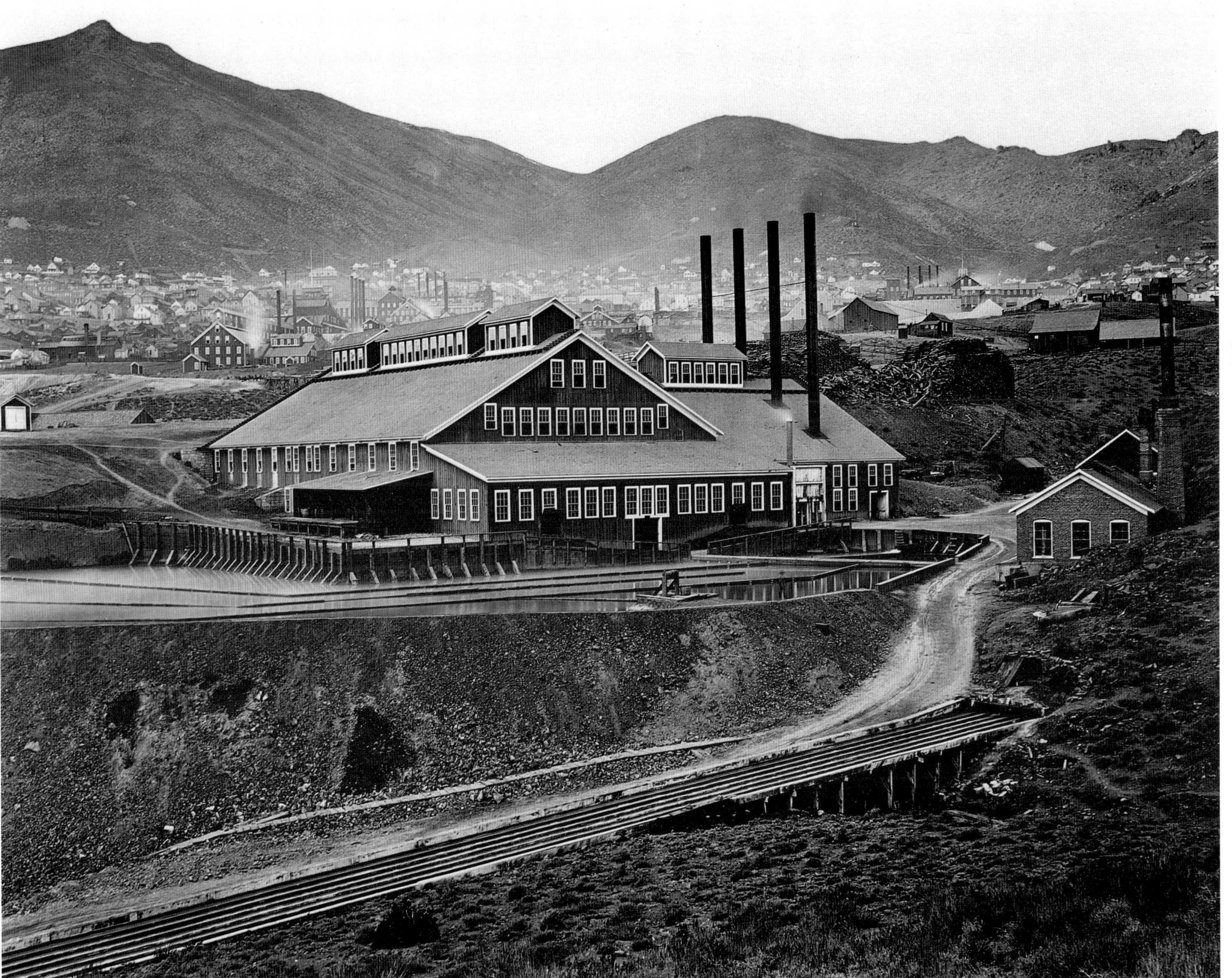

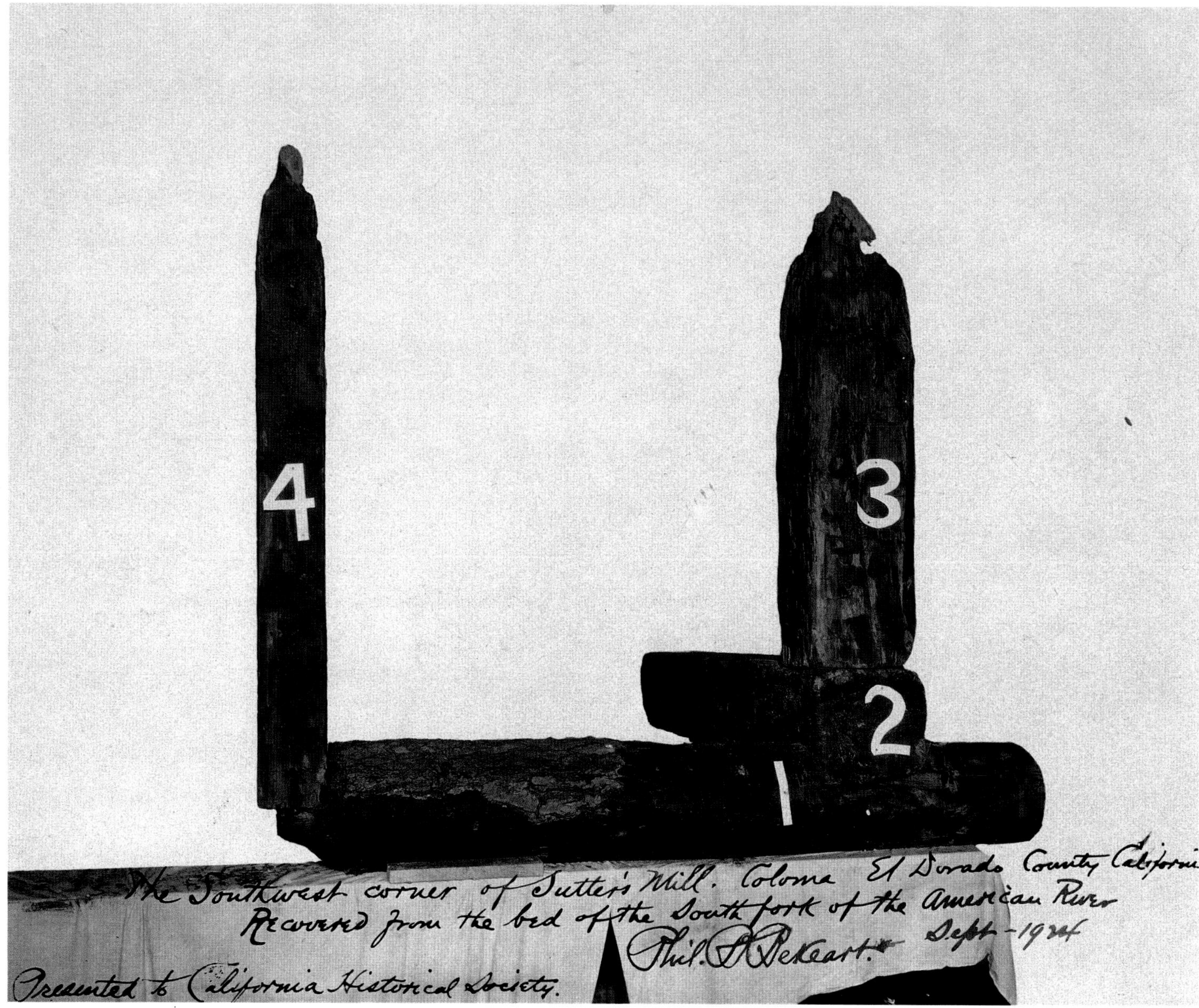

PLATE 22

Unknown

The Southwest Corner of Sutter's Mill, Coloma, El Dorado County, California. Recovered from the Bed of the South Fork of the American River, 1924

gelatin silver print

8¼ x 10¼ in. (21 x 26 cm)

Collection of the California Historical Society, San Francisco

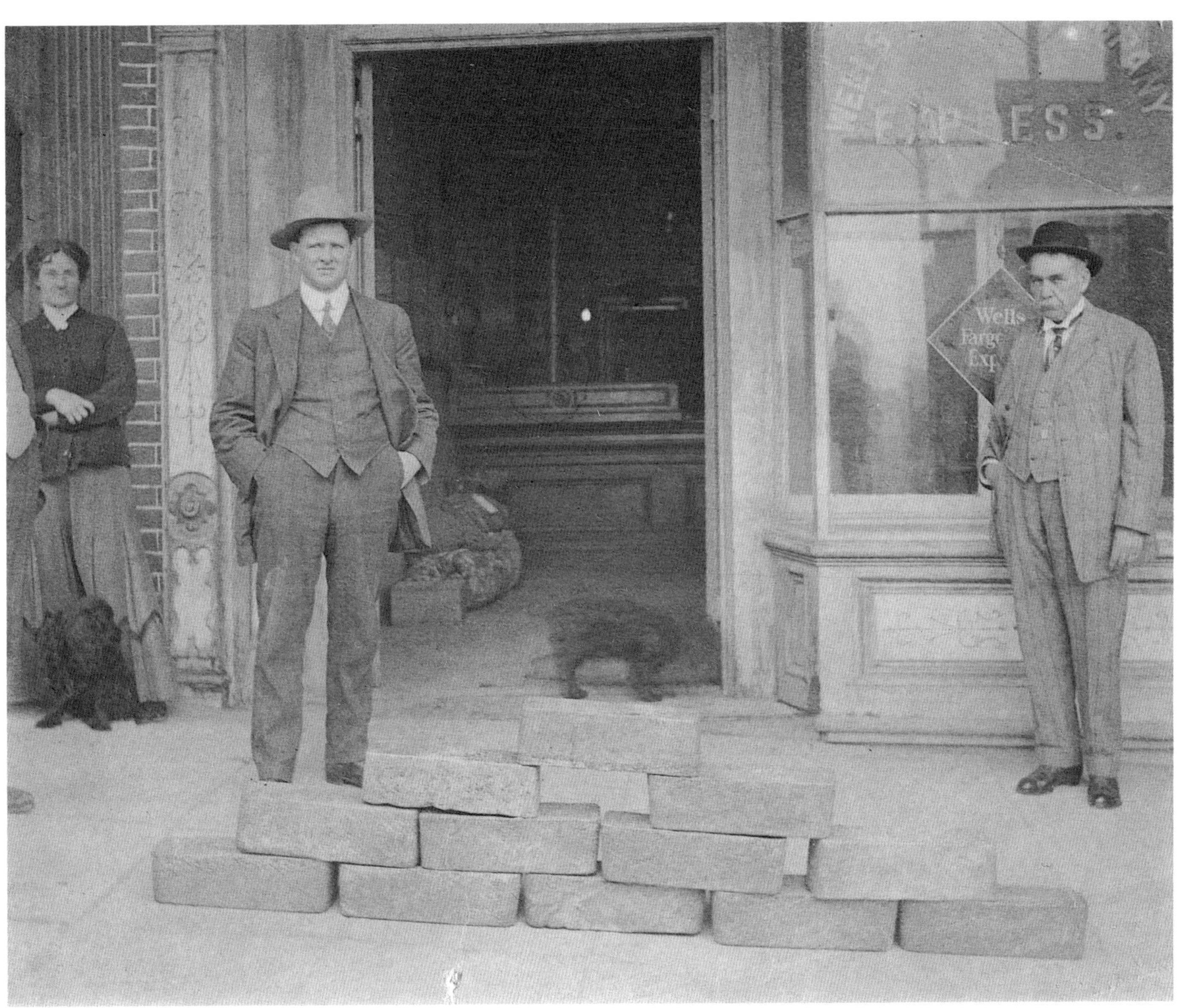

PLATE 23

Unknown

Con Ahern and McHenry, Express Agent, with a Stack of Silver Bullion Being Shipped to Carson Mint in Front of Wells Fargo and Co. Office, Virginia City, Nevada, 1870s

cyanotype

4½ x 6½ in. (11.4 x 16.5 cm)

Collection of the Nevada Historical Society, Reno

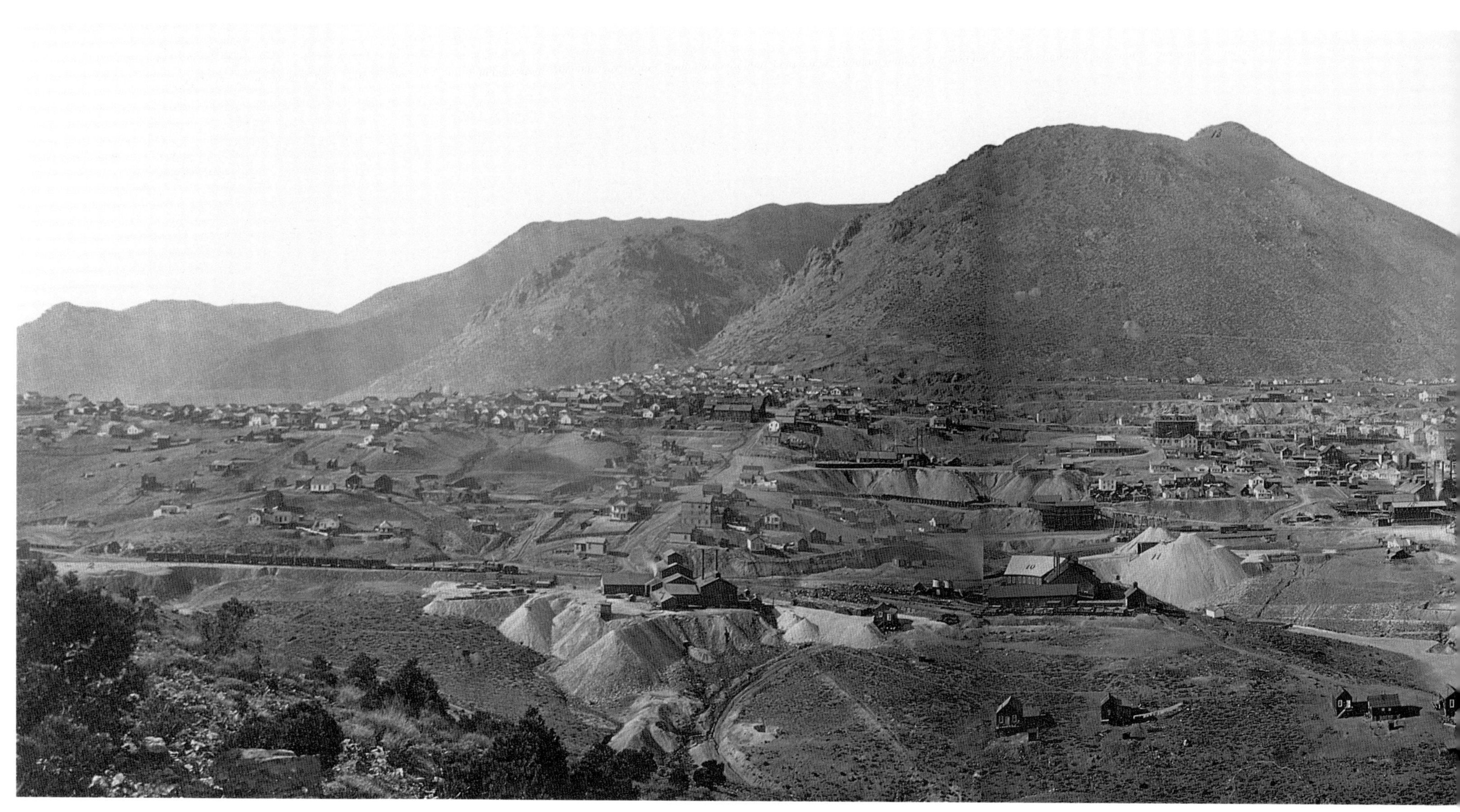

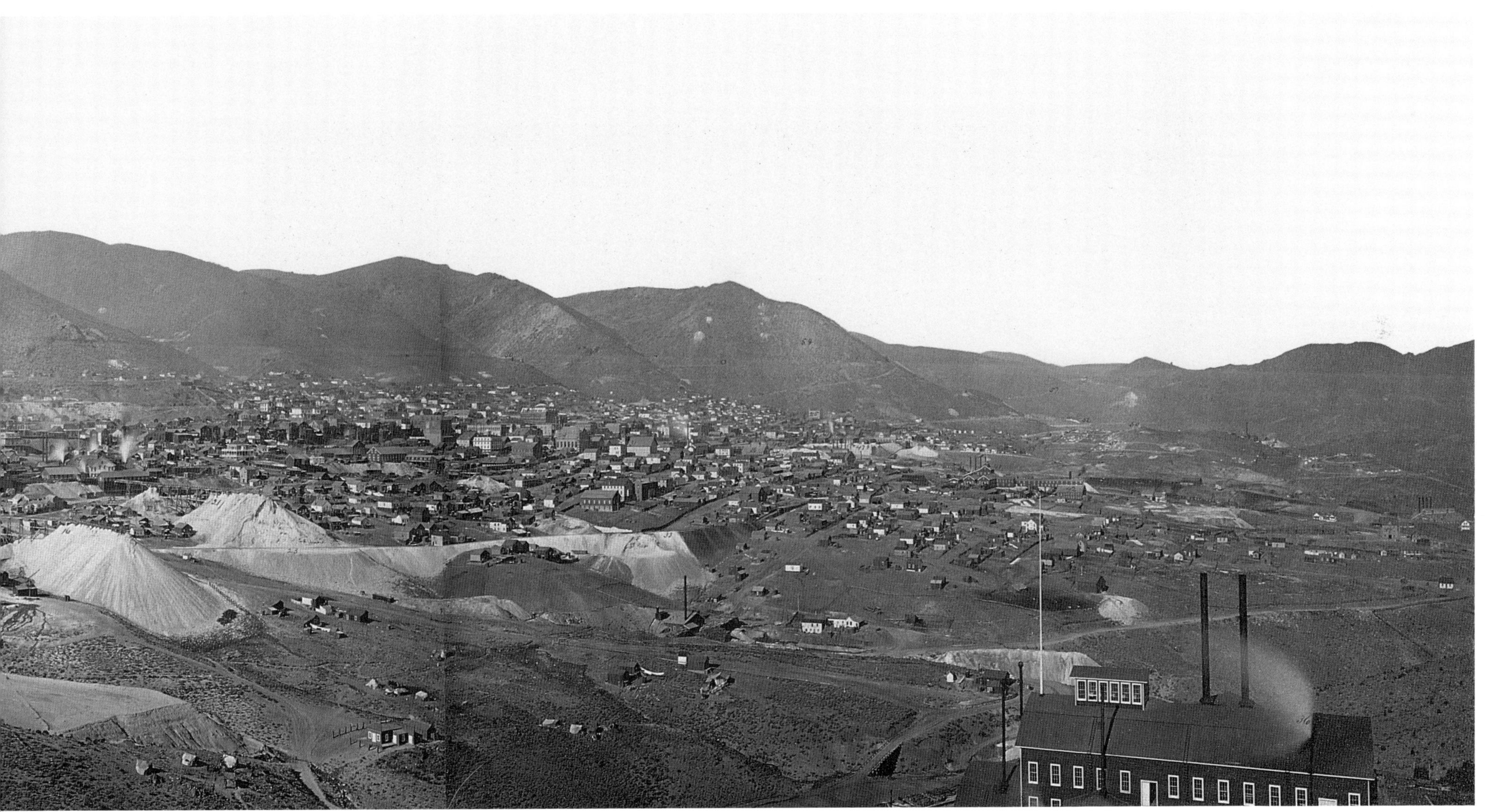

PLATE 24

Carleton E. Watkins
Virginia City. Photographed Oct. 26, 1876. One Year from the date of the Great Fire, 1876
3 albumen prints
16½ x 62¼ in. (41.9 x 158.1 cm) overall
Collection of Ron Bommarito

PLATE 25

Charles Weitfle
No. 225 Gold Retorts, ca. 1865–70
stereographic albumen prints
3 15/16 x 7 1/16 in. (10 x 17.9 cm)
Denver Public Library,
Western History Collection

"This interesting pile of gold is the result of four weeks' run of the 'Hidden Treasure' Mining Co. Weight, 1,370 ozs.; value, $22,500."

PLATE 26

Carleton E. Watkins
Golden Feather Mining Claim, no. 7, Feather River, Butte County, California, 1891
albumen print
15 1/2 x 21 in. (39.4 x 53.3 cm)
Collection of The Bancroft Library, University of California, Berkeley

Looking downstream, showing head-dam during construction. Sub-flume carrying power and seepage water in foreground

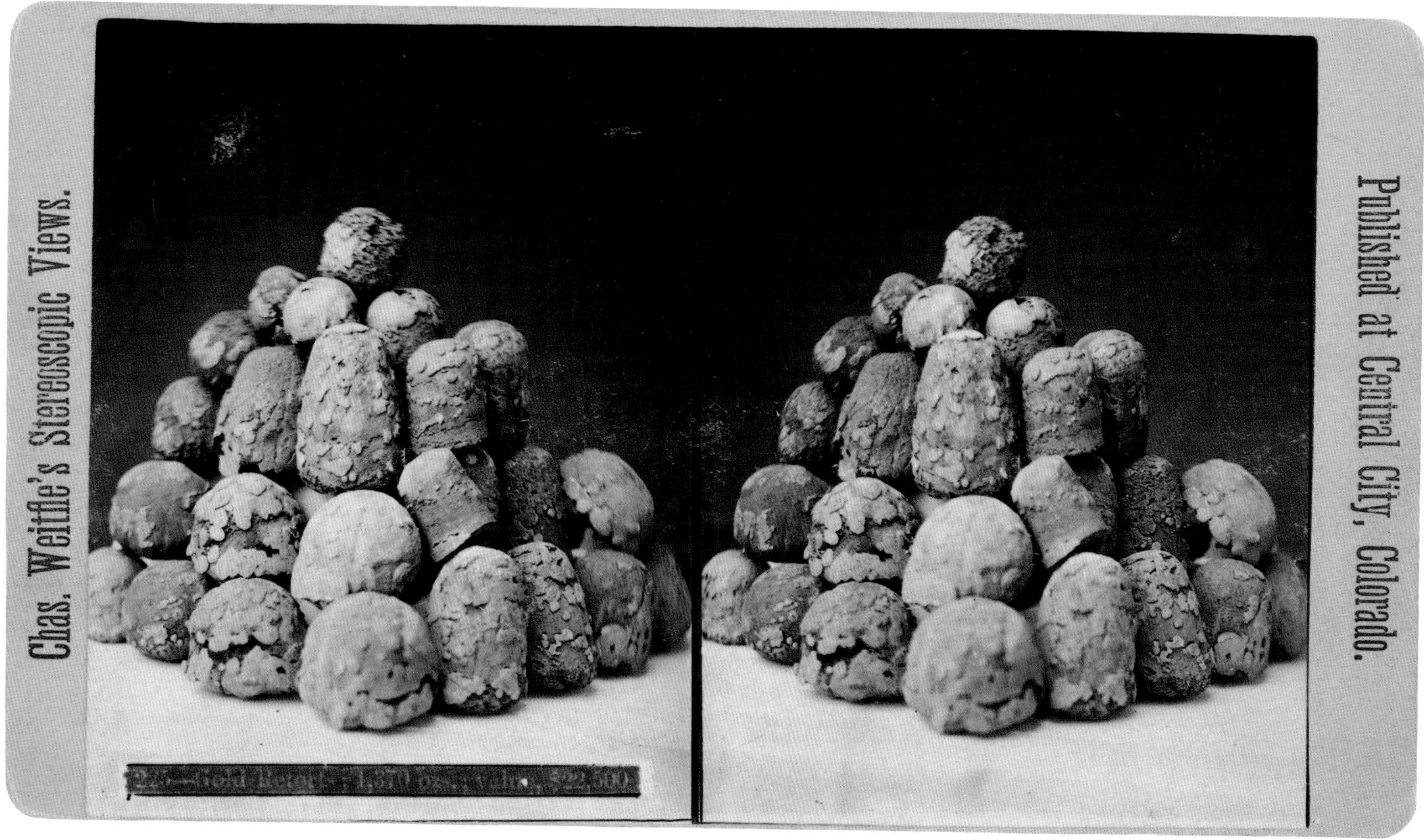

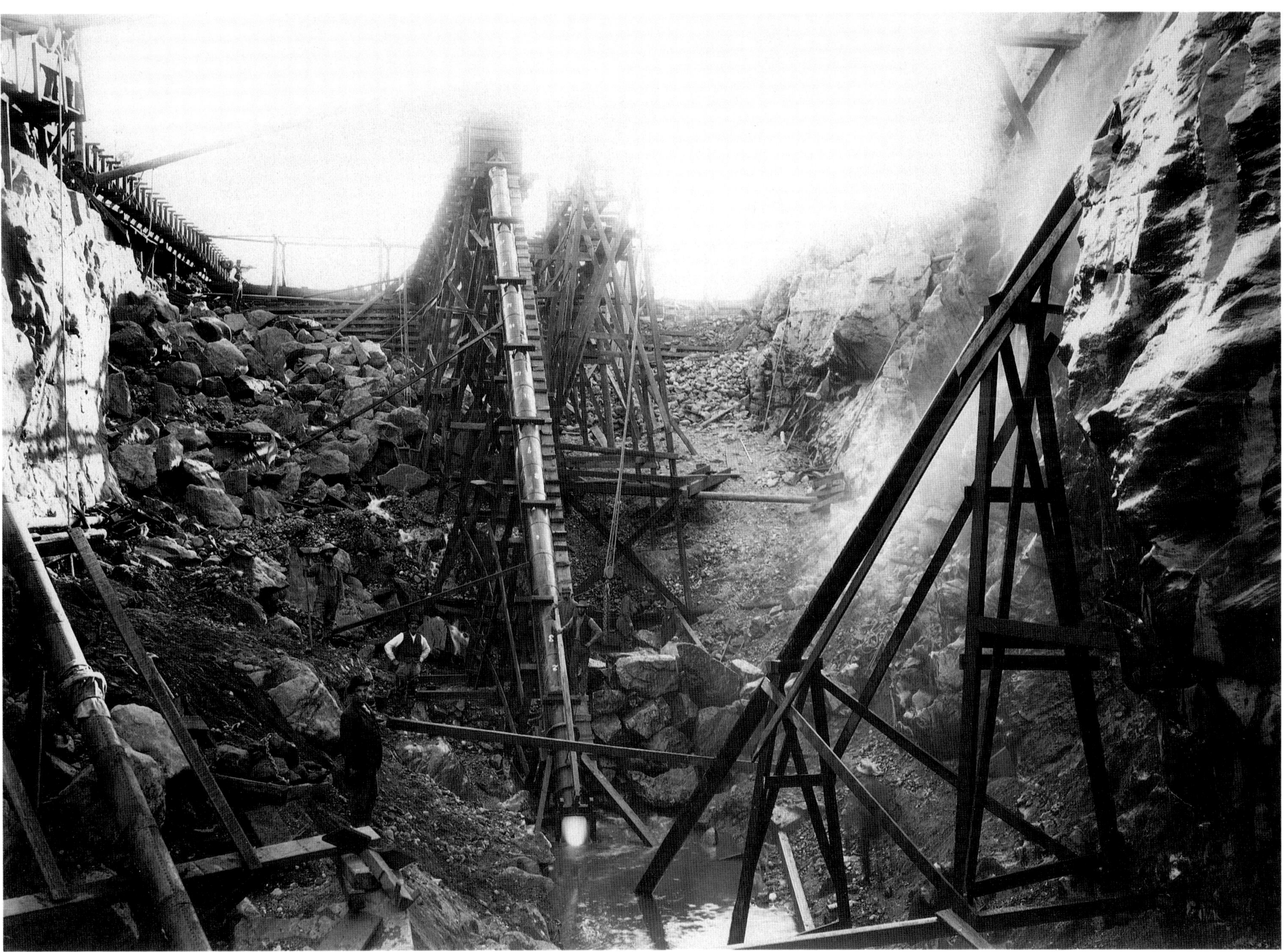

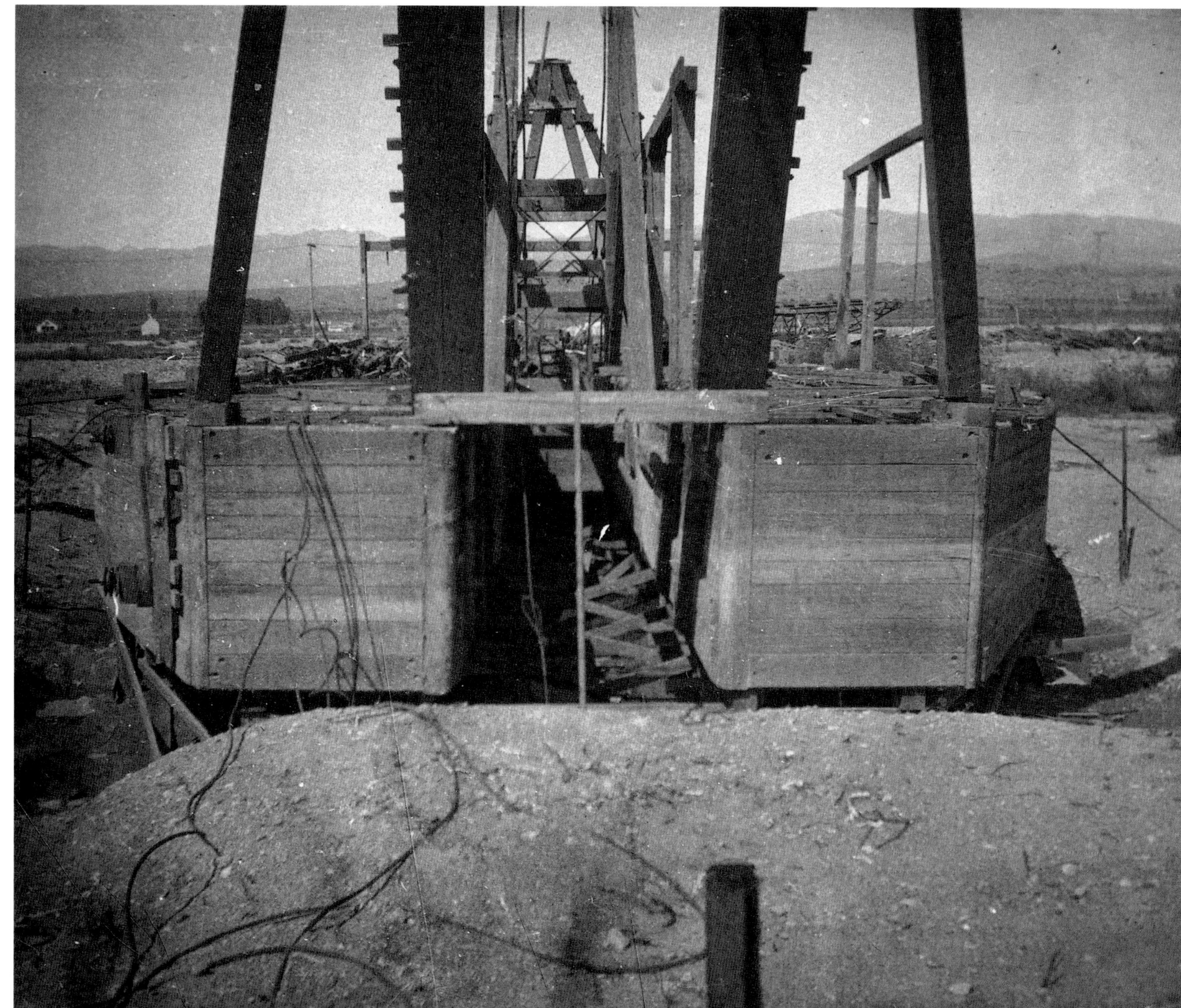

PLATE 27

Unknown
Untitled, ca. 1905
silver bromide print
25 x 30 in. (63.5 x 76.2 cm)
Collection of the San Francisco Museum of Modern Art.
Accessions Committee Fund, 96.123

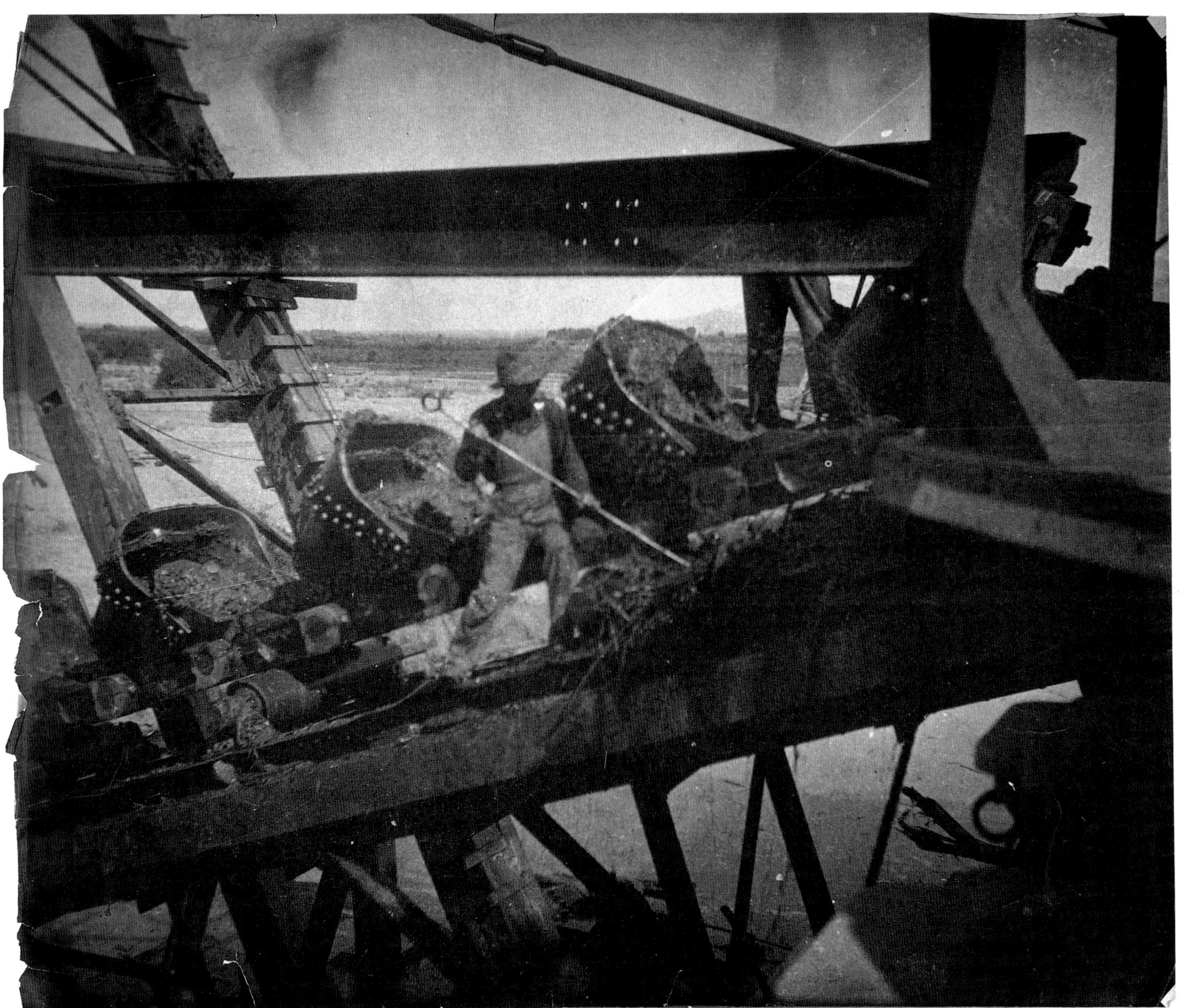

PLATE 28

Unknown
Untitled, ca. 1905
silver bromide print
25½ x 30½ in. (64.8 x 77.5 cm)
Collection of the San Francisco Museum of Modern Art.
Accessions Committee Fund, 96.124

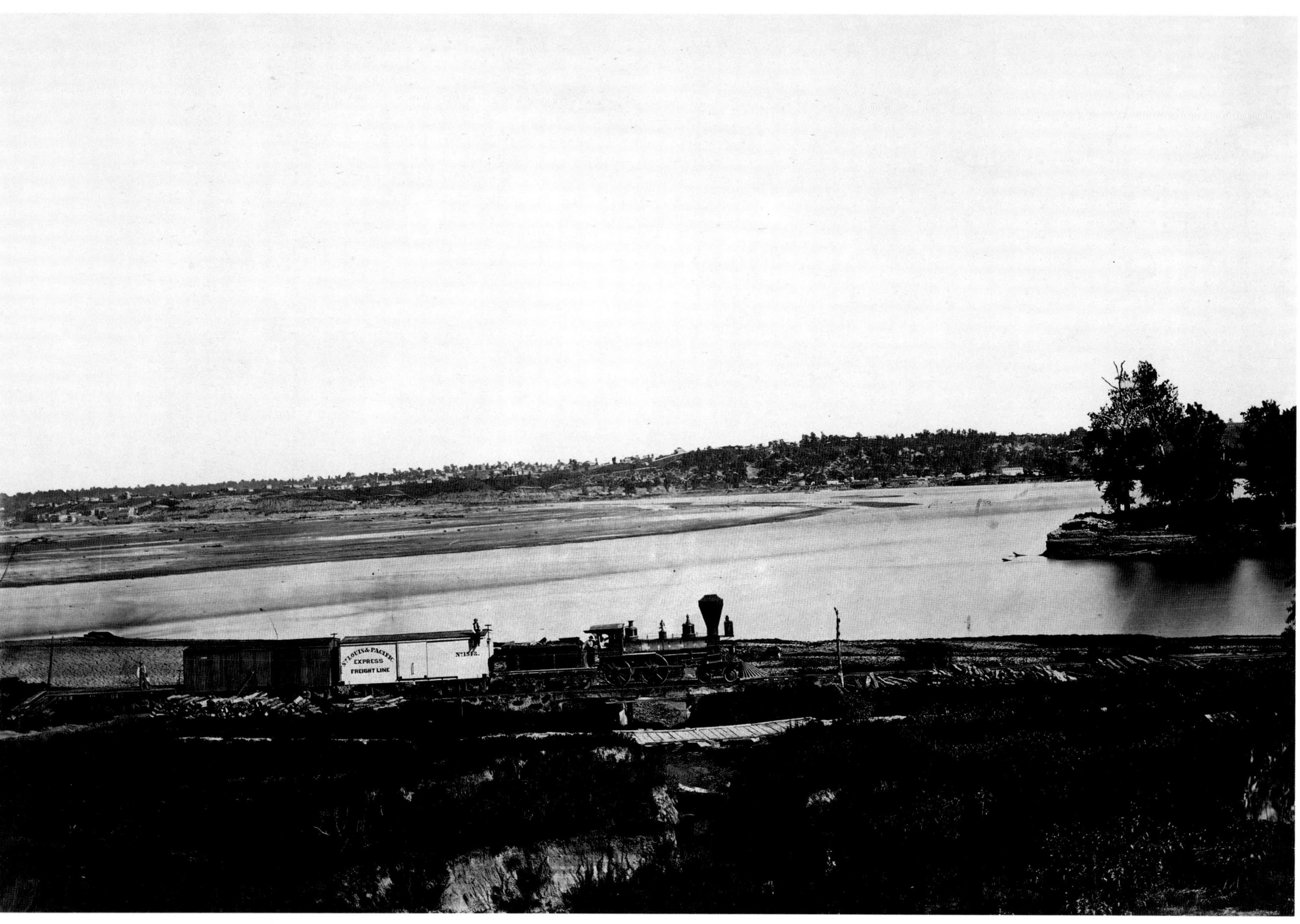
St LOUIS & PACIFIC
EXPRESS
FREIGHT LINE

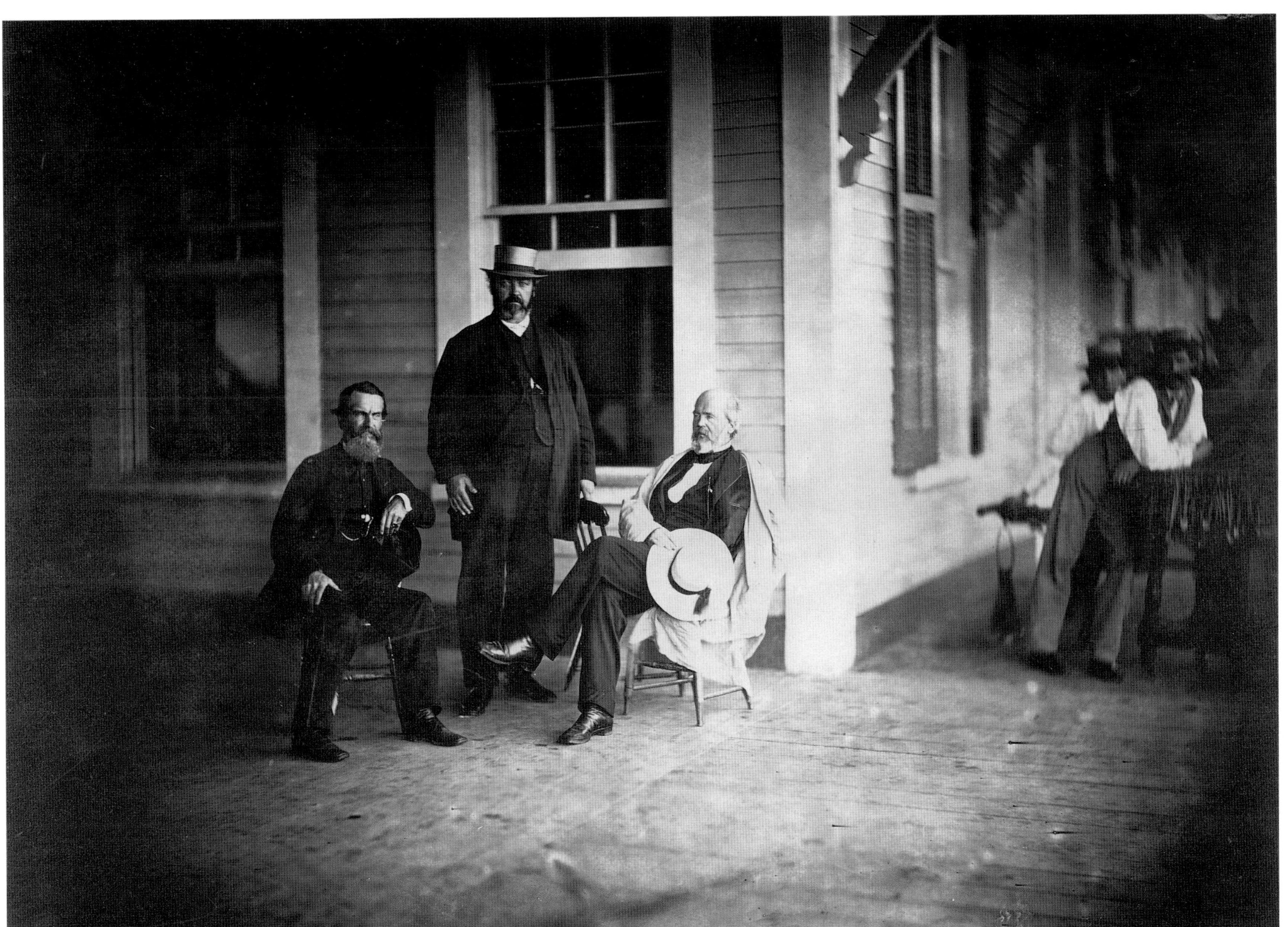

PLATE 29

Alexander Gardner
Confluence of Kaw and Missouri Rivers at Wyandotte, Kansas, from the album *Across the Continent on the Union Pacific Railway, E.D.*, 1867
albumen print
13 x 18$^{11}/_{16}$ in. (33 x 47.5 cm)
Collection of the J. Paul Getty Museum, Los Angeles, California

PLATE 30

Alexander Gardner
Railroad Commissioners at State Line, Kansas, from the album *Across the Continent on the Union Pacific Railway, E.D.*, 1867
albumen print
13 x 18$^{11}/_{16}$ in. (33 x 47.5 cm)
Collection of the J. Paul Getty Museum, Los Angeles, California

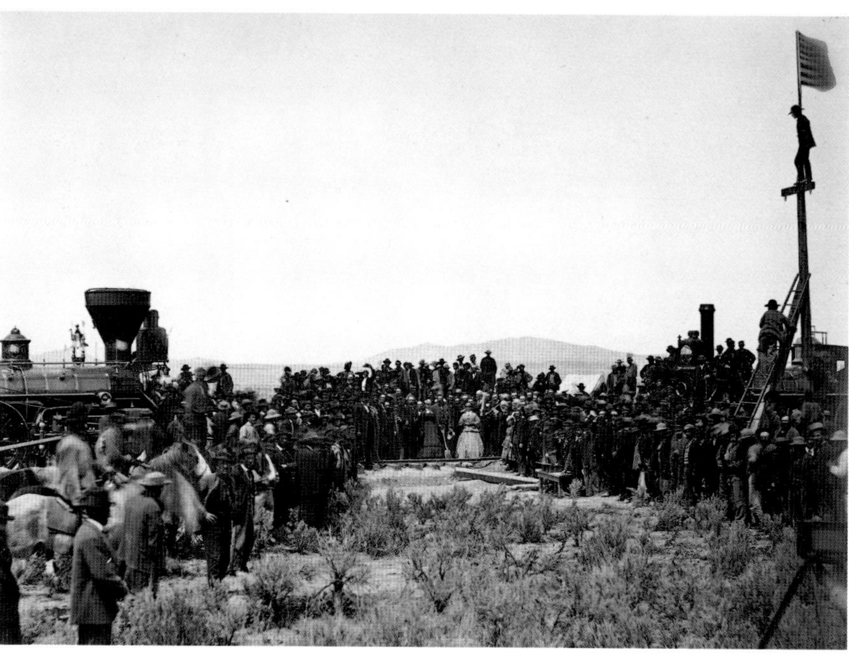

PLATE 31

Andrew Joseph Russell
Laying of Last Rail
(Promontory Summit), 1869
albumen print
8$\frac{5}{8}$ x 11$\frac{3}{4}$ in. (21.9 x 29.8 cm)
Union Pacific Museum Collection

PLATE 32

J. E. Stimson
Temporary Trestle Work for Large Fill across Papio Valley, near Omaha, from an untitled album of railroad views, 1908
platinum print
7$\frac{5}{8}$ x 9$\frac{1}{2}$ in. (19.4 x 24.1 cm)
Union Pacific Museum Collection

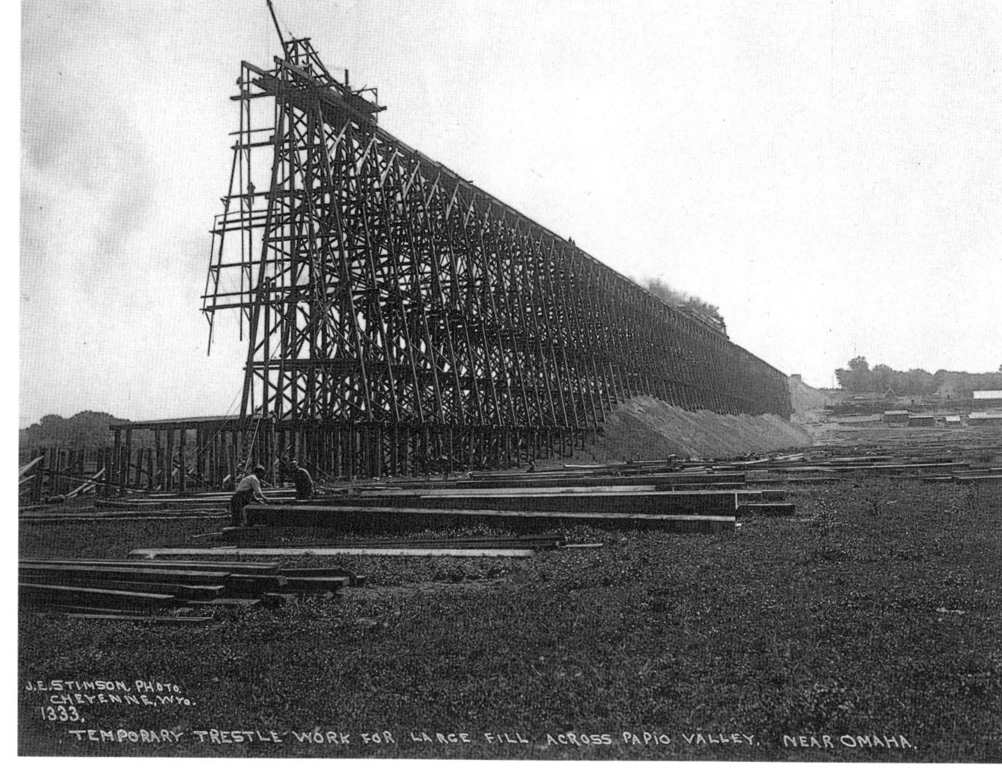

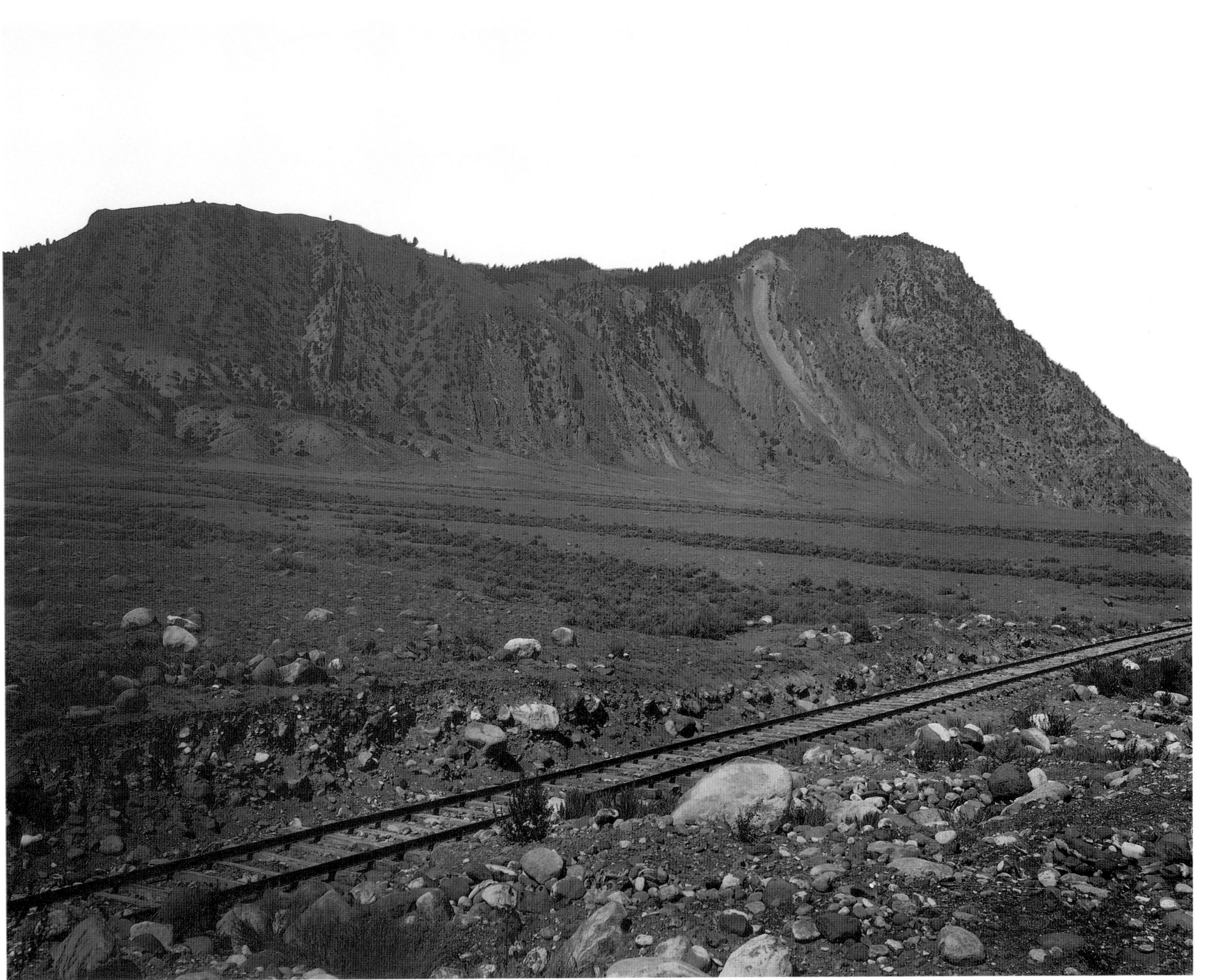

PLATE 33

Frank Jay Haynes
Cinnabar Mountain, Devil's Slide,
1890
albumen print
17⅜ x 21⅝ in. (44.1 x 54.9 cm)
Collection of the San Francisco Museum of Modern Art.
Accessions Committee Fund,
95.178

PLATE 34

Andrew Joseph Russell
Corinne [Utah], 1869
albumen print
8⅝ x 11¾ (21.9 x 29.8 cm)
Union Pacific Museum Collection

PLATE 35

Andrew Joseph Russell
Dale Creek Bridge, from above, from the album *The Great West Illustrated in a Series of Photographic Views Across the Continent; Taken Along the Line of the Union Pacific Railroad, West from Omaha, Nebraska* (Vol. I), 1869
albumen print
9⅜ x 12¼ in. (23.8 x 31.1 cm)
Collection of the San Francisco Museum of Modern Art. Fractional gift of Kathy and Ron Perisho, 94.490

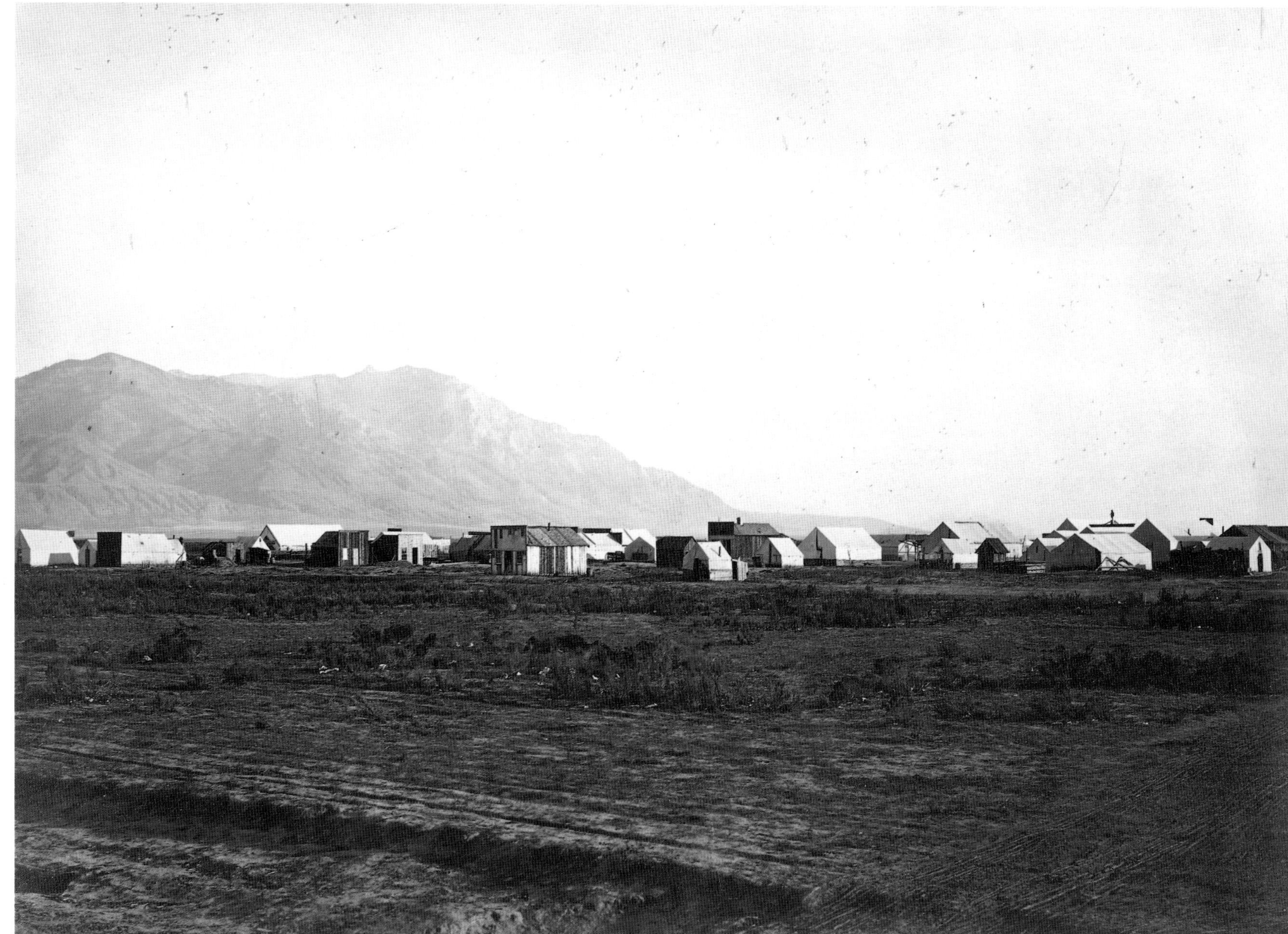

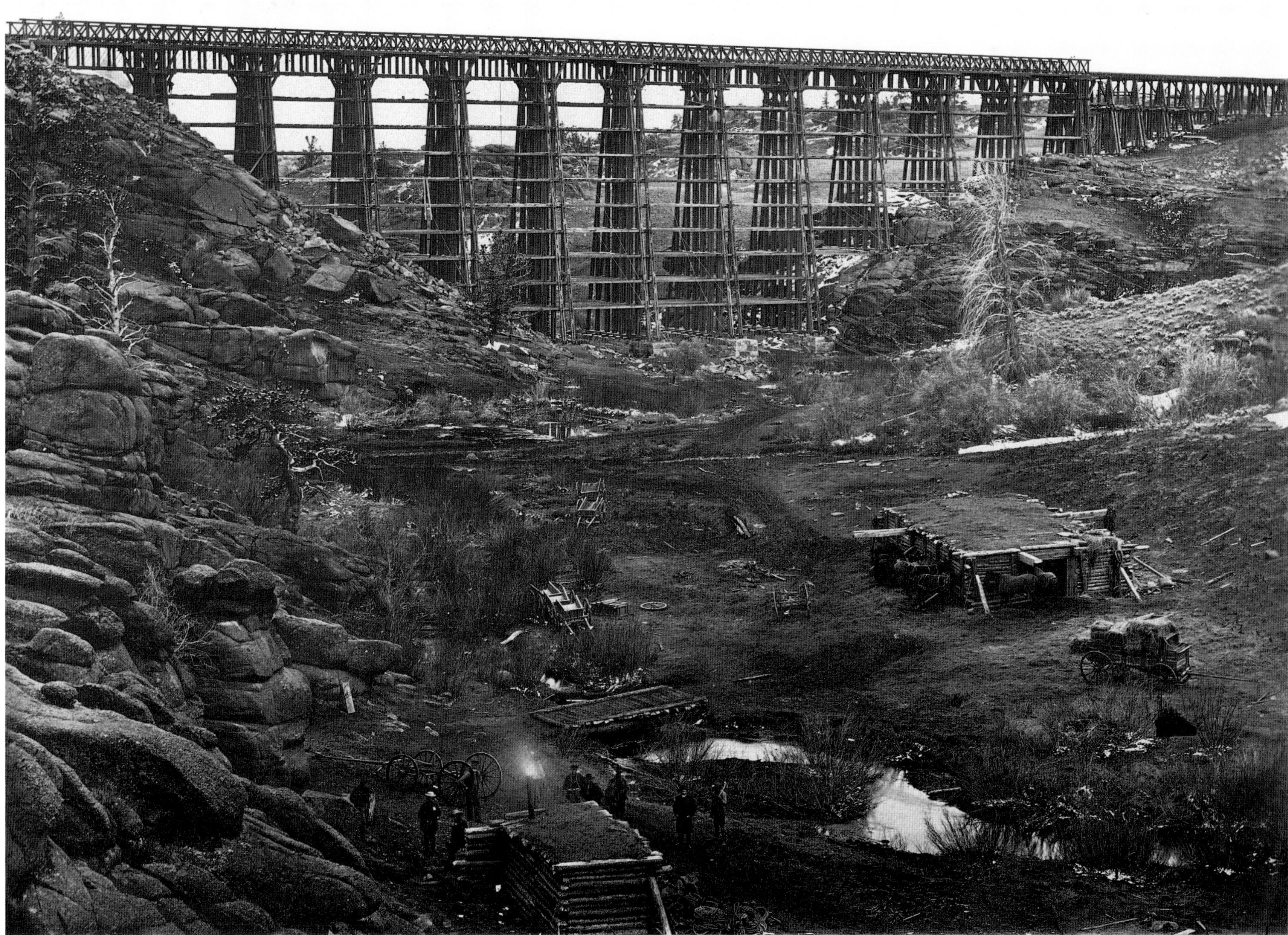

PLATE 36

Evelyn J. Cameron
Work Crew on the Chicago, Milwaukee, and Saint Paul Railway near Terry, Montana, ca. 1907
gelatin silver print on printing out paper
4½ x 6½ in. (11.4 x 16.5 cm)
Collection of the Montana Historical Society, Helena

PLATE 37

William Henry Jackson
Mexico. Tamasopo Cañon. Tunnel 5, from an untitled Detroit Publishing Company album of Colorado, Mexico, and Utah railroad views, 1891
albumen print
15⅝ x 20½ in. (39.7 x 52.1 cm)
Collection of the Colorado Historical Society, Denver

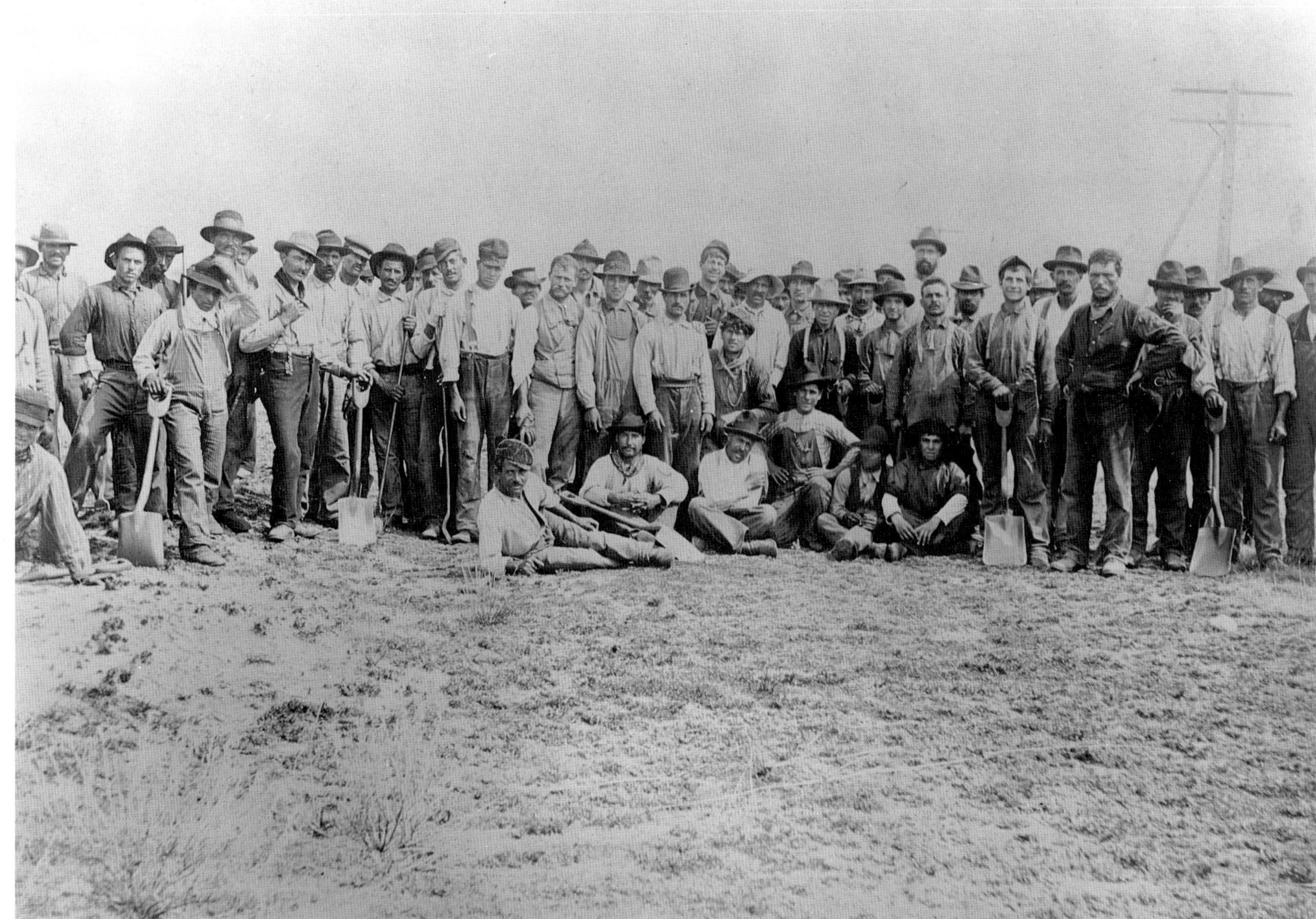

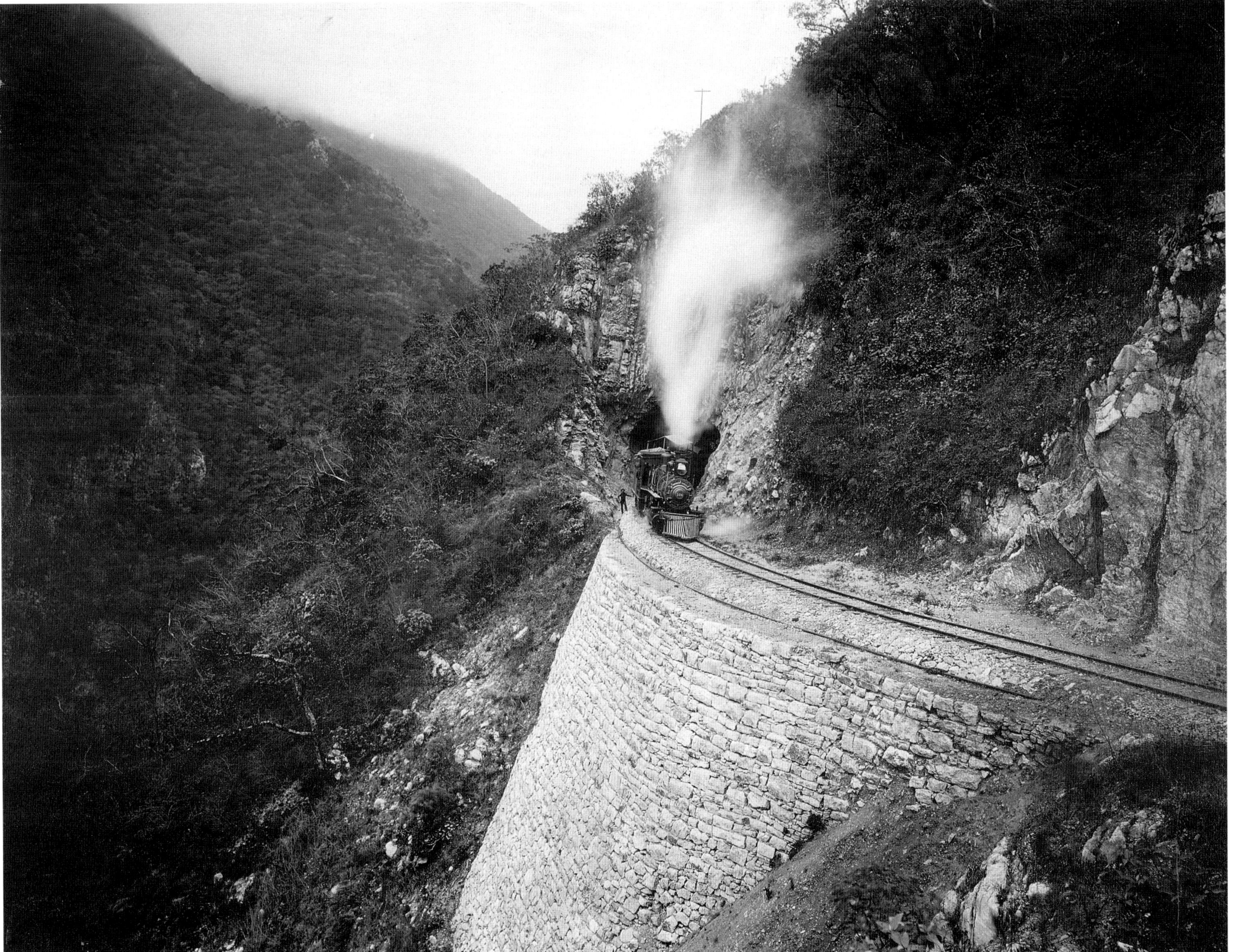

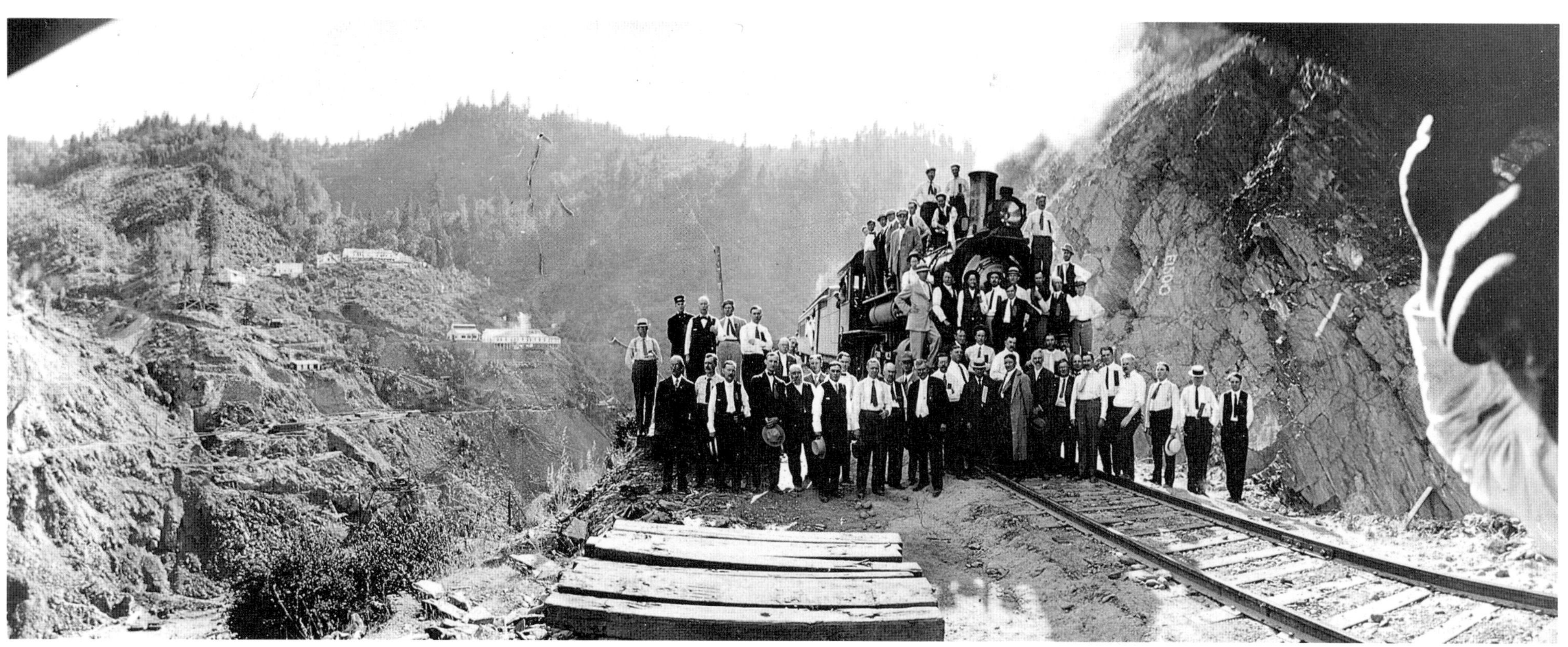

PLATE 38

Unknown

Western Pacific Railroad. Great Western Powerhouse, Feather River Canyon, California, 1910

gelatin silver print

5 x 11⅞ in. (12.7 x 30.2 cm)

Collection of the California State Library, Sacramento

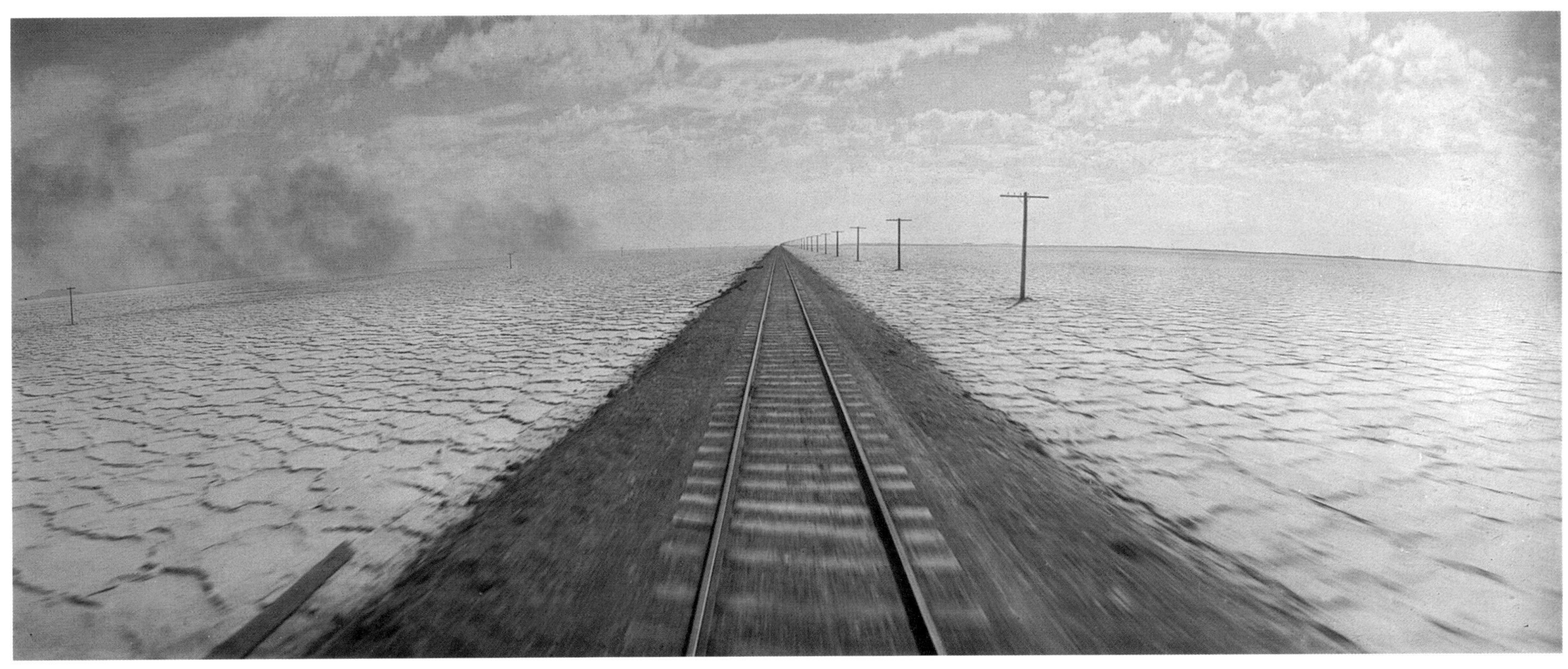

PLATE 39

Unknown
Opening of Western Pacific Passenger Service between San Francisco and Salt Lake City, Sea of Salt, Utah, 1910
gelatin silver print
5 x 11⅞ in. (12.7 x 30.2 cm)
Collection of the California State Library, Sacramento

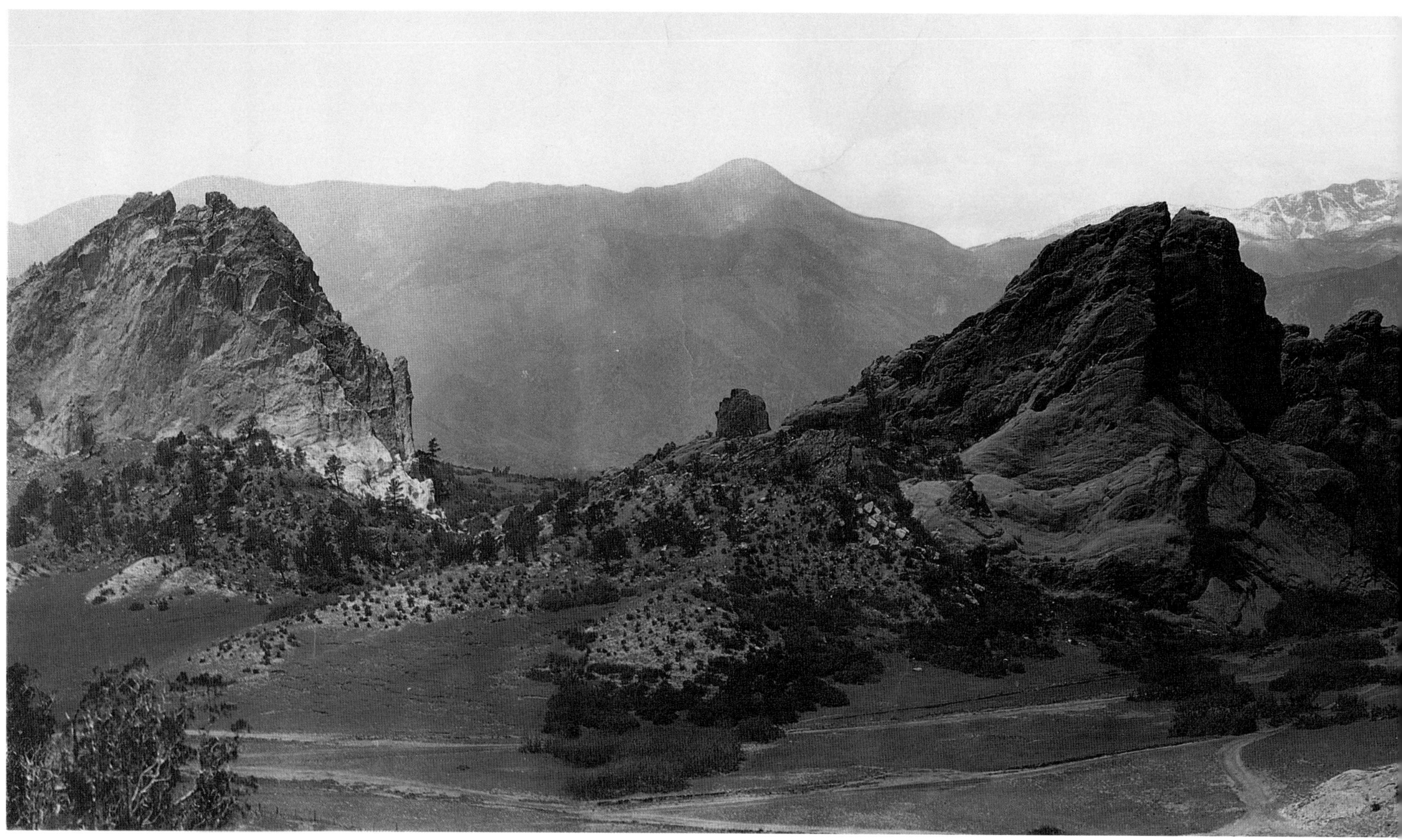

PLATE 40

William Henry Jackson
Pike's Peak from the Garden of the Gods, 1888
albumen print
20¼ x 70¼ in. (51.4 x 178.4 cm)
Collection of the San Francisco Museum of Modern Art.
Purchased through a gift of the Judy Kay Memorial Fund

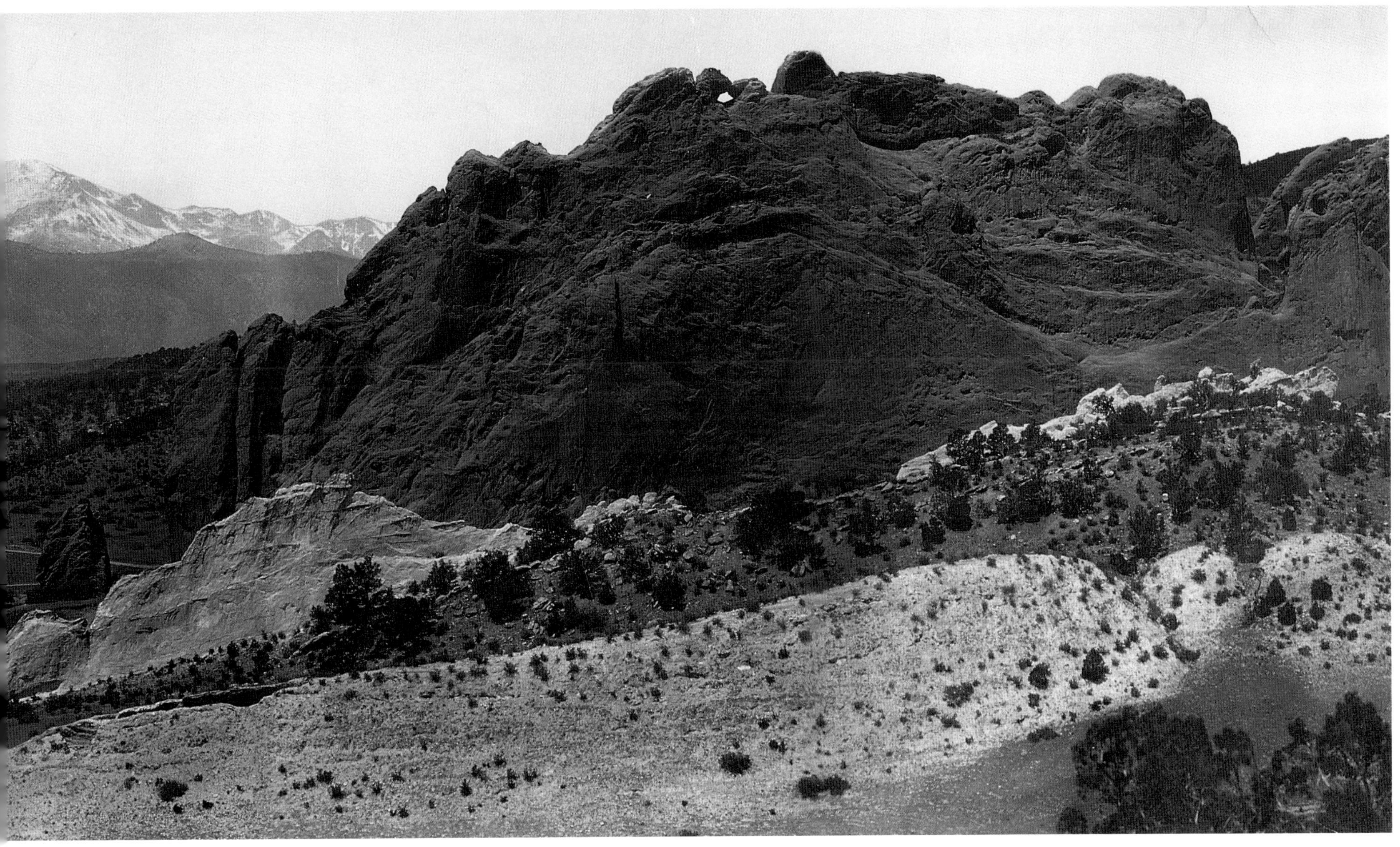

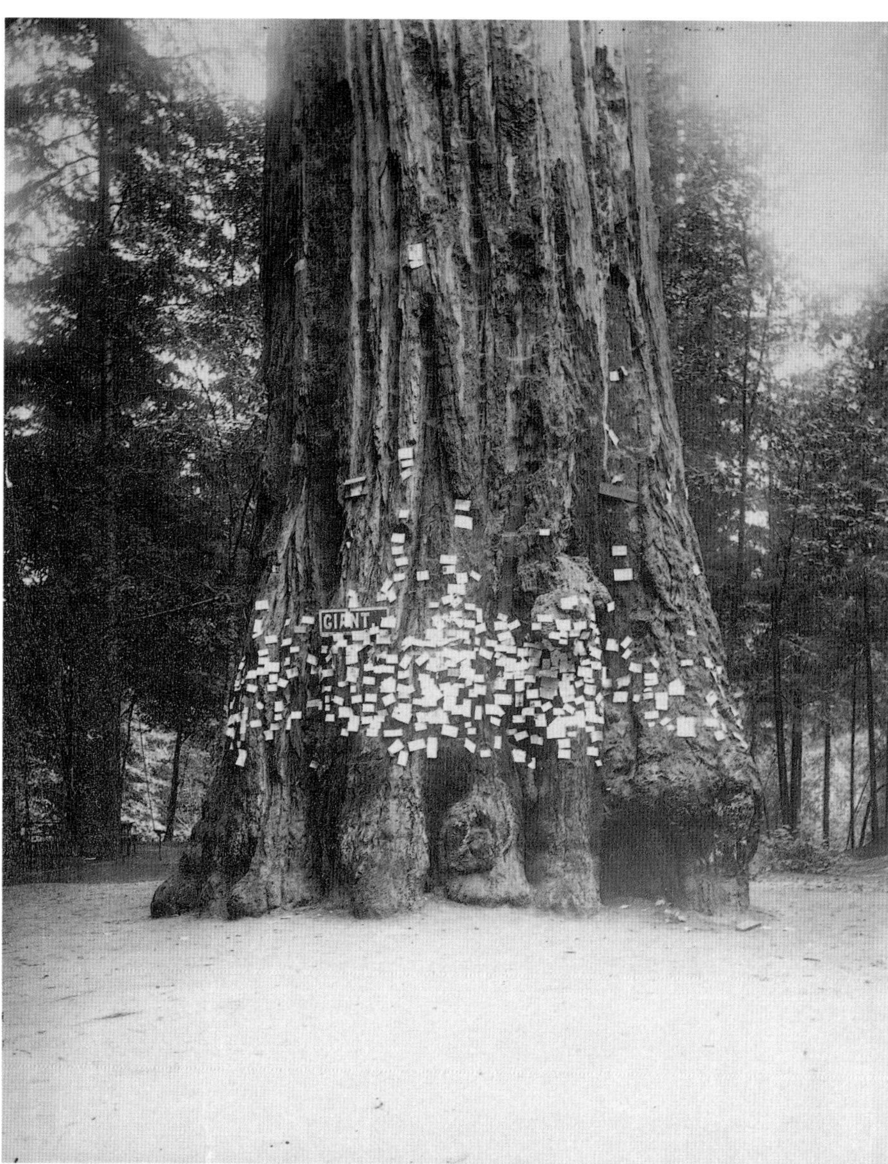

PLATE 41

Taber Studio (attributed to Carleton E. Watkins)
Big Trees, Felton, Santa Cruz, ca. 1880
albumen print
9⅝ x 7⅝ in. (24.5 x 19.4 cm)
Collection of the San Francisco Museum of Modern Art.
Purchased through a gift of Frederick P. Currier, 95.141

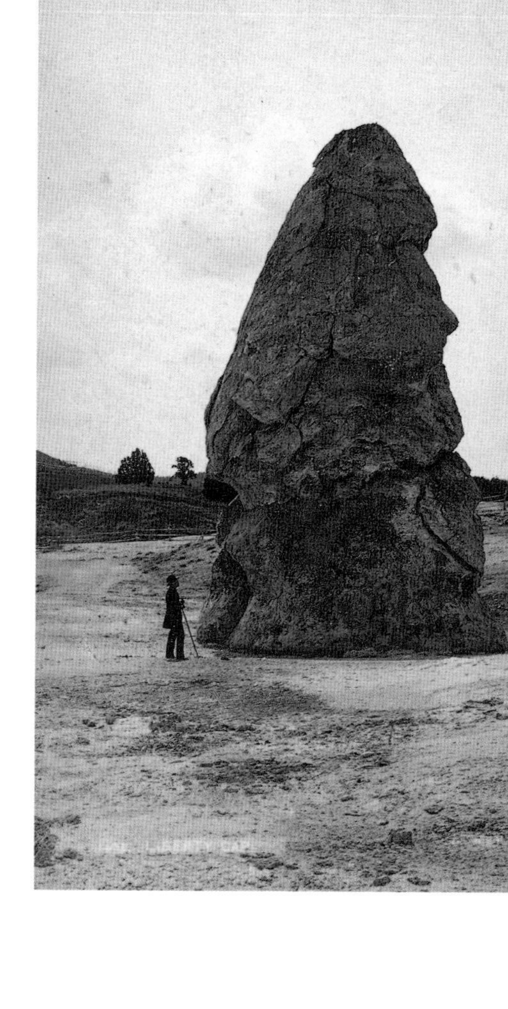

PLATE 42

Frank Jay Haynes
Liberty Cap (Yellowstone National Park), ca. 1900
albumen print
6⅛ x 3⅞ in. (15.6 x 9.8 cm)
Collection of the San Francisco Museum of Modern Art.
Members of Foto Forum, 95.398

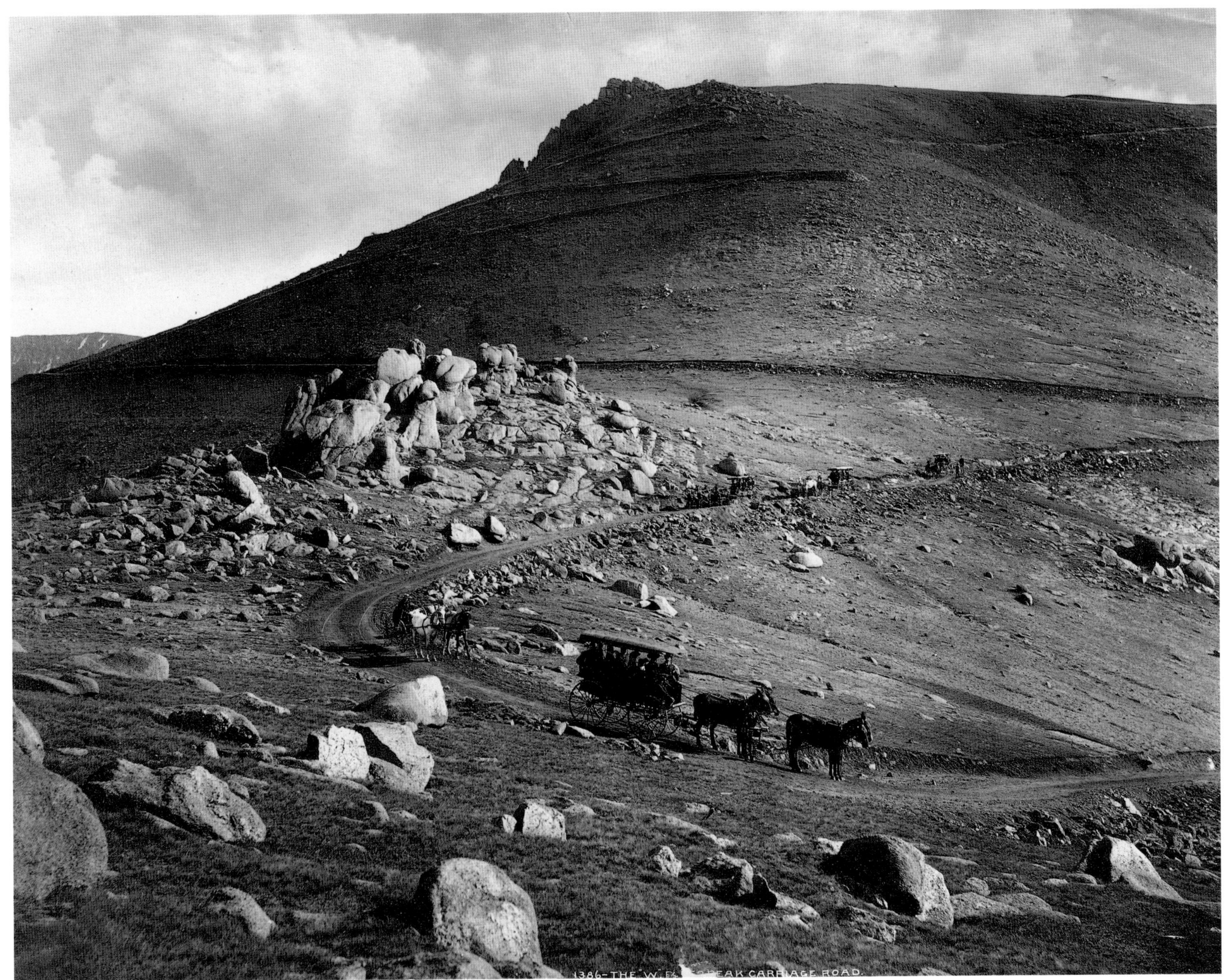

PLATE 43

William Henry Jackson
The "W." Pikes Peak Carriage Road, after 1891
albumen print
15¾ x 20½ in. (40 x 52 cm)
Collection of the Colorado Historical Society, Denver

PLATE 44

Unknown
7½ Pounds, n.d.
sixth-plate daguerreotype
approx. 2¾ x 3¼ in. (7 x 8.3 cm)
Collection of the California
Historical Society, San Francisco

PLATE 45

Evelyn J. Cameron
Sheep Crossing on Scott's Ferry, Yellowstone River, 1905
gelatin silver print on
printing out paper
7½ x 9½ in. (19.1 x 24.1 cm)
Collection of the Montana
Historical Society, Helena

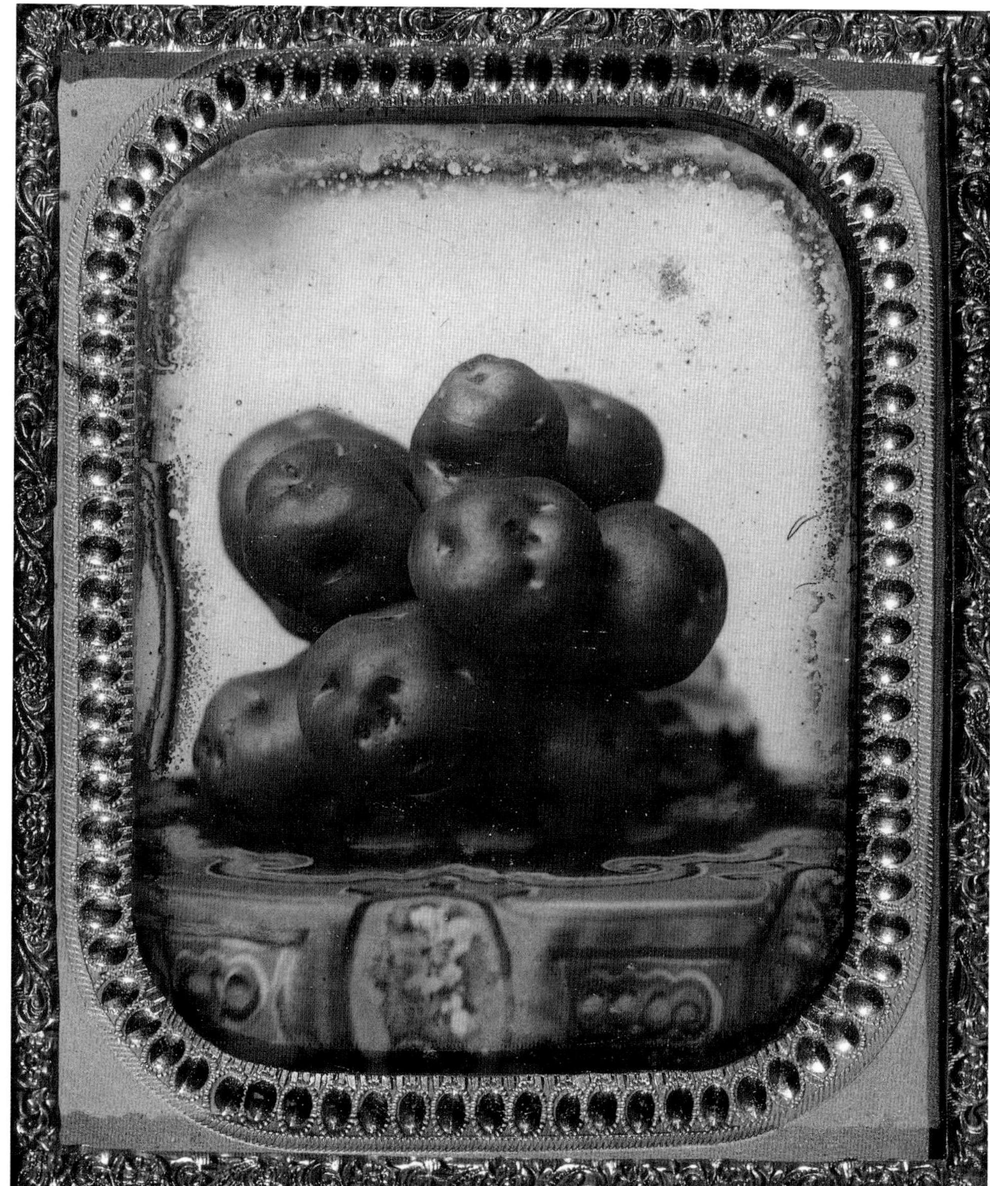

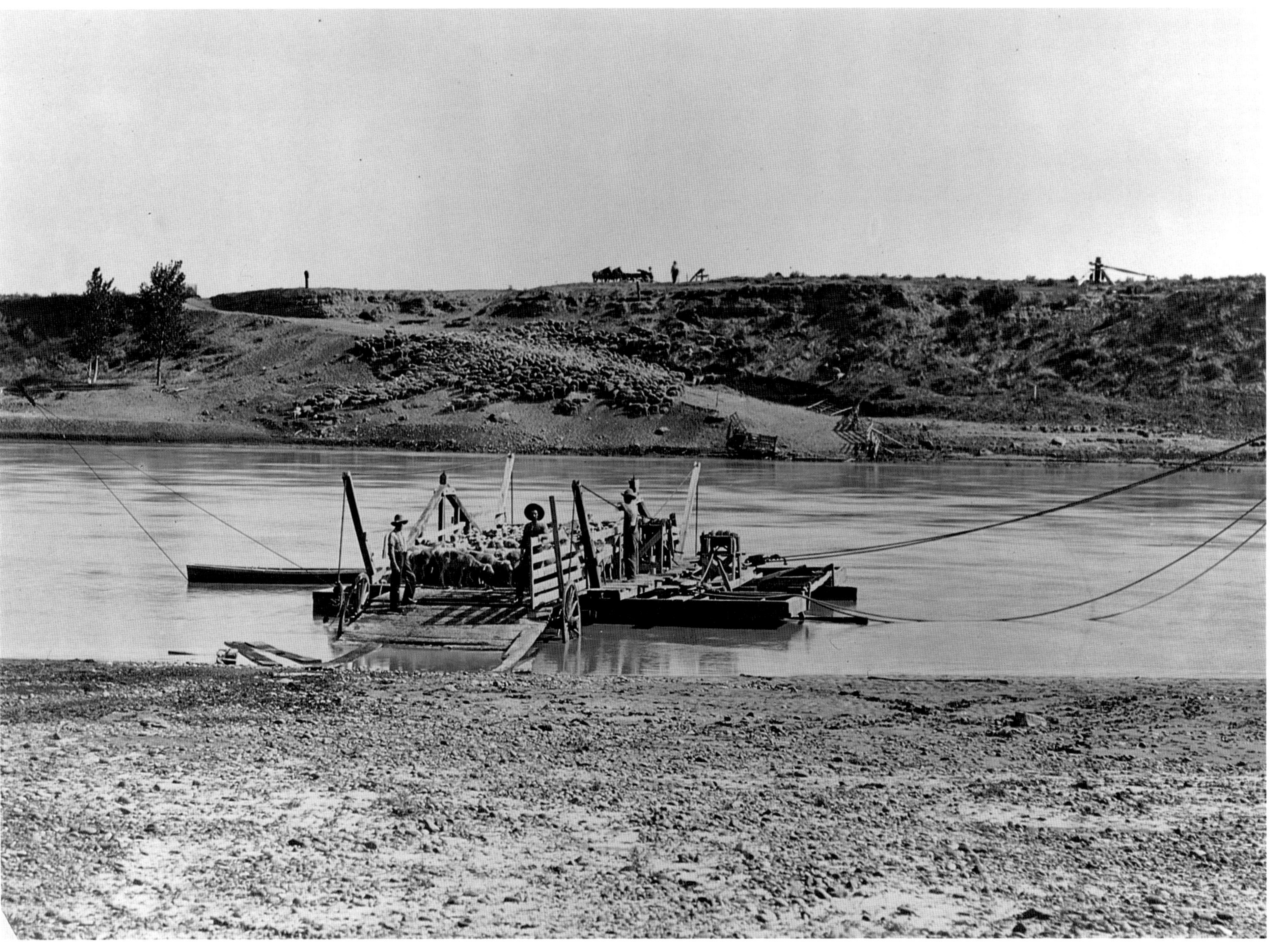

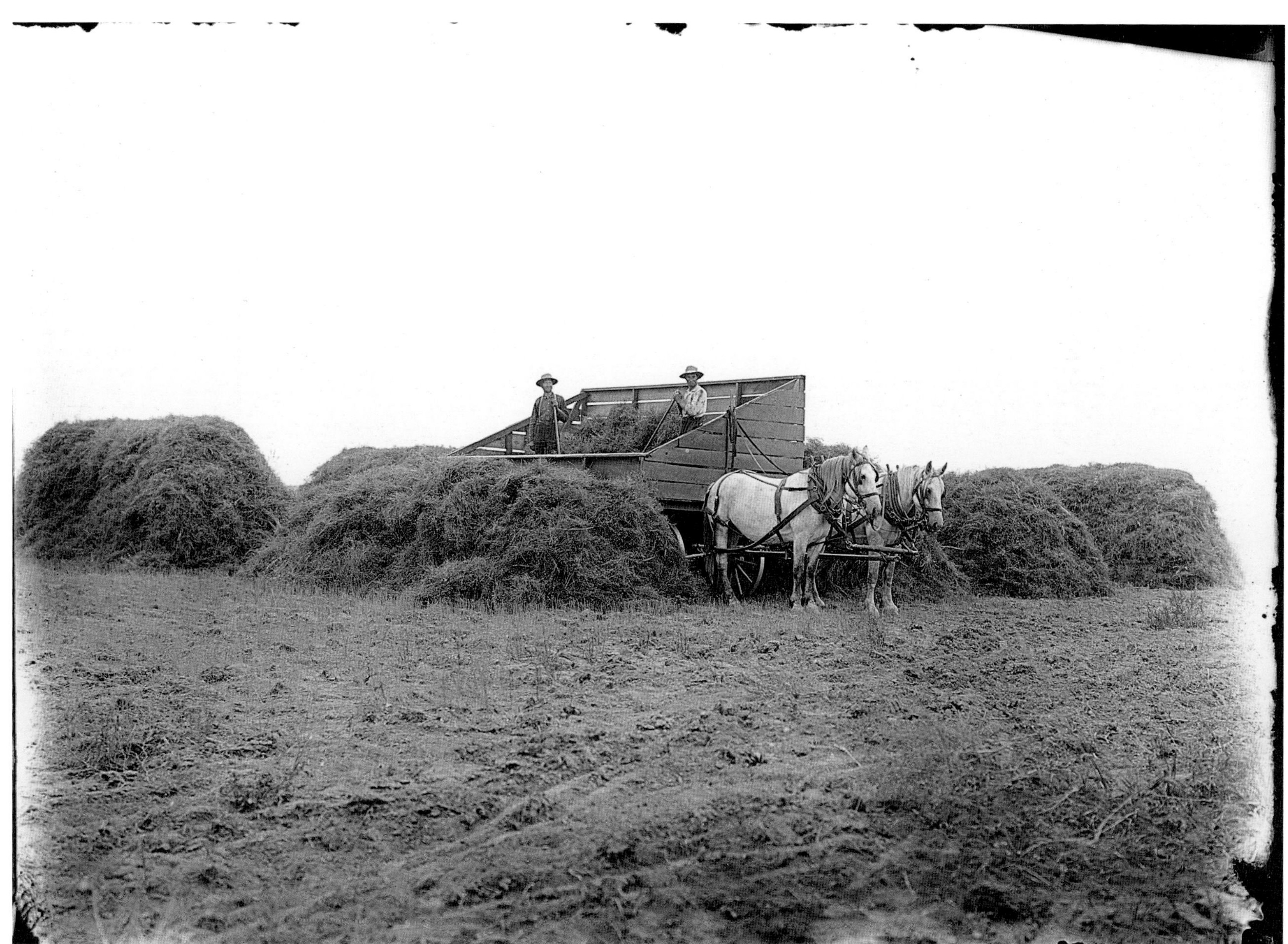

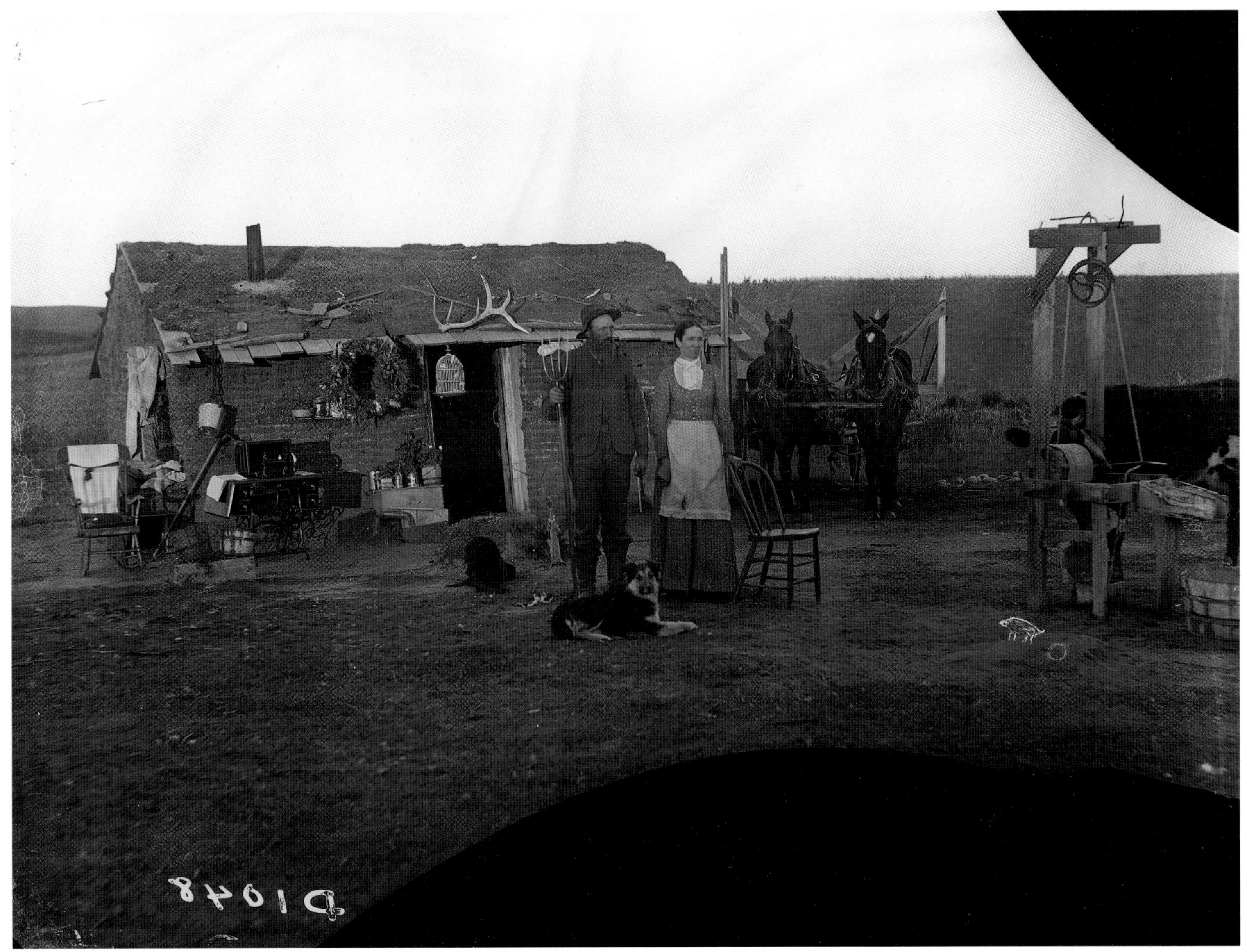

PLATE 46

Evelyn J. Cameron
Men Loading Horse-drawn Wagon with Hay, Eastern Montana, ca. 1910
gelatin silver print on printing out paper
4½ x 6½ in. (11.4 x 16.5 cm)
Collection of the Montana Historical Society, Helena

PLATE 47

Solomon D. Butcher
Untitled (Nebraska Gothic), 1886
albumen print
5¾ x 9 in. (14.6 x 22.9 cm)
Solomon D. Butcher Collection, B983-1048, Nebraska State Historical Society

The John Curry Sod House near Old West Union, Nebraska

BUCK.

My favorite cattle horse.

Died Sept.20th,1884,aged

18 years & six months.

In adversity
faithful.

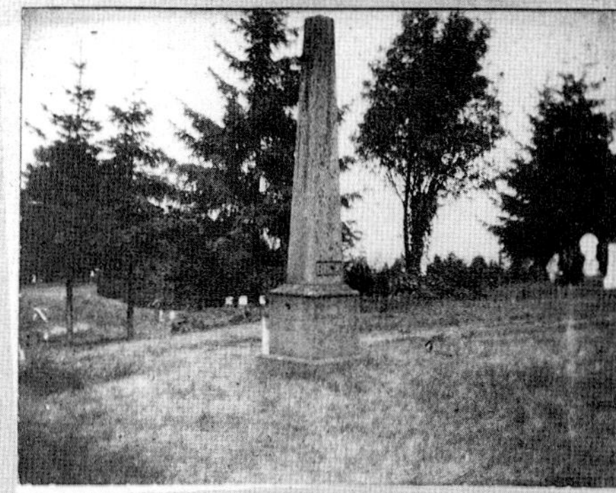

For thirteen year
my trusted friend
and companion,in
blackness of nigh
in storm,sunshine
and danger.

CORRALD.

PLATE 48

Unknown
Monument to a Horse, ca. 1940
gelatin silver print
5 x 7 in. (12.7 x 17.8 cm)
Merrill G. Burlingame Special Collections, Montana State University–Bozeman

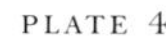

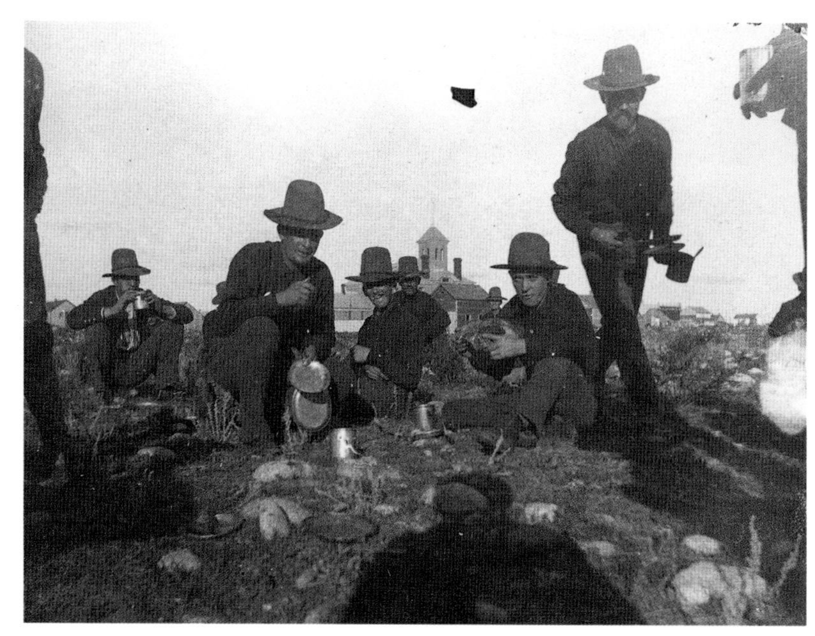

PLATE 49

Unknown
76 Ranch, ca. 1940
sepia-toned gelatin silver print
4 x 5 in. (10.2 x 12.7 cm)
Merrill G. Burlingame Special Collections, Montana State University–Bozeman

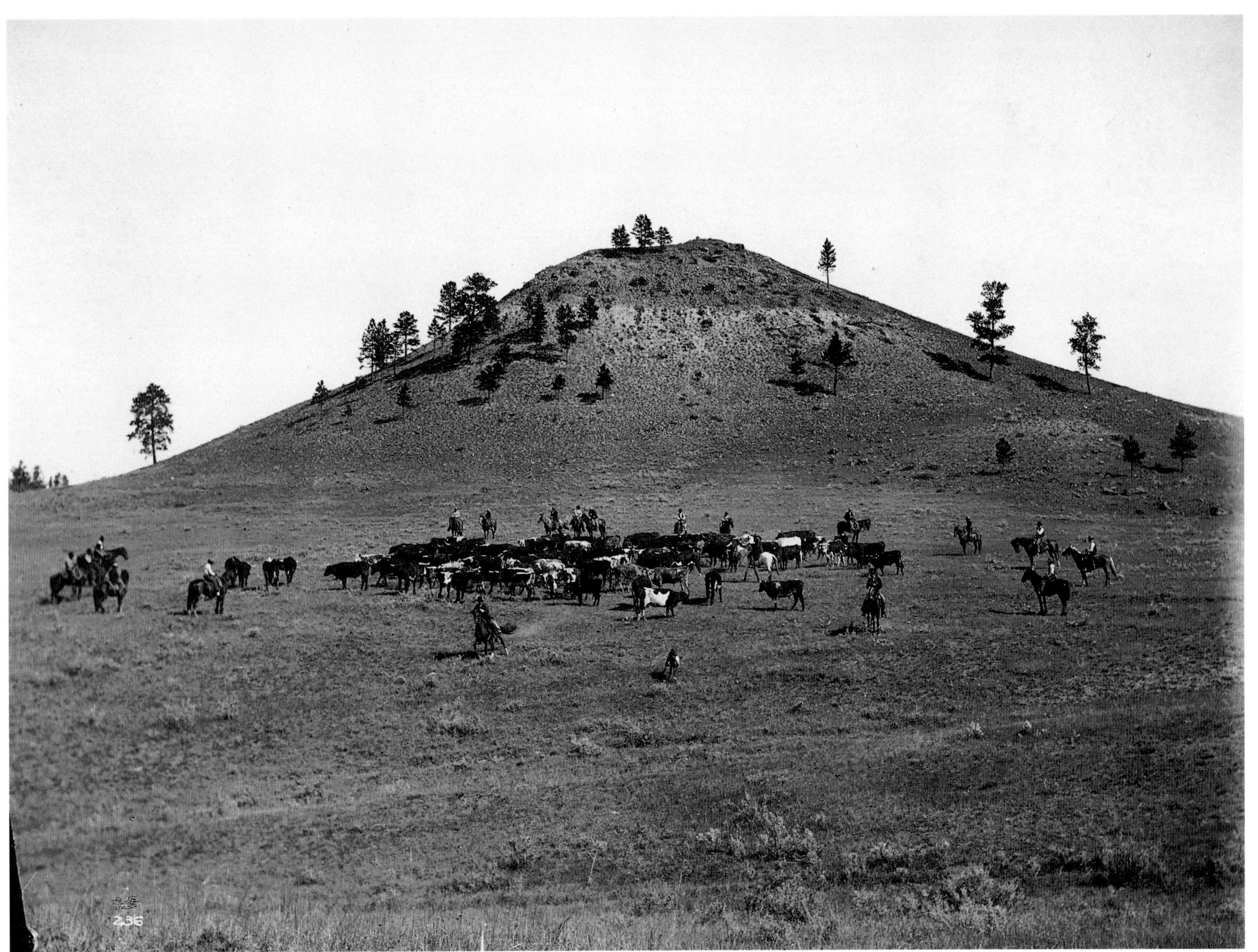

PLATE 50

Laton Alton Huffman
Working a Small Herd, ca. 1890
albumen print
6 x $8\frac{3}{16}$ in. (15.2 x 20.8 cm)
Collection of the San Francisco Museum of Modern Art.
Purchased through a gift of the Judy Kay Memorial Fund

PLATE 51

Bryan Studio
Untitled (Pile of Tails), ca. 1886
albumen print
5½ x 4 in. (14 x 10.2 cm)
Collection of the San Francisco Museum of Modern Art. Members of Foto Forum, 94.465

PLATE 52

Unknown
Invasion of Mice Repelled by Government Forces, 1927
gelatin silver print
$5\frac{11}{16}$ x 7⅞ in. (14.5 x 20 cm)
Collection of the California Historical Society, San Francisco

"Los Angeles . . . The Federal Bureau of Pest Control has been asked to assume the role of the Pied Piper of Hamelin in checking the invasion of mice in Kern County, in and around Taft, Cal. Thousands upon thousands of mice are dead and other thousands prowl about night and day, feeding on the dead rodents, wreaking havoc among wheat and grain fields and barns. Extreme means have been adopted to eliminate this plague. Lengthy trenches filled with poisonous wheat have been dug; volunteers beat about various sections, killing the mice in droves. Some progress has been made in the battle against the mice, but further greater efforts on the part of the government bureaus is expected. 1-24-27"

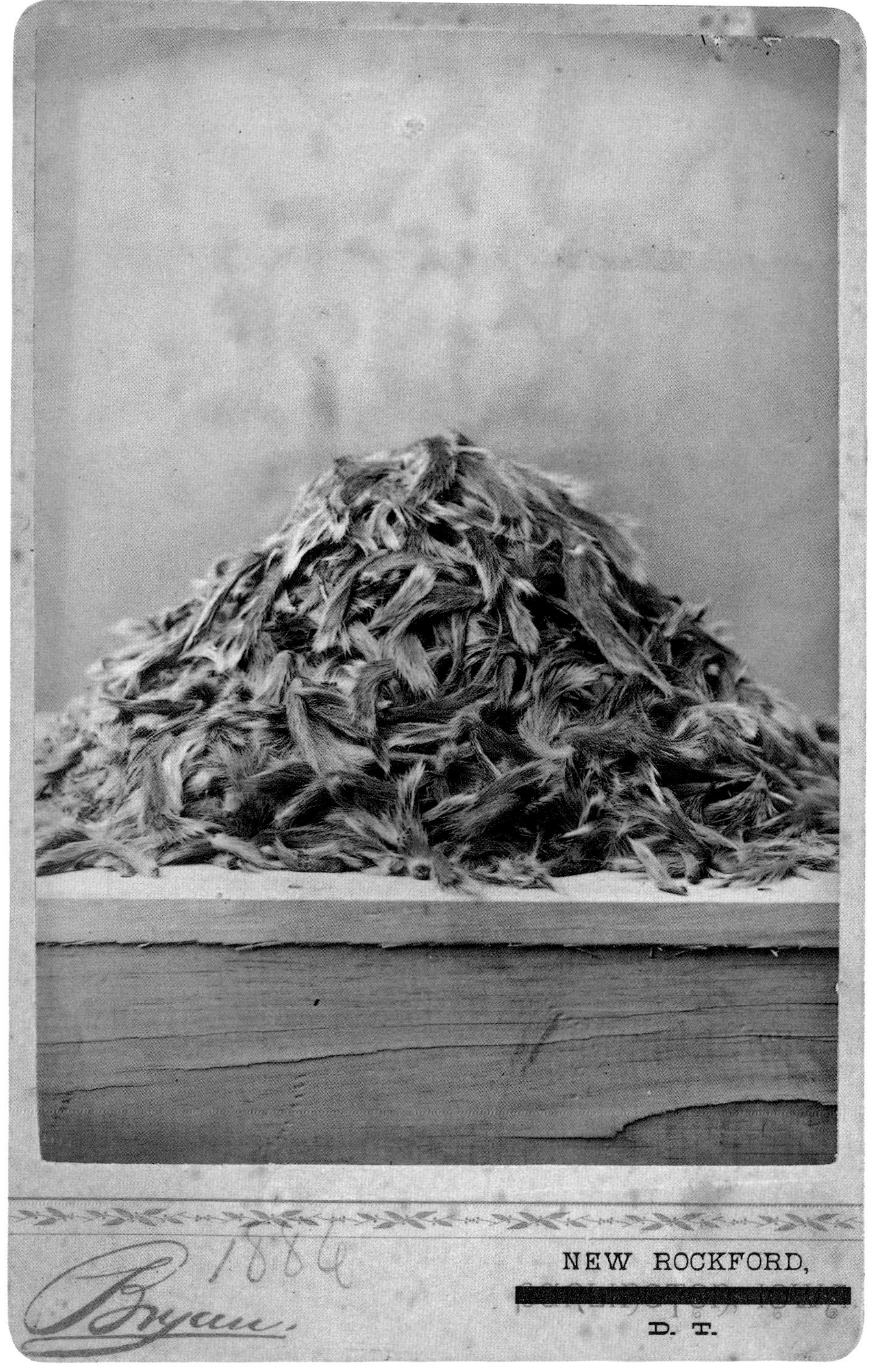

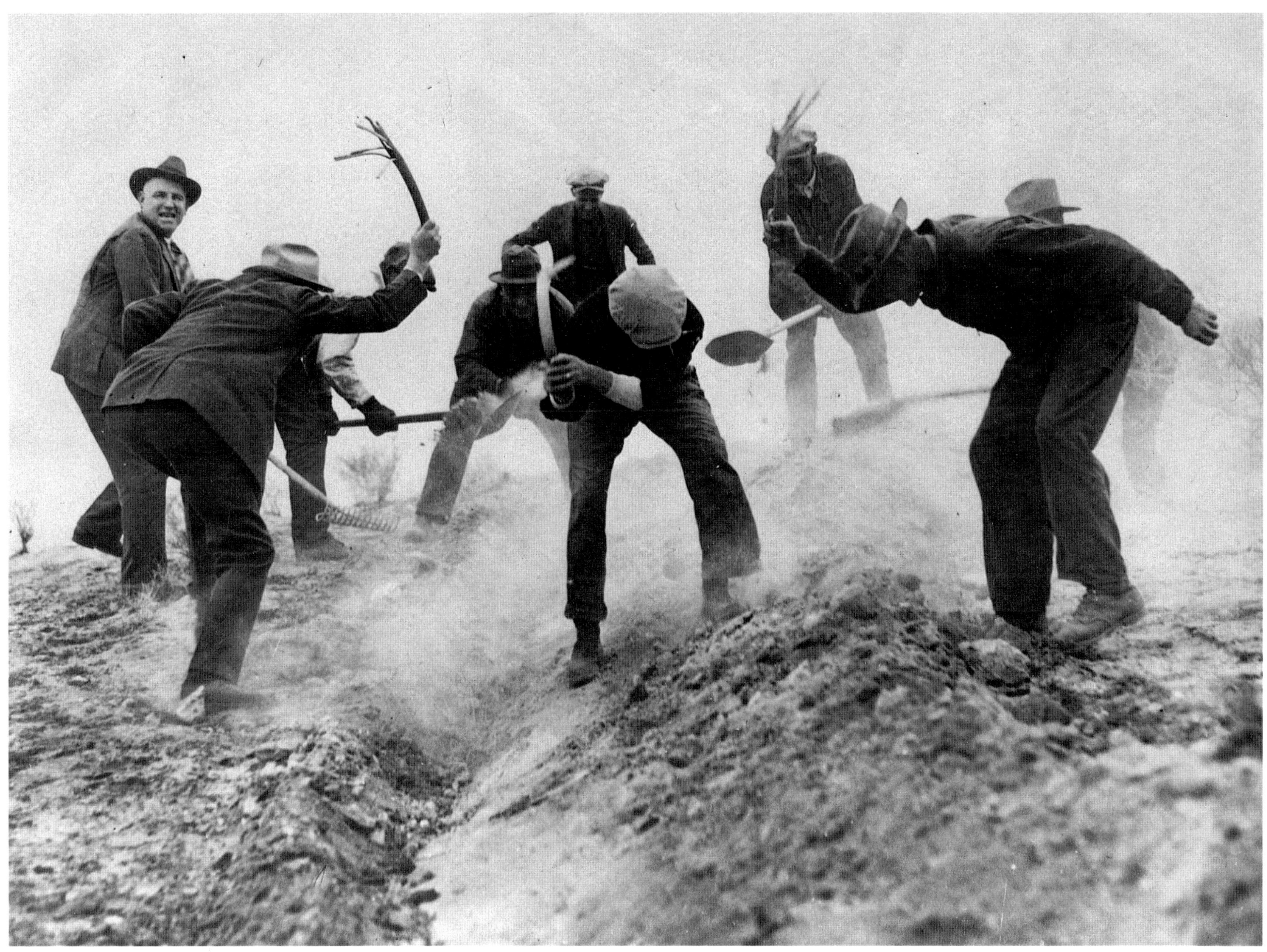

PLATE 53

L. C. McClure
Barley Raised without Irrigation, Skelton Ranch, Woodland Park, Colorado Midland Railway, ca. 1910
gelatin silver print
7⅞ x 9⅞ in. (20 x 24.9 cm)
Denver Public Library, Western History Collection

PLATE 54

Unknown
Moering Bros. Fleet of Steam Oil Burning Holt Combines with steam tractors. Sacramento Valley, 1917
gelatin silver print
15⅜ x 19¼ in. (39.1 x 48.9 cm)
Department of Special Collections, University of California Library, Davis, California

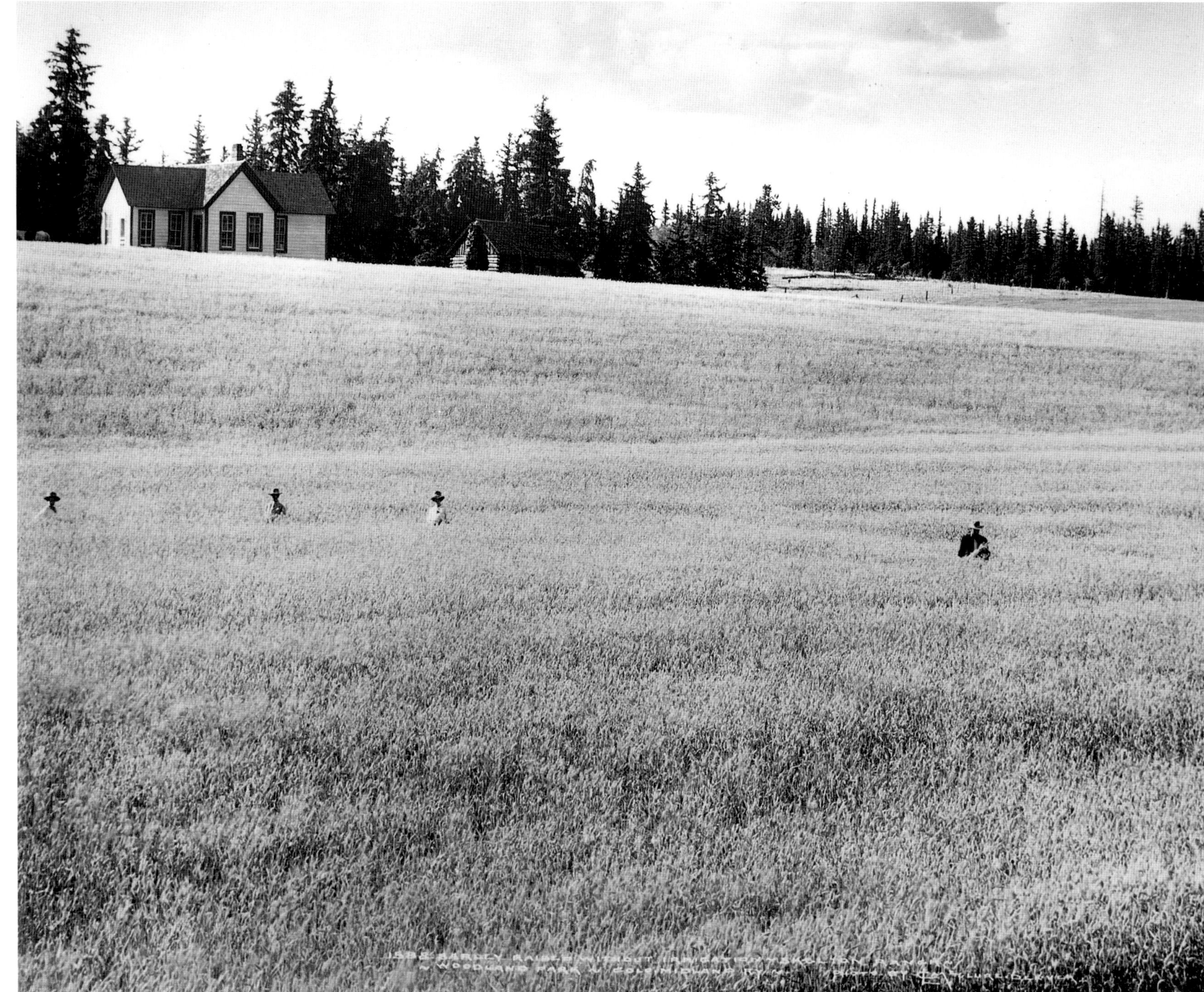

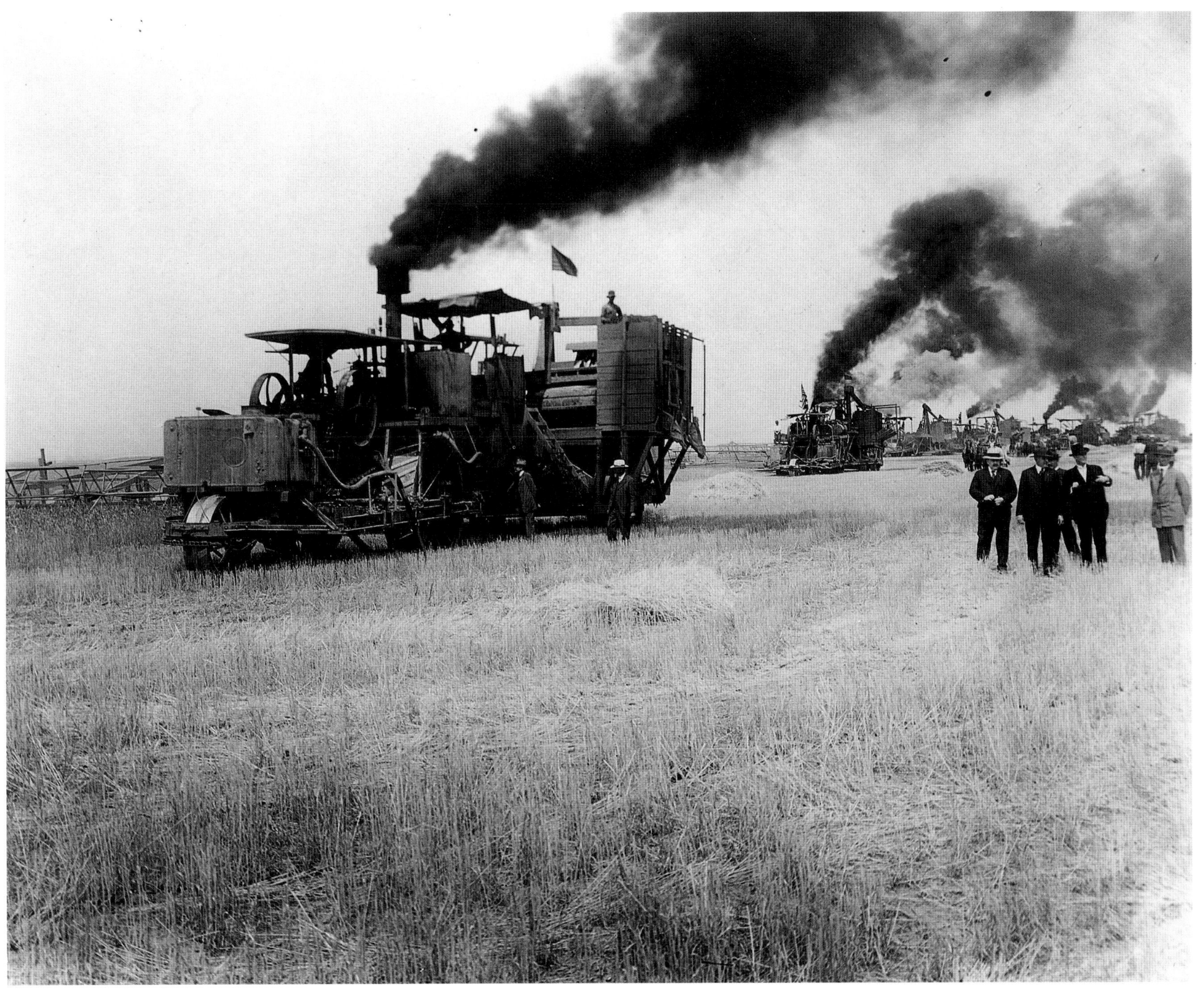

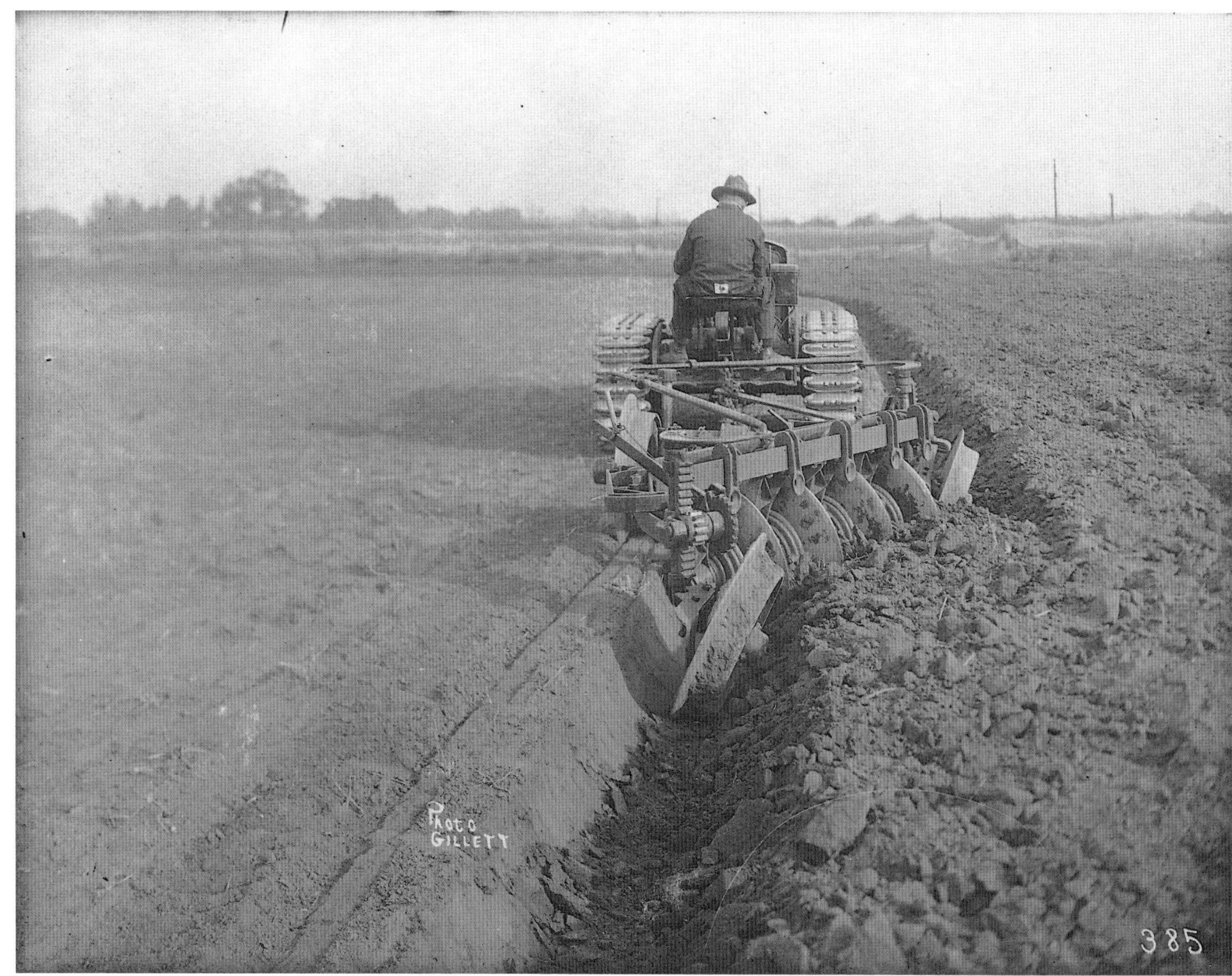

PLATE 55

Unknown [Gillett?]
Untitled photo no. 385 of a Yuba Ball Tread Tractor from a proof book made for the Yuba Manufacturing Company, ca. 1910
cyanotype
7⅝ x 9⅝ in. (19.4 x 24.5 cm)
Department of Special Collections, University of California Library, Davis, California

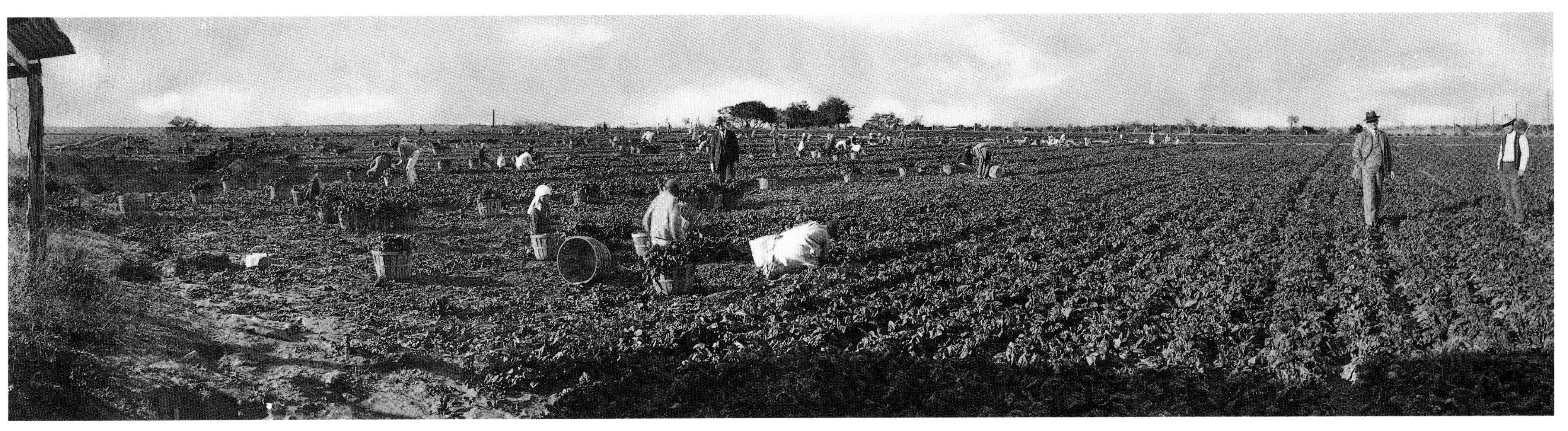

PLATE 56

Harvey and Julius Patteson
Untitled (South Texas), ca. 1920
hand-colored gelatin silver print
8⅝ x 35½ in. (21.8 x 90.2 cm)
Harvey and Julius Patteson
Collection, Harry Ransom
Humanities Research Center,
The University of Texas at
Austin

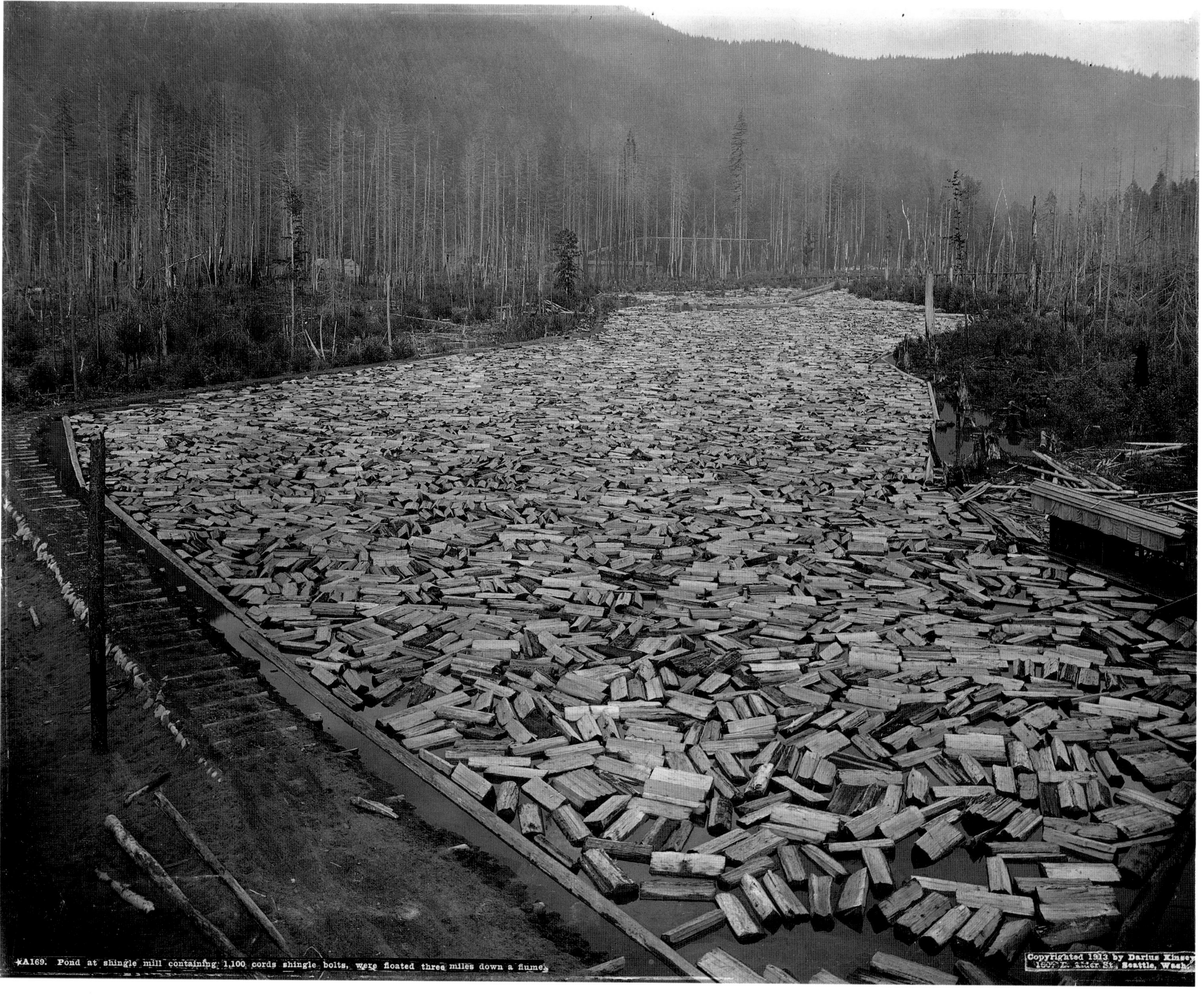
★A169. Pond at shingle mill containing 1,100 cords shingle bolts, were floated three miles down a flume.
Copyrighted 1913 by Darius Kinsey
Seattle, Wash.

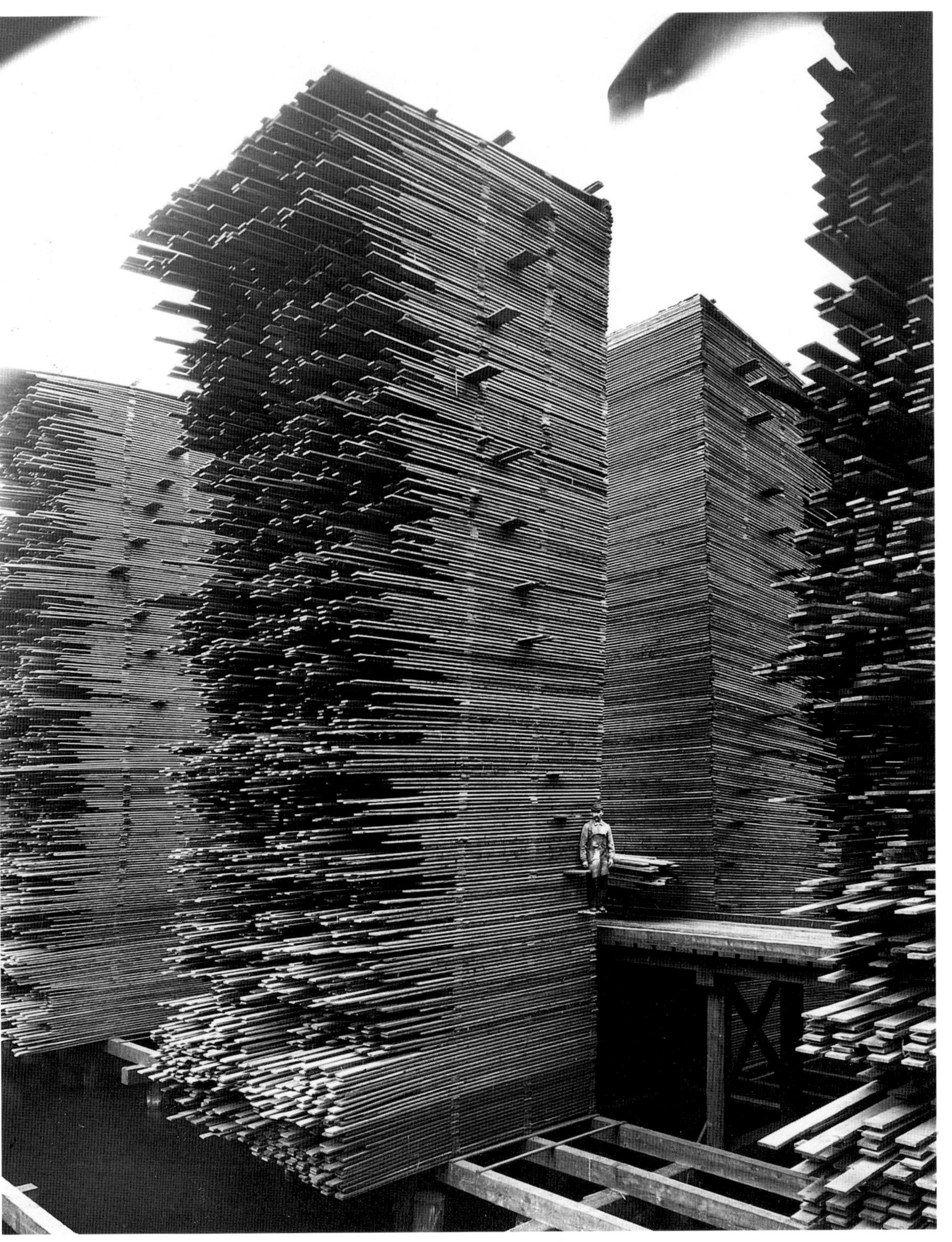

PLATE 57

Darius R. Kinsey
Pond at shingle mill containing 1,100 cords shingle bolts, were floated three miles down a flume, 1913
gelatin silver print
11 x 14 in. (27.9 x 35.6 cm)
D. Kinsey Collection, 10169 (A169), Whatcom Museum of History and Art, Bellingham, Washington

PLATE 58

Webster and Stevens
Seattle Cedar Mill's Drying Stacks, 1919
modern gelatin silver print
10 x 8 in. (25.4 x 20.3 cm)
Collection of the Museum of History and Industry, Seattle

Ballard's largest cedar mill, located just west of the bridge, created an impressive sight with its stacks of lumber over fifty feet high. The cedar was left to air dry for at least nine months before being sold. In May 1958, these stacks kindled a huge fire still vivid in the memories of many Ballard residents.

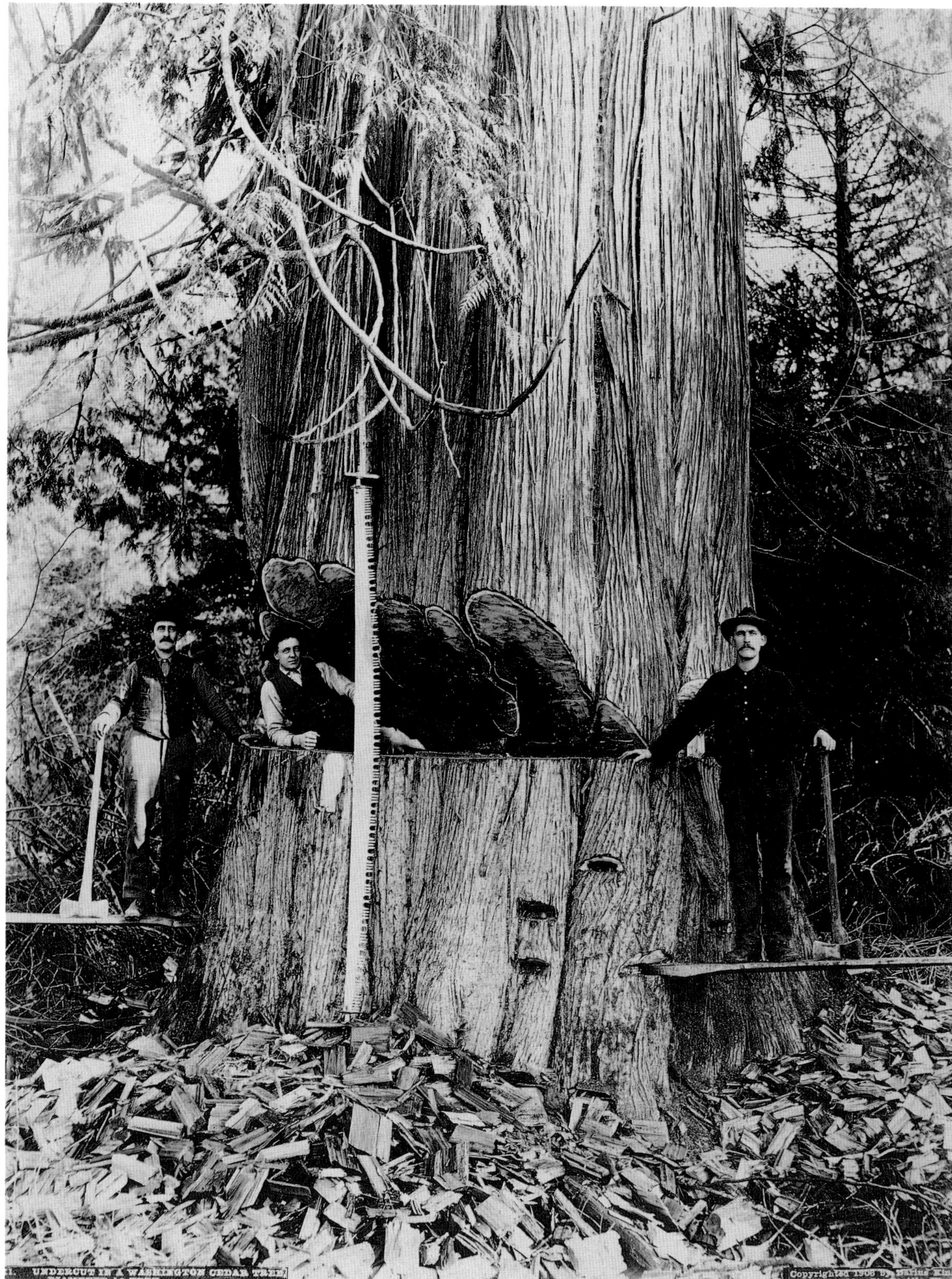

PLATE 59

Darius R. Kinsey
Undercuts in a Washington Cedar Tree, Diameter 16 Feet, from an untitled album, 1906
gelatin silver print
13½ x 10½ in. (34.3 x 26.7 cm)
Collection of the San Francisco Museum of Modern Art

PLATE 60

Bunnell Studio
Untitled (Men with Redwood Planks), ca. 1890
gelatin silver print
8³⁄₁₆ x 13¼ in. (20.8 x 33.7 cm)
Collection of the San Francisco Museum of Modern Art. Purchased through a gift of Sidney Goldstein, 95.115

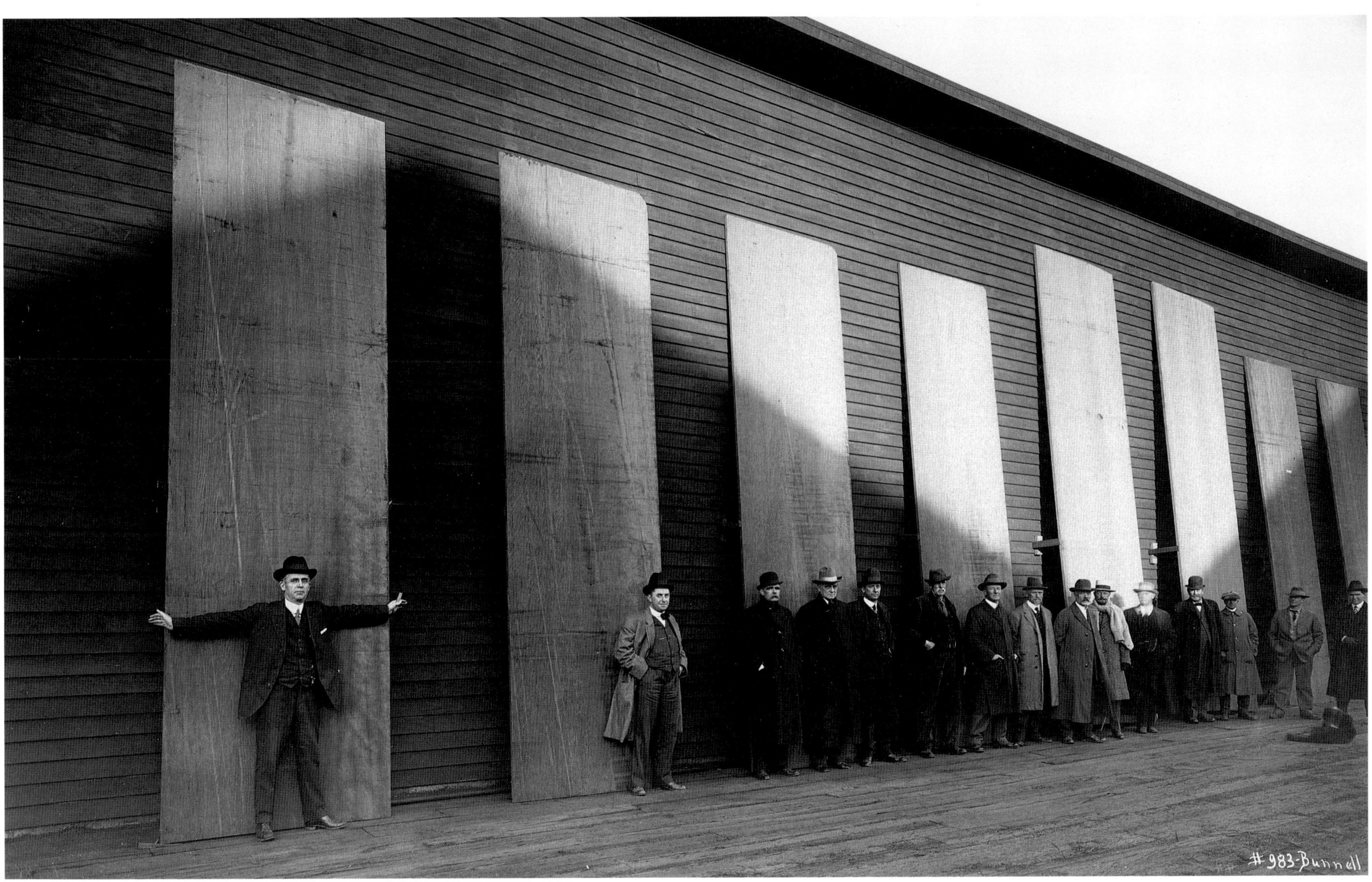
#983-Bunnell

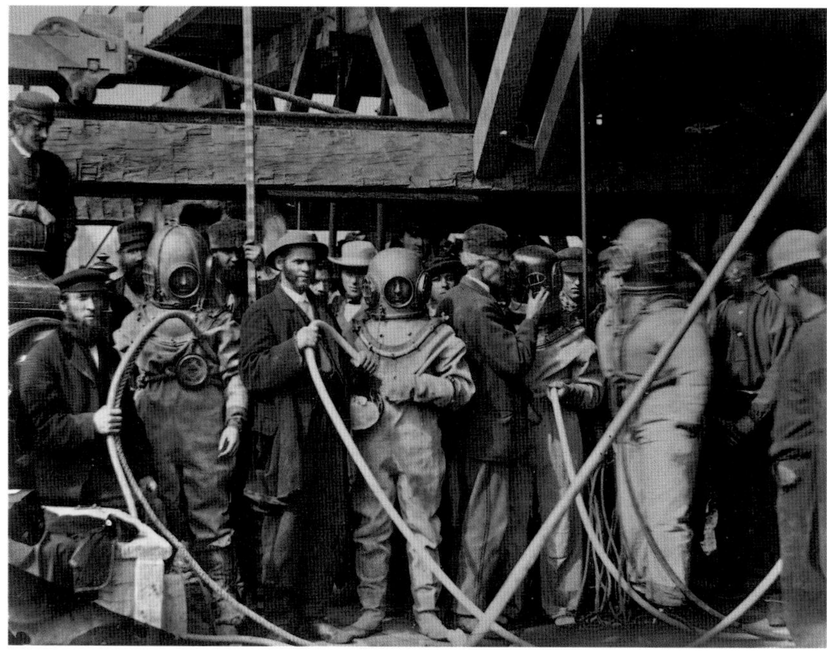

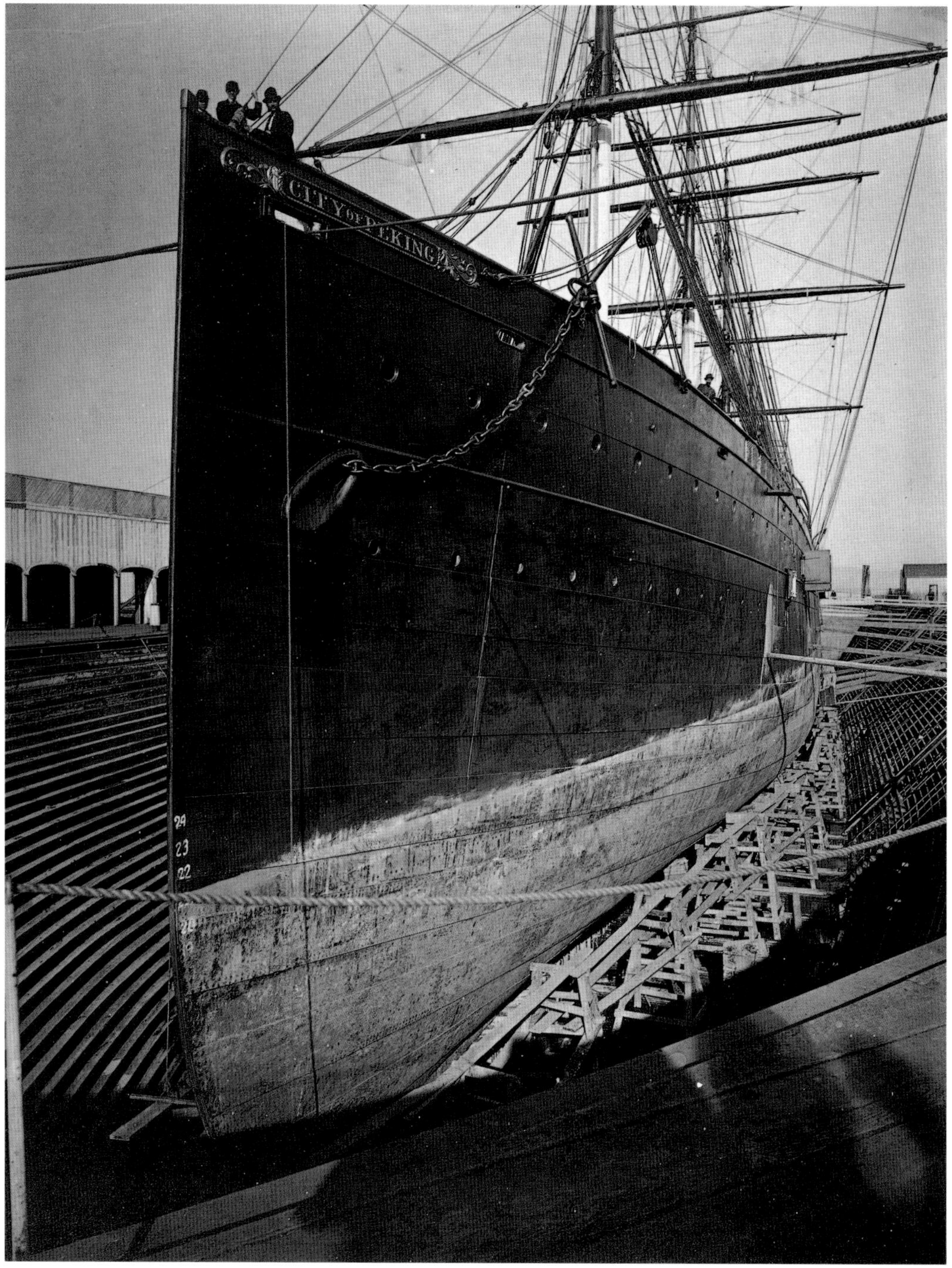

PLATE 61

Thomas Houseworth & Co.
P.M.S.S. Co's. Steamer "City of Peking," ca. 1870
albumen print
20⅜ x 15¾ in. (51.8 x 40 cm)
Collection of the California State Library, Sacramento

"In the California Dry Dock at Hunters' Point. Length 423 feet, Breadth 45 feet, Depth 38 feet, Total Capacity 5,500 Tons."

PLATE 62

J. P. Babbitt
Divers at Pier No. 4, March 2, 1869, from the book *The Kansas City Bridge, with an Account of the Regimen of the Missouri River, and a Description of Methods Used for Founding in that River,* 1870
7 x 9 in. (17.7 x 22.9 cm)
Collection of the DeGolyer Library, Southern Methodist University, 95.1 1248

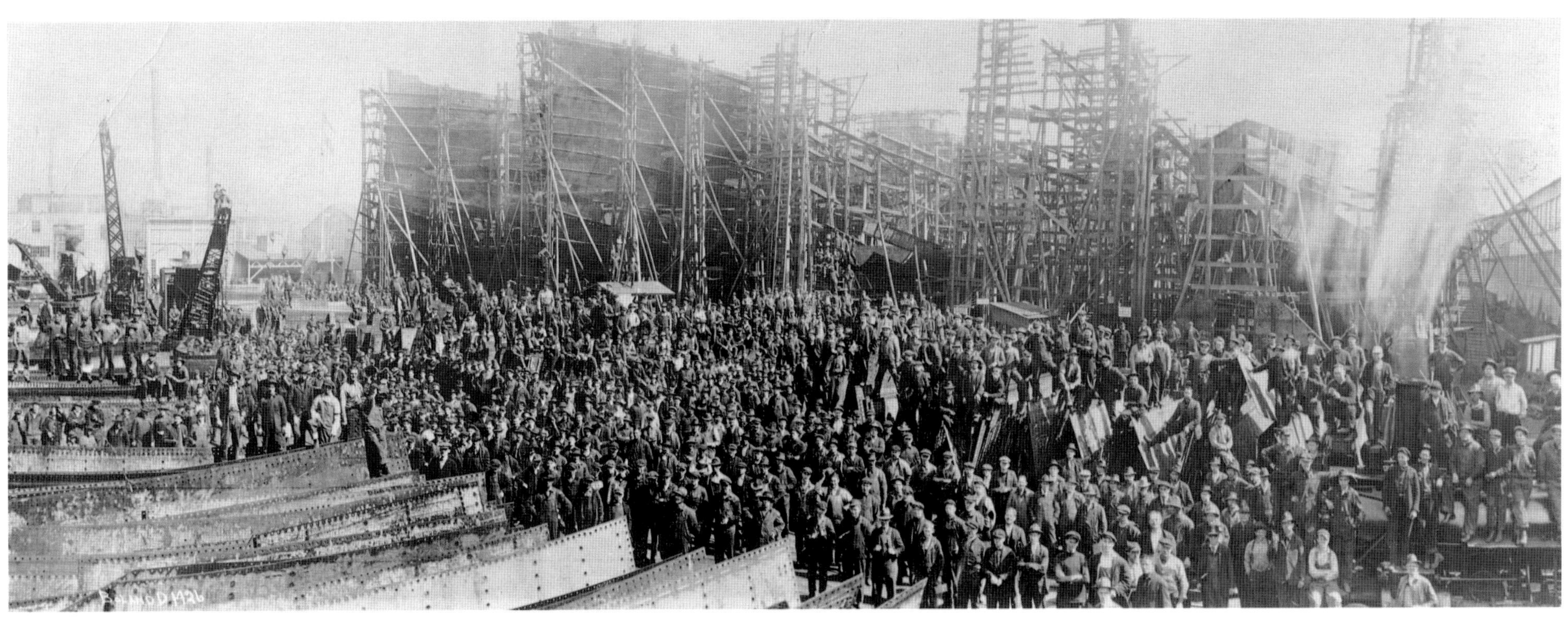

PLATE 63

M. D. Boland
Untitled (J. F. Duthie & Company Shipyard, Seattle), ca. 1918
gelatin silver print
7⅛ x 18⅞ (18 x 48 cm)
Collection of the Museum of History and Industry, Seattle, 94.31.1

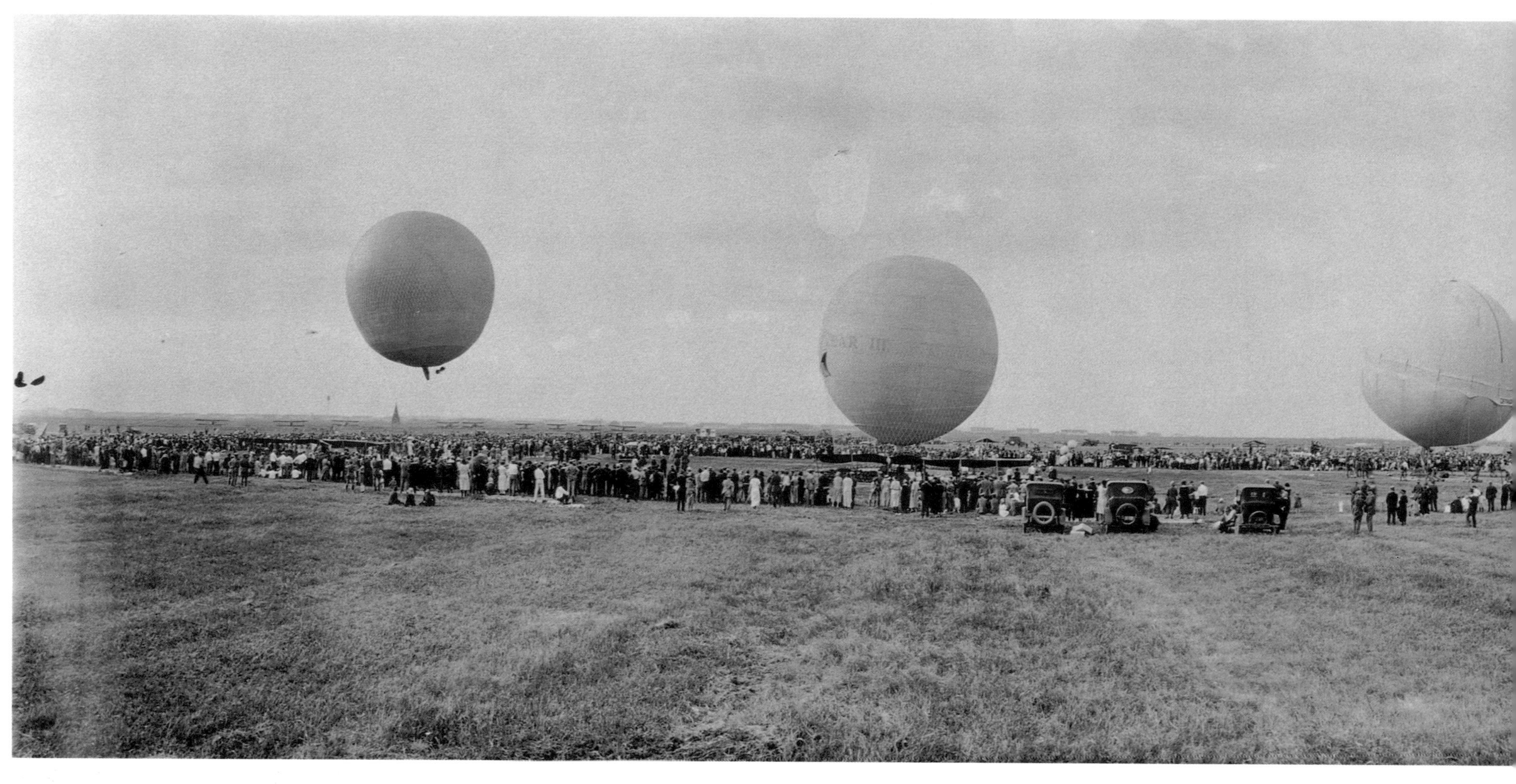

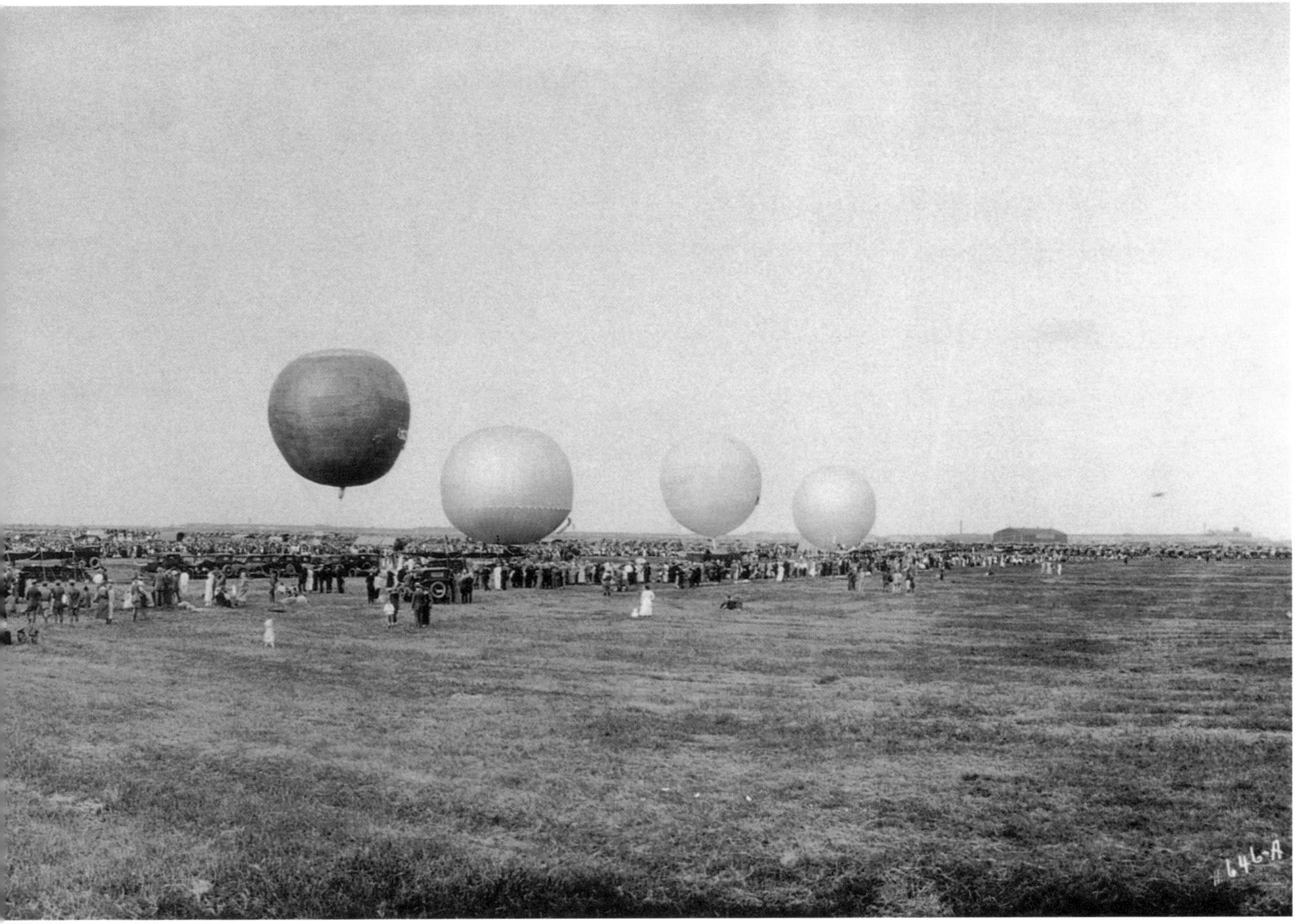

PLATE 64

Eugene O. Goldbeck
National Balloon Race, April 23, 1924, 1924
modern gelatin silver print on printing out paper
$9\frac{3}{4}$ x $35\frac{1}{4}$ in. (23.8 x 89.54 cm)
Photography Collection, Harry Ransom Humanities Research Center, The University of Texas at Austin

PLATE 65

Unknown
First Airplane that Landed in Denver, 1910
gelatin silver print
$4\frac{7}{16}$ x $3\frac{7}{16}$ in. (11.3 x 8.7 cm)
Denver Public Library, Western History Collection

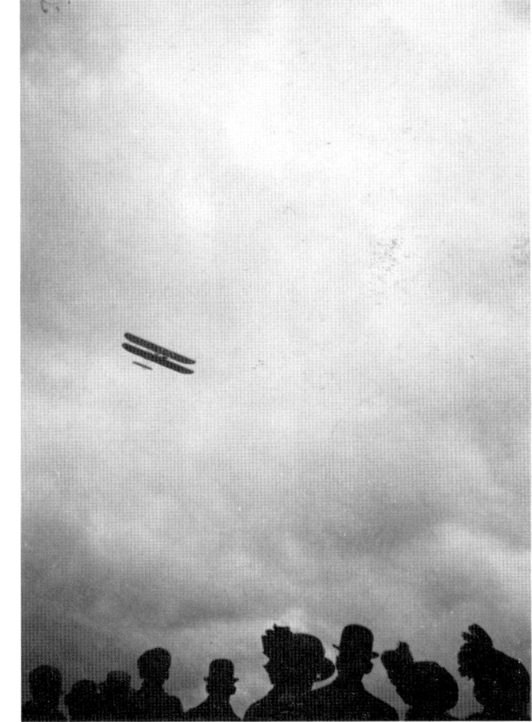

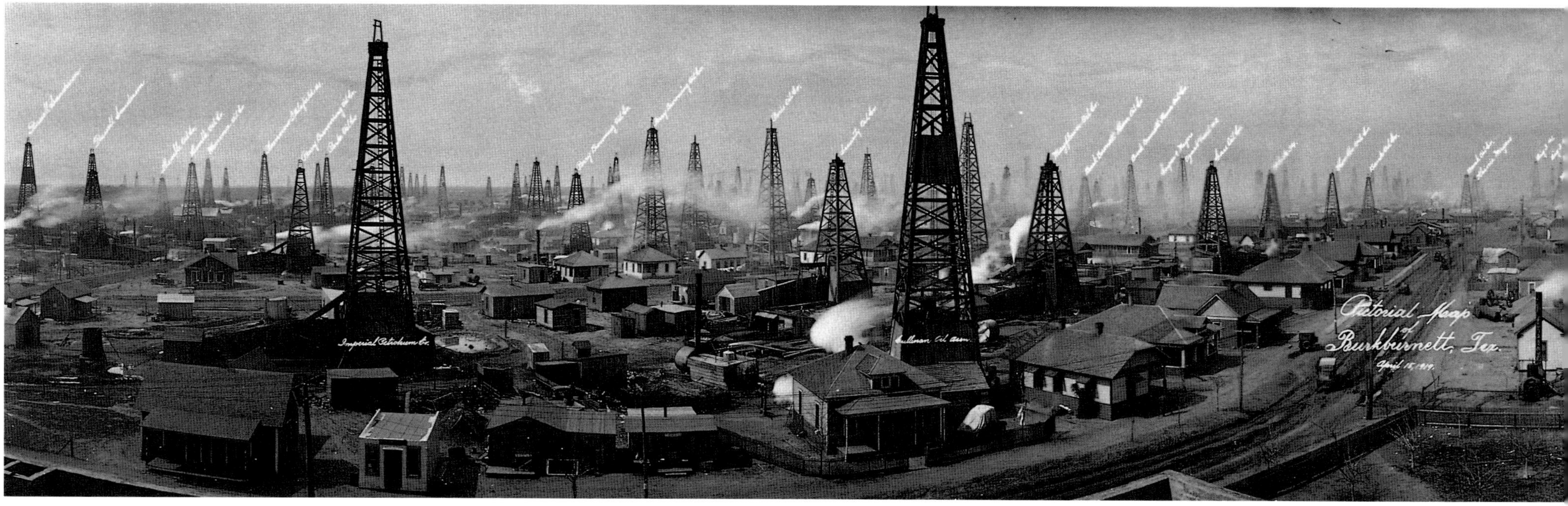

Imperial Petroleum Co.

Bullman Oil Assn.

Pictorial Map
of
Burkburnett, Tex.
April 15, 1919.

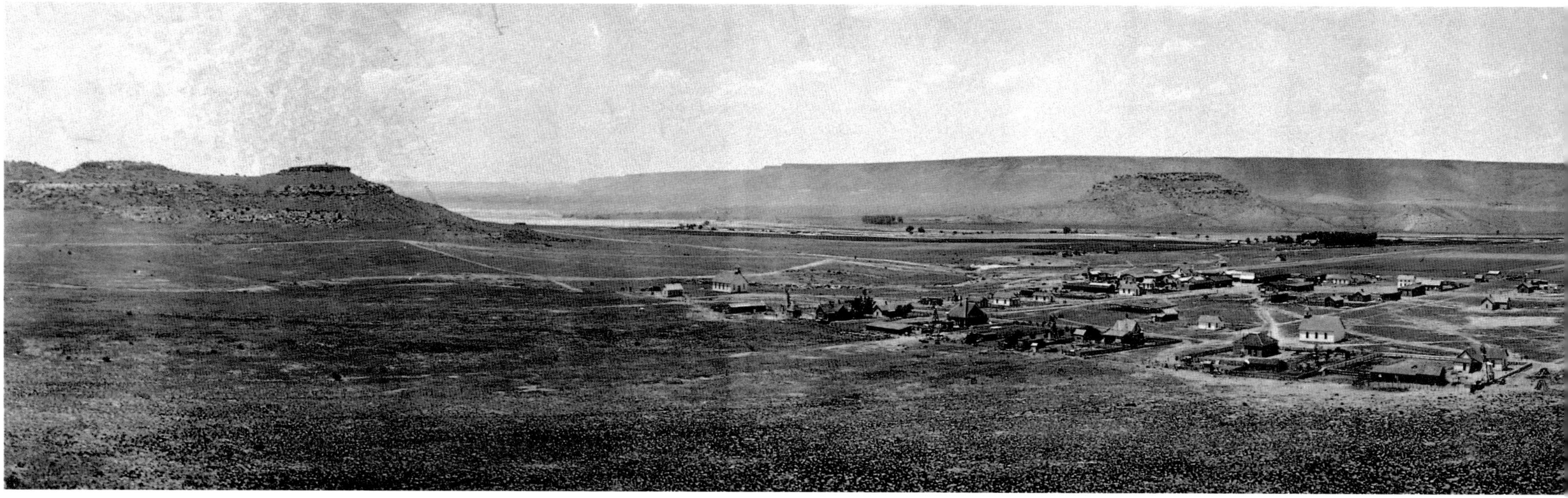

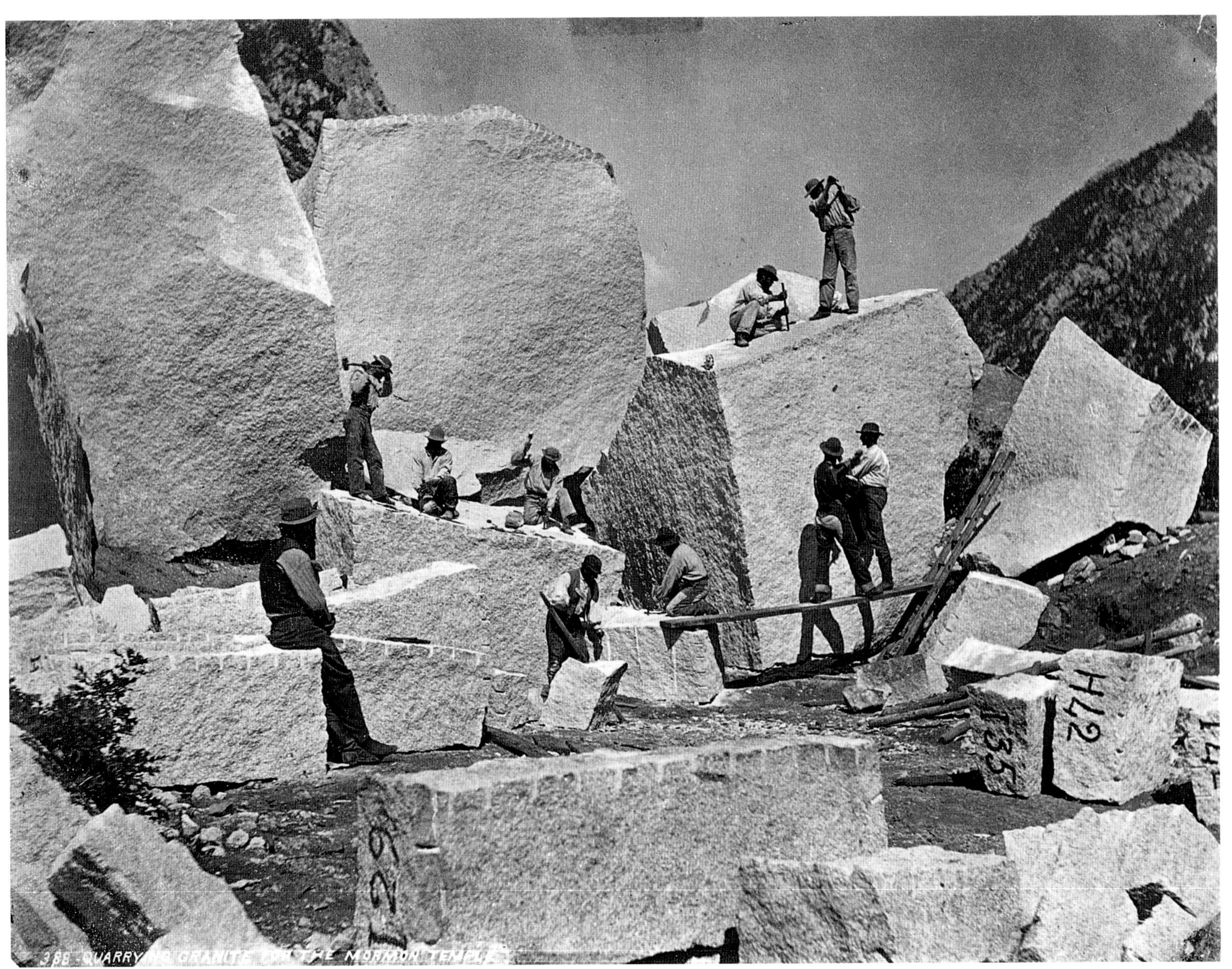

PLATE 74

Charles Roscoe Savage (printed by William Henry Jackson)
Quarrying Granite for the Mormon Temple, Little Cottonwood Cañon, Utah,
ca. 1870
albumen print
6½ x 8⅞ (16.5 x 22.5 cm)
Monsen Collection

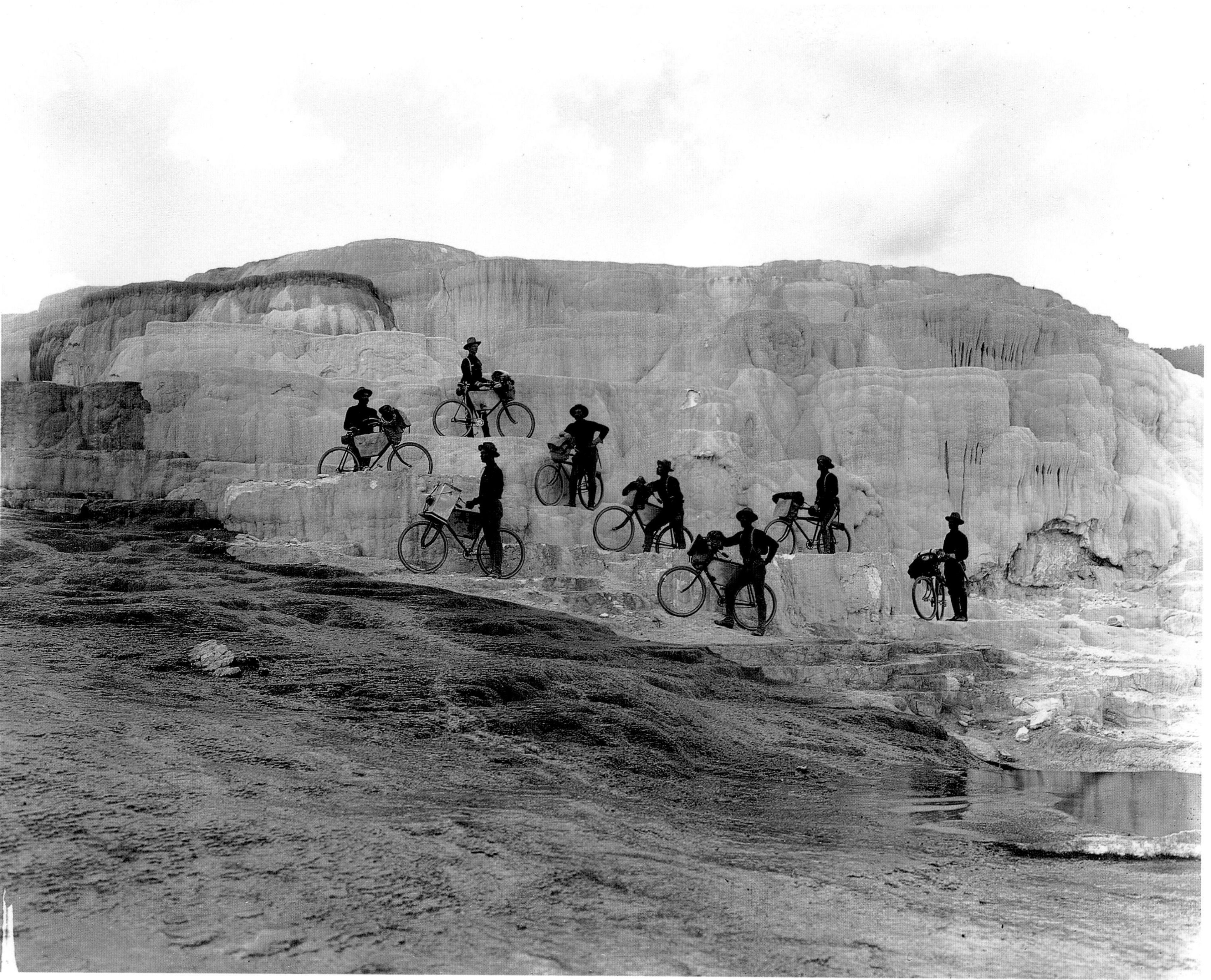

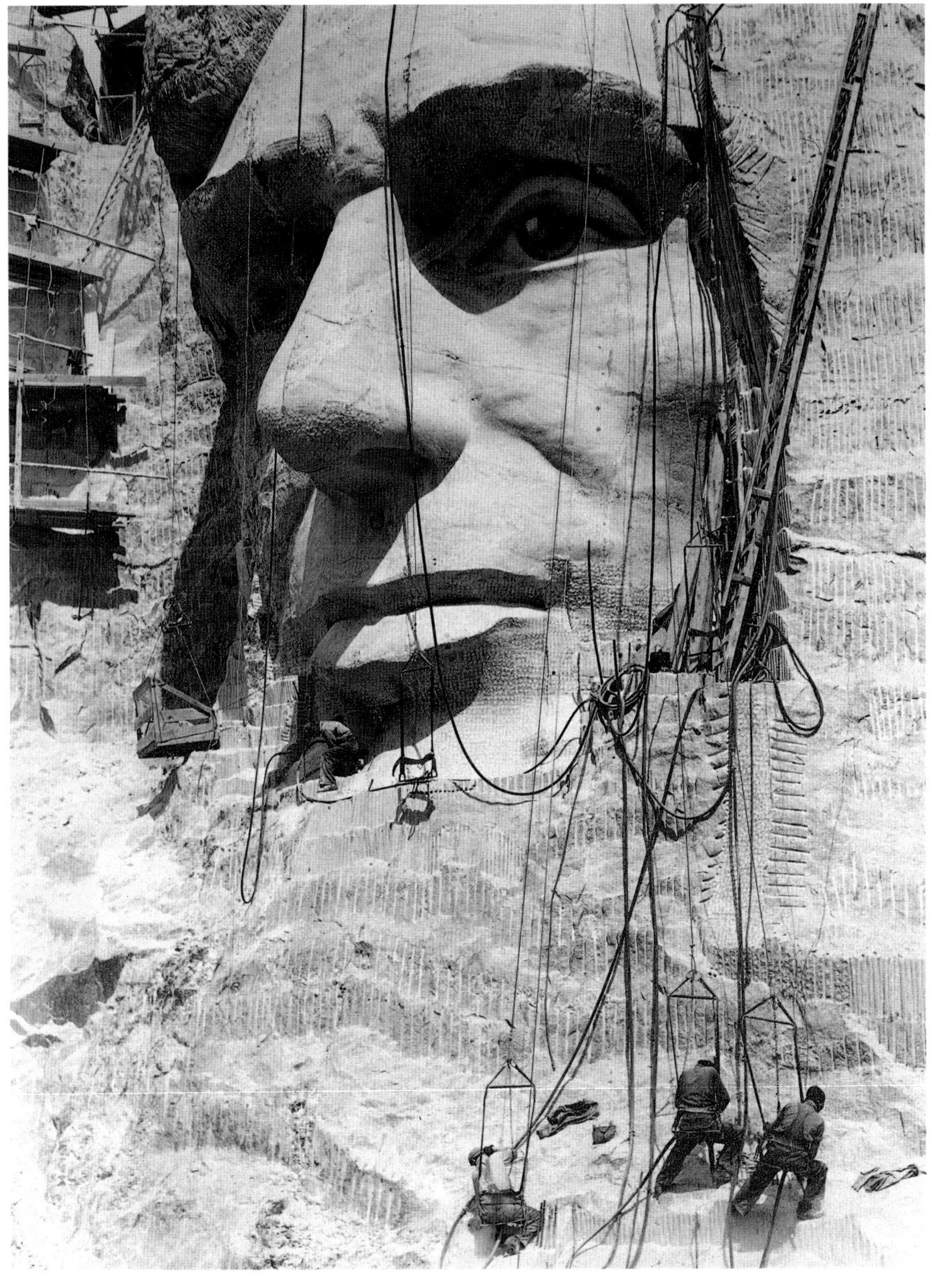

PLATE 75

Frank Jay Haynes

Bicyclist's Group on Minerva Terrace, Yellowstone Park, October 7, 1896, 1896

modern gelatin silver print on printing out paper

8 x 10 in. (20.3 x 25.4 cm)

Collection of the Montana Historical Society, Helena

Lt. James A. Moss and his company of the 25th Infantry, U.S. Army Bicycle Corps, posed on the terraces during a trip through the park.

PLATE 76

Alfred Palmer

Mt. Rushmore, President Lincoln, 1938

gelatin silver print

13½ x 10⅜ in. (34.3 x 26.4 cm)

Collection of the San Francisco Museum of Modern Art. Accessions Committee Fund, 93.72

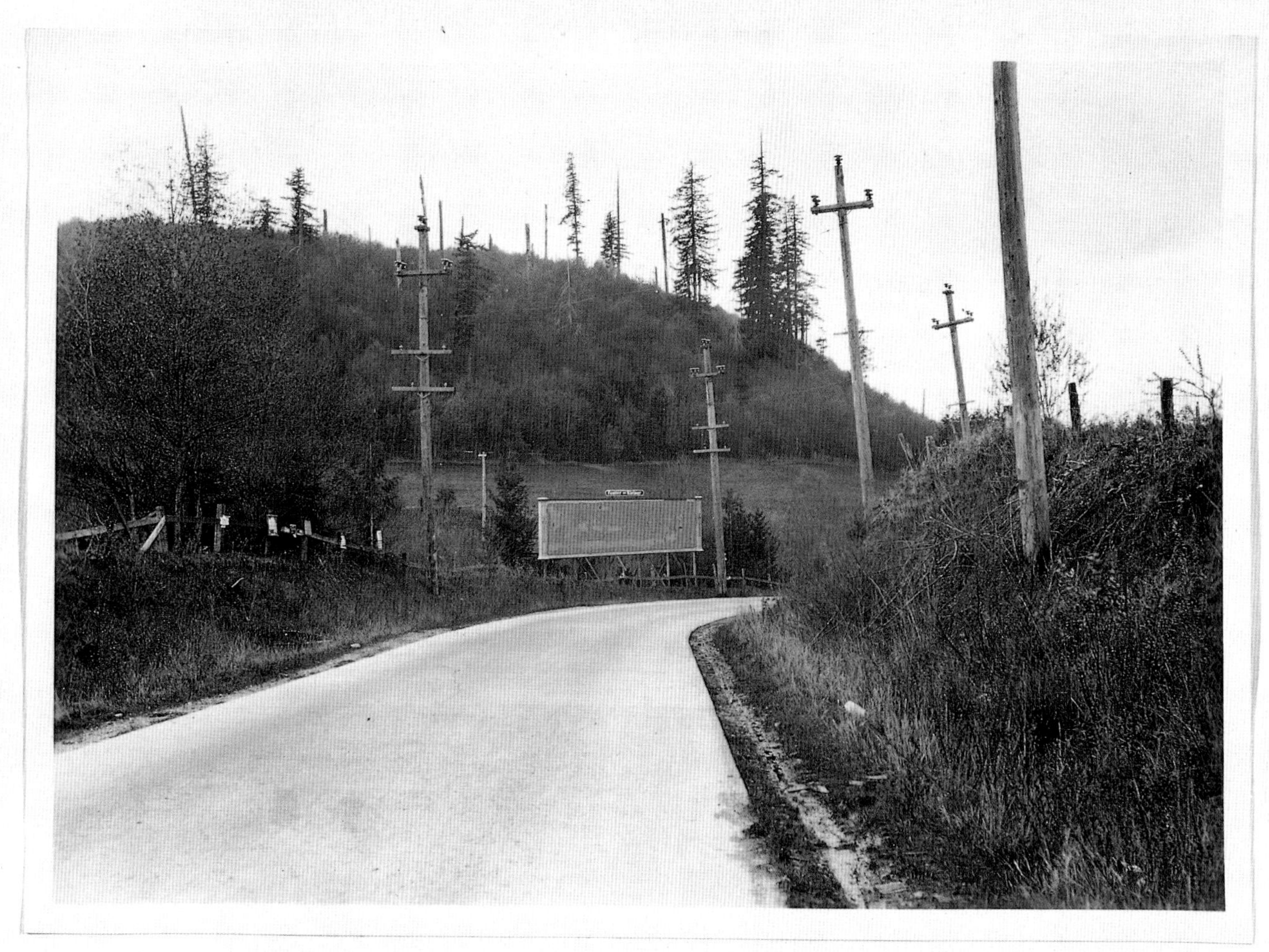

Foster Road

1/10 Mi. West of Jenne Road

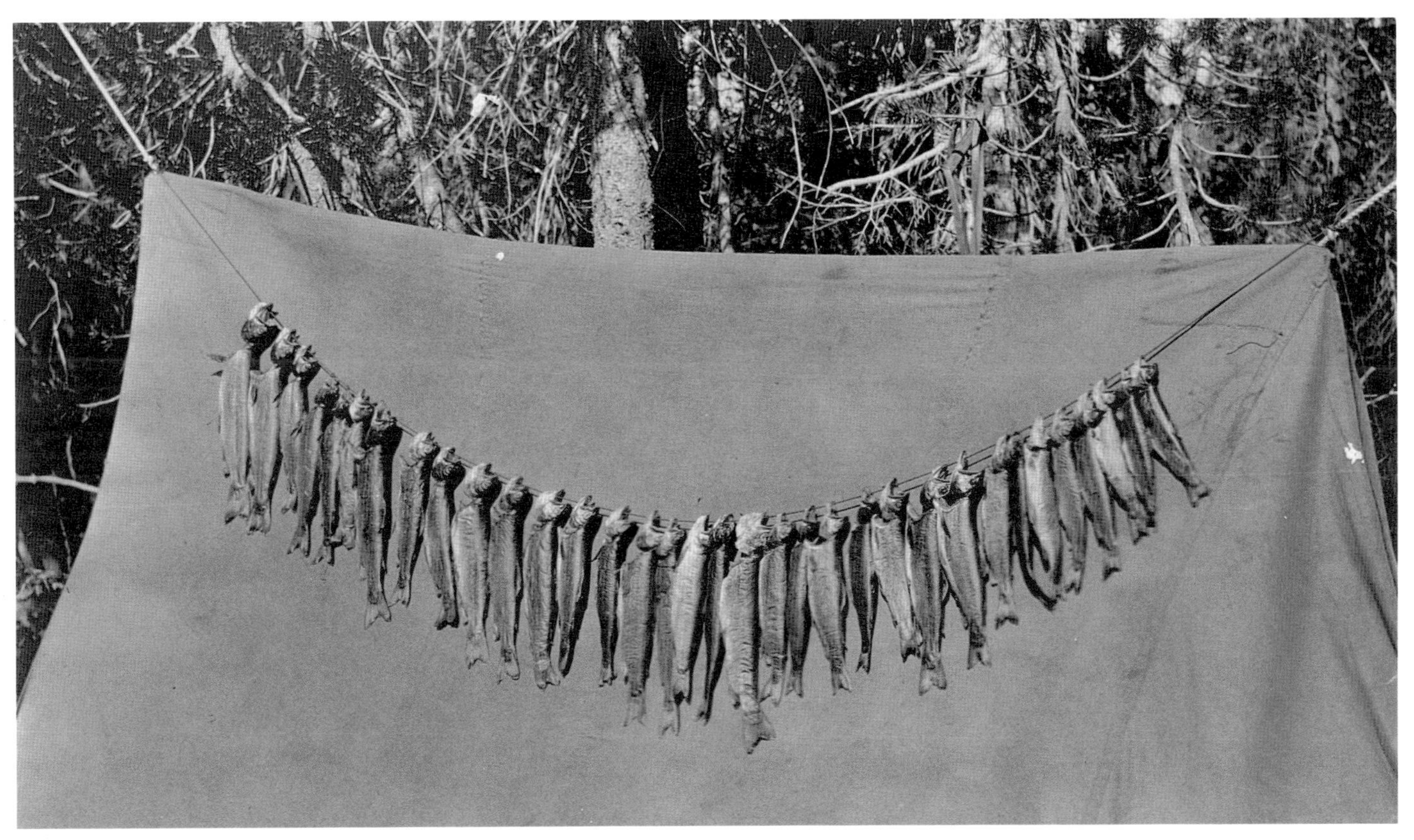

PLATE 77

Unknown
Foster Road, 1/10 Mi. West of Jenne Road, from an untitled album of Foster and Kleiser billboards, ca. 1920
water-based paint on gelatin silver print on paper
8 x 11 in. (20.3 x 27.9 cm)
Stephen White Collection II

PLATE 78

Unknown
A String of Fish, ca. 1910
gelatin silver print postcard
3⅝ x 5¾ in. (9.2 x 14.6 cm)
Collection of the San Francisco Museum of Modern Art.
Members of Foto Forum, 95.422

State Route Signs

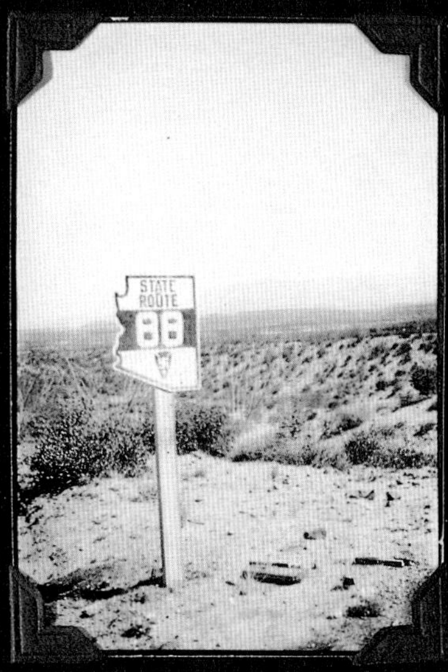

Arizona

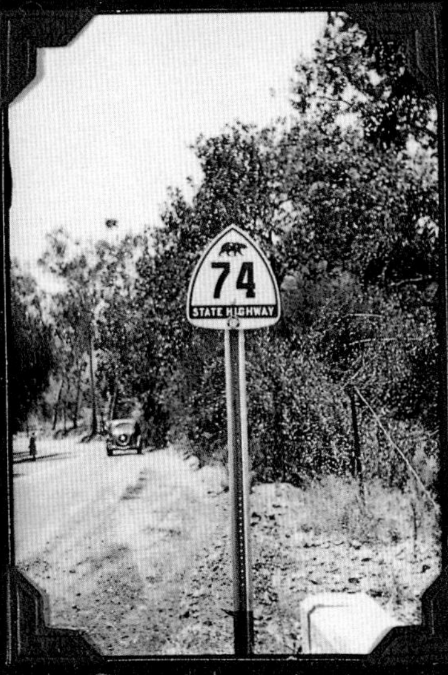

California

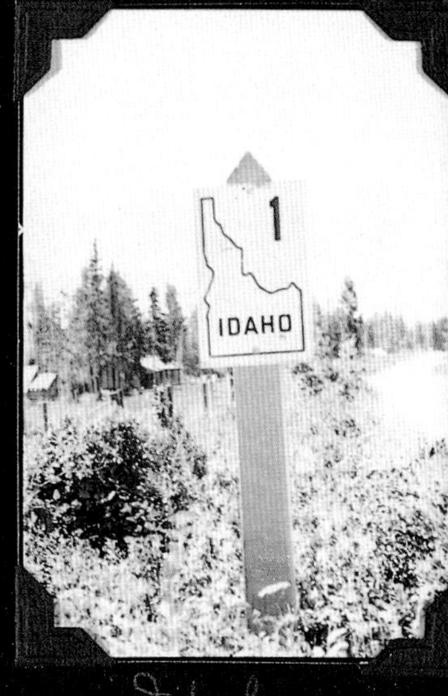

Idaho

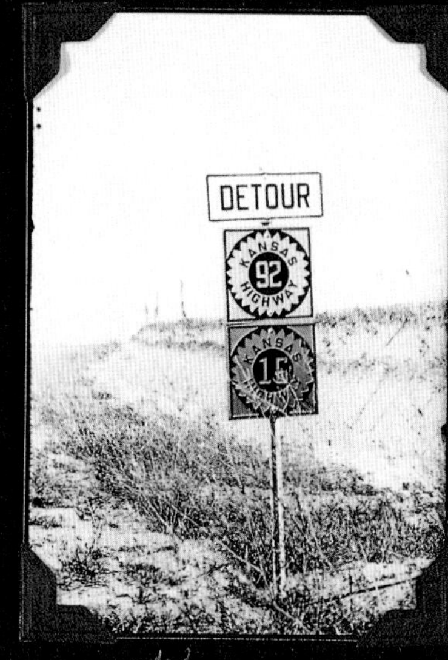

Kansas

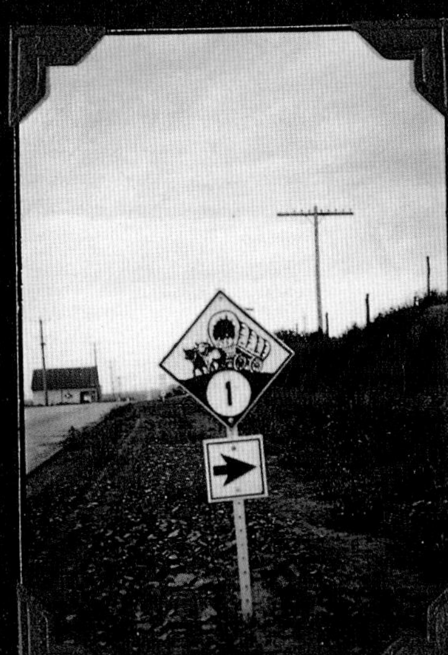

Nebraska

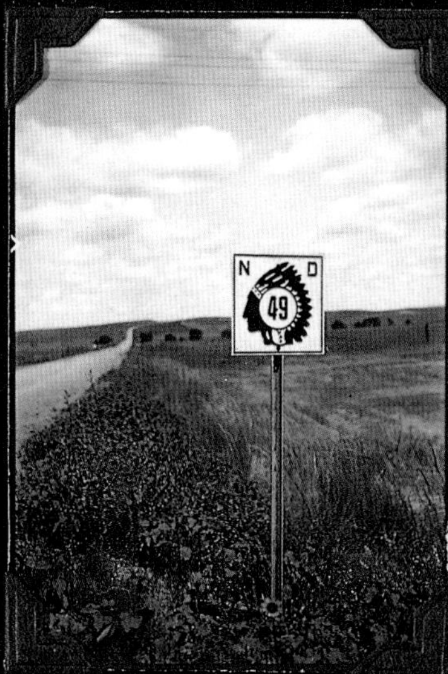

North Dakota

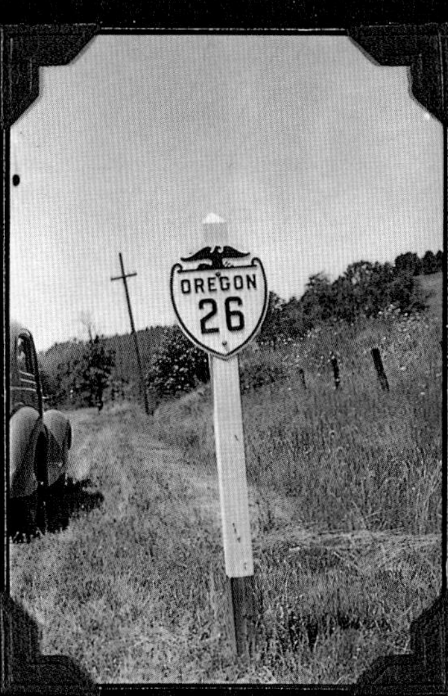

Oregon

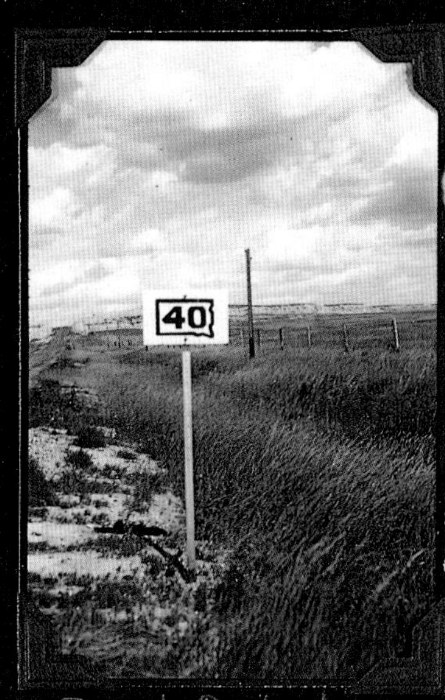

South Dakota

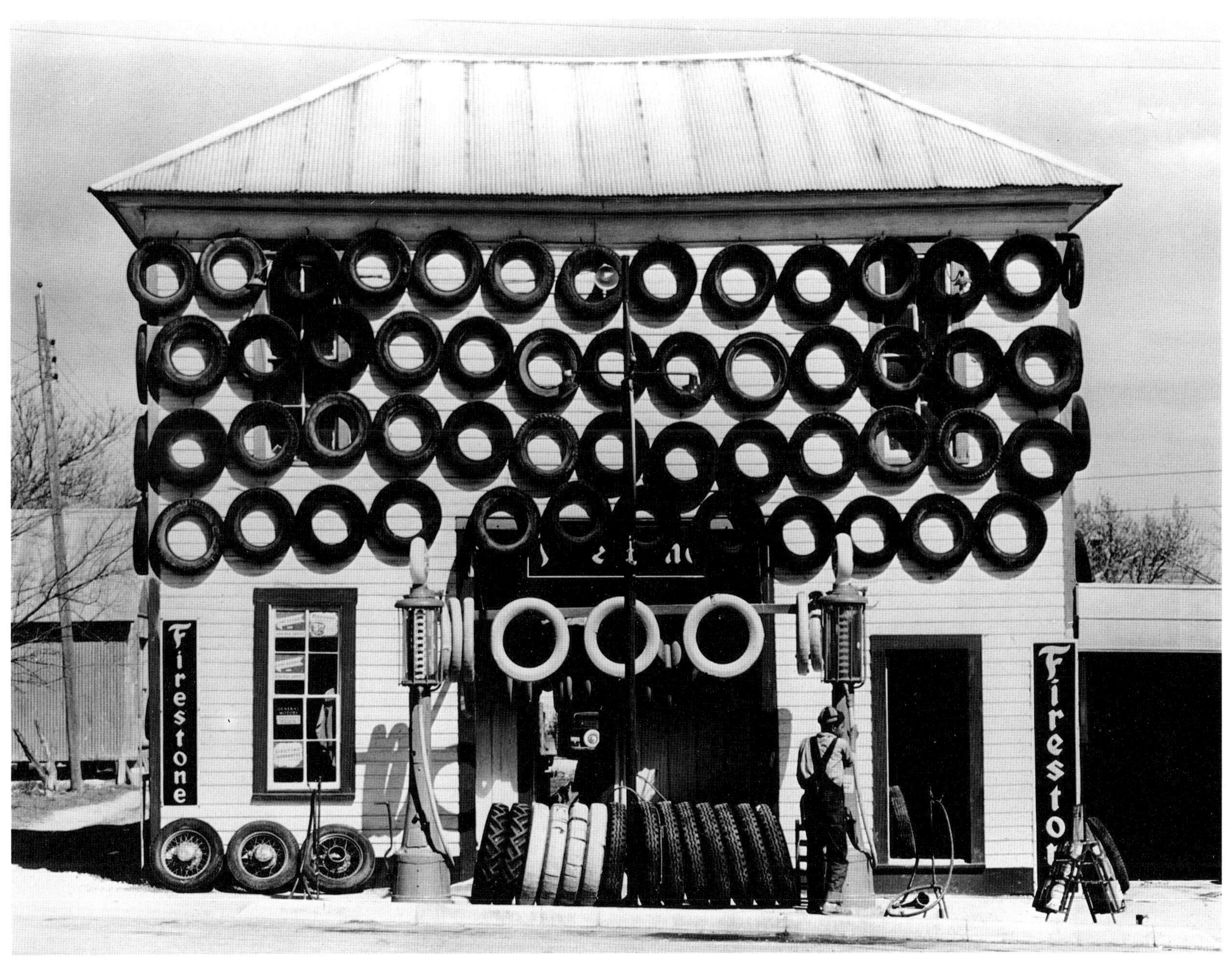

PLATE 79

Unknown
State Route Signs, from an untitled album, ca. 1930
gelatin silver prints on black paper
3½ x 2¼ in. (8.9 x 5.7 cm) each
Collection of Gordon L. Bennett

PLATE 80

Russell Lee
San Marcos, Texas, 1940
modern gelatin silver print
8 x 10 in. (20.3 x 25.4 cm)
Collection of the Museum of Fine Arts, Museum of New Mexico, Pinewood Collection of FSA Photography, 1990

PLATE 81

Unknown
Truckee Canal Chute, Churchill County, Nevada, 1911
gelatin silver print
$4\frac{3}{4}$ x $6\frac{1}{8}$ in. (12.1 x 15.6 cm)
Collection of the Nevada Historical Society, Reno

PLATE 82

Darius R. Kinsey
Diablo Dam, ca. 1912
toned gelatin silver print
$19\frac{3}{4}$ x 26 in. (50.2 x 66 cm)
Collection of the San Francisco Museum of Modern Art. Purchased through a gift of Marsha Smollens, 95.401

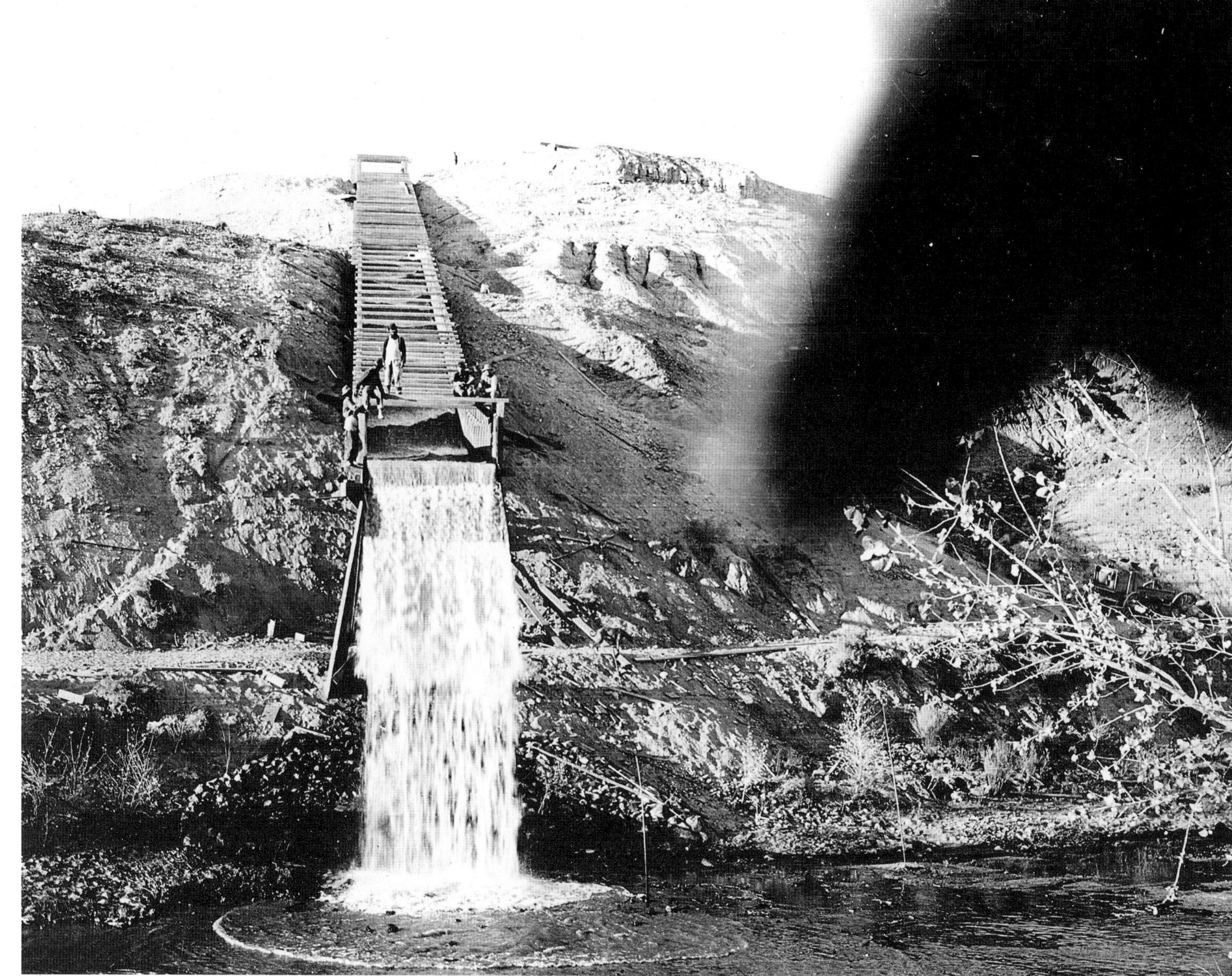

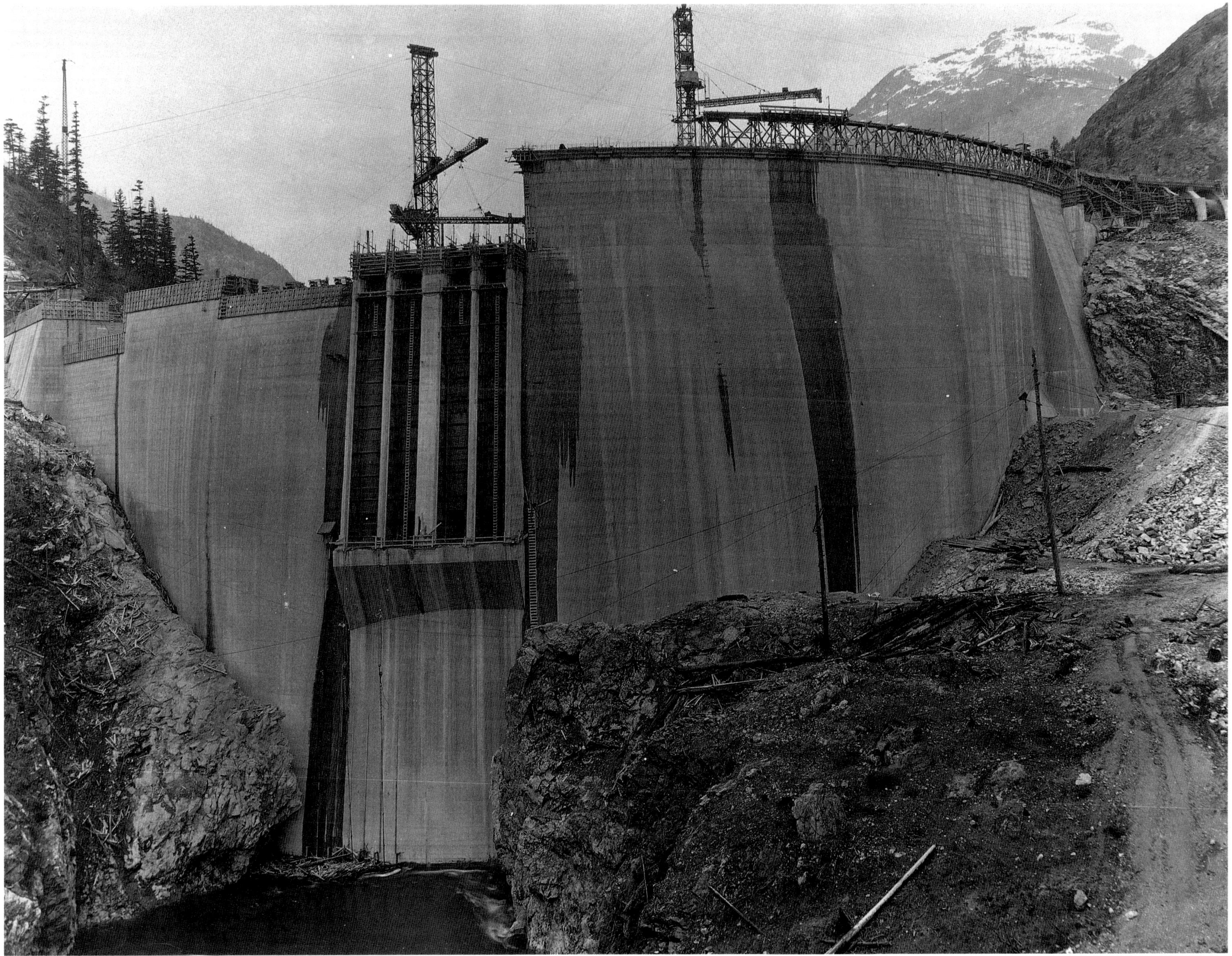

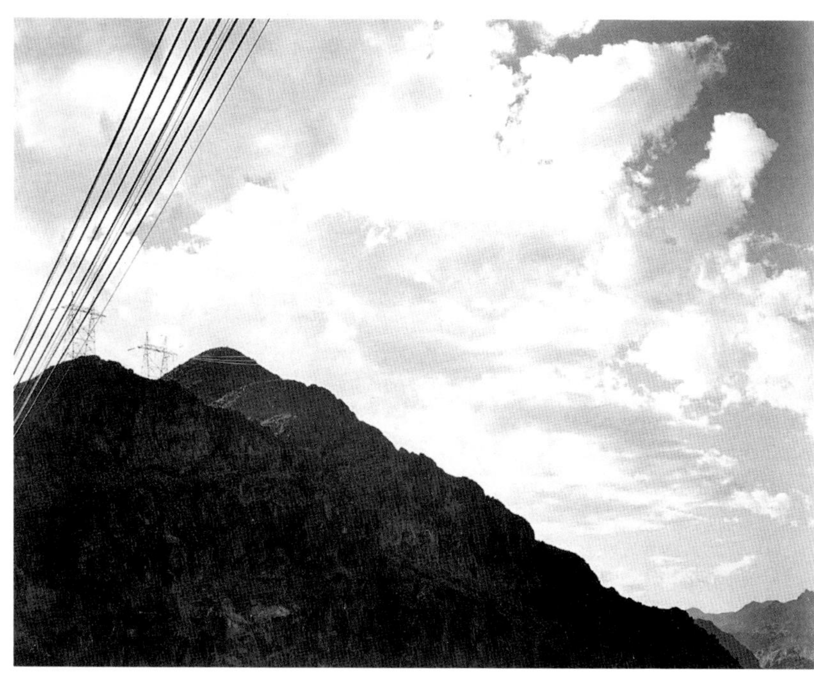

PLATE 83

Ansel Adams
Boulder Dam, 1941. Looking Toward Transmission Lines on Mountains, Clouded Sky, 1941
gelatin silver print
2¾ x 4⅞ in. (7 x 12.4 cm)
Collection of the Nevada Historical Society, Reno

PLATE 84

Unknown
All Valves Open, Boulder Dam; Taken from Nevada Power House, 1936
gelatin silver print
2¾ x 4⅞ in. (7 x 12.4 cm)
Collection of the Nevada Historical Society, Reno

OPPOSITE PAGE:
PLATE 85

Herm Wilson
Boulder Dam During Construction, 1930s
gelatin silver print
7¾ x 9½ in. (19.7 x 24.1 cm)
Collection of the Nevada Historical Society, Reno

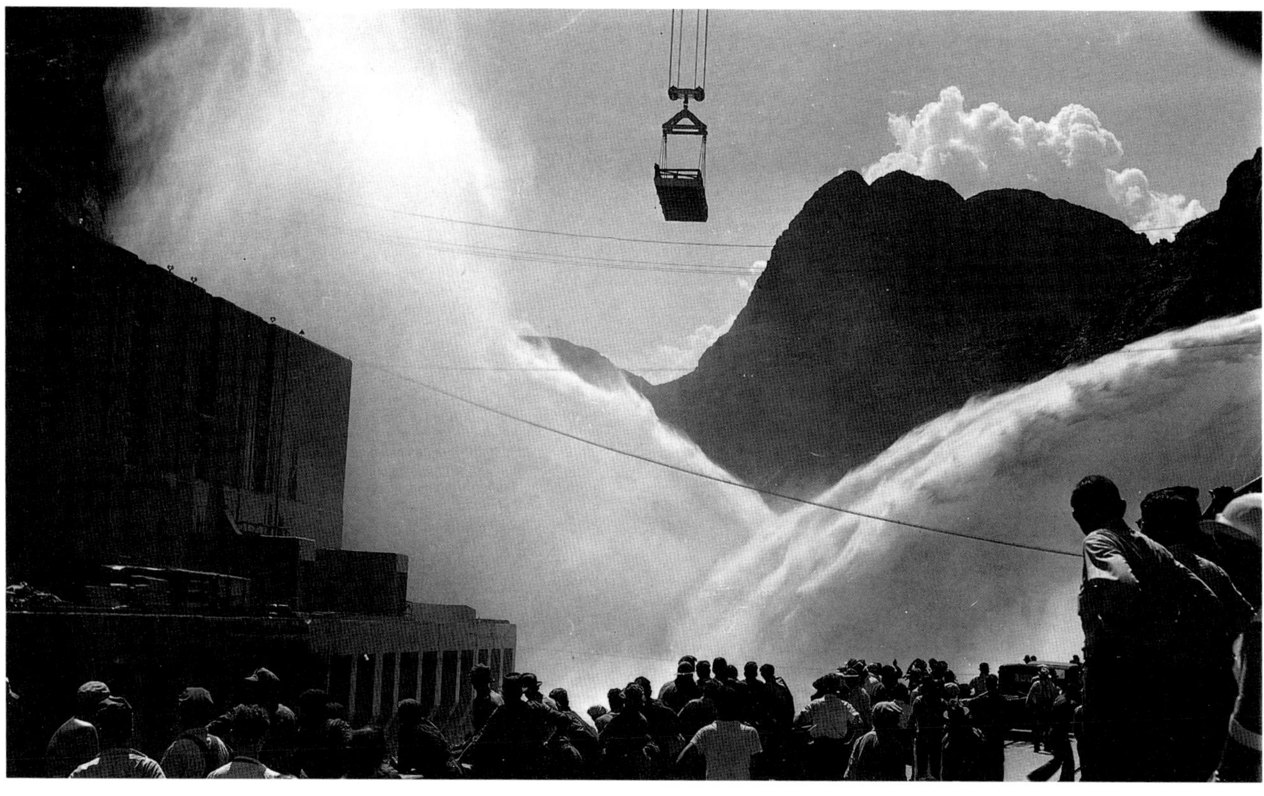

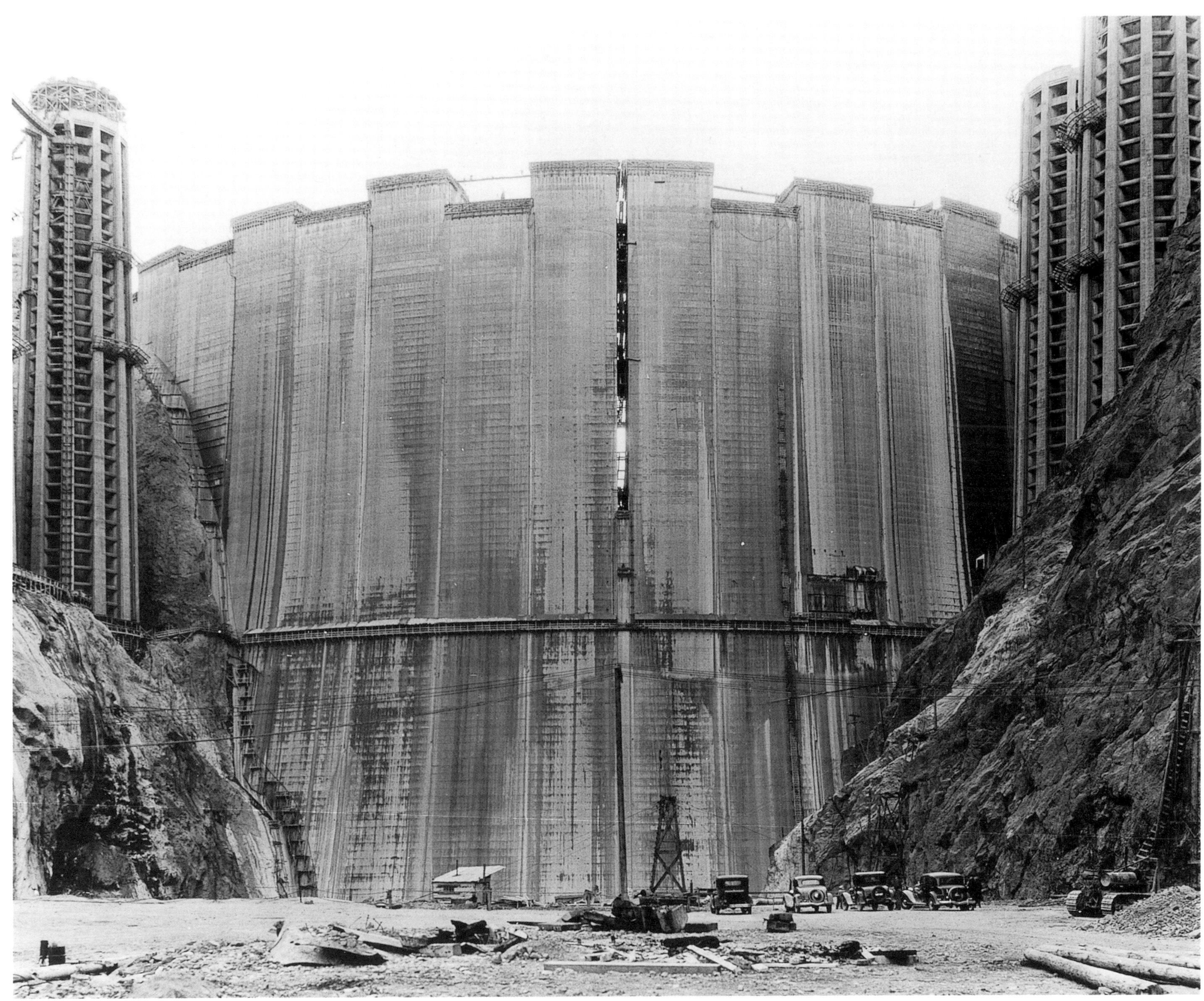

PLATE 86

Unknown

Sample of Silt Showing Thickness of Deposit Formed at Pierce's Farm Since Development of Lake, 1930s
gelatin silver print
4⅜ x 6½ in. (11.1 x 16.5 cm)
Scrugham Collection, Nevada Historical Society, Reno

PLATE 87

Unknown

Hoover Dam, side of Canyon for blasting, 1935
gelatin silver print
8 x 10 in. (20.3 x 25.4 cm)
Union Pacific Museum Collection

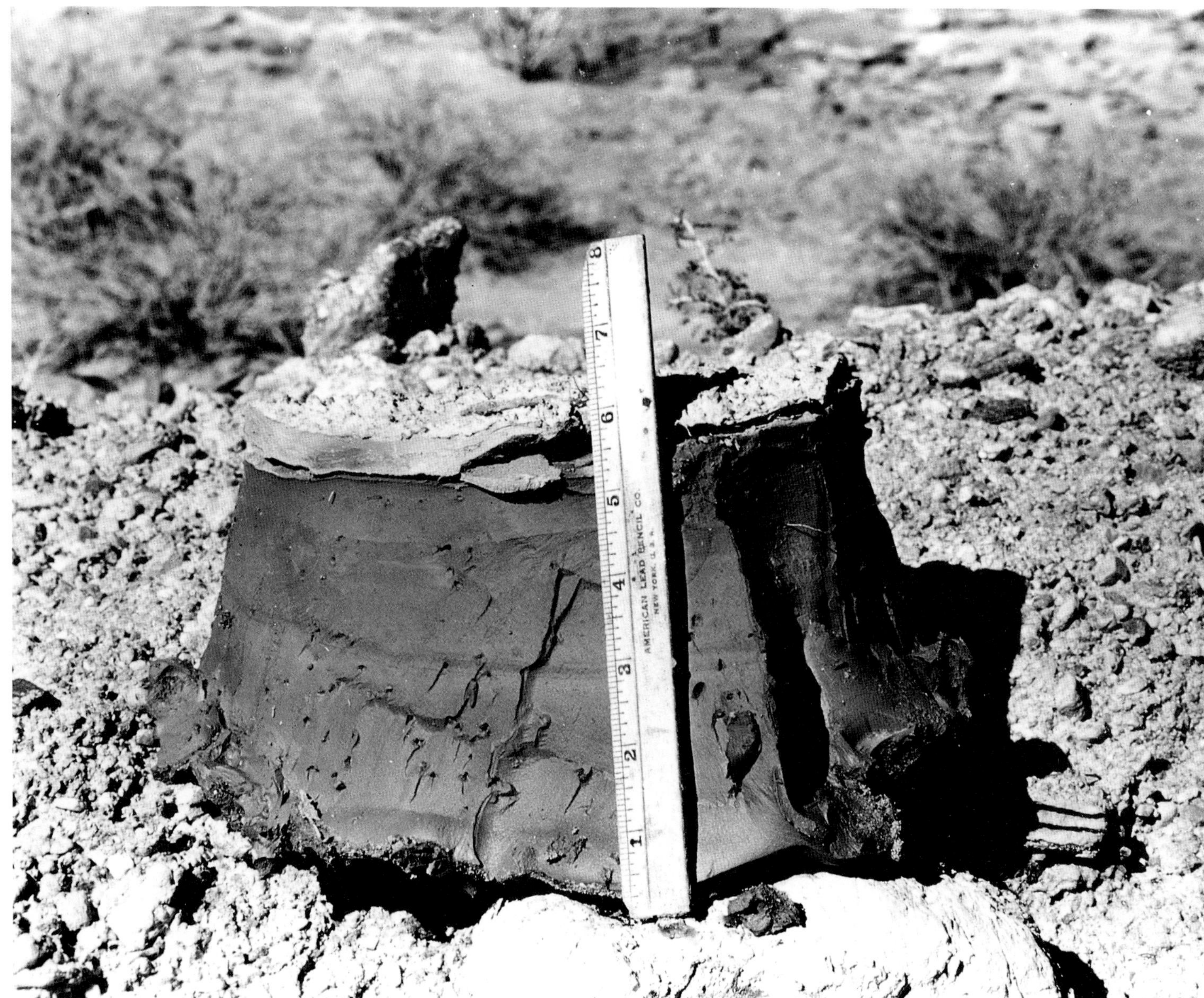

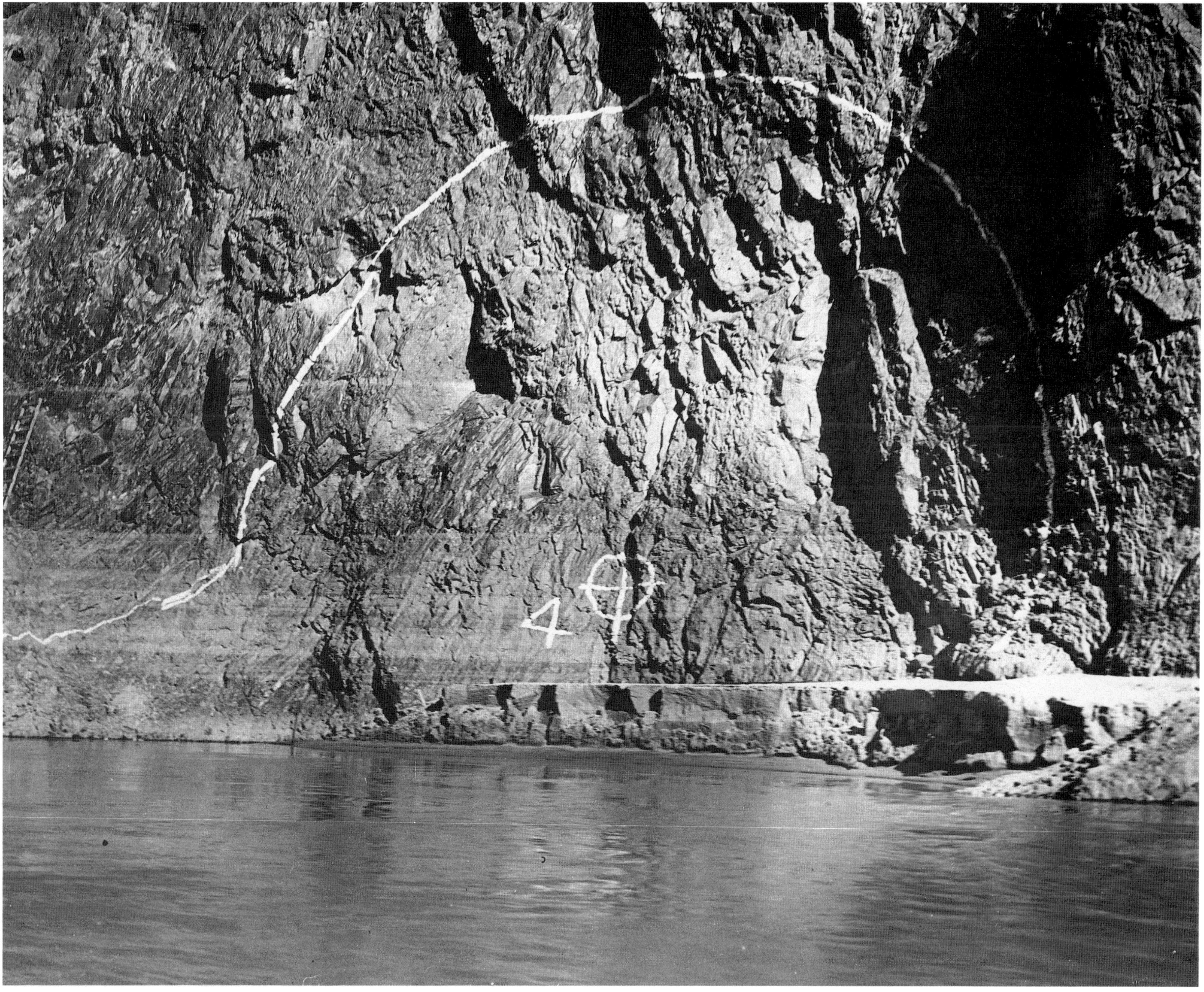
4

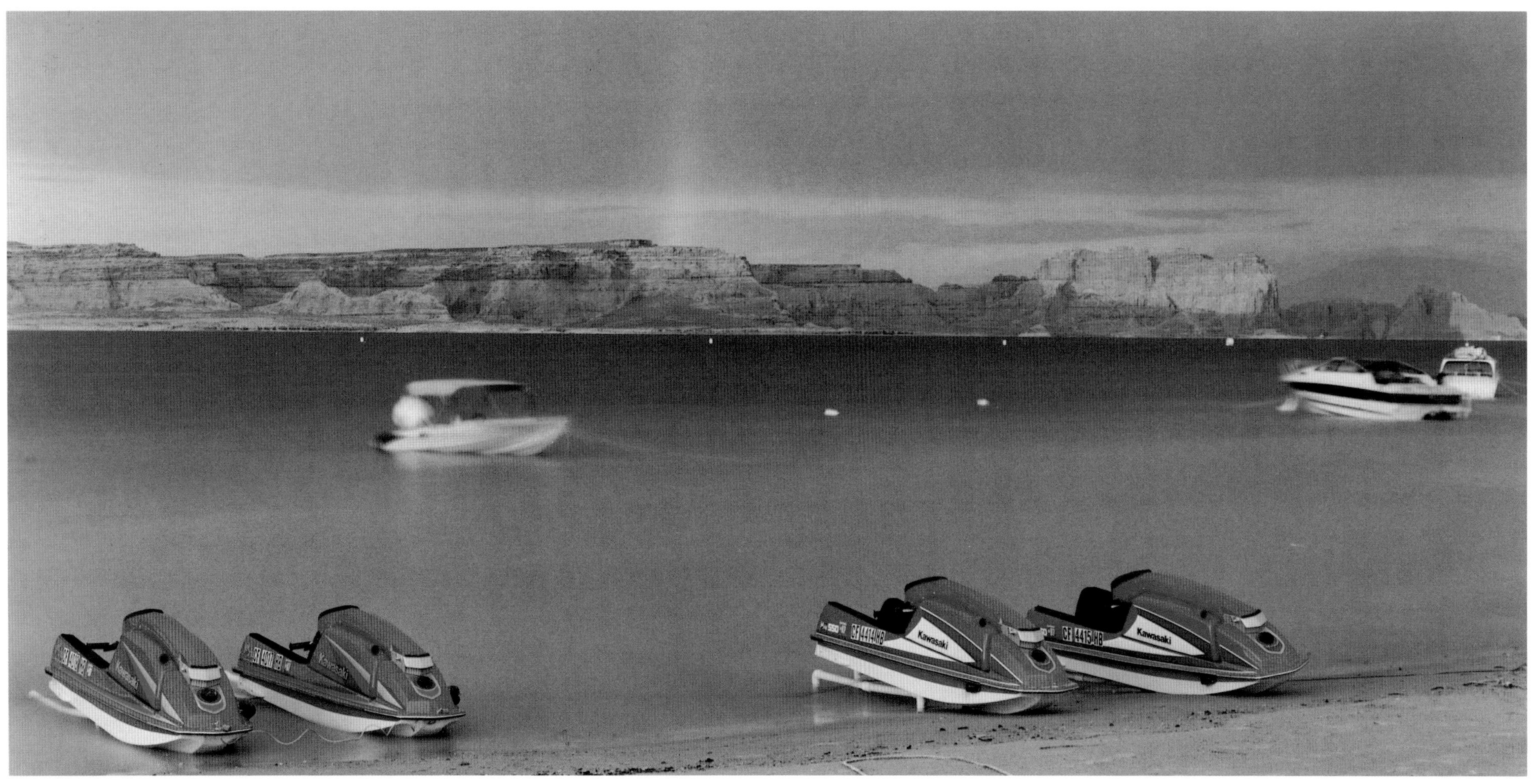

PLATE 88

Karen Halverson
Lake Powell, near Page, Arizona, 1987
chromogenic development print
11½ x 22$\frac{9}{16}$ in. (29.2 x 57.3 cm)
Collection of the San Francisco Museum of Modern Art.
Purchased through a gift of Linda Gruber

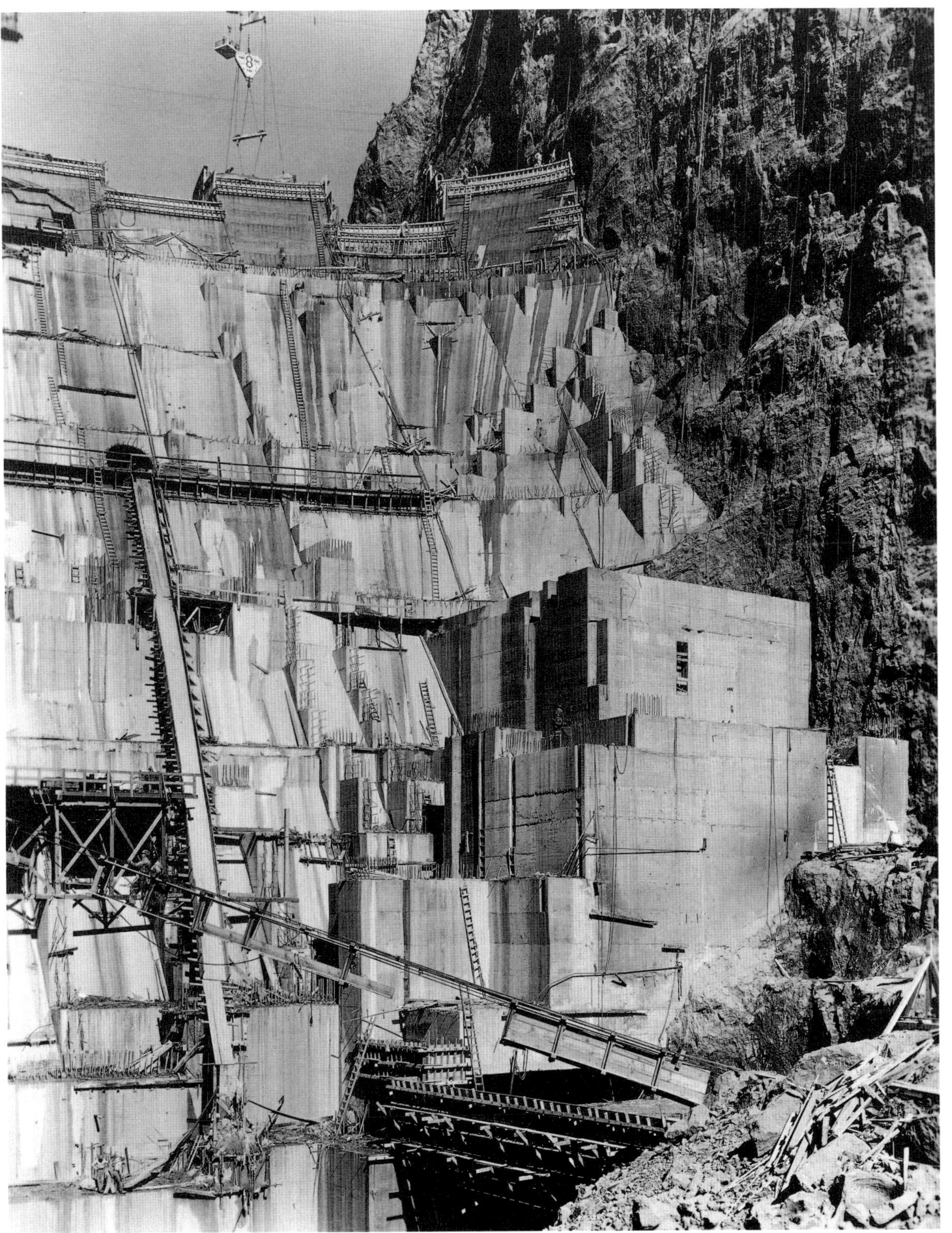

PLATE 89

Unknown

Hoover Dam During Construction, 1935
gelatin silver print
8 x 10 in. (20.3 x 25.4 cm)
Union Pacific Museum Collection

PLATE 90

Tseng Kwong Chi
Lightning Field, 1980–85
gelatin silver print
36 x 36 in. (91.4 x 91.4 cm)
Collection of the San Francisco Museum of Modern Art. Purchased through a gift of Linda Gruber

PLATE 91

Lee Friedlander
Mt. Rushmore, South Dakota, 1969
gelatin silver print
7⅝ x 11⁵⁄₁₆ in. (19.4 x 28.7 cm)
Collection of the San Francisco Museum of Modern Art. Purchased through a gift of the Judy Kay Memorial Fund

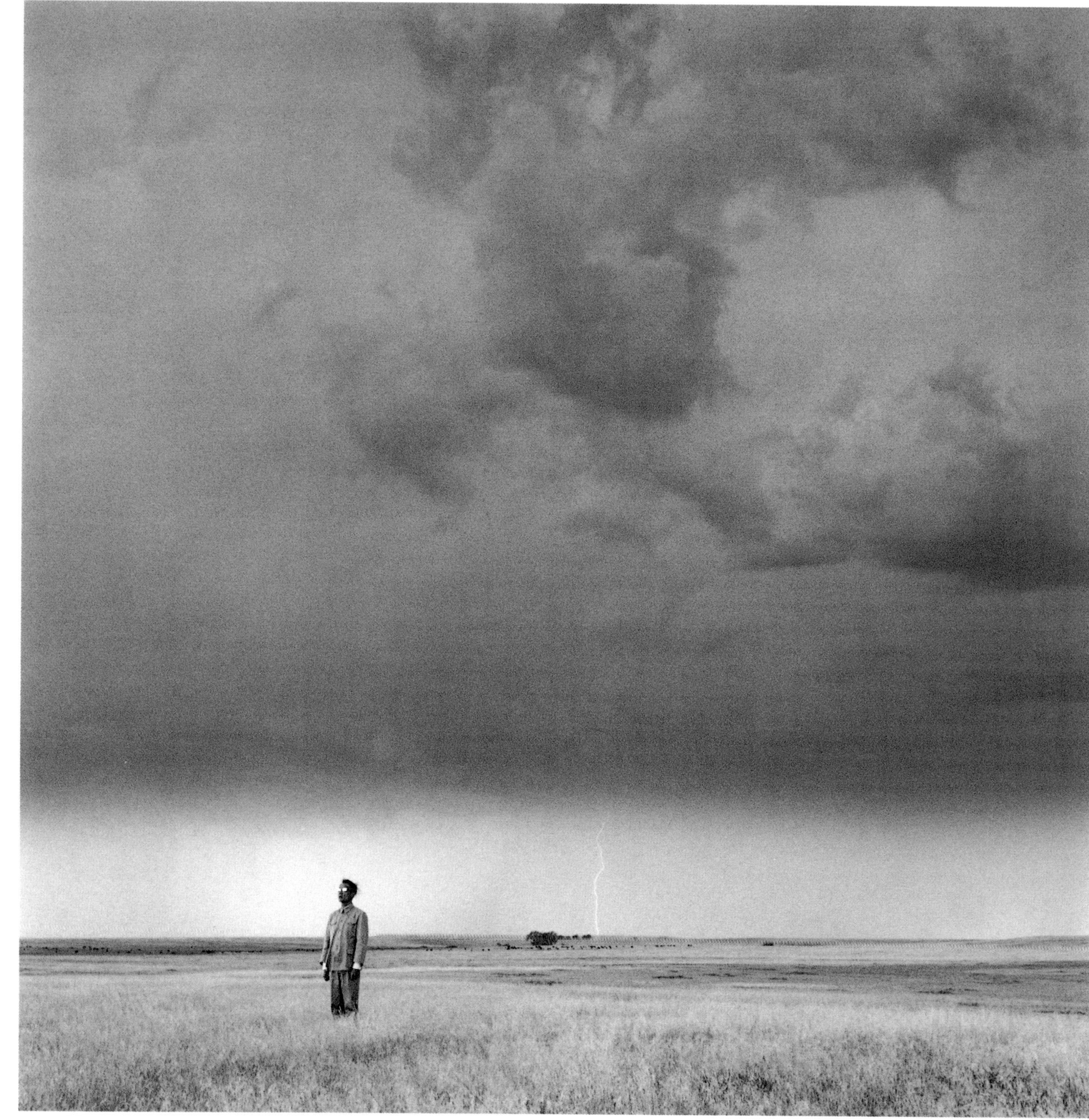

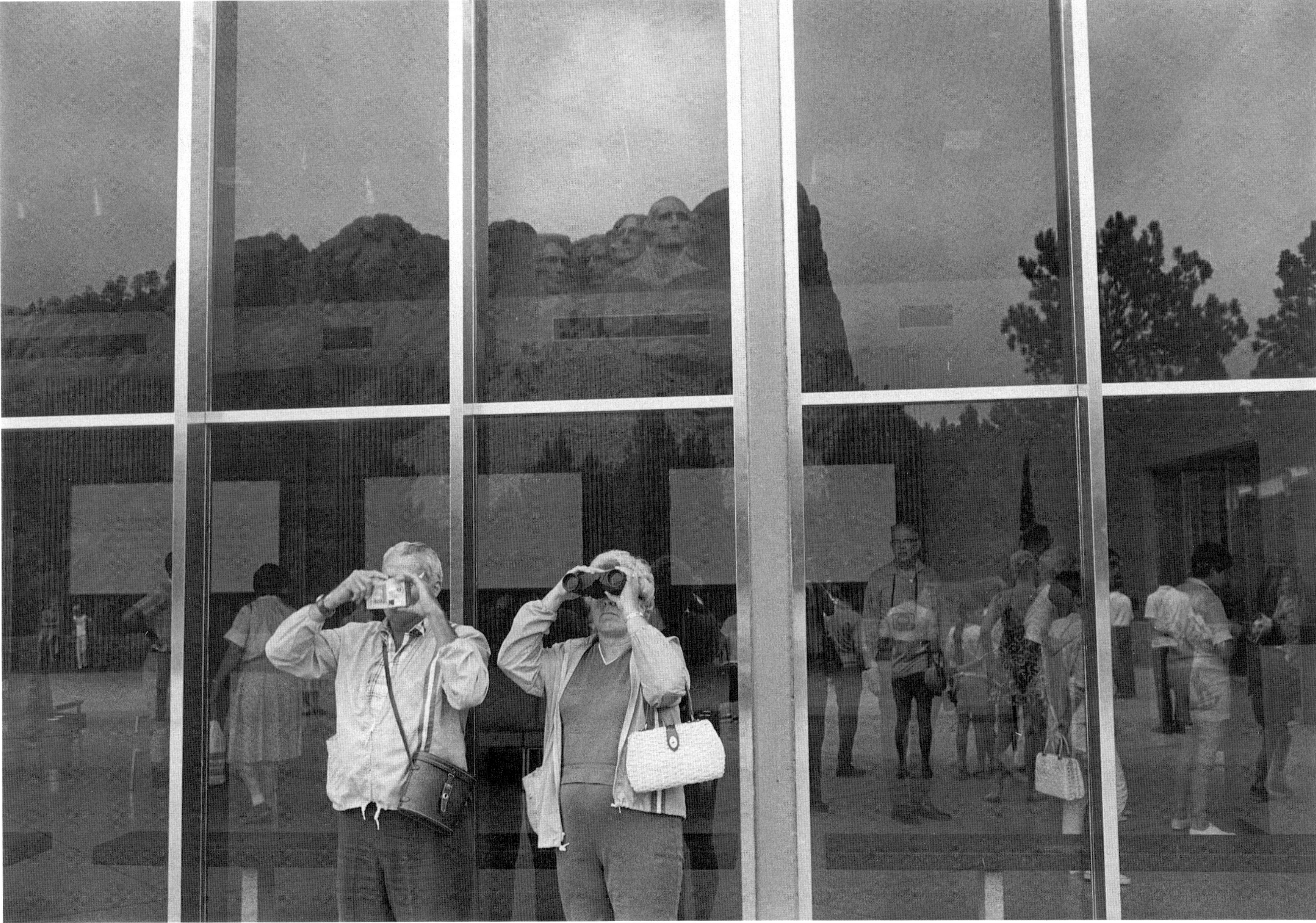

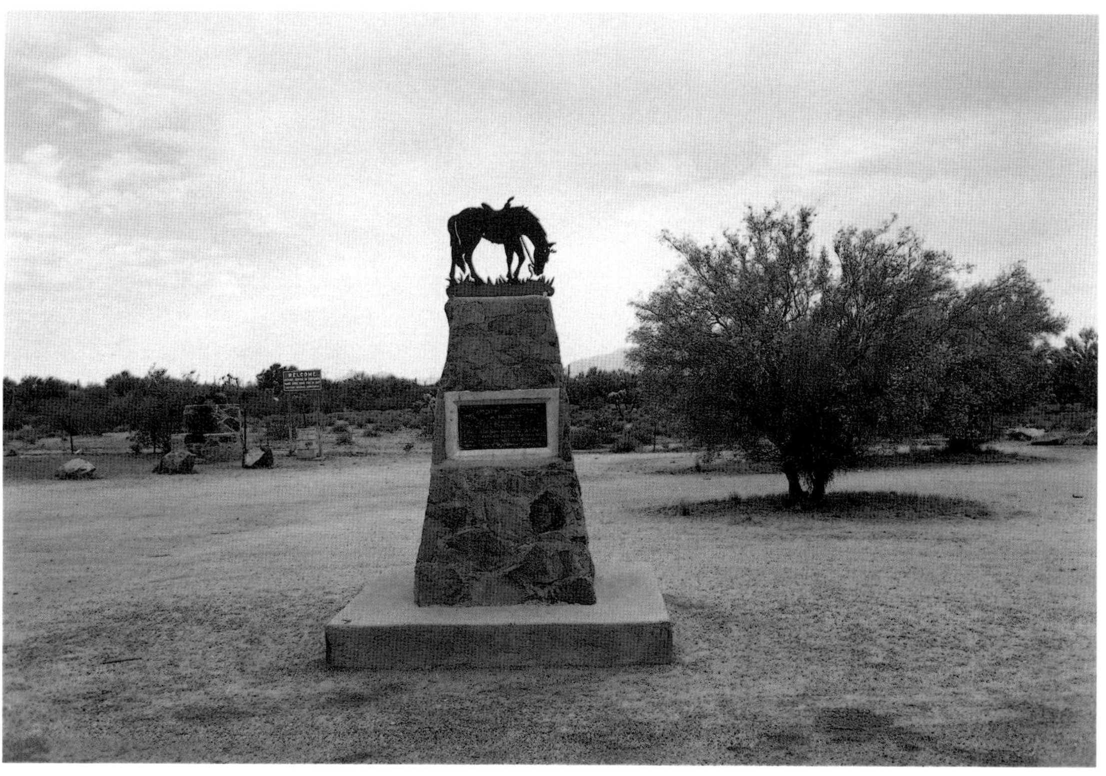

PLATE 92

Lee Friedlander
Florence, Arizona, ca. 1975
gelatin silver print
8⅝ x 13 in. (21.9 x 33 cm)
Collection of the San Francisco Museum of Modern Art. Purchased through a gift of the Judy Kay Memorial Fund

PLATE 93

Greg MacGregor
Milo J. Ayer, age 29, 1849, Graffiti, Independence Rock, Wyoming, 1988
gelatin silver print
16 x 20 in. (40.6 x 50.8 cm)
Collection of the San Francisco Museum of Modern Art

OPPOSITE PAGE:
PLATE 94

Len Jenshel
Route 127 near Death Valley National Monument, California, 1990
chromogenic development print
15 x 22 in. (38.1 x 55.9 cm)
Collection of the San Francisco Museum of Modern Art. Gift of the artist, 95.277

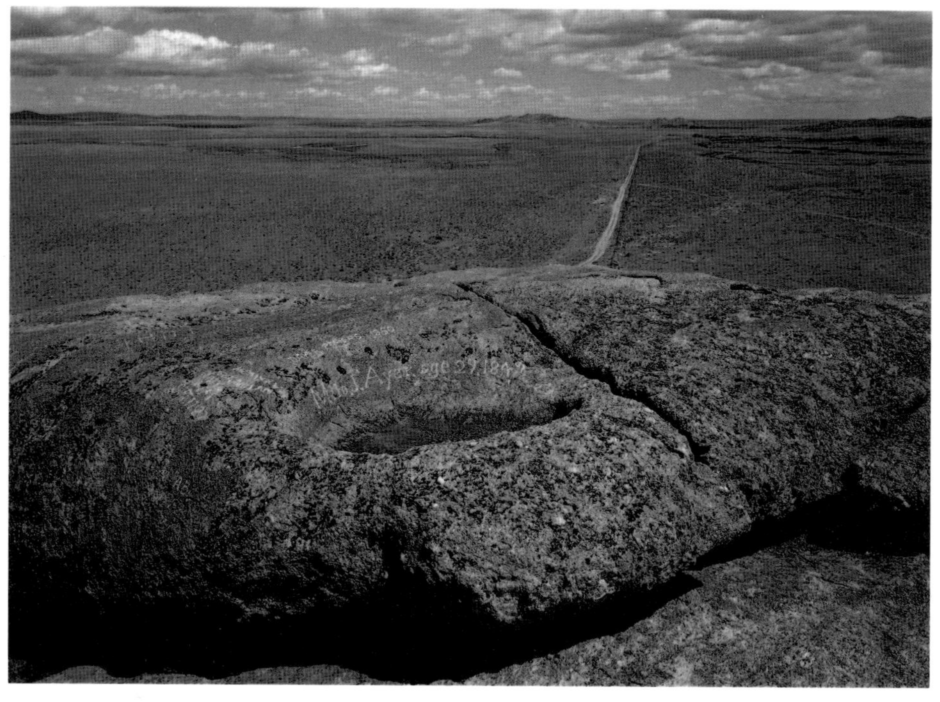

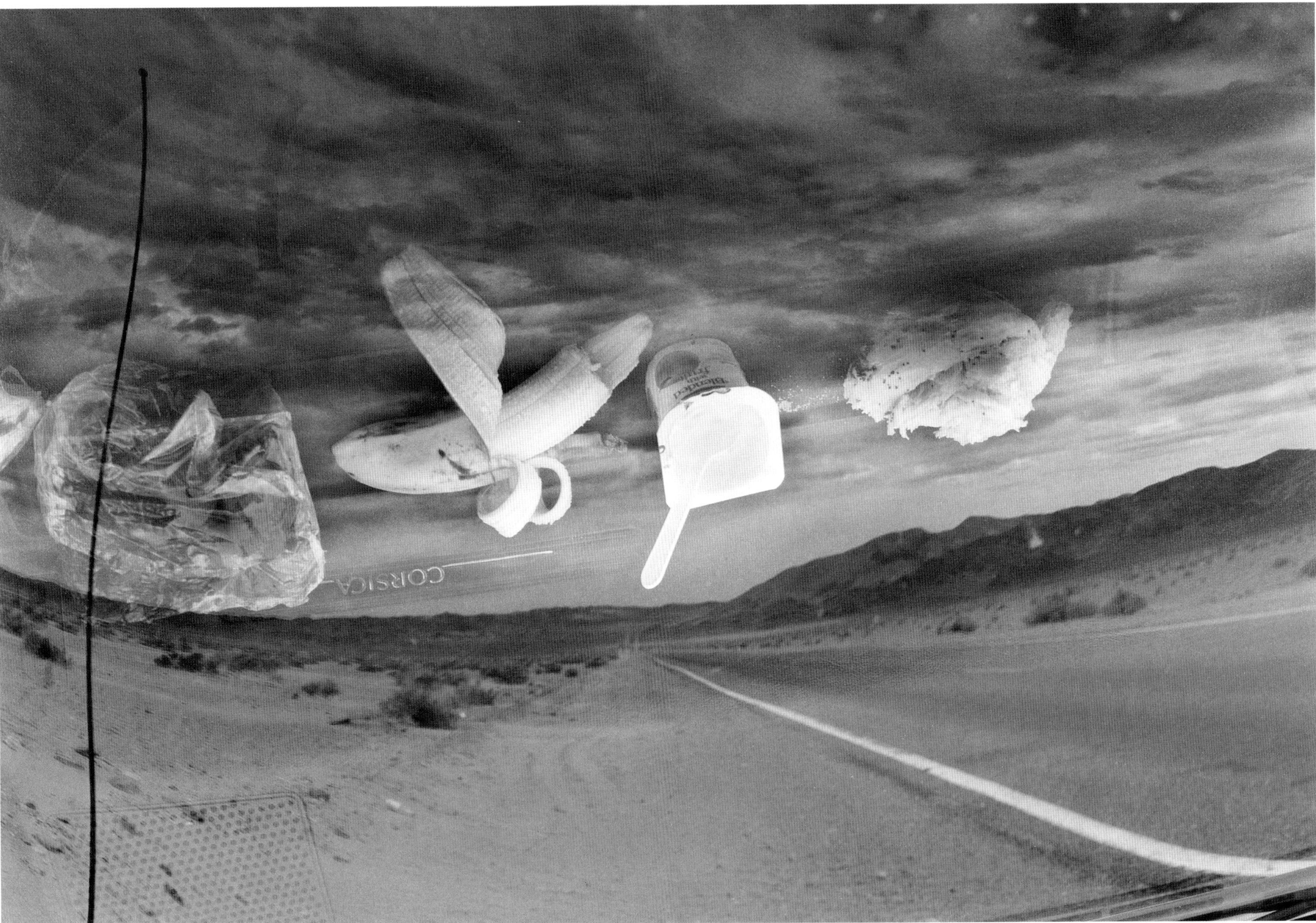
CORSICA

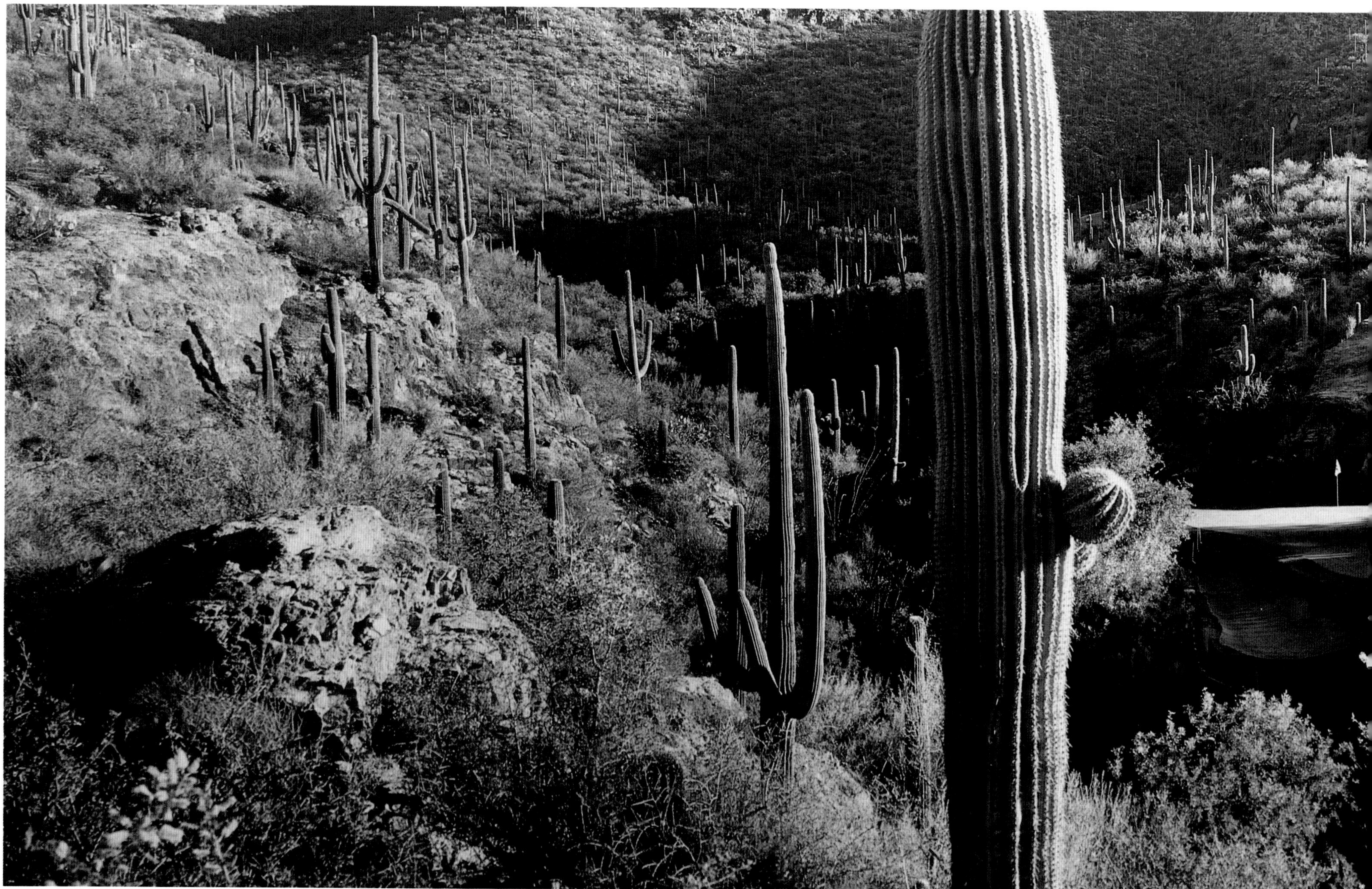

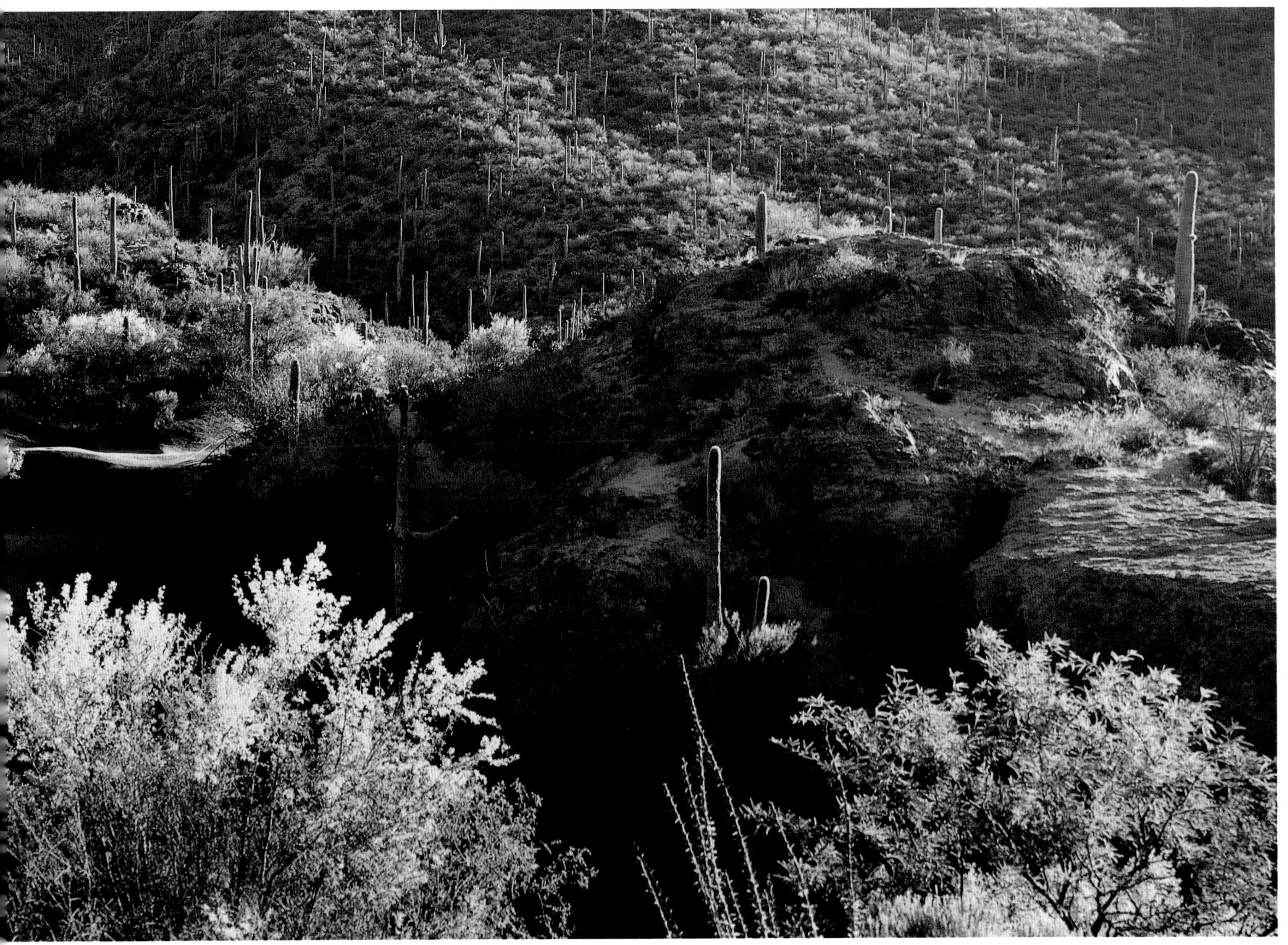

PLATE 95

Skeet McAuley

Ventana Canyon, Tucson, Mountain Course, Third Green, 1991
chromogenic development print
28 x 84 in. (71.1 x 213.4 cm)
Collection of the San Francisco Museum of Modern Art. Gift of Bruce Velick in honor of Harris Stewart, 96.104

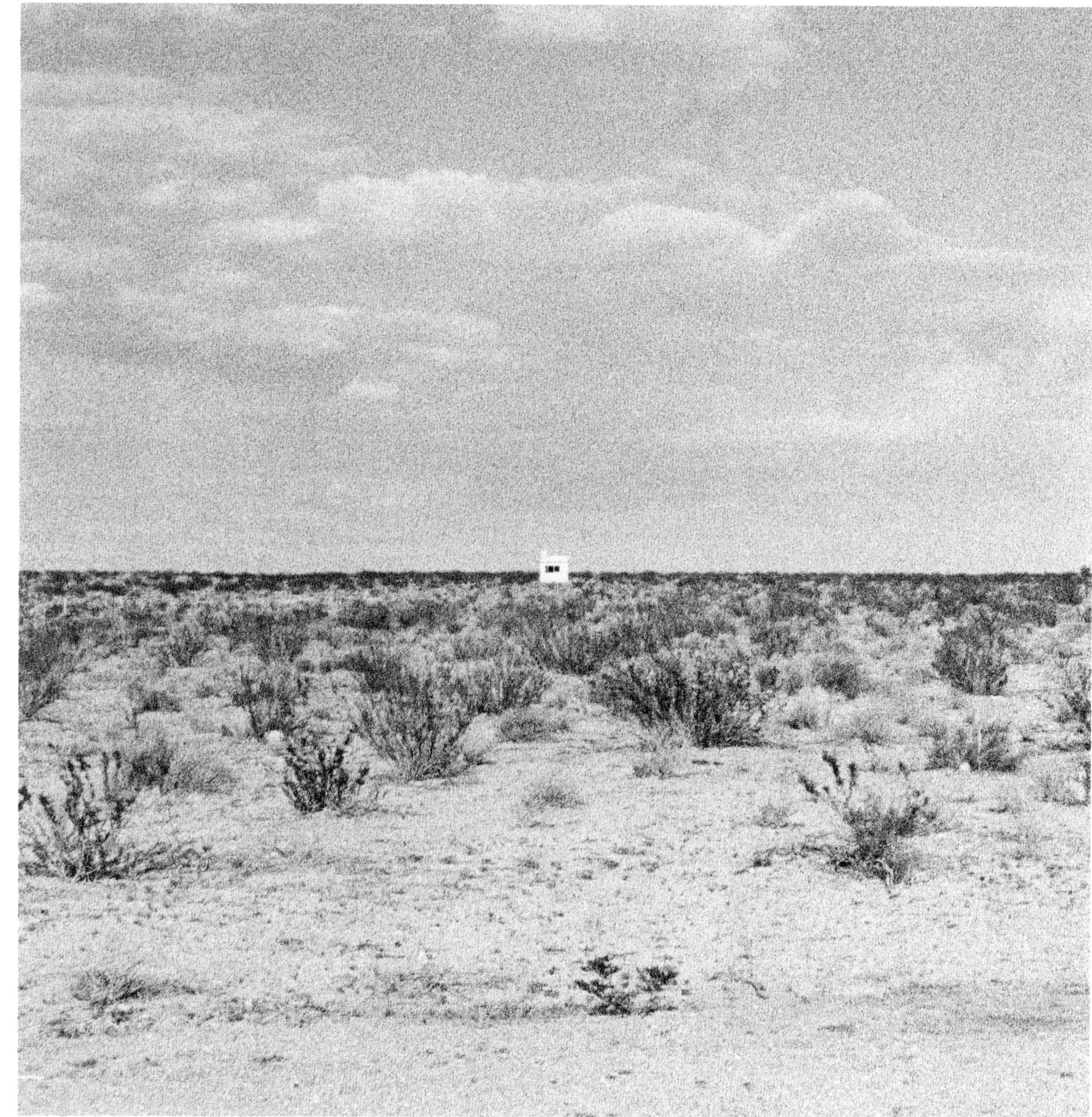

PLATE 96

John Divola
Untitled print #5, from *Isolated Houses: High Desert*, 1992
gelatin silver print
16 x 20 in. (40.6 x 50.8 cm)
Collection of the San Francisco Museum of Modern Art.
Members of Foto Forum,
94.471.5

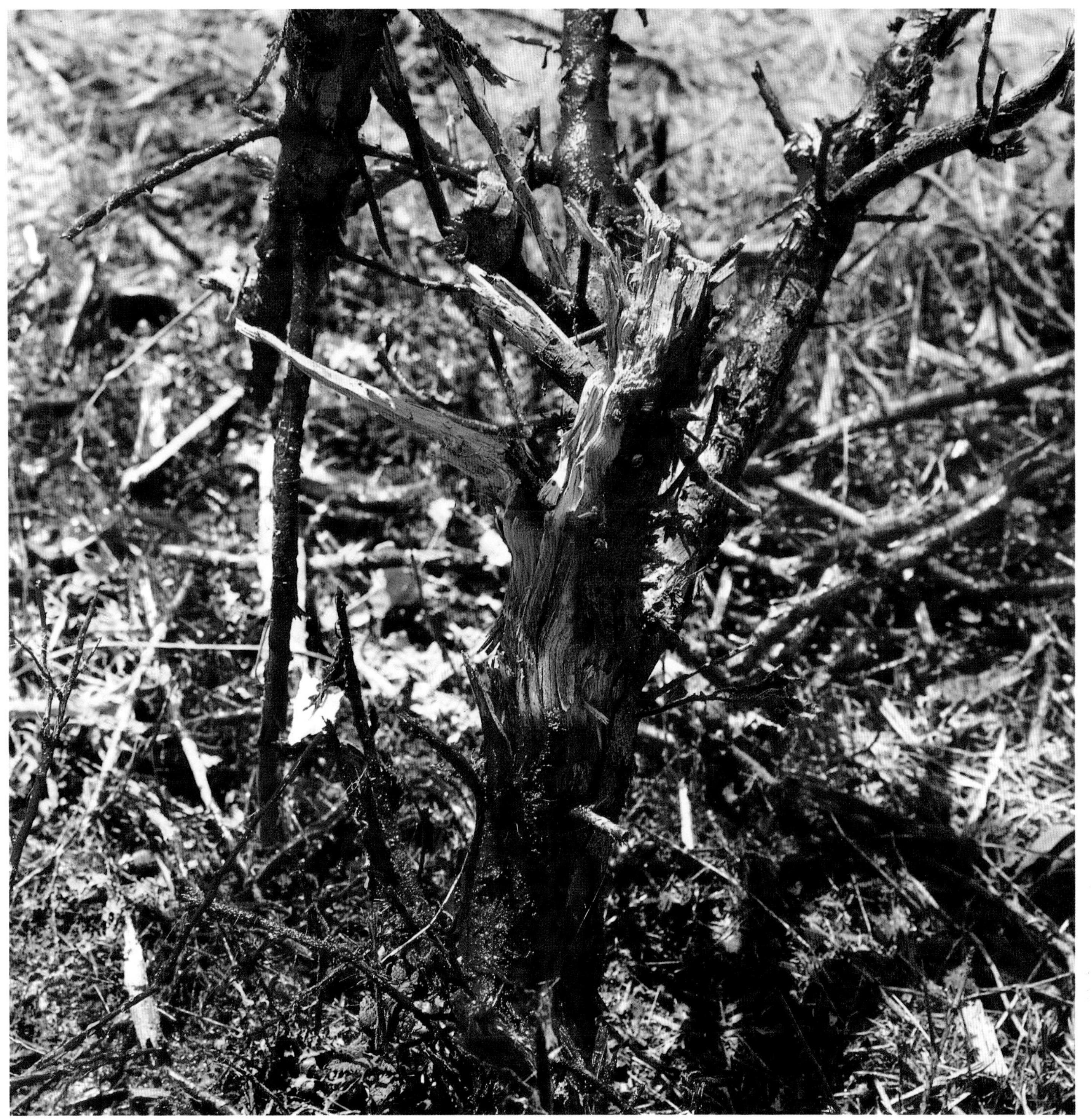

PLATE 97

Anthony Hernandez
Angeles National Forest #19, from the series *Shooting Sites*, 1988
silver dye bleach print
28¾ x 28⅜ in. (73 x 72.1 cm)
Collection of the San Francisco Museum of Modern Art. Gift of the artist and Craig Krull Gallery, Santa Monica, 95.270

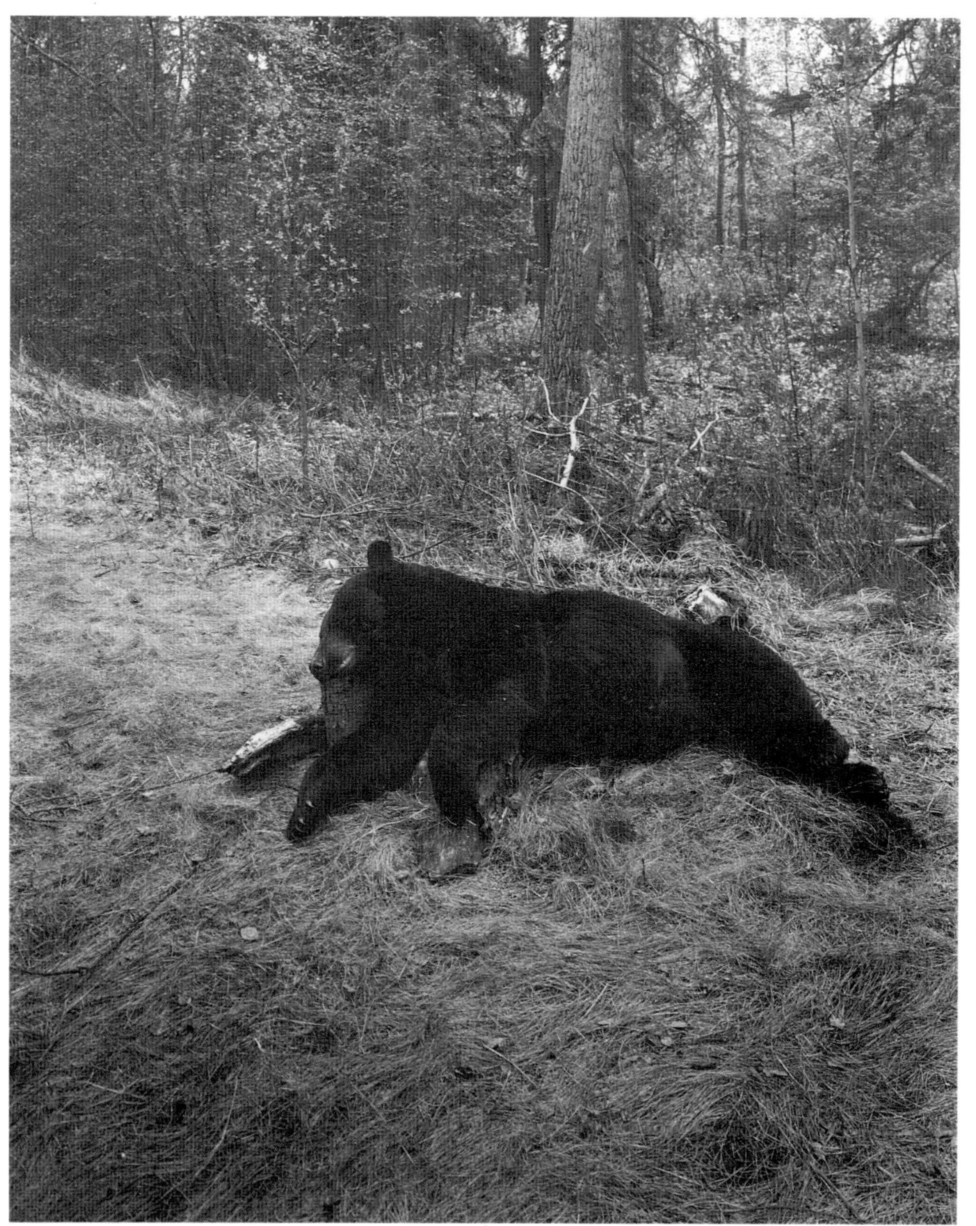

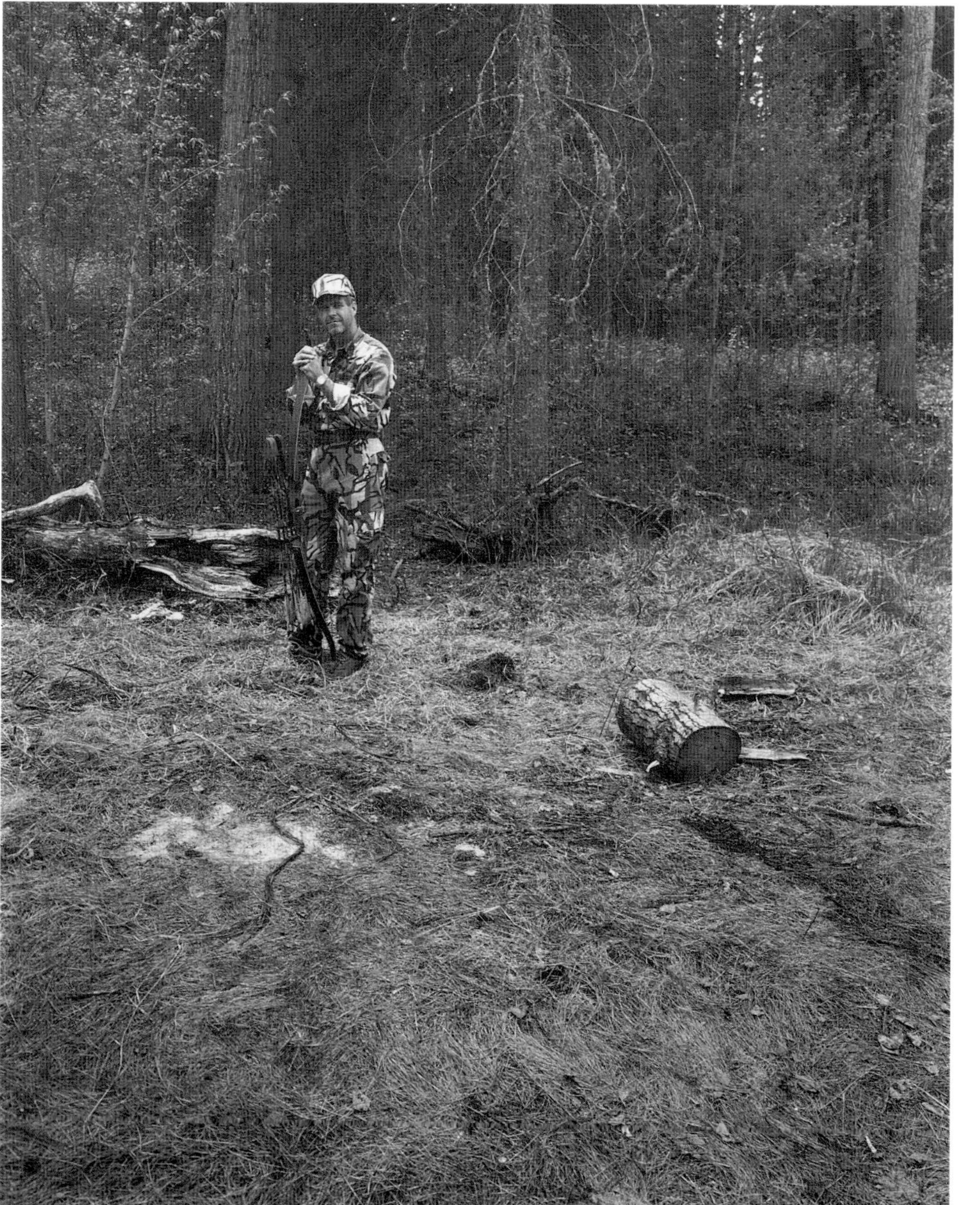

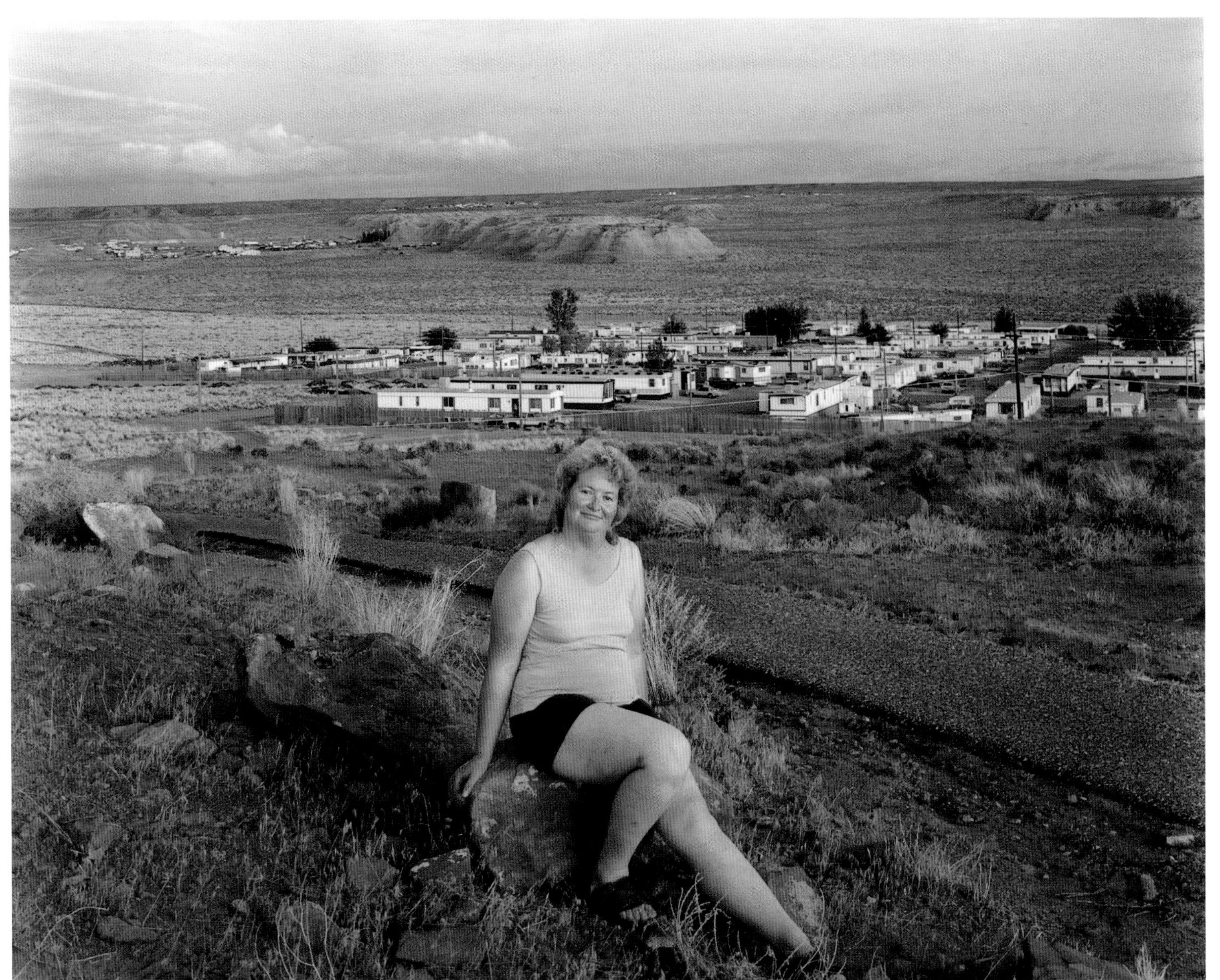

PLATE 98

Barbara Bosworth
Black Bear Hunter, Peace River, Alberta, 1994
gelatin silver print
$9^{11}/_{16}$ x $15^{1}/_{2}$ in. (24.6 x 39.4 cm)
Collection of the San Francisco Museum of Modern Art

PLATE 99

Joel Sternfeld
Page Arizona, August 1983, 1983
chromogenic development print
$13^{3}/_{8}$ x $16^{15}/_{16}$ in. (34 x 43 cm)
Collection of the San Francisco Museum of Modern Art

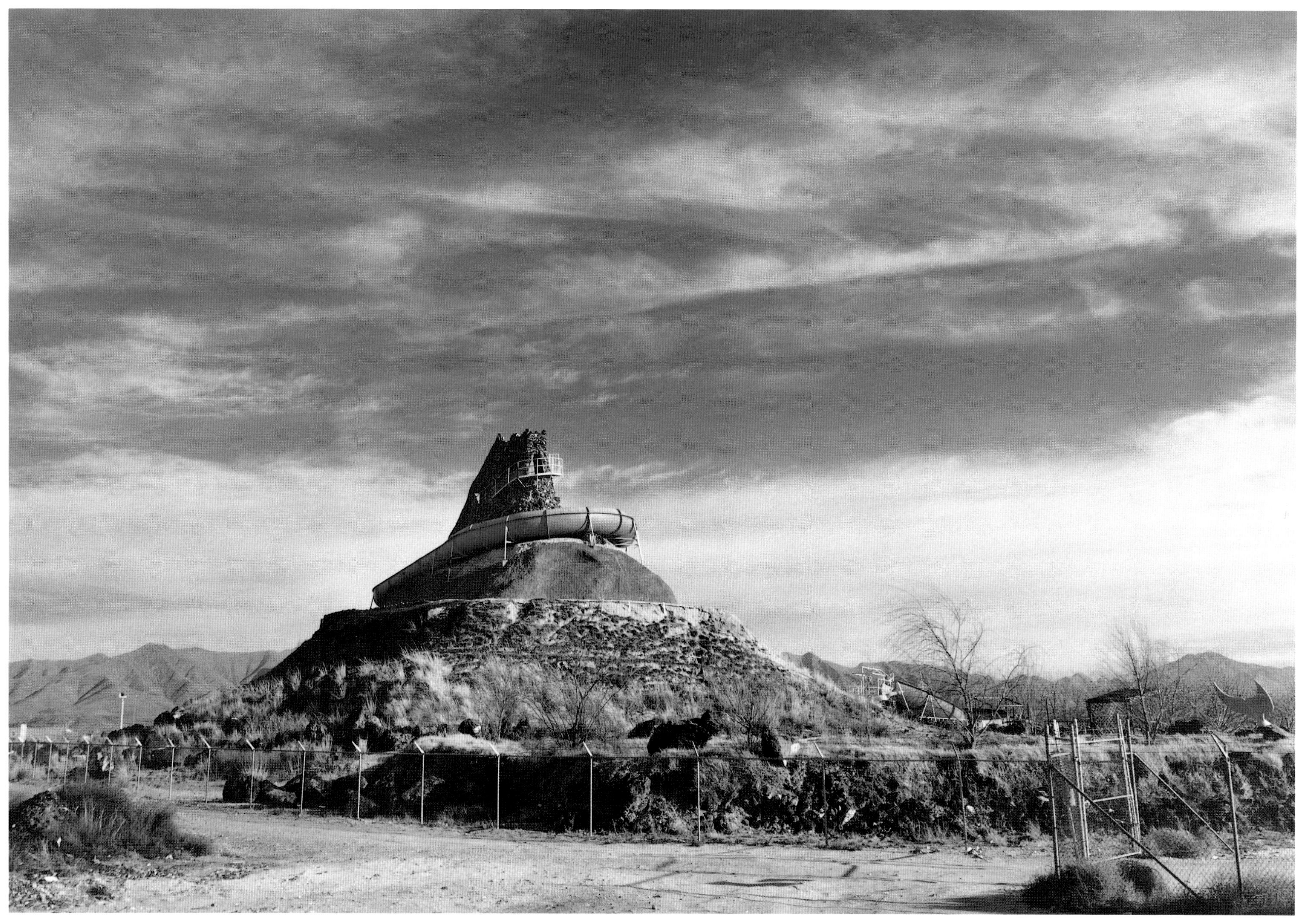

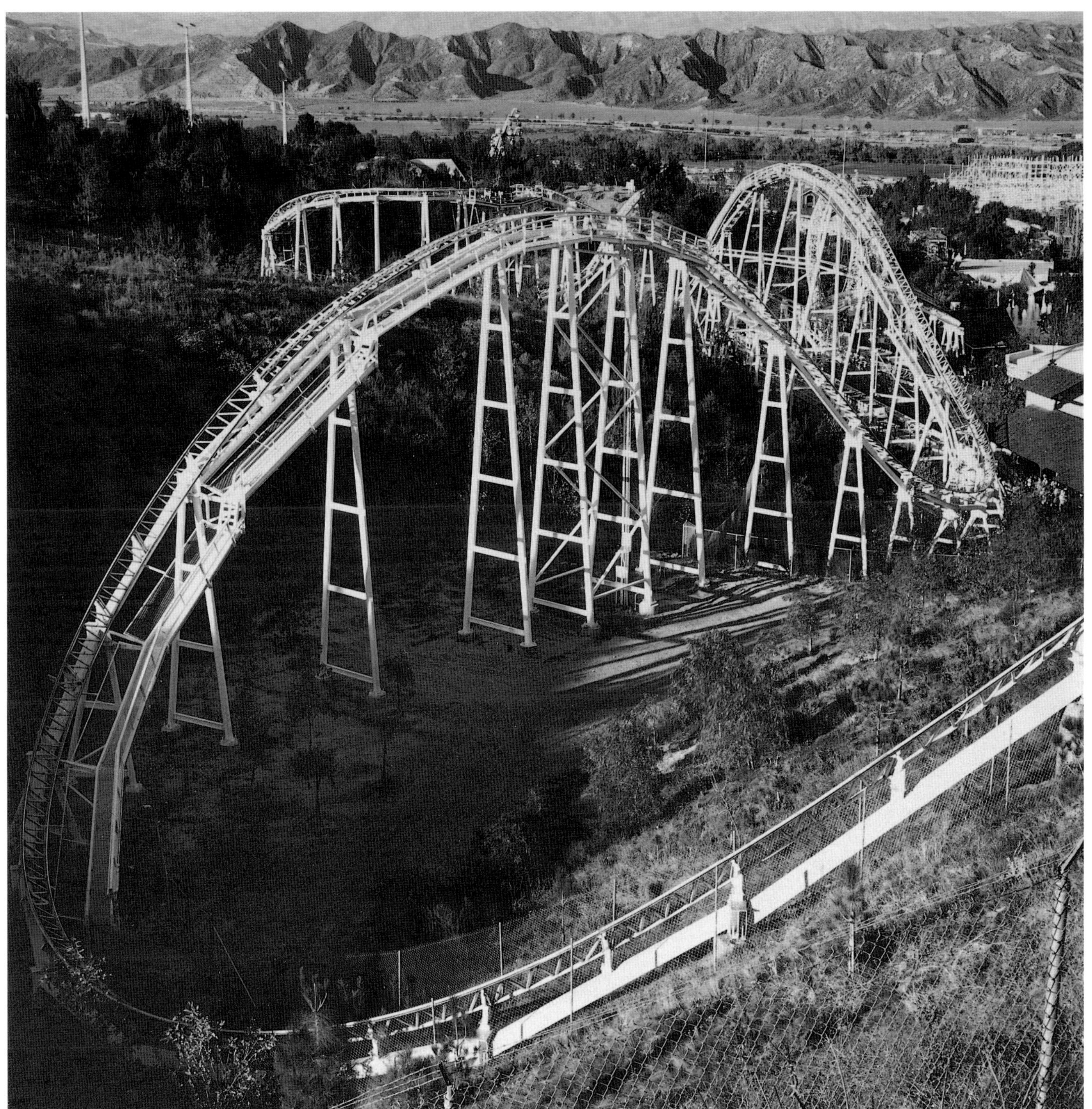

PLATE 100

John Ganis
Texas Water Slide, 1987
chromogenic development print
13 x 18¹³⁄₁₆ in. (33 x 47.8 cm)
Collection of the San Francisco Museum of Modern Art. Purchased through a gift of the Judy Kay Memorial Fund, 96.96

PLATE 101

Joe Deal
View, Magic Mountain, Valencia, California, 1977
gelatin silver print
11⅛ x 11⅜ in. (28.3 x 28.9 cm)
Collection of the San Francisco Museum of Modern Art

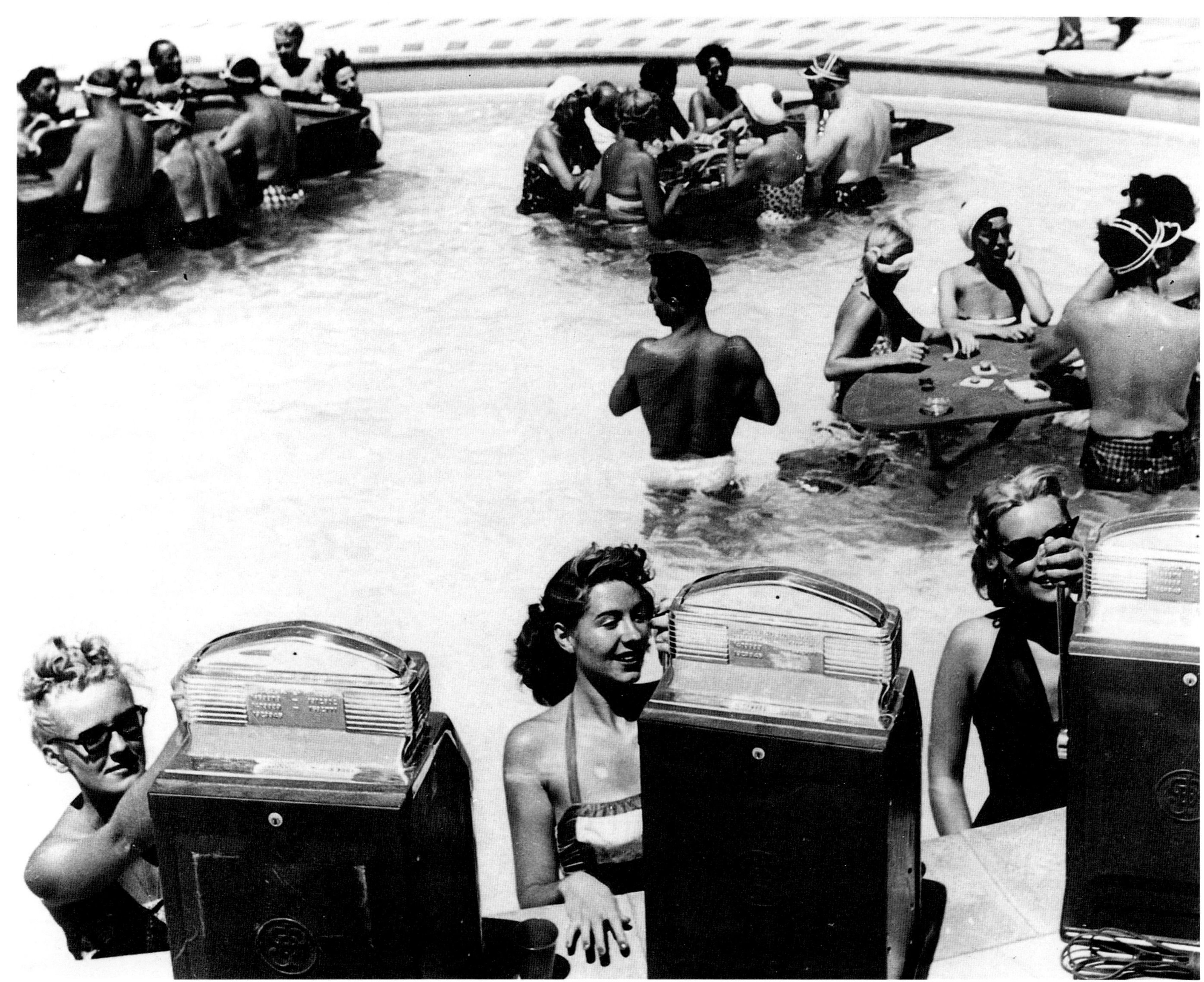

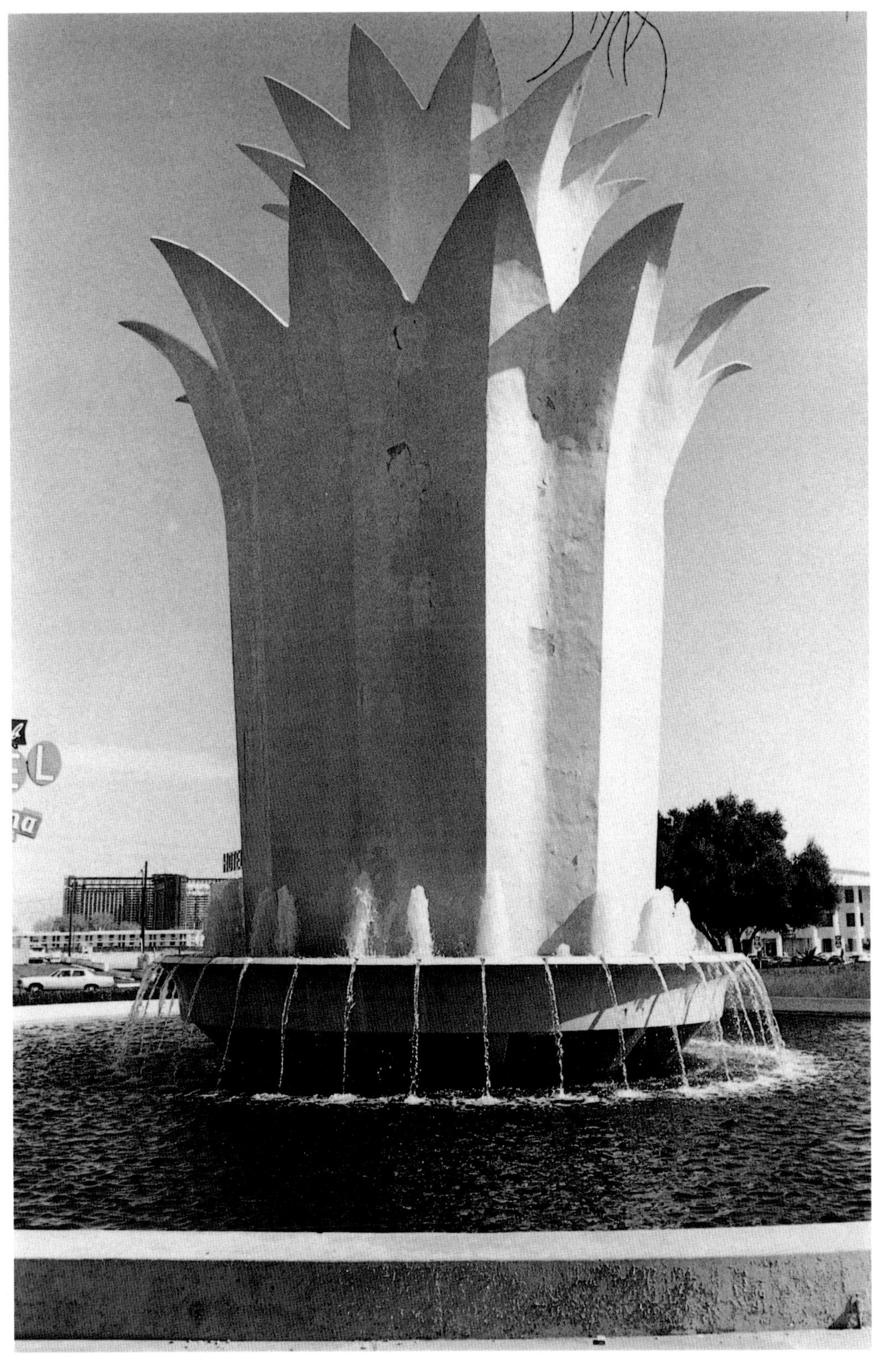

PLATE 102

Las Vegas News Bureau
Untitled, 1950s
gelatin silver print
7¾ x 9½ in. (19.7 x 24.1 cm)
Collection of the Nevada Historical Society, Reno

PLATE 103

William Thacher Dane
Las Vegas, 1973
gelatin silver print
$6\frac{11}{16}$ x $4\frac{7}{16}$ in. (17 x 11.3 cm)
Collection of the San Francisco Museum of Modern Art

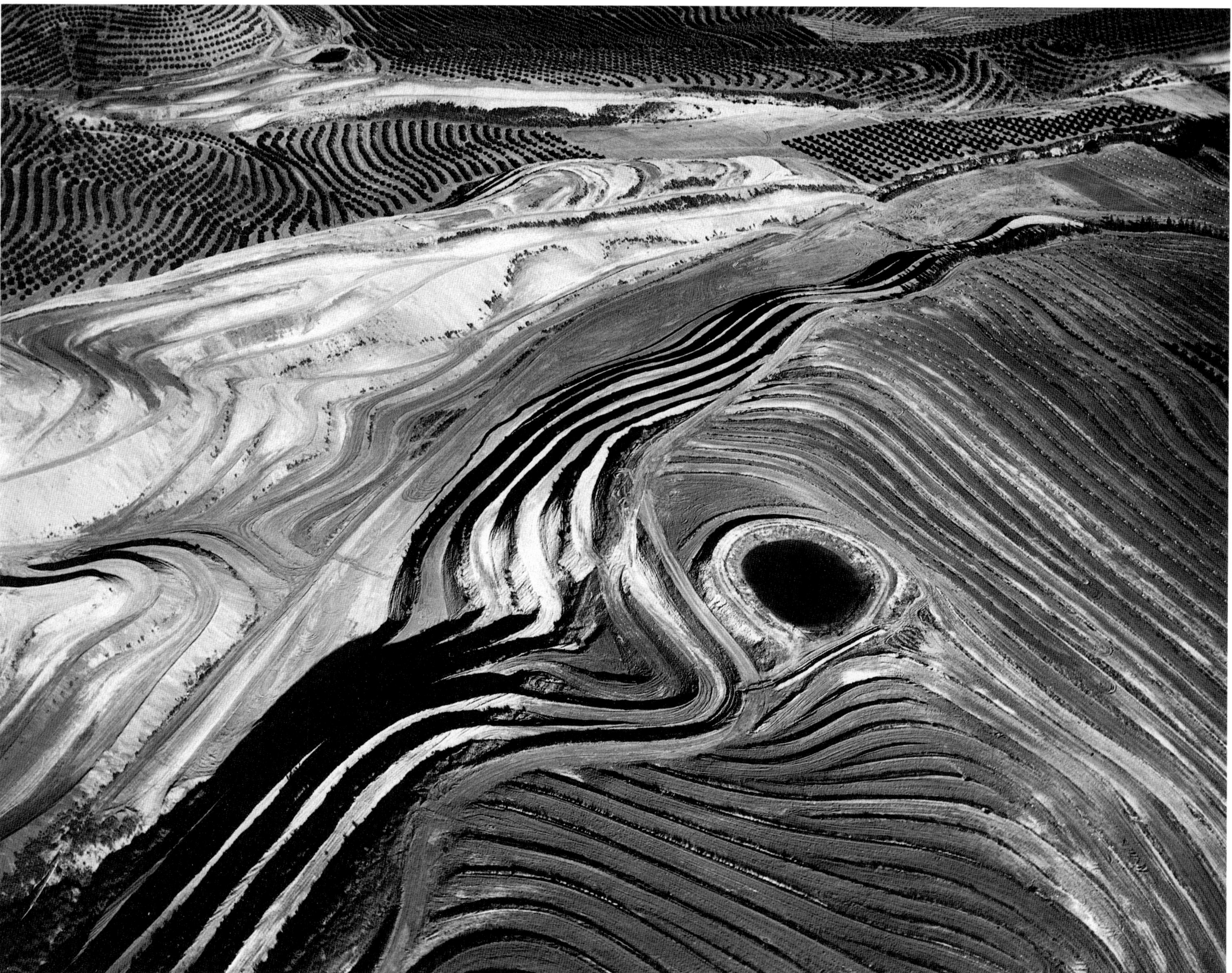

PLATE 104

William Garnett
Contour Graded Hills, Ventura County, California, 1953
gelatin silver print
10½ x 13½ in. (26.7 x 34.3 cm)
Collection of the San Francisco Museum of Modern Art.
Accessions Committee Fund, 93.394

PLATE 105

Gregory Conniff
Cattle Water, Sand Hills, Merrill County, Nebraska (Aerial 1), 1990
gelatin silver print
18⅛ x 17⅞ in. (46 x 45.4 cm)
Collection of the San Francisco Museum of Modern Art.
Purchased through a gift of Linda Gruber

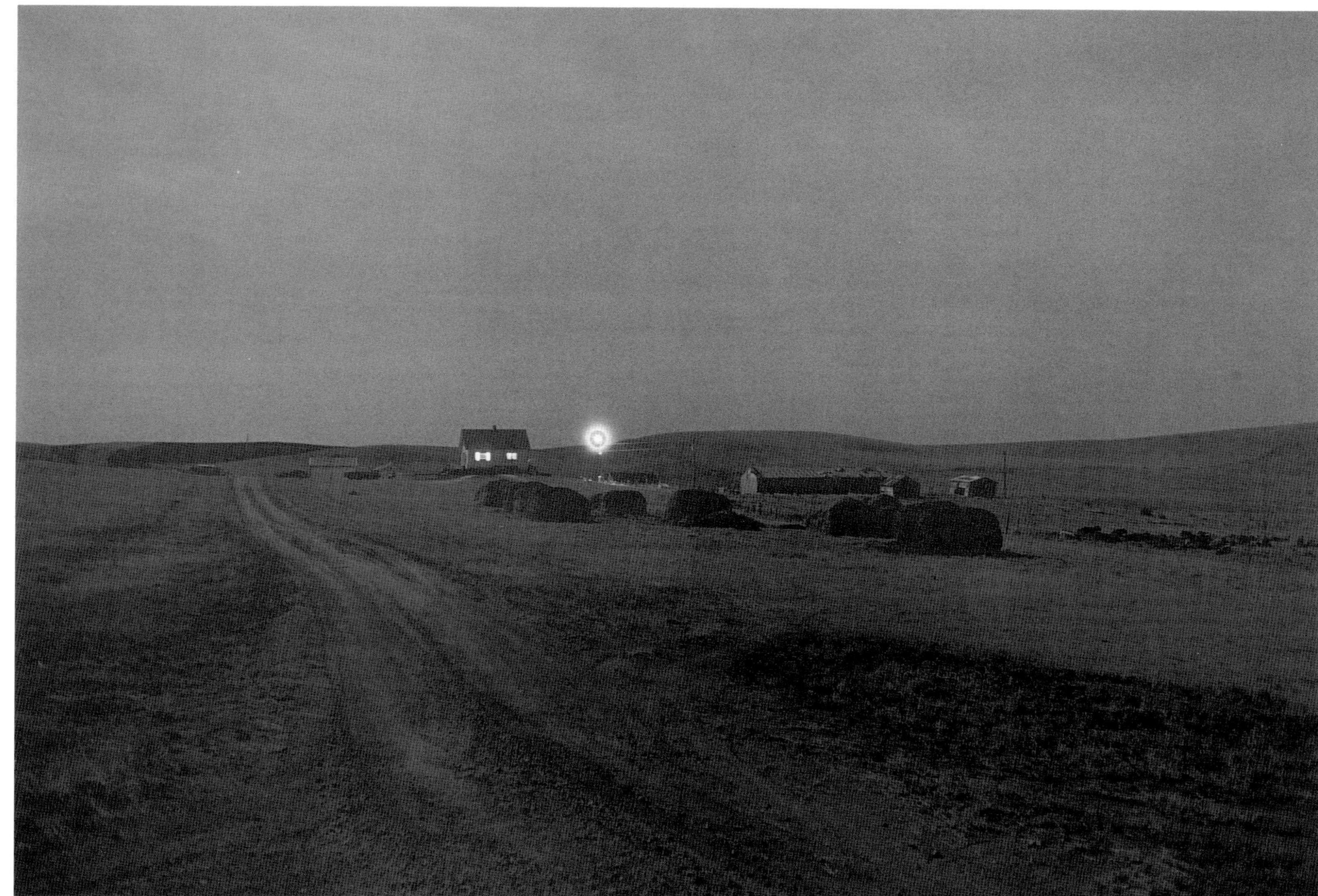

PLATE 106

Thomas Frederick Arndt
Farmyard with Yardlight South Dakota, 1982
gelatin silver print
15⅞ x 19⅞ in. (40.3 x 50.5 cm)
Collection of the San Francisco Museum of Modern Art. Gift of the artist, 93.14

PLATE 107

Joseph Bartscherer
Detail of *Untitled*, from the series *Pioneering Mattawa*, 1984–93
8 gelatin silver prints with 1 text panel
23¼ x 28¼ in. (59.1 x 71.8 cm) each
Collection of the San Francisco Museum of Modern Art

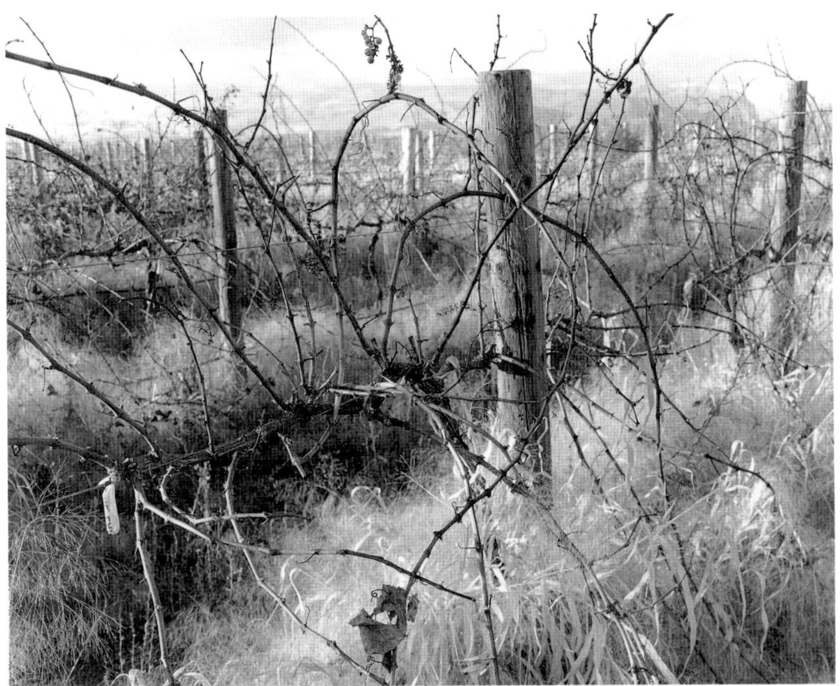

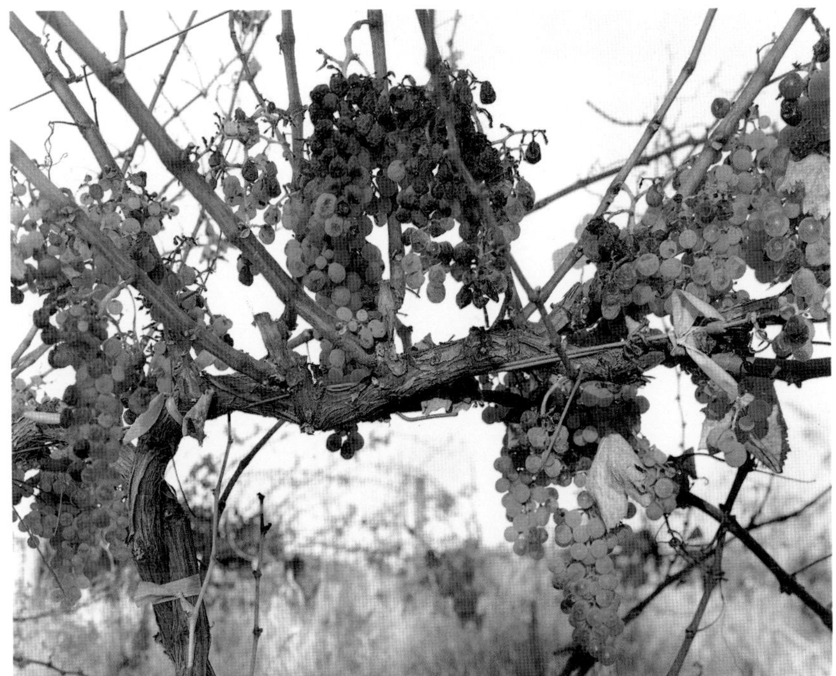

There were mustang here in the beginning I know because Leon Nunnally got off the train to Seattle in 1937 and took a job chasing them for the Northern Pacific. Even before the railroad they ran cattle on this land and when it came they pastured sheep too. Wild rye, shoulder and head tall, grew right to the river. Spiked wheat, Idaho fescue, Indian rice spread everywhere. The Wahluke Slope was serviceable range until the bunchgrass was finished. Once the horses were gone it was empty country.

On the map the Grand Coulee Dam brought water to the entire Columbia Basin from day one, but it was not until after the war that they ever filled Banks Lake and not until 1961 that we saw any water on this side of Saddle Mountain. That was way over on the eastern end of the Slope. Every few years then would come another extension of the canal, another block of sage broken out. You could climb the basalts at the top of O Road and see in the wind just how far the water had come by watching where the dust blew up over new ground.

To anyone contemplating apples or especially vines the Mattawa acreage has laid like the promised land awaiting the blessing of regular rain. Its soil is sand on a gravel bed, textbook sterile and full of air. No root rot, no grubs, no past. Make it what you need. It sits high with a long southern face tipped to the sun, inclined enough to spill the cold. One hundred and ninety frost-free days.

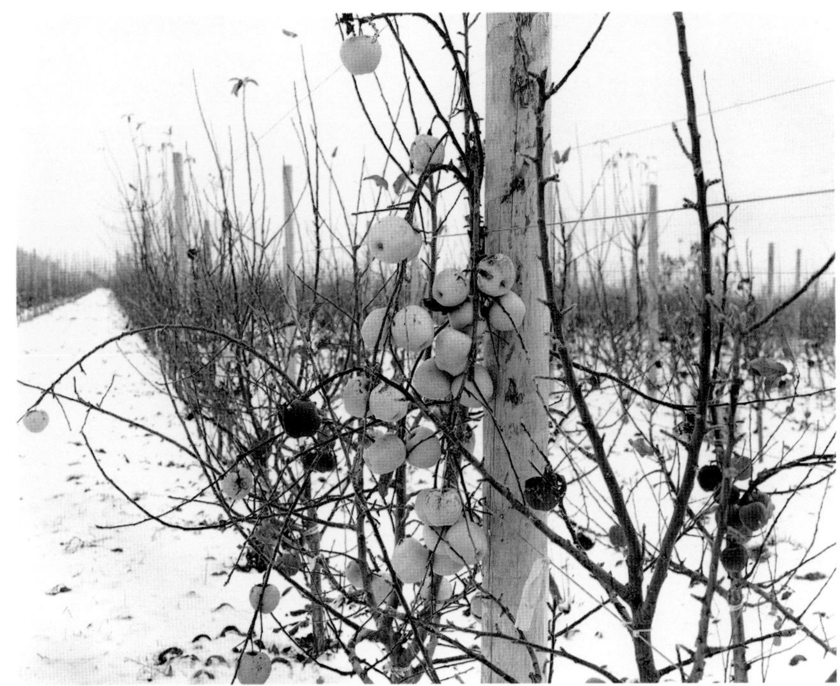

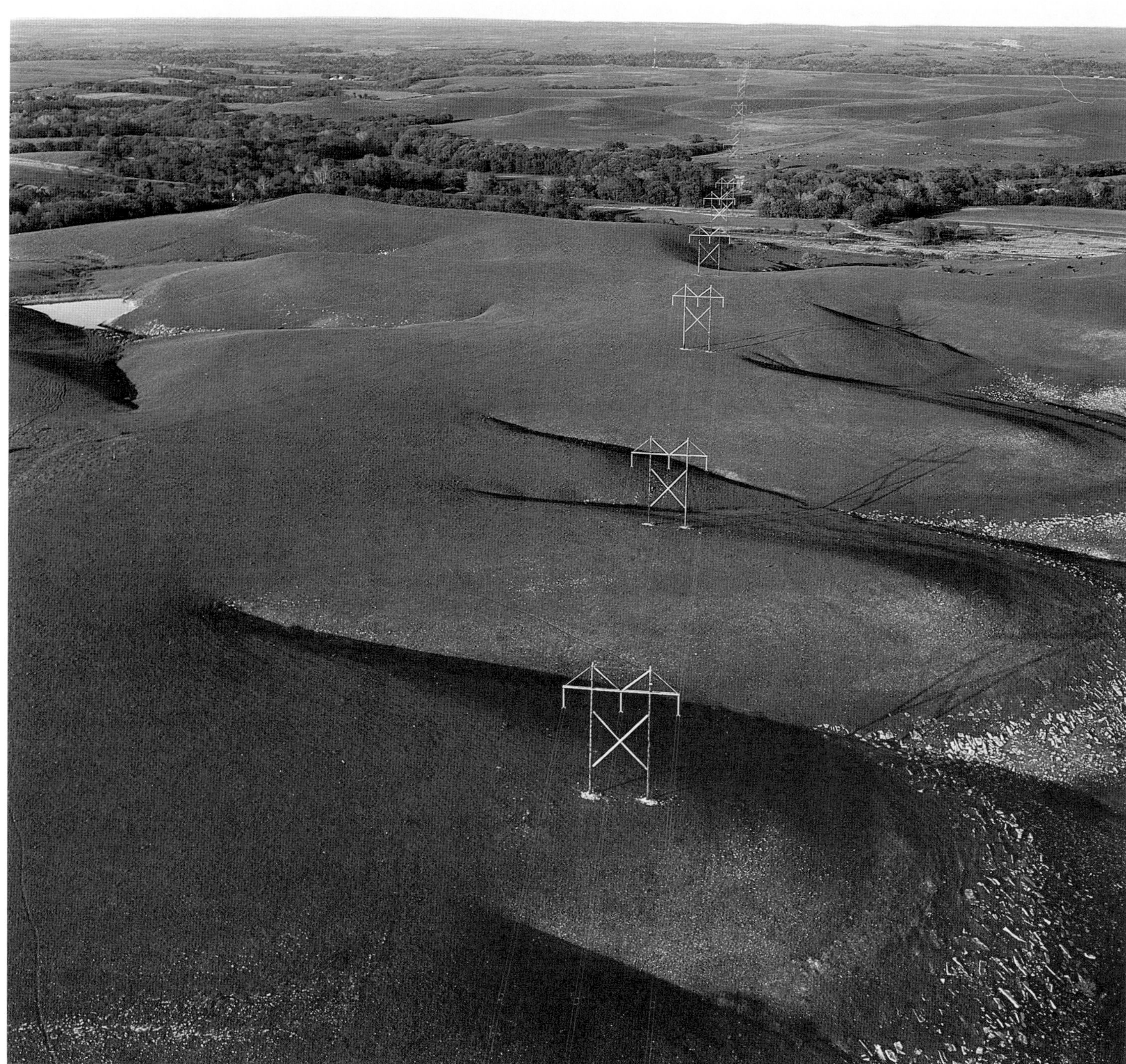

PLATE 108

Terry Evans
Power Lines Intersecting the Flint Hills East of Matfield Green, Chase County, Kansas, 1994
gelatin silver print
42¼ x 41½ in. (107.3 x 105.4 cm)
Collection of the San Francisco Museum of Modern Art

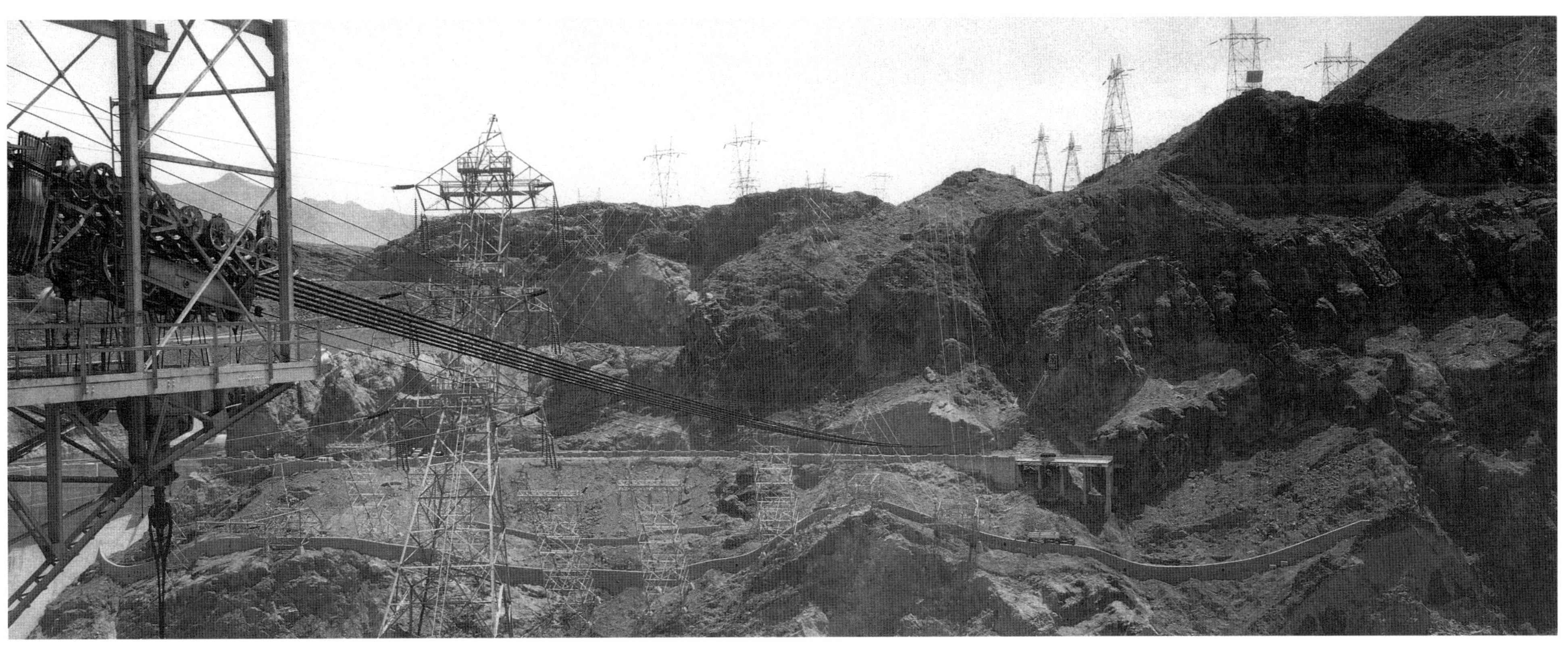

PLATE 109

Lois Conner
Hoover Dam, Arizona, 1989
platinum print
6⅝ x 16⅝ in. (16.8 x 42.1 cm)
Collection of the San Francisco Museum of Modern Art. Accessions Committee Fund

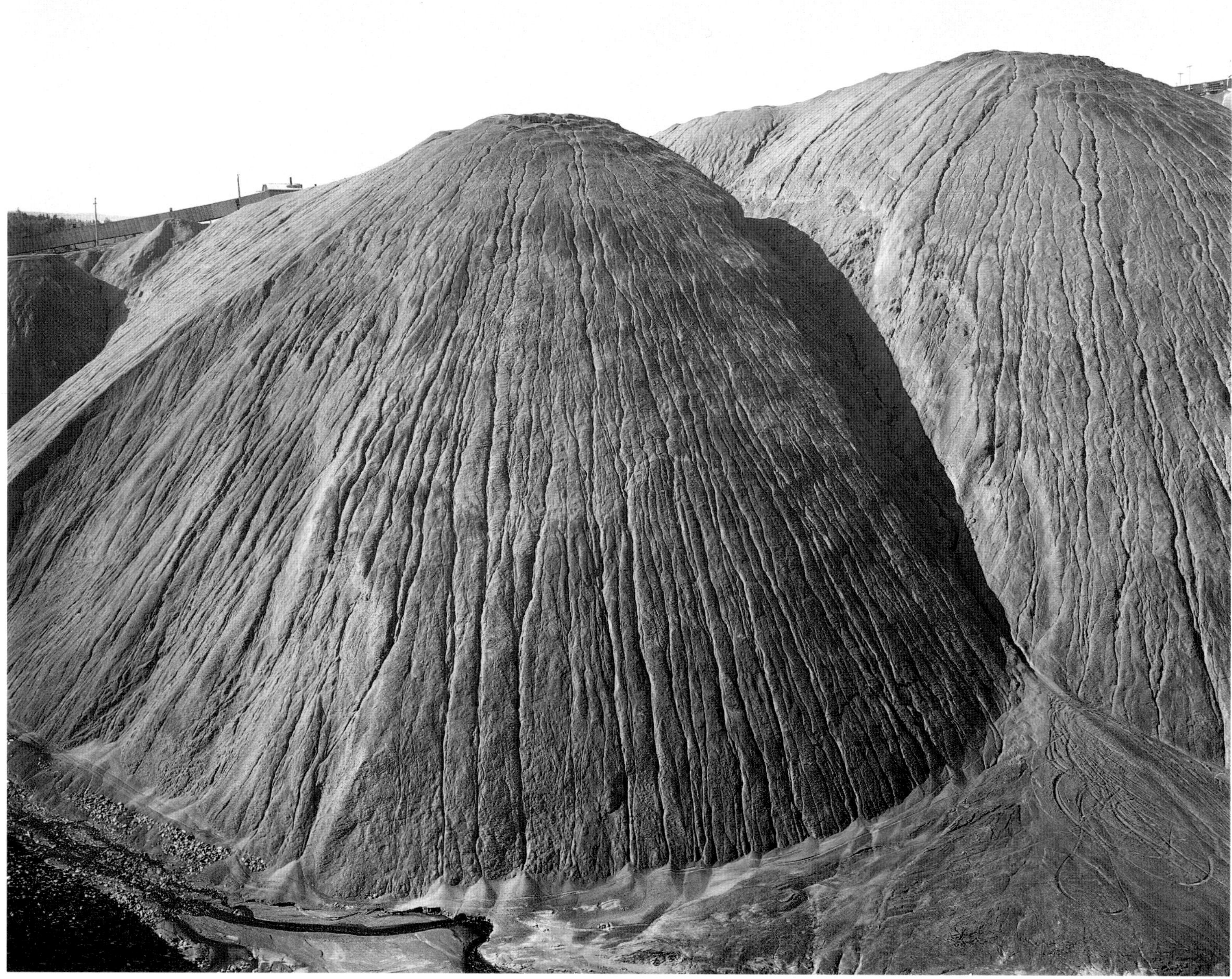

PLATE 110

Geoffrey James
Vimy Ridge, 1993
gelatin silver print
18½ x 23½ in. (47 x 59.7 cm)
Collection of the San Francisco Museum of Modern Art.
Accessions Committee Fund, 95.274

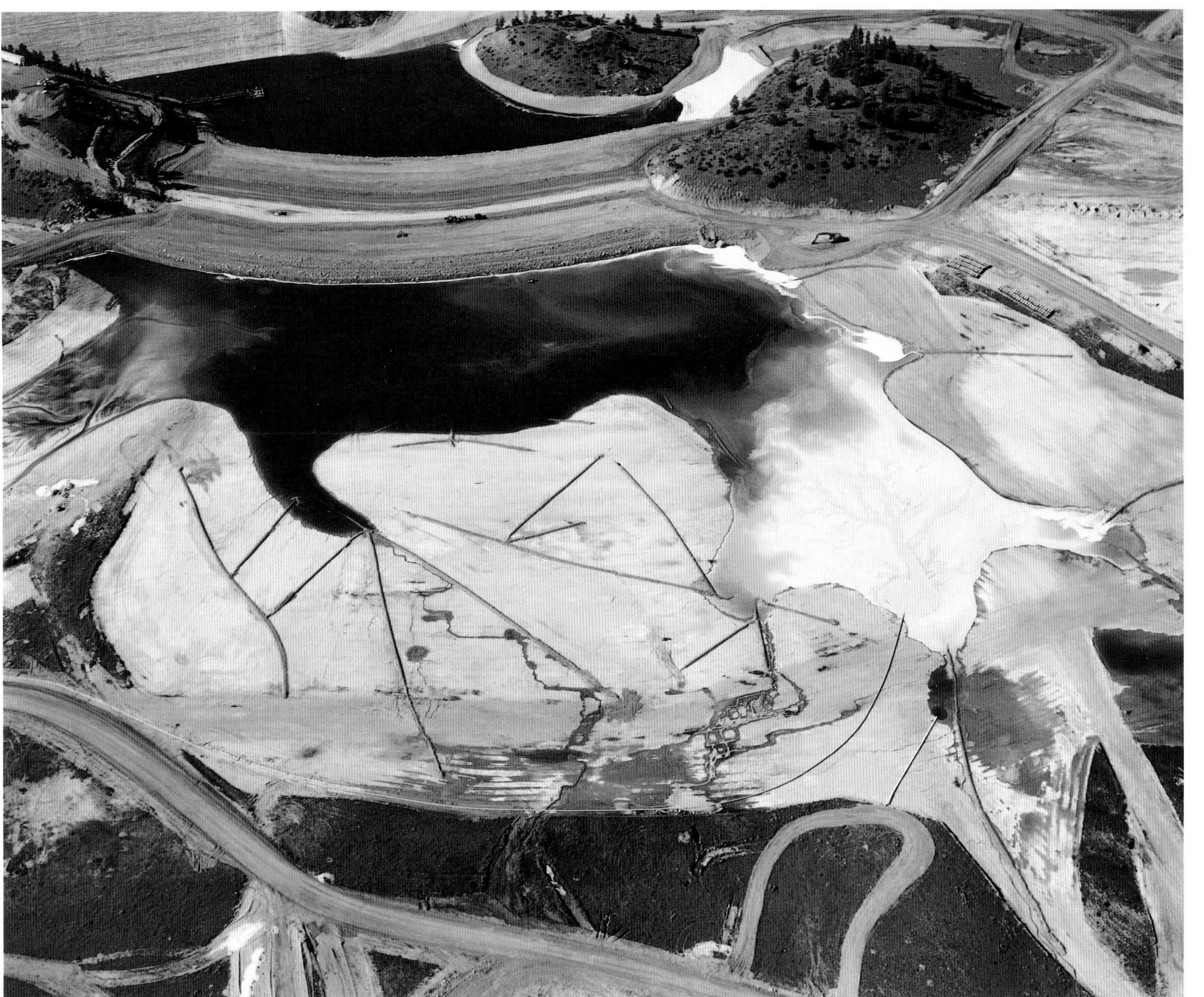

PLATE 111

David T. Hanson
Waste Ponds: June 1984, from the series *Colstrip, Montana*, 1984
Ektacolor print
16 x 20 in. (40.6 x 50.8 cm)
Collection of the San Francisco Museum of Modern Art

FOLLOWING PAGES:
PLATE 112

Mark Ruwedel
Hanford Town Site, Columbia River, A Nez Perce Meeting Place, from the series *The Hanford Stretch*, 1992–93
gelatin silver prints
24 x 48 in. (61 x 121.9 cm) overall
Collection of the San Francisco Museum of Modern Art.
Purchased through a gift of Jane and Larry Reed

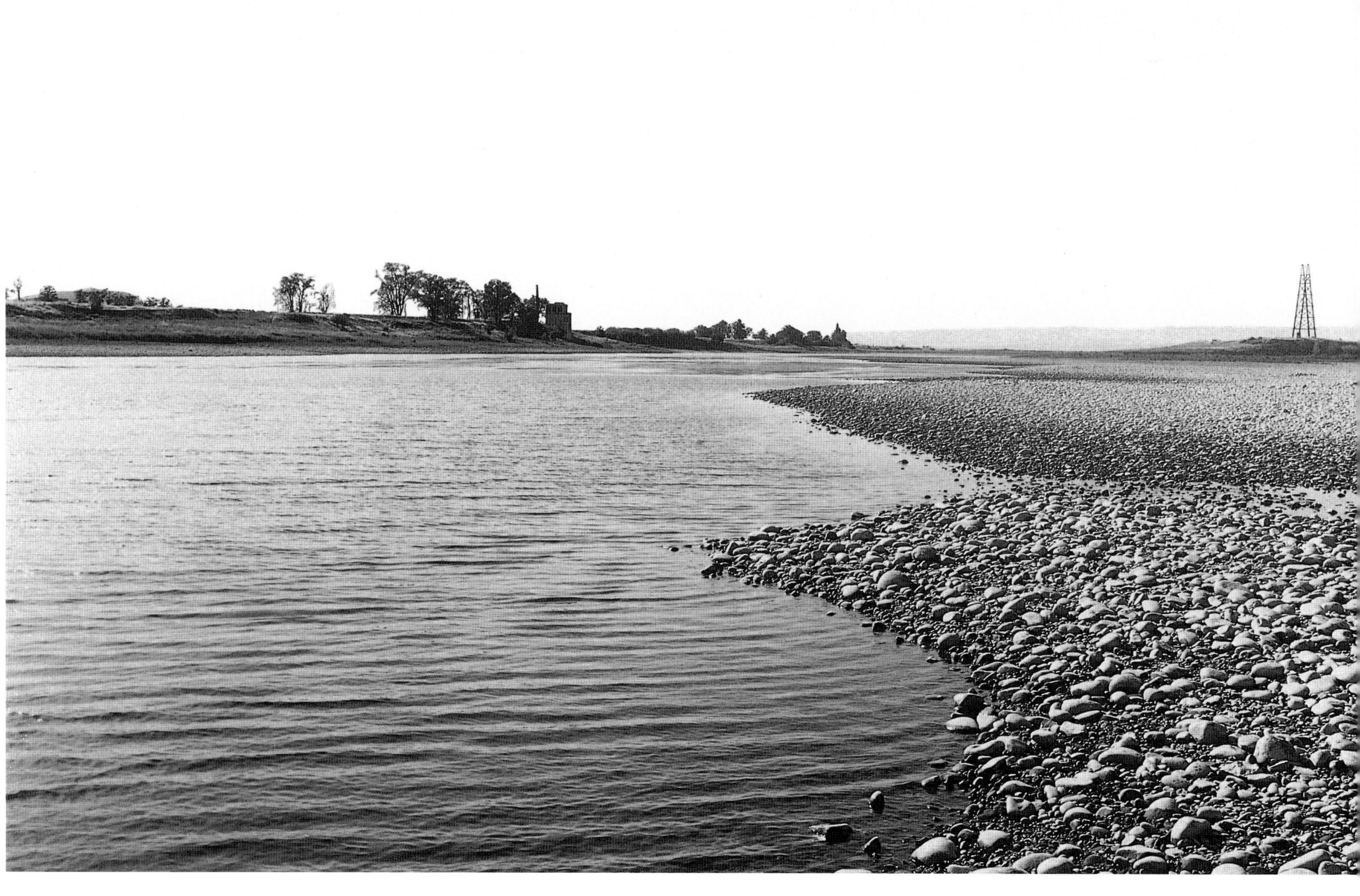

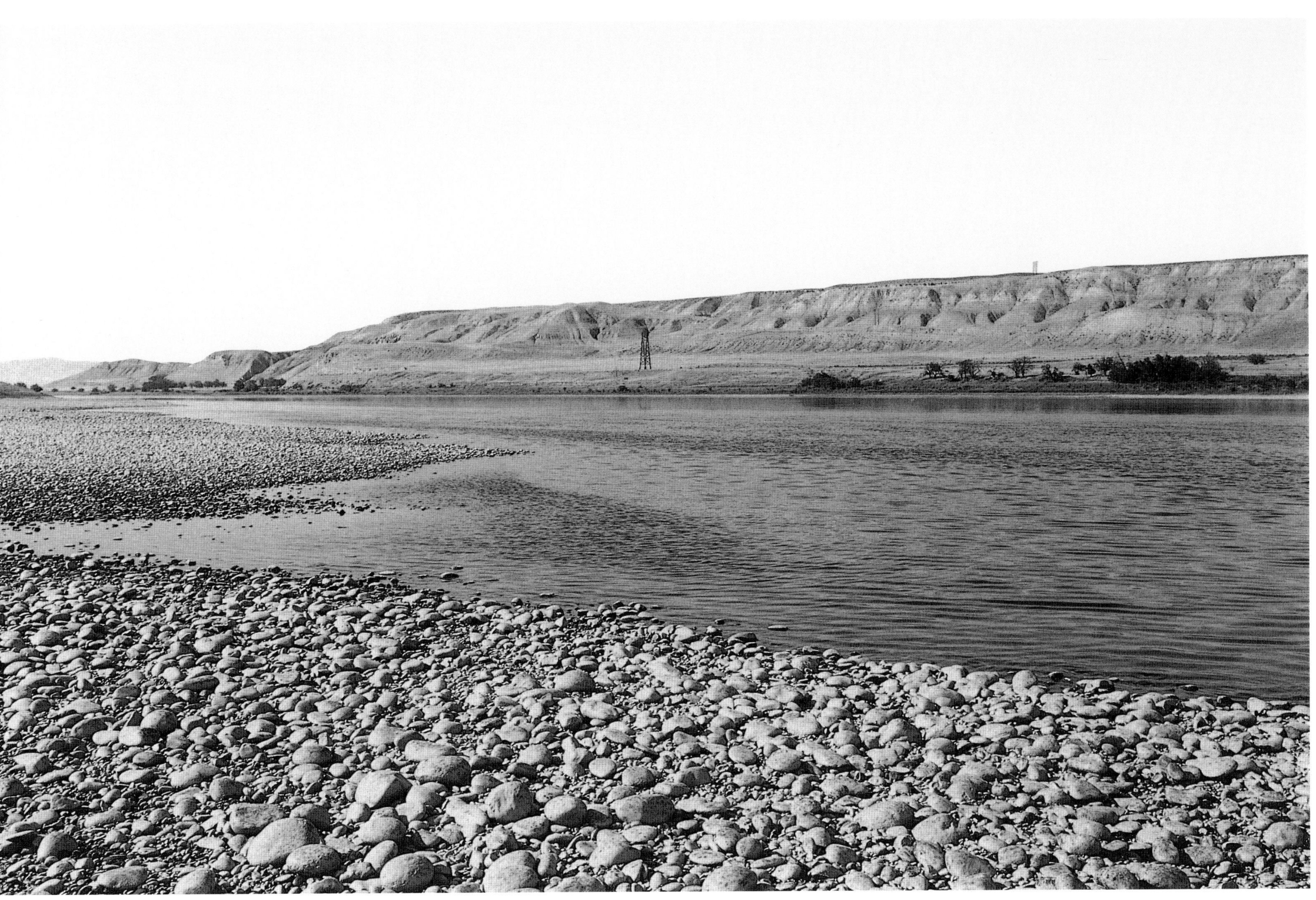

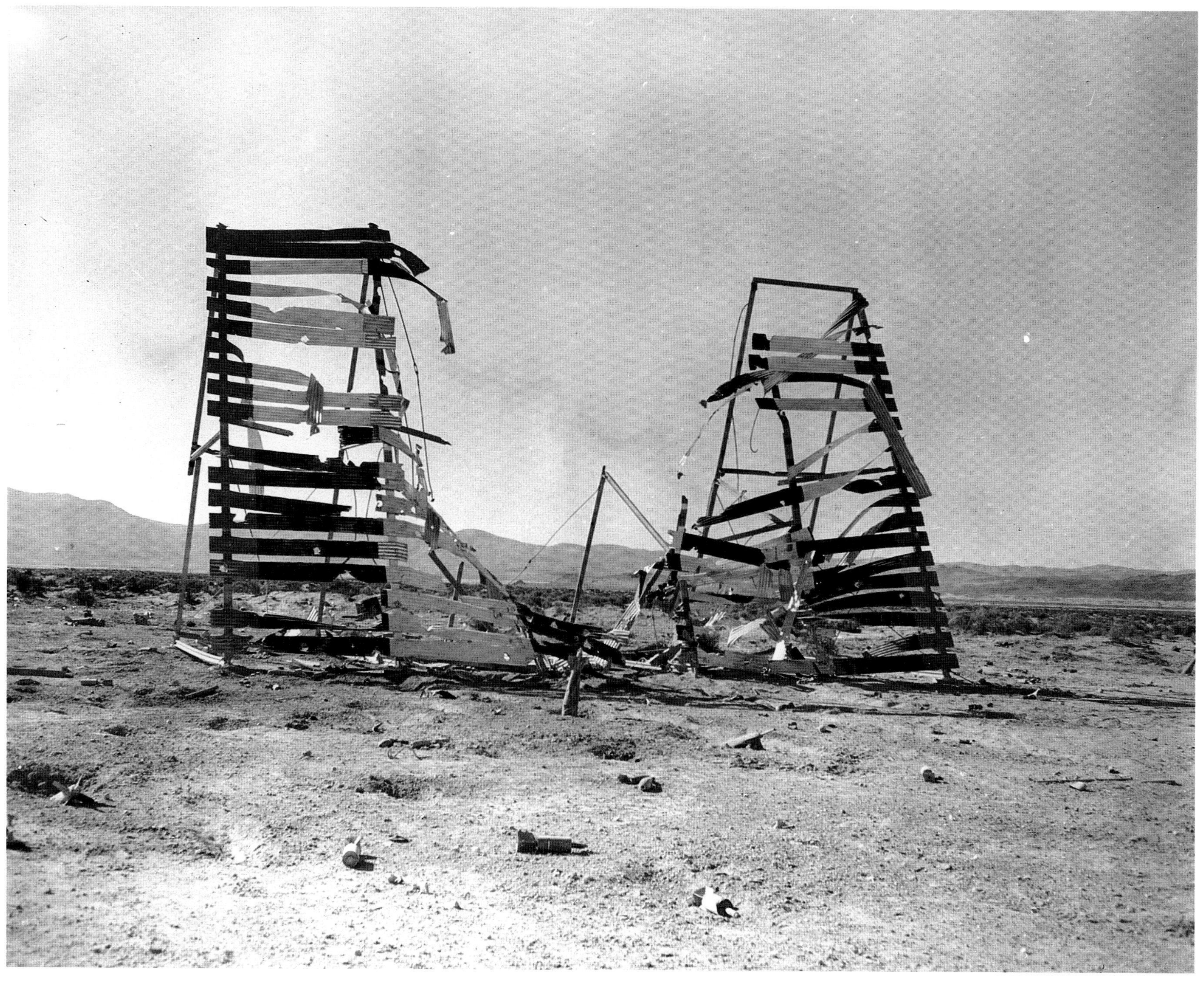

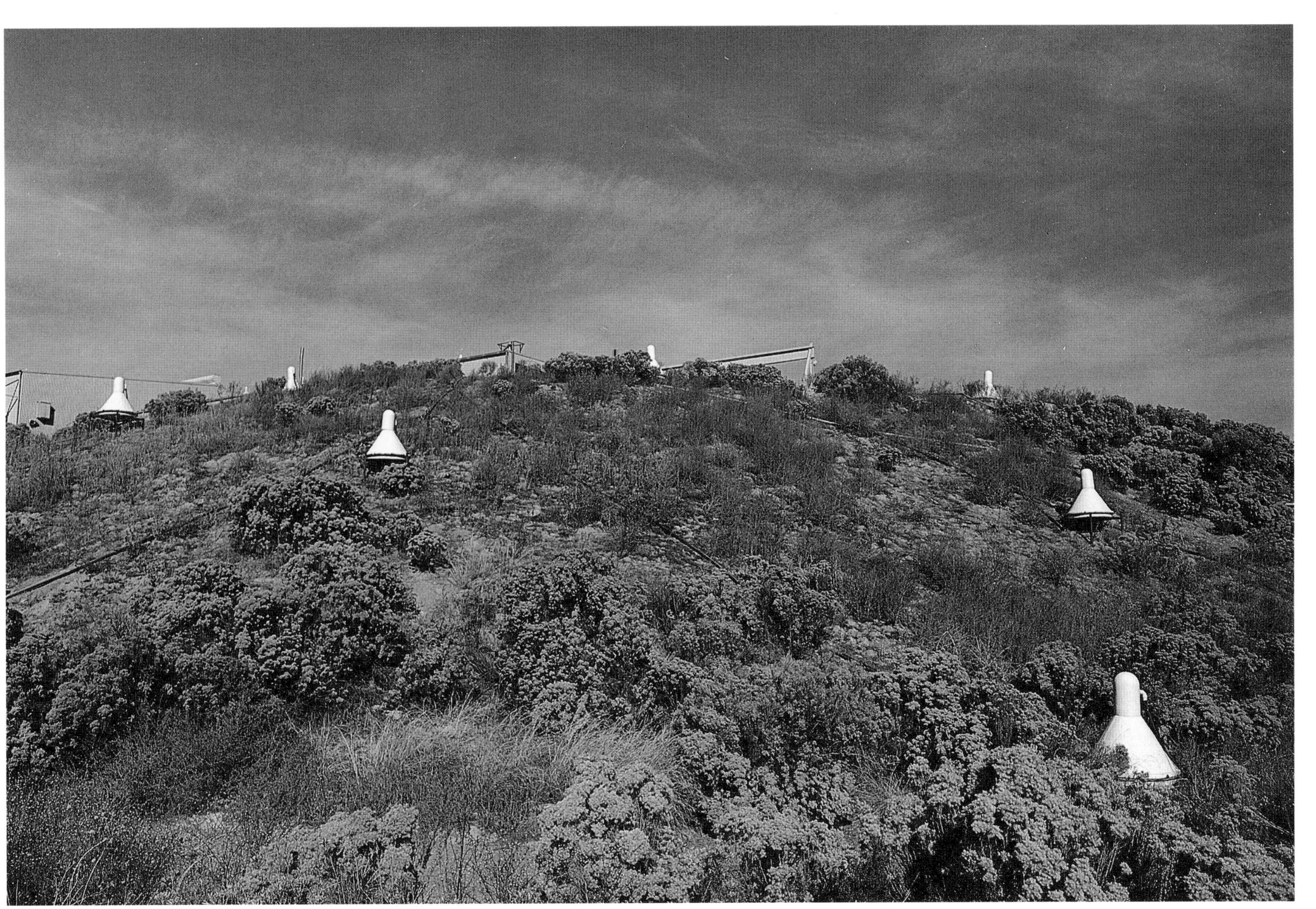

PLATE 113

Unknown U.S. Navy Photographer
Front View of B-16 Target After Accident. Pilot: Winterbottom, A. W., 1960
gelatin silver print
8⅛ x 10 in. (20.6 x 25.4 cm)
Special Collections, University of Nevada-Reno Library

PLATE 114

Barbara Norfleet
Measuring Cosmic Rays, Los Alamos National Laboratory: 43 square miles, Los Alamos, NM, 1988
gelatin silver print
11³⁄₁₆ x 16¹¹⁄₁₆ in. (28.4 x 42.4 cm)
Collection of the San Francisco Museum of Modern Art. Members of Foto Forum, 94.171

PLATE 115

Edgerton, Germeshausen & Grier, Inc.
Color View of Atomic Weapons Explosions at the Nevada Nuclear Testing Site, Nye County, Nevada, ca. 1950
chromogenic development print
8½ x 10½ in. (21.6 x 26.7 cm)
Special Collections, University of Nevada–Reno Library

PLATE 116

Richard Misrach
Bomb Crater and Destroyed Convoy, 1986 (printed 1991)
chromogenic development print
18⅜ x 23³⁄₁₆ in. (46.7 x 58.9 cm)
Collection of the San Francisco Museum of Modern Art. Purchased through a gift of the Judy Kay Memorial Fund

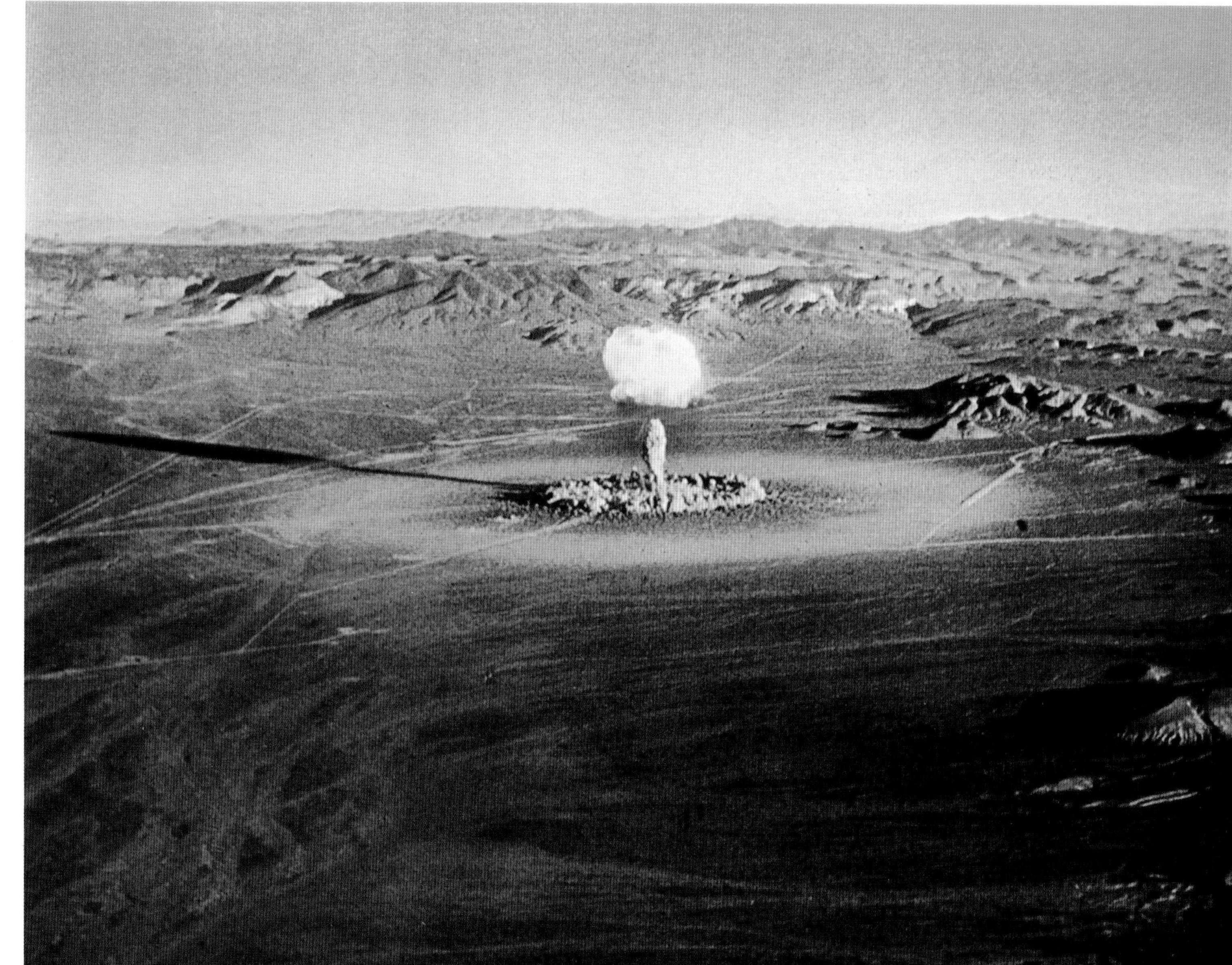

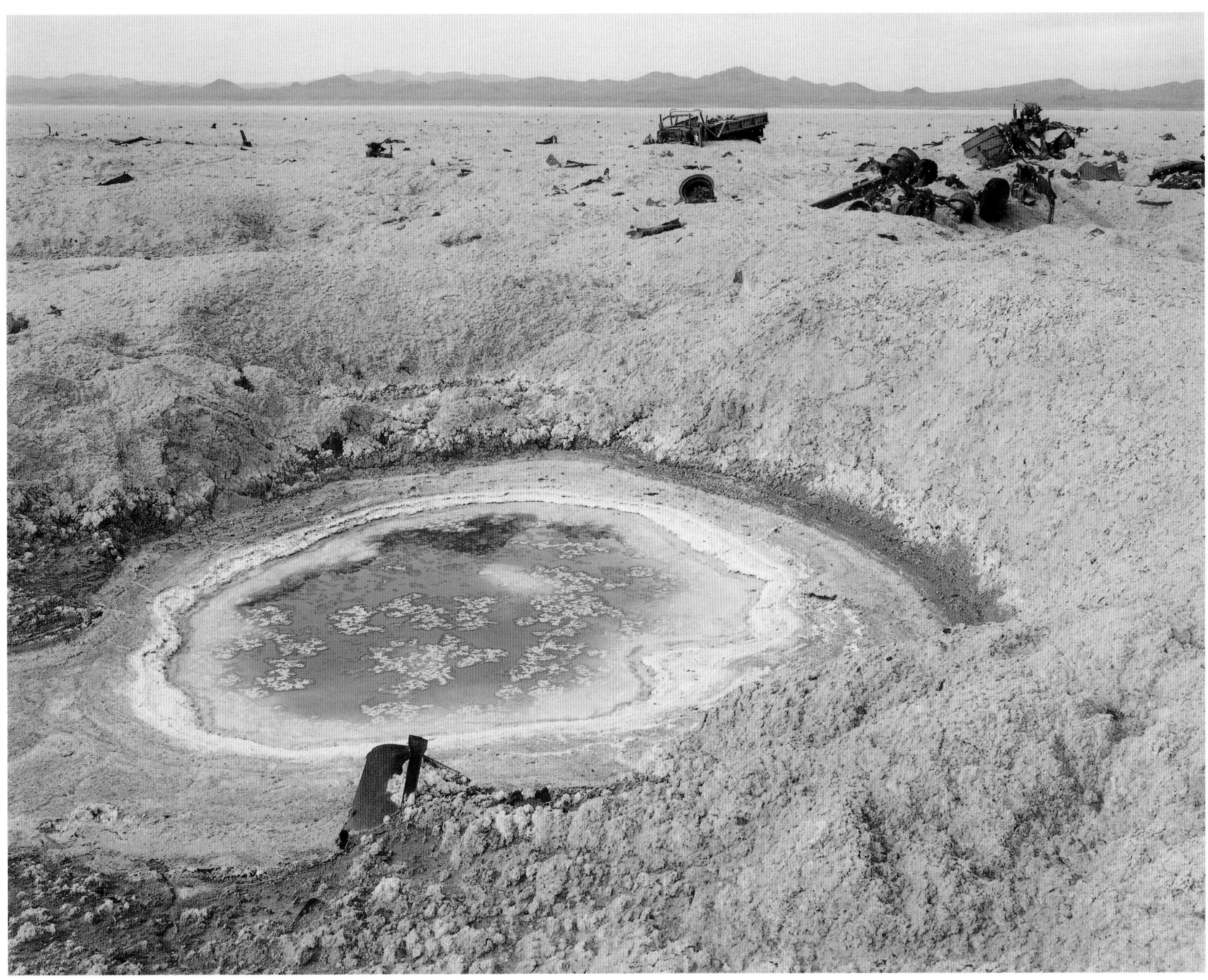

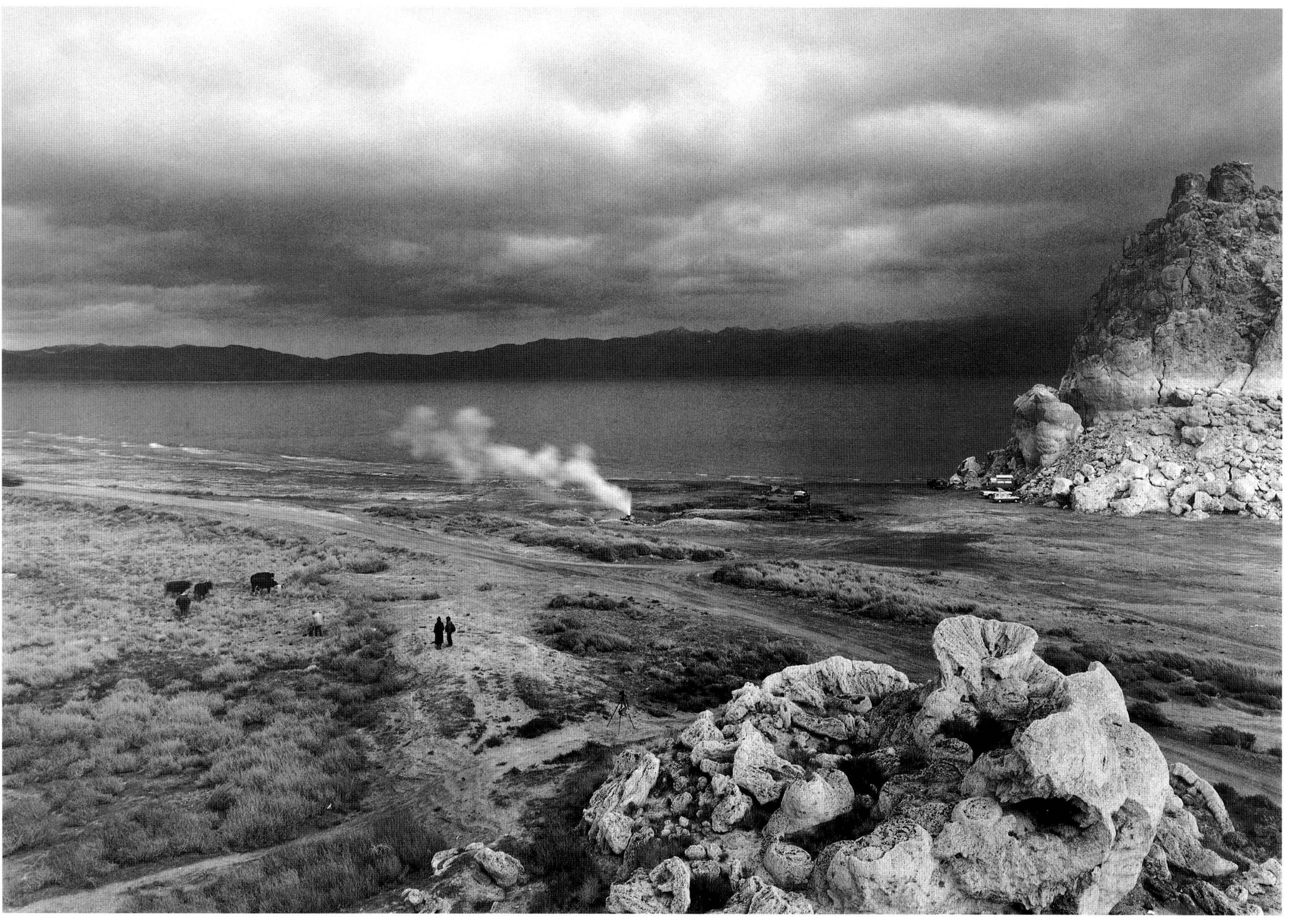

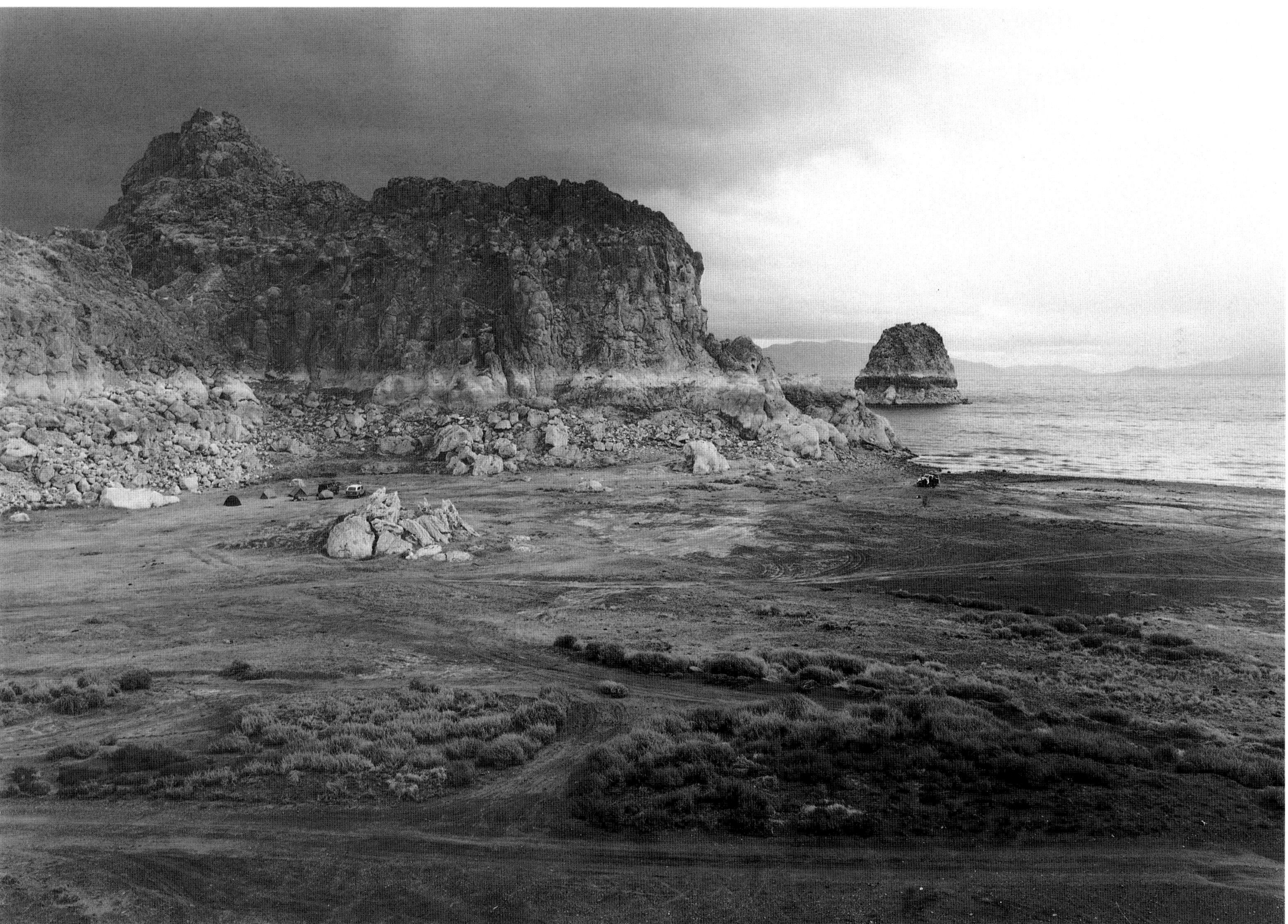

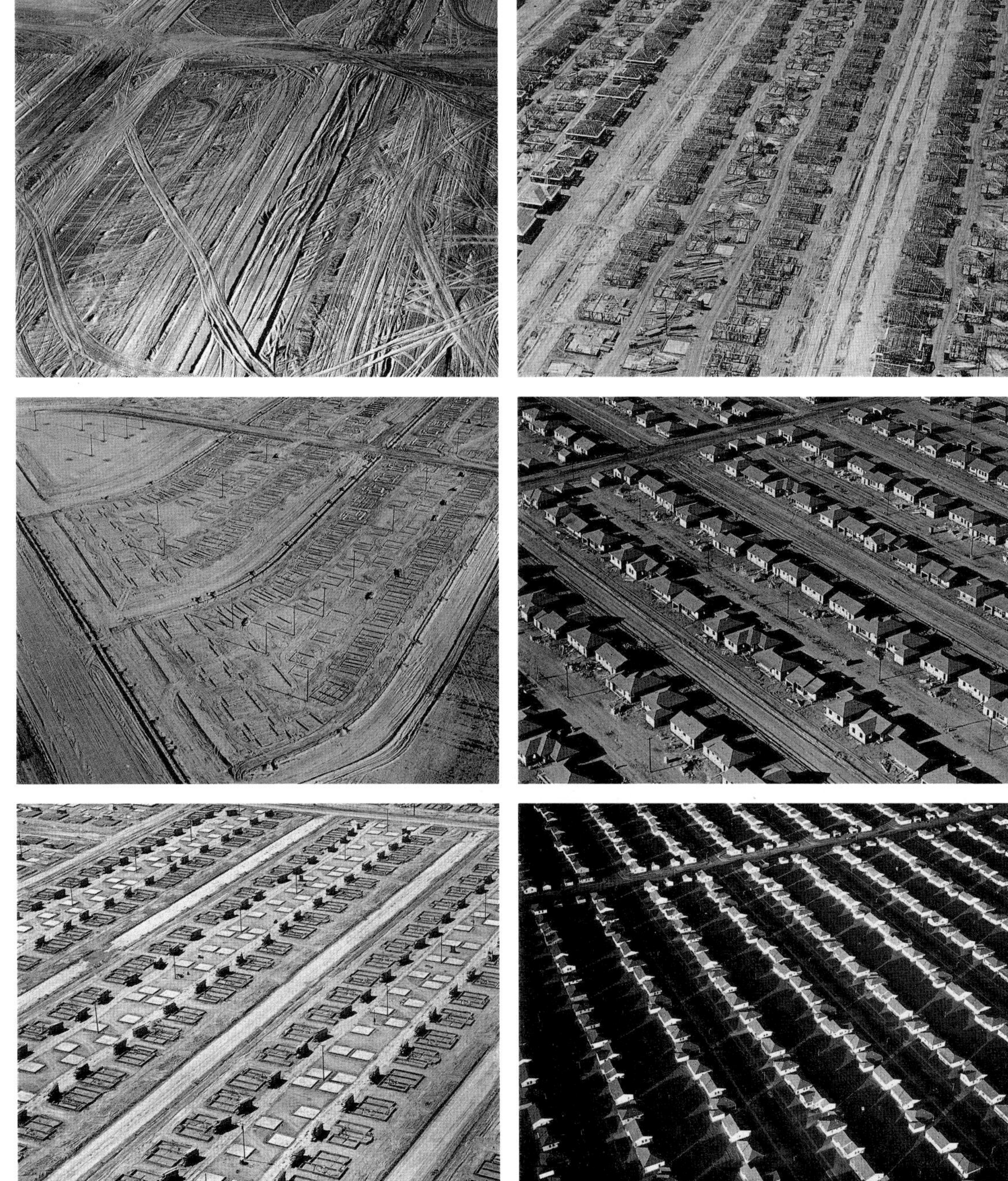

PREVIOUS PAGES:
PLATE 117

Robert Dawson
Pinnacles, Pyramid Lake, 1990
gelatin silver prints
13 x 18$^{15}/_{16}$ in. (33 x 48.1 cm) each
Collection of the San Francisco
Museum of Modern Art.
Accessions Committee Fund,
90.38.a-b

PLATE 118

William Garnett
Lakewood Housing Project
(six views), 1950
gelatin silver prints
8 x 10 in. (20.3 x 25.4 cm) each
Collection of the San Francisco
Museum of Modern Art

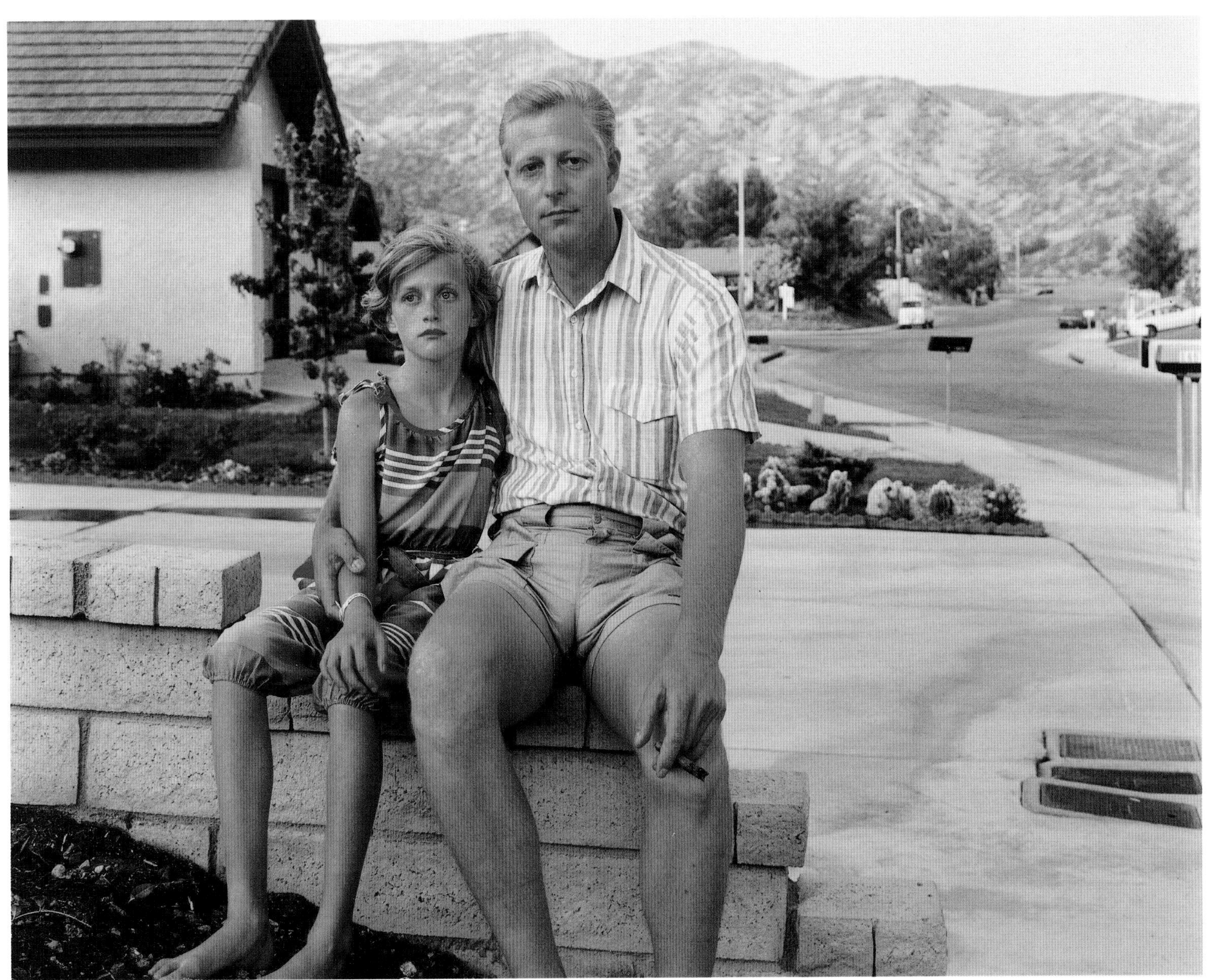

PLATE 119

Joel Sternfeld
Canyon Country, California, June 1983, 1983
Ektacolor print
13½ x 17⅛ in. (34.3 x 43.5 cm)
Collection of the San Francisco Museum of Modern Art.
Gift of the artist

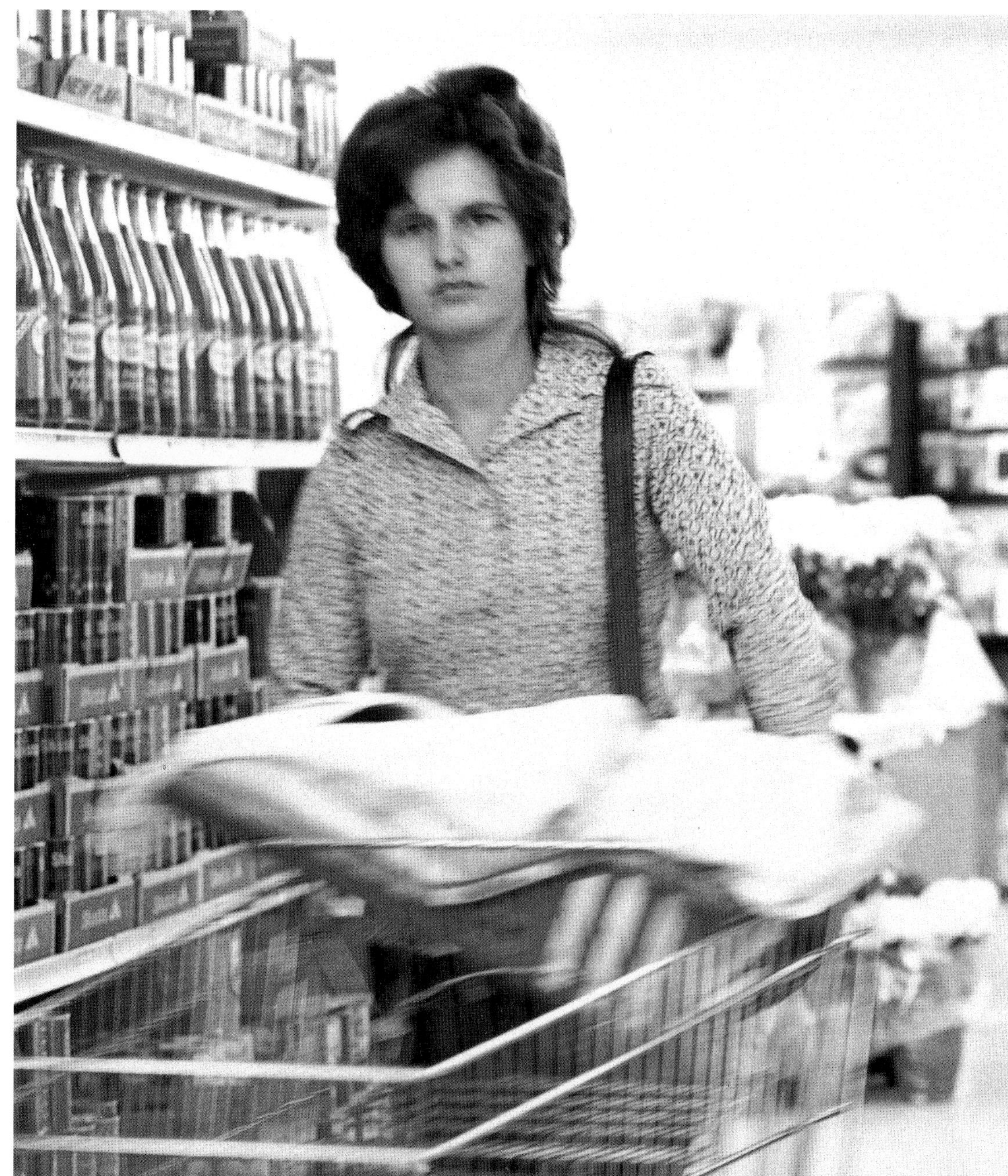

PLATE 120

Robert Adams

Longmont, 1973–74
gelatin silver print
6¾ x 6 in. (17.1 x 15.2 cm)
Collection of the San Francisco Museum of Modern Art. Accessions Committee Fund

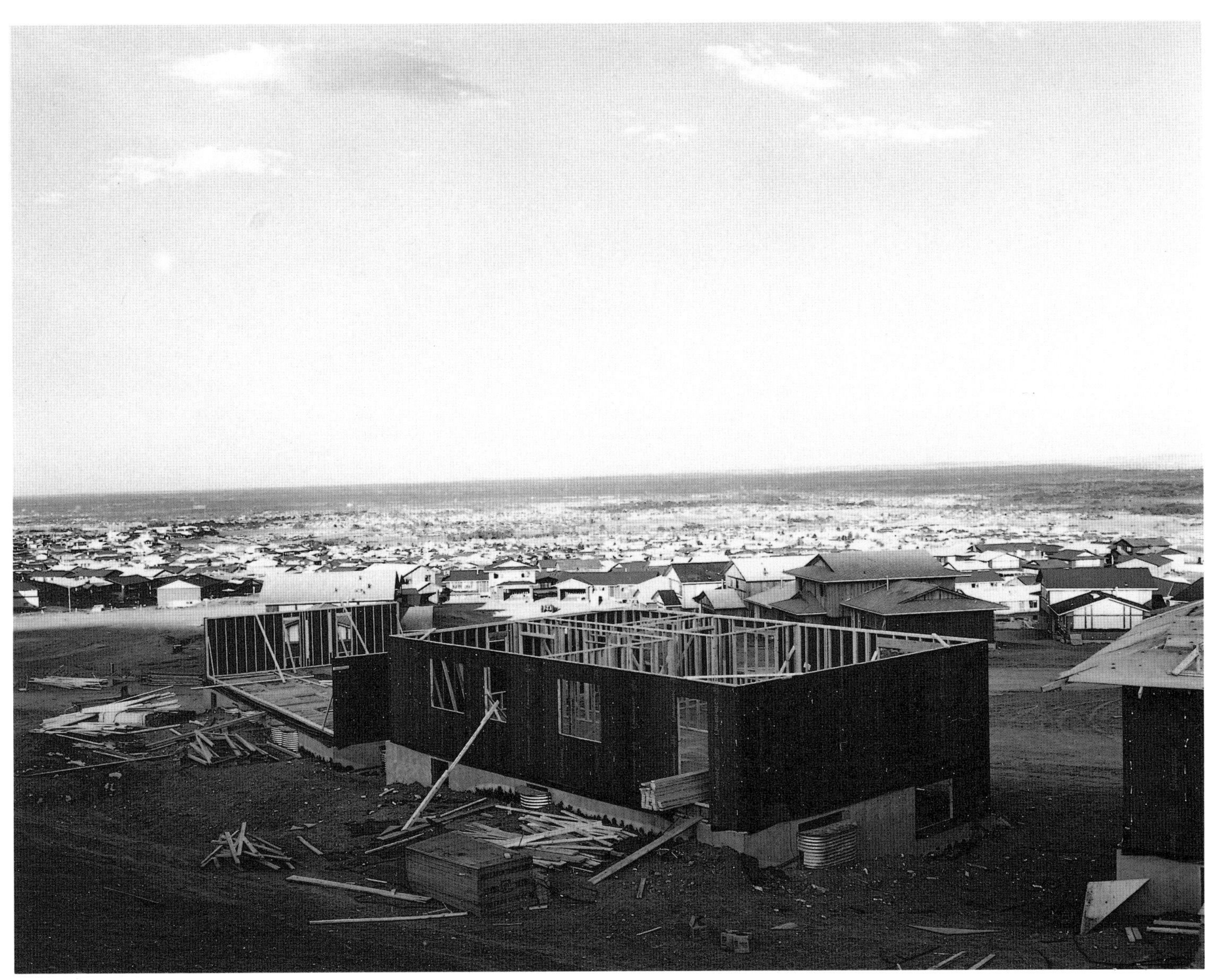

PLATE 121

Robert Adams
Lakewood, 1973–74
gelatin silver print
6 x 7½ in. (15.2 x 19 cm)
Paul Sack Collection

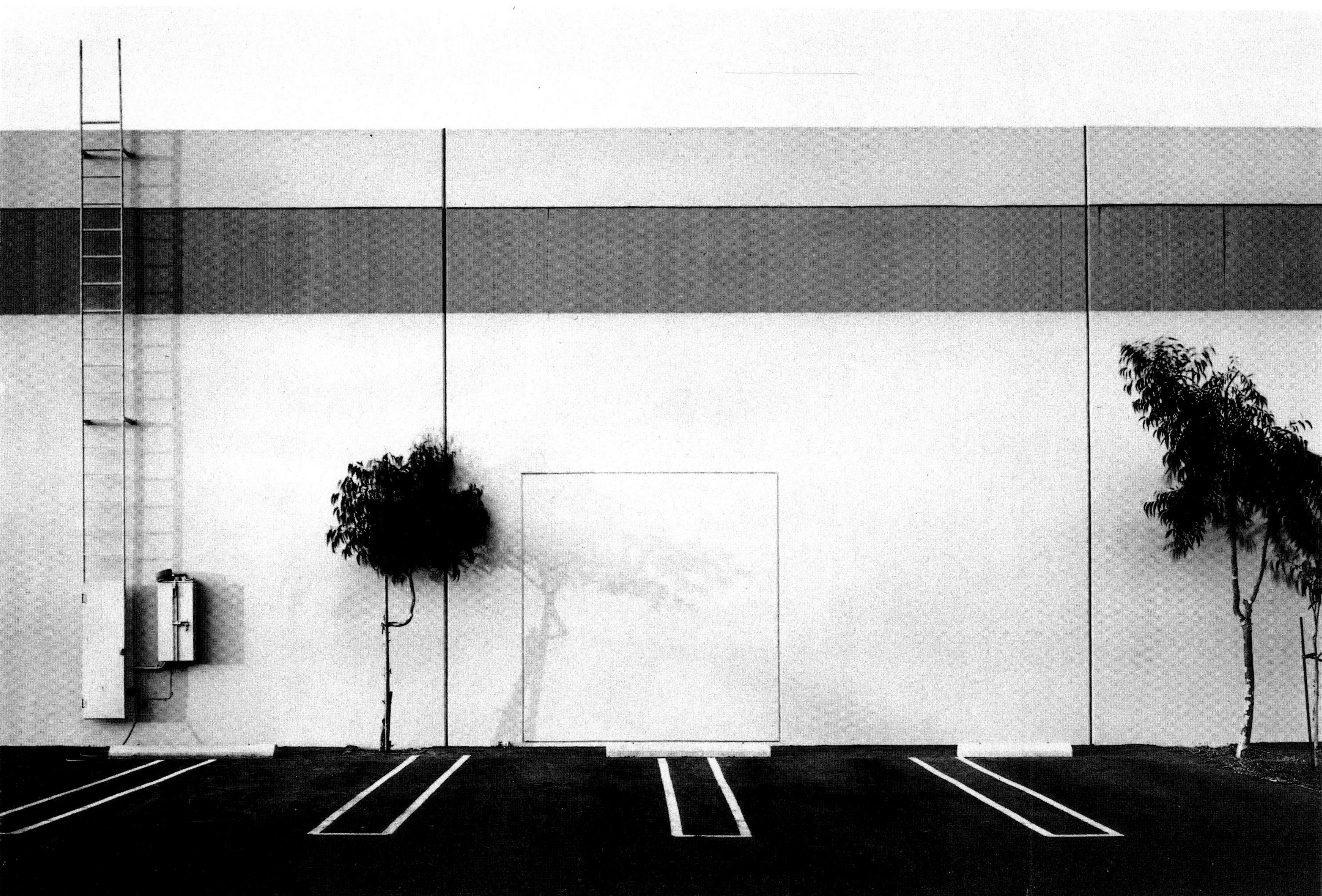

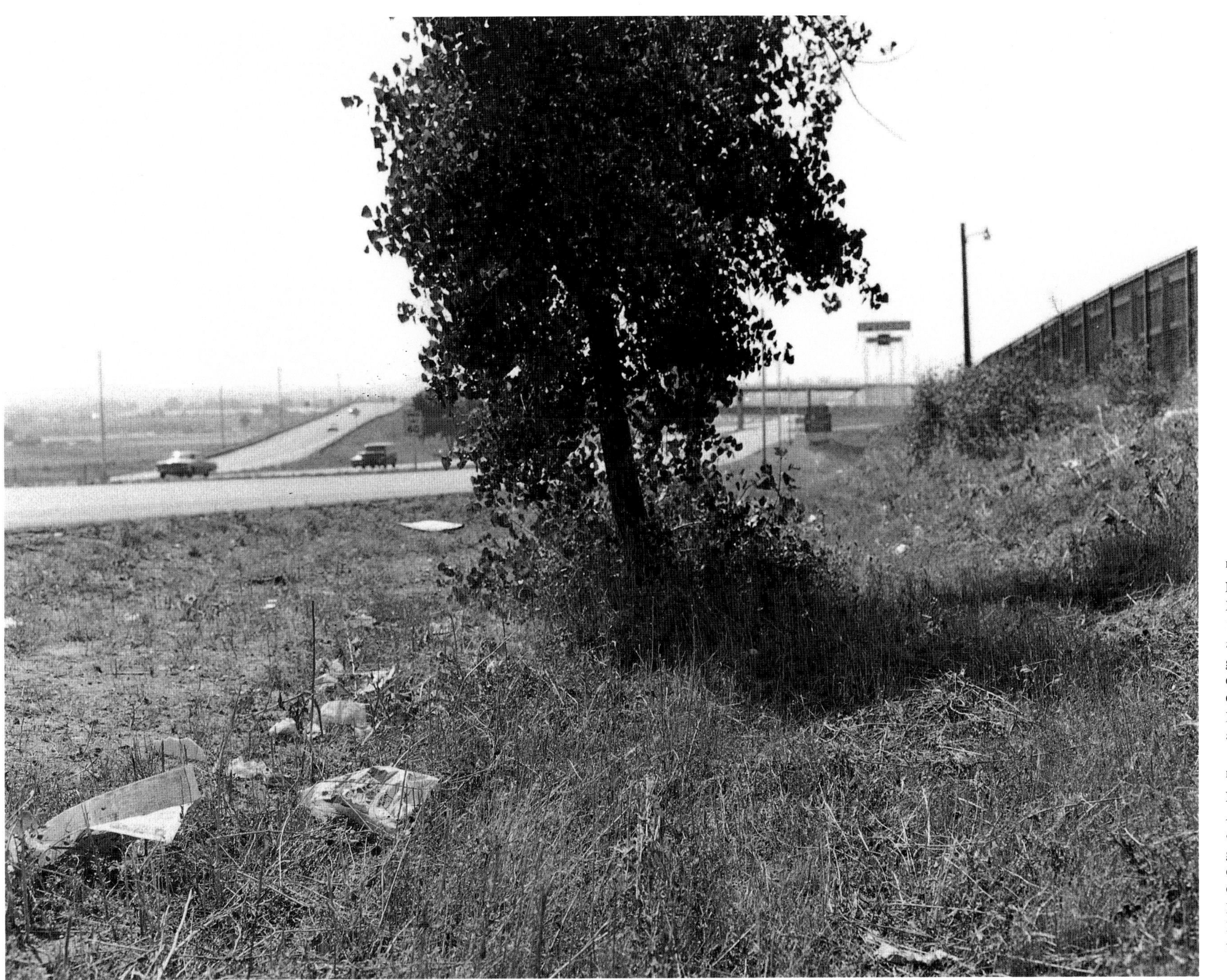

PLATE 122

Lewis Baltz
Element number 5 from
The New Industrial Parks near Irvine, California, 1974
gelatin silver print
6¹⁄₁₆ x 9¹⁄₁₆ in. (15.4 x 23 cm)
Collection of the San Francisco Museum of Modern Art,
80.472.5

PLATE 123

Robert Adams
Along Interstate 25 North of Denver, 1973–74
gelatin silver print
6 x 7½ in. (15.2 x 19 cm)
Collection of the San Francisco Museum of Modern Art.
Purchased through a gift of the Judy Kay Memorial Fund

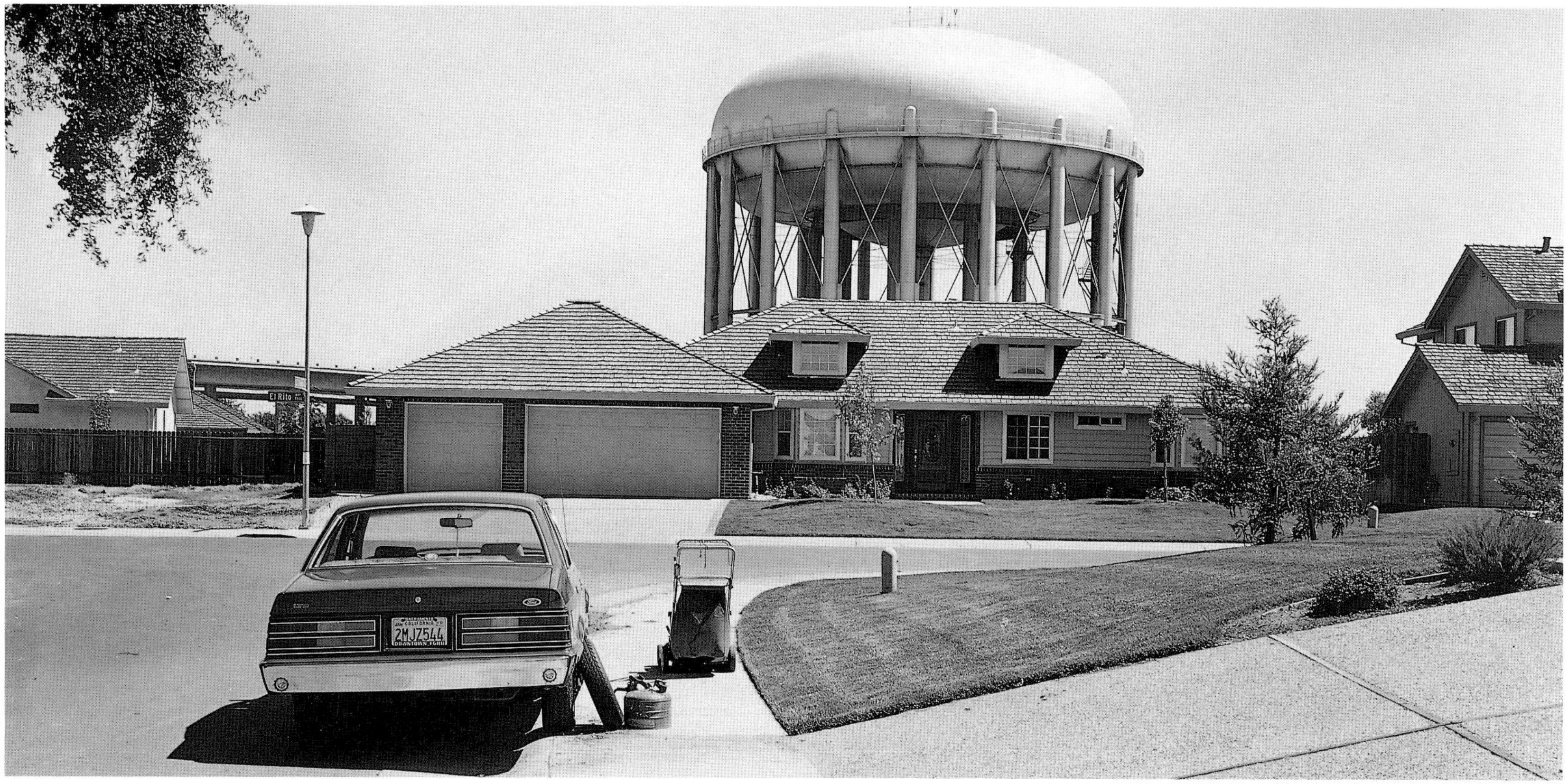

PLATE 124

Richard Meisinger, Jr.
The New American Suburbs: Still Life with Water Tank—Sacramento, CA, 1989
gelatin silver print
9⅜ x 19 in. (23.8 x 48.3 cm)
Collection of the San Francisco Museum of Modern Art. Gift of the artist, 93.111

PLATE 125

Gene Kennedy
Bernardo Heights Golf Course, Rancho Bernardo, San Diego County, California, from the series *California Carcinoma*, 1982
gelatin silver print
8⅞ x 18⅛ in. (22.5 x 46 cm)
Collection of the San Francisco Museum of Modern Art

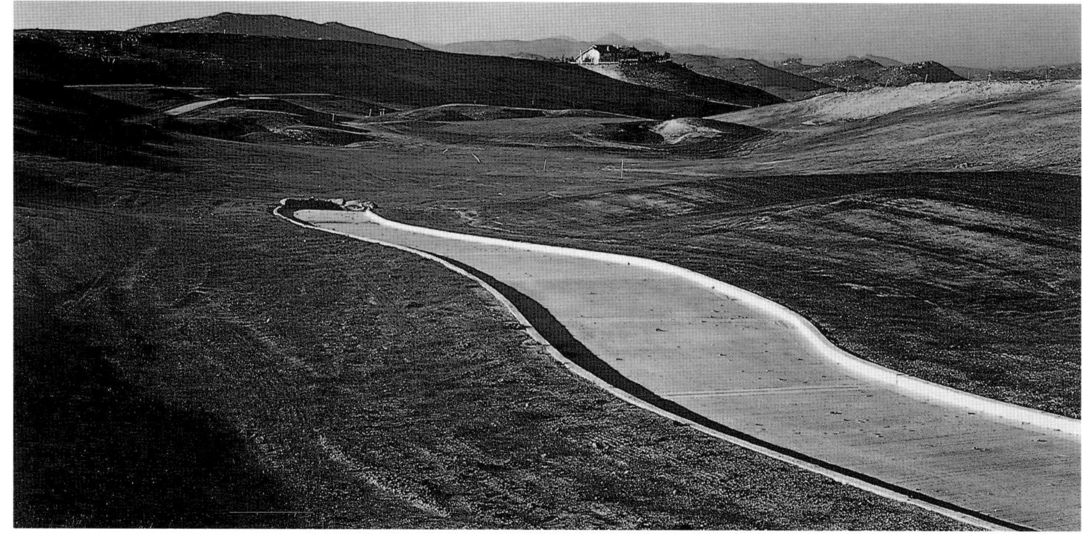

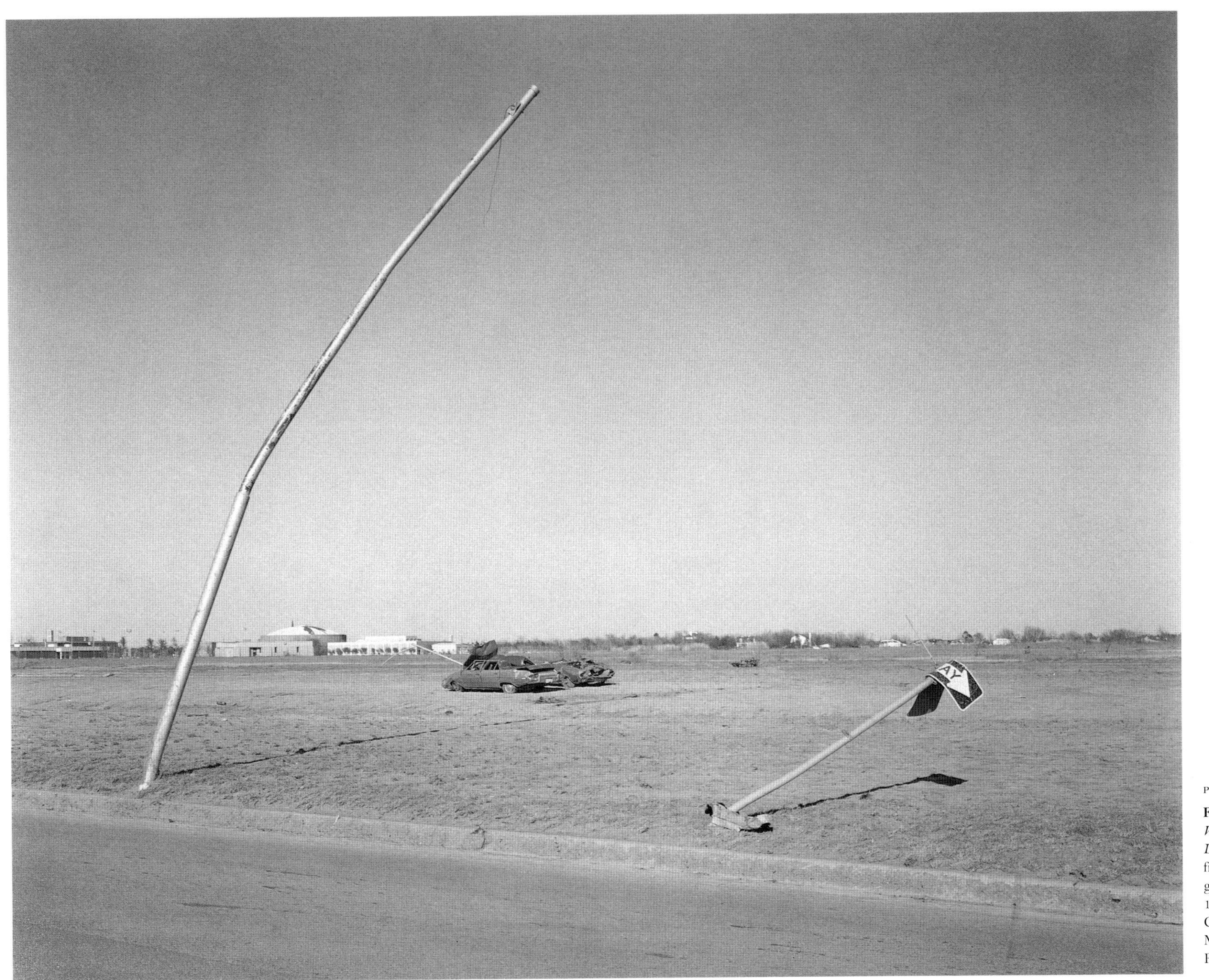

PLATE 126

Frank Gohlke
Wichita Falls, Texas, April 14, 1979, Looking northeast from Sikes Center, from the series *Aftermath*, 1979
gelatin silver print
16 x 20 in. (40.6 x 50.8 cm)
Collection of the San Francisco Museum of Modern Art. Gift of Robert Adams

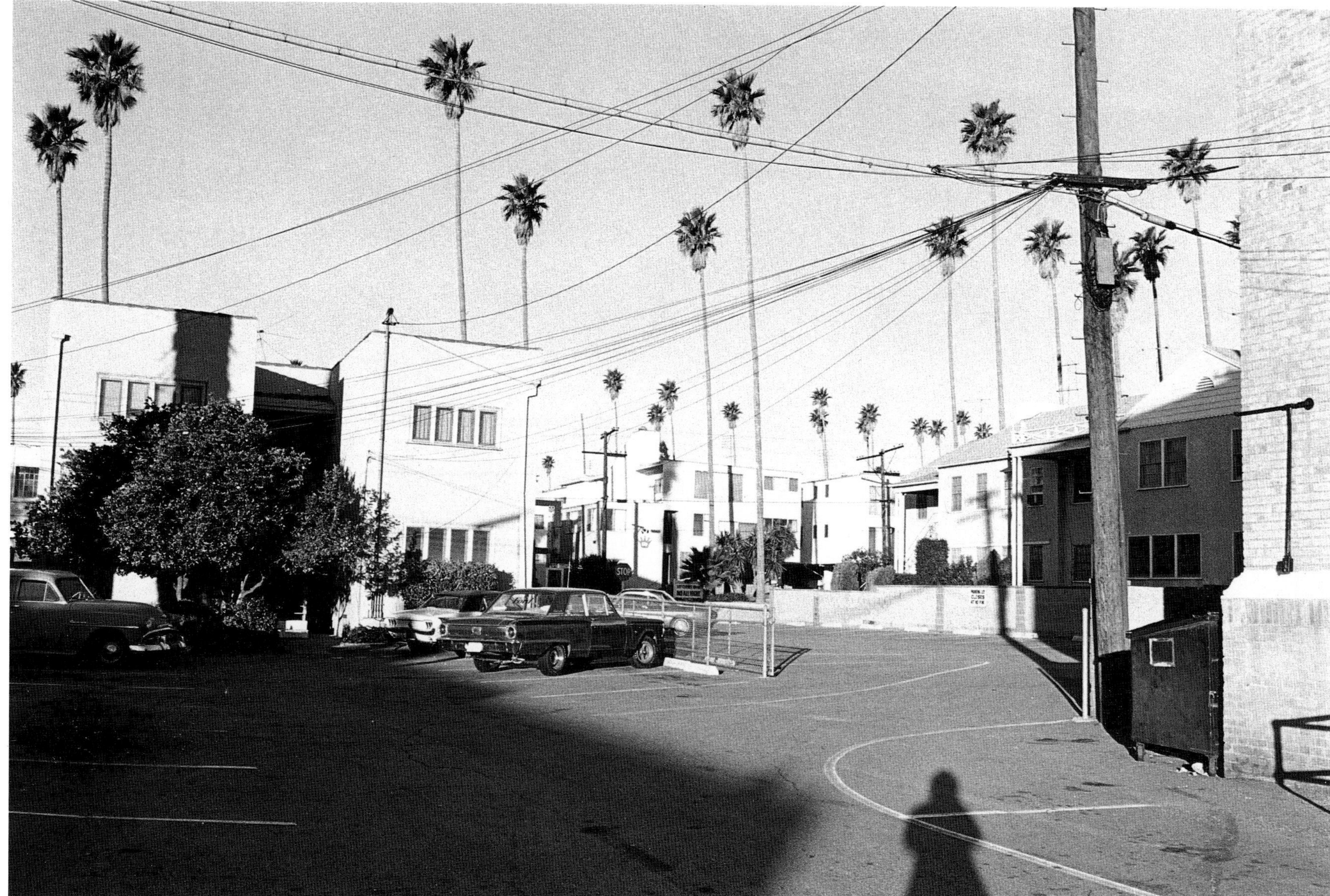

PLATE 127

Henry Wessel
Hollywood, California, 1972
gelatin silver print
10⅞ x 13⅞ in. (27.6 x 35.2 cm)
Collection of the San Francisco Museum of Modern Art. Gift of Maggie Keating, 91.277

PLATE 128

Garry Winogrand
Santa Monica, California, 1982–83
gelatin silver print
14¾ x 22 in. (37.5 x 55.9 cm)
Collection of the San Francisco Museum of Modern Art. Gift of the Estate of Garry Winogrand and Fraenkel Gallery

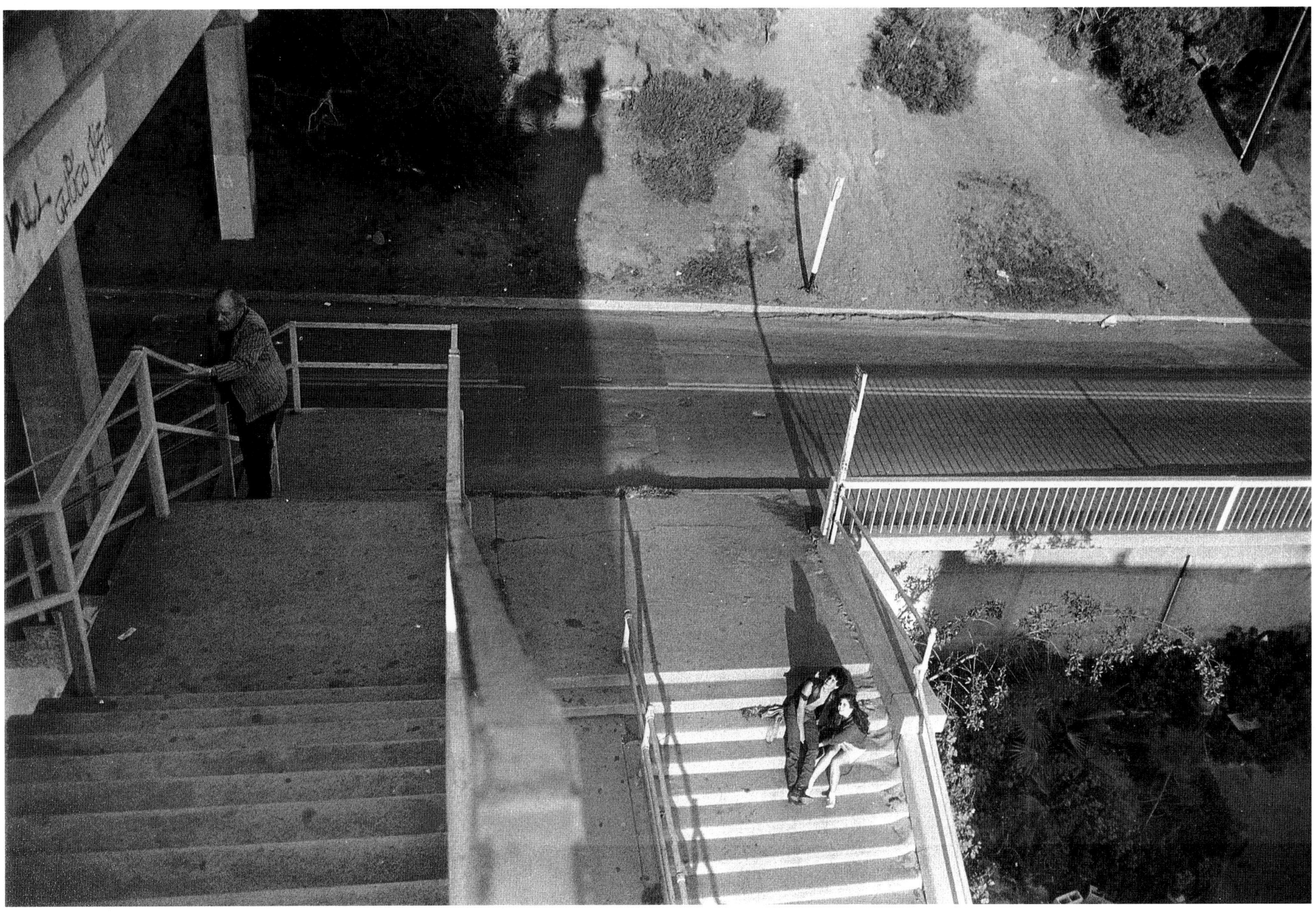

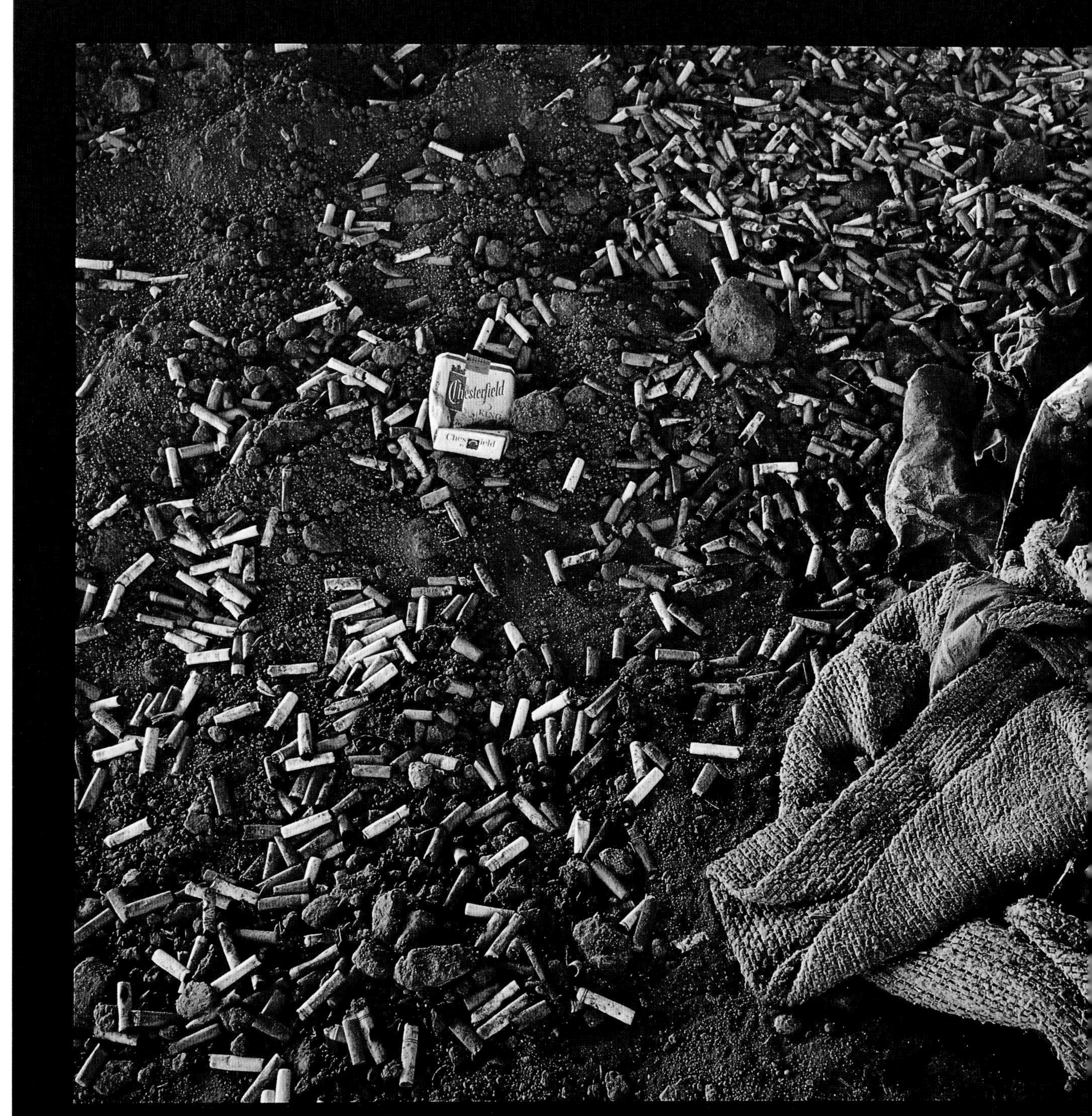
Chesterfield

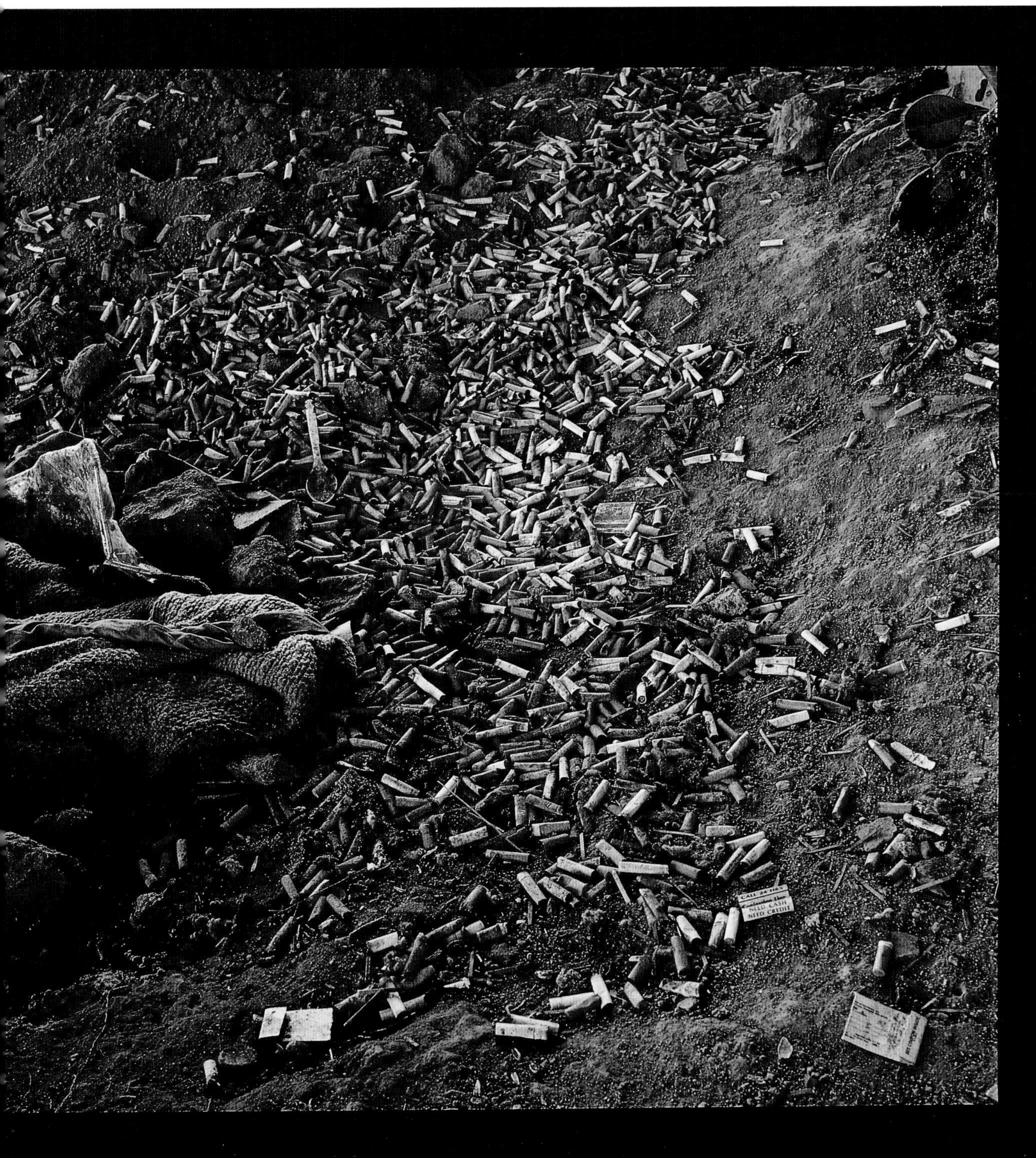

PLATE 129

Anthony Hernandez
Landscapes for the Homeless, 1990
silver dye bleach print
33 x 66 in. (83.8 x 167.6 cm)
Collection of the San Francisco Museum of Modern Art, 93.203

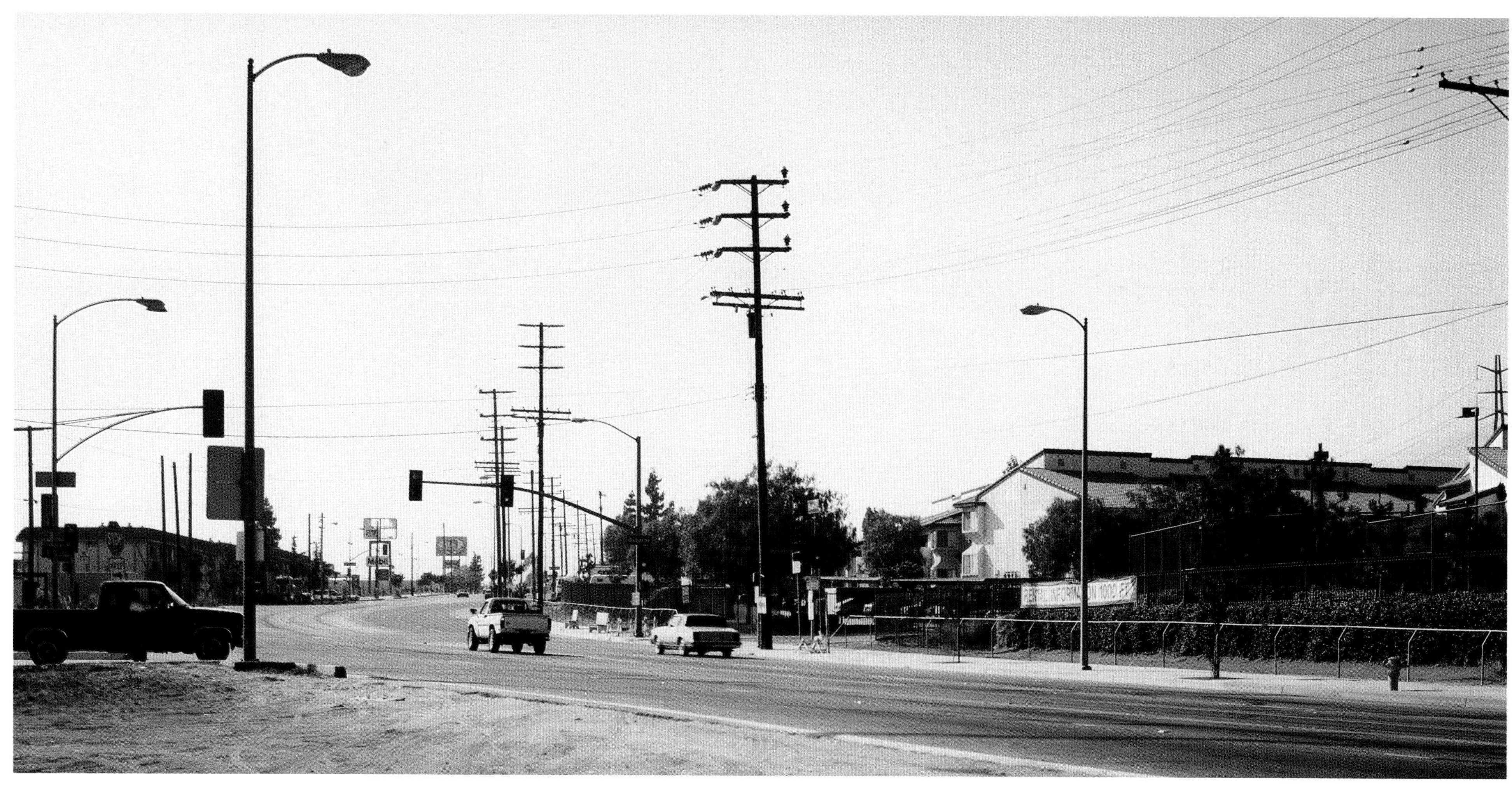

PLATE 130

Lewis Baltz
11777 Foothill Boulevard, Los Angeles, CA, 1991
silver dye bleach print
29⅜ x 49¾ in. (74.6 x 126.4 cm)
Collection of the San Francisco Museum
of Modern Art

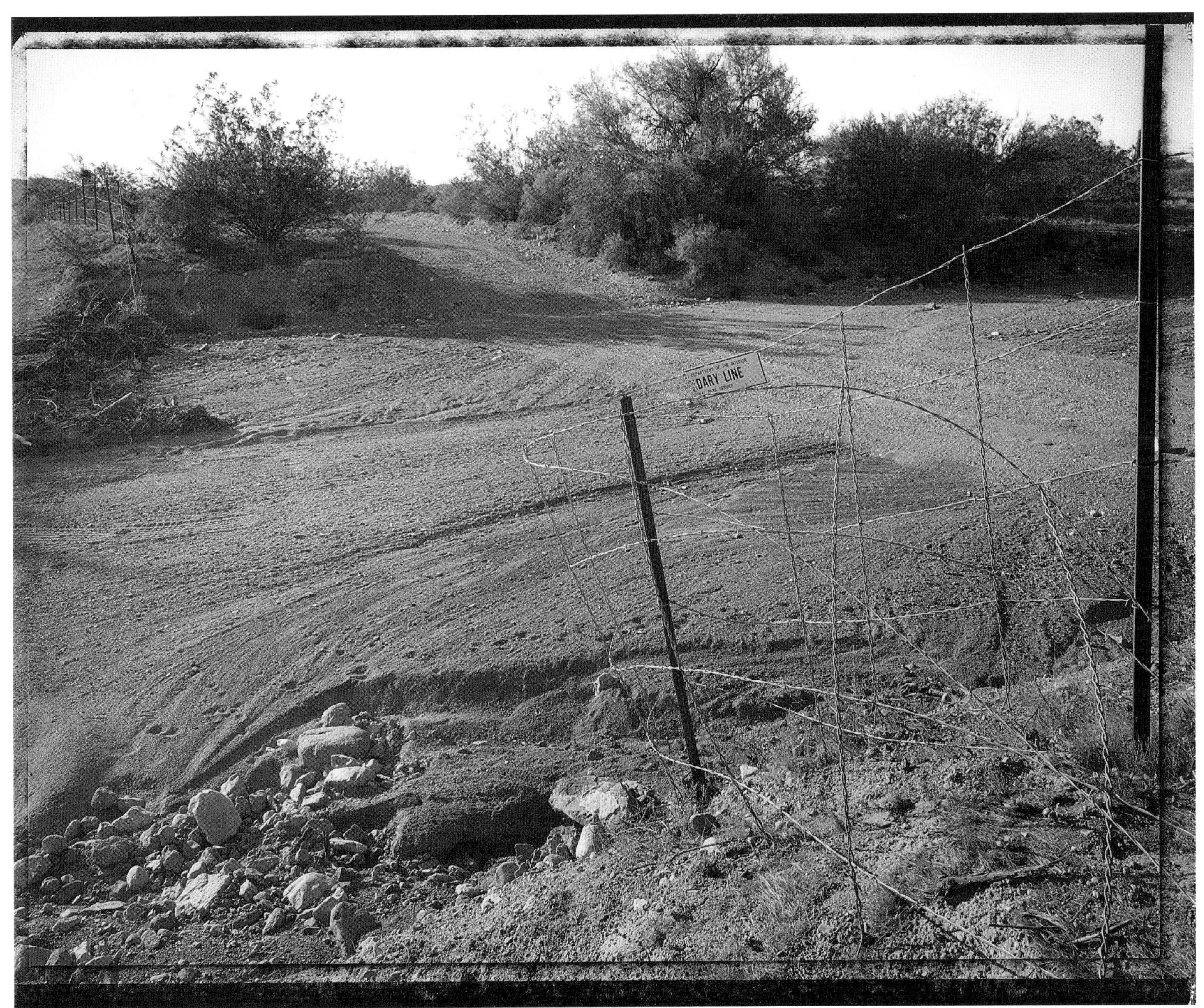

PLATE 131

Mark Klett
Border Fence Cut by Flash Flood, near Sonoyta, from *Desert Legends*, 1993
gelatin silver print
16 x 20 in. (40.6 x 50.8 cm)
Collection of the San Francisco Museum of Modern Art.
Purchased through a gift of the Judy Kay Memorial Fund

Illustration Credits

Many of the photographs reproduced in this catalogue were created as historical documents and as such were accompanied by extended explanatory texts. Whenever this information exists it has been included below the caption for the work.

Unless otherwise indicated below, illustrations have been supplied by the artist or by the owner of the work named in the caption.

Photo by Ian Reeves: figs. 4, 11, 15, 17, 21 and pls. 2, 6–8, 13–15, 17, 20, 22, 24, 27–28, 33, 35, 40–42, 44, 50–52, 55, 59–60, 66, 71, 76–79, 82, 90–92, 94–101, 103–106, 109–112, 116–129.

Figures

Fig. 3: photo by Ben Blackwell; fig. 7: courtesy Jim Crain and Chronicle Books; fig. 12: ©1995 by the Trustees of the Ansel Adams Publishing Rights Trust. All Rights Reserved; fig. 13: photo by Sotheby's, Inc.; fig. 14: ©Robert Frank, Courtesy PaceWildensteinMacGill, New York; fig. 15 ©The Estate of Garry Winogrand; fig. 18: Venturi, Scott Brown and Associates, Inc.; fig. 19: courtesy Alan Hess and Chronicle Books; fig. 20 ©Alex S. MacClean; fig. 23: reprinted from *Industrial Chicago* (Chicago: Goodspeed Publishing Co., 1891); fig. 25: reprinted from Charles H. Singer et al. (eds.), *A History of Technology* (London: Oxford University Press, 1954–58) by permission of Oxford University Press; fig. 26: photo by Grady Clay from his book *Real Places: An Unconventional Guide to America's Generic Landscape* (©1994 by the University of Chicago); fig. 27: photo by Aaron Betsky; figs. 28–30, 32–34: Janice C. Fong; fig. 31: courtesy of the United States Geological Survey.

Plates

Pl. 2: ©Joel Sternfeld, Courtesy PaceWildensteinMacGill, New York; pl. 9: photo by Adam Reich, courtesy of Basilico Fine Arts, New York; pl. 12: photo ©1996 The Cleveland Museum of Art. Edwin R. and Harriet Pelton Perkins Memorial Fund, 1992.242; pls. 38–39, 61: photo by Nikki Pahl; pl. 72: Frank Wing Photography; pl. 73: courtesy of Bradley W. Richards, M.D.; pl. 74: Richard Nicol Photography; pls. 99, 119: ©Joel Sternfeld, Courtesy PaceWildensteinMacGill, New York; pl. 130: Los Angeles County Museum of Art, Commissioned by funds provided by Michael R. Kaplan, M.D., Gary B. Sokol, and the Horace W. Goldsmith Foundation.